THE LOEB CLASSICAL LIBRARY

FOUNDED BY JAMES LOEB

EDITED BY

G. P. GOOLD

STRABO

III

LCL 182

STRABO

GEOGRAPHY

BOOKS 6–7

WITH AN ENGLISH TRANSLATION BY

HORACE LEONARD JONES

HARVARD UNIVERSITY PRESS

CAMBRIDGE, MASSACHUSETTS

LONDON, ENGLAND

First published 1924
Reprinted 1954, 1961, 1967, 1983, 1995

ISBN 0-674-99201-6

Printed in Great Britain by St Edmundsbury Press Ltd,
Bury St Edmunds, Suffolk, on acid-free paper.
Bound by Hunter & Foulis Ltd, Edinburgh, Scotland.

CONTENTS

THE

GEOGRAPHY OF STRABO

BOOK VI

ΣΤΡΑΒΩΝΟΣ ΓΕΩΓΡΑΦΙΚΩΝ

ϛ′

I

1. Μετὰ δὲ τὸ στόμα τοῦ Σιλάριδος Λευκανία καὶ τὸ τῆς Ἥρας ἱερὸν τῆς Ἀργῴας,[1] Ἰάσονος ἵδρυμα, καὶ πλησίον ἐν πεντήκοντα σταδίοις ἡ Ποσειδωνία.[2] ἐντεῦθεν δ' ἐκπλέοντι τὸν κόλπον[3] νῆσος Λευκωσία, μικρὸν ἔχουσα πρὸς τὴν ἤπειρον διάπλουν, ἐπώνυμος μιᾶς τῶν Σειρήνων, ἐκπεσούσης δεῦρο μετὰ τὴν μυθευομένην ῥίψιν αὐτῶν εἰς τὸν βυθόν. τῆς δὲ νήσου πρόκειται τὸ ἀντακρωτήριον ταῖς Σειρηνούσσαις ποιοῦν τὸν Ποσειδωνιάτην κόλπον. κάμψαντι δ' ἄλλος συνεχὴς κόλπος, ἐν ᾧ πόλις, ἣν οἱ μὲν κτίσαντες Φωκαιεῖς Ὑέλην, οἱ δὲ Ἔλην ἀπὸ κρήνης τινός, οἱ δὲ νῦν Ἐλέαν ὀνομάζουσιν, ἐξ ἧς Παρμενίδης καὶ Ζήνων ἐγένοντο, ἄνδρες Πυθαγόρειοι. δοκεῖ δέ μοι καὶ δι' ἐκείνους καὶ ἔτι πρότερον εὐνομηθῆναι· διὸ καὶ

---

[1] Ἀργῴας, Meineke (from conj. of Casaubon), for Ἀργονίας.

[2] Most of the editors, including Meineke, transfer the words Συβαρῖται . . . ἀναχεόμενος (5. 4. 13) to a position after Ποσειδωνία.

[3] κόλπον, Kramer, for πόντον; so Meineke.

2

THE GEOGRAPHY OF STRABO

BOOK VI

I

1. After the mouth of the Silaris one comes to
Leucania, and to the temple of the Argoan Hera,
built by Jason, and near by, within fifty stadia, to
Poseidonia. Thence, sailing out past the gulf, one
comes to Leucosia,[1] an island, from which it is only
a short voyage across to the continent. The island
is named after one of the Sirens, who was cast
ashore here after the Sirens had flung themselves,
as the myth has it, into the depths of the sea. In
front of the island lies that promontory[2] which is
opposite the Sirenussae and with them forms the
Poseidonian Gulf. On doubling this promontory
one comes immediately to another gulf, in which
there is a city which was called "Hyele" by the
Phocaeans who founded it, and by others "Ele,"
after a certain spring, but is called by the men of
to-day "Elea." This is the native city of Parmenides and Zeno, the Pythagorean philosophers.
It is my opinion that not only through the influence
of these men but also in still earlier times the city

[1] Now Licosa.
[2] Poseidium, now Punta Della Licosa.

πρὸς Λευκανοὺς ἀντέσχον καὶ πρὸς Ποσειδωνιάτας
καὶ κρείττους ἀπῇεσαν, καίπερ ἐνδεέστεροι καὶ
χώρᾳ καὶ πλήθει σωμάτων ὄντες. ἀναγκάζονται
γοῦν διὰ τὴν λυπρότητα τῆς γῆς τὰ πολλὰ θαλατ-
τουργεῖν καὶ ταριχείας συνίστασθαι καὶ ἄλλας
τοιαύτας ἐργασίας. φησὶ δ᾽ Ἀντίοχος Φωκαίας
ἁλούσης ὑφ᾽ Ἁρπάγου, τοῦ Κύρου στρατηγοῦ,
τοὺς δυναμένους ἐμβάντας εἰς τὰ σκάφη πανοικίους
πλεῦσαι πρῶτον εἰς Κύρνον καὶ Μασσαλίαν μετὰ
Κρεοντιάδου, ἀποκρουσθέντας δὲ τὴν Ἐλέαν κτίσαι.
ἔνιοι δὲ τοὔνομα ἀπὸ ποταμοῦ Ἐλέητος· διέχει δὲ
τῆς Ποσειδωνίας ὅσον διακοσίους σταδίους ἡ πόλις.
μετὰ δὲ ταύτην ἀκρωτήριον Παλίνουρος. πρὸ δὲ
τῆς Ἐλεάτιδος αἱ Οἰνωτρίδες νῆσοι δύο, ὑφόρμους
C 253 ἔχουσαι. μετὰ δὲ Παλίνουρον Πυξοῦς ἄκρα καὶ
λιμὴν καὶ ποταμός· ἓν γὰρ τῶν τριῶν ὄνομα·
ᾤκισε δὲ Μίκυθος, ὁ Μεσσήνης ἄρχων τῆς ἐν
Σικελίᾳ, πάλιν δ᾽ ἀπῆραν οἱ ἱδρυθέντες πλὴν
ὀλίγων. μετὰ δὲ Πυξοῦντα ἄλλος[1] κόλπος καὶ
ποταμὸς Λᾶος καὶ πόλις, ἐσχάτη τῶν Λευκανίδων,
μικρὸν ὑπὲρ τῆς θαλάττης, ἄποικος Συβαριτῶν,
εἰς ἣν ἀπὸ Ἕλης στάδιοι τετρακόσιοι· ὁ δὲ πᾶς
τῆς Λευκανίας παράπλους ἑξακοσίων πεντήκοντα.
πλησίον δὲ τὸ τοῦ Δράκοντος ἡρῷον, ἑνὸς τῶν
Ὀδυσσέως ἑταίρων, ἐφ᾽ οὗ ὁ χρησμὸς τοῖς
Ἰταλιώταις ἐγένετο,

---

[1] ἄλλος, Unger (*Philologus*, 1881, p. 537), for Λᾶος.

[1] Antiochus Syracusanus, the historian. Cp. Herodotus
l. 167.
[2] The Latin form is " Hales " (now the Alento).
[3] The Greek inhabitants of Italy were called " Italiotes."

4

was well governed; and it was because of this good
government that the people not only held their own
against the Leucani and the Poseidoniatae, but even
returned victorious, although they were inferior to
them both in extent of territory and in population.
At any rate, they are compelled, on account of the
poverty of their soil, to busy themselves mostly
with the sea and to establish factories for the salting
of fish, and other such industries. According to
Antiochus,[1] after the capture of Phocaea by Harpagus, the general of Cyrus, all the Phocaeans who
could do so embarked with their entire families on
their light boats and, under the leadership of Cre-
ontiades, sailed first to Cyrnus and Massalia, but
when they were beaten off from those places founded
Elea. Some, however, say that the city took its
name from the River Elees.[2] It is about two
hundred stadia distant from Poseidonia After Elea
comes the promontory of Palinurus. Off the territory of Elea are two islands, the Oenotrides, which
have anchoring-places. After Palinurus comes Pyxus
—a cape, harbour, and river, for all three have the
same name. Pyxus was peopled with new settlers
by Micythus, the ruler of the Messene in Sicily,
but all the settlers except a few sailed away again.
After Pyxus comes another gulf, and also Laüs—
a river and city; it is the last of the Leucanian
cities, lying only a short distance above the sea,
is a colony of the Sybaritae, and the distance thither
from Ele is four hundred stadia. The whole voyage
along the coast of Leucania is six hundred and fifty
stadia. Near Laüs is the hero-temple of Draco, one
of the companions of Odysseus, in regard to which
the following oracle was given out to the Italiotes:[3]

5

STRABO

Λάϊον ἀμφὶ Δράκοντα πολύν ποτε λαὸν ὀλεῖ-
σθαι·

ἐπὶ γὰρ ταύτην λαοί[1] στρατεύσαντες οἱ κατὰ
τὴν Ἰταλίαν Ἕλληνες ὑπὸ Λευκανῶν ἠτύχησαν,
ἐξαπατηθέντες τῷ χρησμῷ.

2. Κατὰ μὲν δὴ τὴν Τυρρηνικὴν παραλίαν
ταῦτ᾿ ἐστὶ τὰ τῶν Λευκανῶν χωρία,[2] τῆς δ᾿
ἑτέρας οὐχ ἥπτοντο θαλάττης πρότερον, ἀλλ᾿ οἱ
Ἕλληνες ἐπεκράτουν οἱ τὸν Ταραντῖνον ἔχοντες
κόλπον. πρὶν δὲ τοὺς Ἕλληνας ἐλθεῖν οὐδ᾿ ἦσάν
πω Λευκανοί, Χῶνες δὲ καὶ Οἰνωτροὶ τοὺς τόπους
ἐνέμοντο. τῶν δὲ Σαυνιτῶν αὐξηθέντων ἐπὶ πολὺ
καὶ τοὺς Χῶνας καὶ τοὺς Οἰνωτροὺς ἐκβαλόντων,
Λευκανοὺς δ᾿ εἰς τὴν μερίδα ταύτην ἀποικισάντων,
ἅμα δὲ καὶ τῶν Ἑλλήνων τὴν ἑκατέρωθεν παραλίαν μέχρι Πορθμοῦ κατεχόντων, πολὺν χρόνον
ἐπολέμουν οἵ τε Ἕλληνες καὶ οἱ βάρβαροι πρὸς
ἀλλήλους. οἱ δὲ τῆς Σικελίας τύραννοι καὶ μετὰ
ταῦτα Καρχηδόνιοι τοτὲ μὲν περὶ τῆς Σικελίας
πολεμοῦντες πρὸς Ῥωμαίους, τοτὲ δὲ περὶ αὐτῆς
τῆς Ἰταλίας, ἅπαντας τοὺς ταύτῃ κακῶς διέθηκαν,
μάλιστα[3] δὲ τοὺς Ἕλληνας. ὕστερον μέν γε καὶ
τῆς μεσογαίας πολλὴν ἀφῄρηντο, ἀπὸ τῶν Τρωικῶν
χρόνων ἀρξάμενοι, καὶ δὴ ἐπὶ τοσοῦτον ηὔξαντο,
ὥστε τὴν μεγάλην Ἑλλάδα ταύτην ἔλεγον καὶ
τὴν Σικελίαν. νυνὶ δὲ πλὴν Τάραντος καὶ Ῥηγίου

[1] λαοί, the reading of the MSS., Jones restores, for Λᾶον.
[2] ἅ, after χωρία, Meineke deletes (Siebenkees and Corais
read οἱ τῆς ἑτέρας).
[3] μάλιστα, Villebrun, for μετά; so the editors in general.

[1] There is a word-play here which cannot be brought out
in translation: the word for "people" in Greek is "laos."

6

"Much people will one day perish about Laïan Draco."[1] And the oracle came true, for, deceived by it, the peoples[2] who made campaigns against Laüs, that is, the Greek inhabitants of Italy, met disaster at the hands of the Leucani.

2. These, then, are the places on the Tyrrhenian seaboard that belong to the Leucani. As for the other sea,[3] they could not reach it at first; in fact, the Greeks who held the Gulf of Tarentum were in control there. Before the Greeks came, however, the Leucani were as yet not even in existence, and the regions were occupied by the Chones and the Oenotri. But after the Samnitae had grown considerably in power, and had ejected the Chones and the Oenotri, and had settled a colony of Leucani in this portion of Italy, while at the same time the Greeks were holding possession of both seaboards as far as the Strait, the Greeks and the barbarians carried on war with one another for a long time. Then the tyrants of Sicily, and afterwards the Carthaginians, at one time at war with the Romans for the possession of Sicily and at another for the possession of Italy itself, maltreated all the peoples in this part of the world, but especially the Greeks. Later on, beginning from the time of the Trojan war, the Greeks had taken away from the earlier inhabitants much of the interior country also, and indeed had increased in power to such an extent that they called this part of Italy, together with Sicily, Magna Graecia. But to-day all parts of it, except Taras,[4] Rhegium, and Neapolis, have become

[2] Literally, "laoi."
[3] The Adriatic.
[4] The old name of Tarentum.

7

STRABO

καὶ Νεαπόλεως ἐκβεβαρβαρῶσθαι συμβέβηκεν
ἅπαντα καὶ τὰ μὲν Λευκανοὺς καὶ Βρεττίους
κατέχειν, τὰ δὲ Καμπανούς, καὶ τούτους λόγῳ,
τὸ δ' ἀληθὲς Ῥωμαίους· καὶ γὰρ αὐτοὶ Ῥωμαῖοι
γεγόνασιν. ὅμως δὲ τῷ πραγματευομένῳ τὴν τῆς
γῆς περίοδον καὶ τὰ νῦν ὄντα λέγειν ἀνάγκη καὶ
τῶν ὑπαρξάντων ἔνια, καὶ μάλιστα ὅταν ἔνδοξα
ᾖ. τῶν δὲ Λευκανῶν οἱ μὲν ἁπτόμενοι τῆς Τυρρηνικῆς θαλάττης εἴρηνται, οἱ δὲ τὴν μεσόγαιαν
ἔχοντές εἰσιν οἱ ὑπεροικοῦντες τοῦ Ταραντίνου
κόλπου. οὕτω δ' εἰσὶ κεκακωμένοι τελέως οὗτοι
καὶ Βρέττιοι καὶ αὐτοὶ Σαυνῖται οἱ τούτων ἀρχη-
γέται, ὥστε καὶ διορίσαι χαλεπὸν τὰς κατοικίας
C 254 αὐτῶν· αἴτιον δ' ὅτι οὐδὲν ἔτι σύστημα κοινὸν
τῶν ἐθνῶν ἑκάστου συμμένει, τά τε ἔθη διαλέκτων
τε καὶ ὁπλισμοῦ καὶ ἐσθῆτος καὶ τῶν παραπλη-
σίων ἐκλέλοιπεν, ἄλλως τε ἄδοξοι παντάπασίν
εἰσιν αἱ καθ' ἕκαστα καὶ ἐν μέρει κατοικίαι.
3. Ἐροῦμεν δὴ [1] κοινῶς ἃ παρειλήφαμεν, οὐδὲν
παρὰ τοῦτο ποιούμενοι τοὺς τὴν μεσόγαιαν οἰκοῦντας, Λευκανούς τε καὶ τοὺς προσεχεῖς αὐτοῖς
Σαυνίτας. Πετηλία μὲν οὖν μητρόπολις νομίζεται
τῶν Χώνων [2] καὶ συνοικεῖται μέχρι νῦν ἱκανῶς.
κτίσμα δ' ἐστὶ Φιλοκτήτου, φυγόντος τὴν Μελί-
βοιαν κατὰ στάσιν. ἐρυμνὴ δ' ἐστίν, ὥστε καὶ
Σαυνῖταί ποτε Θουρίοις [3] ἐπετείχισαν αὐτήν.

---

[1] δή, Jones, for δέ.
[2] Corais and Meineke emend Χώνων to Λευκανῶν.
[3] Θουρίοις, Meineke, for φρουρίοις.

---

[1] "Barbarised," in the sense of "non-Greek" (cp. 5. 4. 4
and 5. 4. 7).

completely barbarised,[1] and some parts have been
taken and are held by the Leucani and the Brettii,
and others by the Campani—that is, nominally by
the Campani but in truth by the Romans, since the
Campani themselves have become Romans.   However, the man who busies himself with the description of the earth must needs speak, not only of the
facts of the present, but also sometimes of the facts
of the past, especially when they are notable.   As
for the Leucani, I have already spoken of those
whose territory borders on the Tyrrhenian Sea,
while those who hold the interior are the people
who live above the Gulf of Tarentum.   But the
latter, and the Brettii, and the Samnitae themselves
(the progenitors of these peoples) have so utterly
deteriorated that it is difficult even to distinguish
their several settlements; and the reason is that no
common organisation longer endures in any one of
the separate tribes; and their characteristic differences in language, armour, dress, and the like, have
completely disappeared; and, besides, their settlements, severally and in detail, are wholly without
repute.

3. Accordingly, without making distinctions between them, I shall only tell in a general way what
I have learned about the peoples who live in the
interior, I mean the Leucani and such of the Samnitae as are their next neighbours.   Petelia, then,
is regarded as the metropolis of the Chones, and has
been rather populous down to the present day.
It was founded by Philoctetes after he, as the result
of a political quarrel, had fled from Meliboea.   It
has so strong a position by nature that the Samnitae
once fortified it against the Thurii.   And the old

9

Φιλοκτήτου δ' ἐστὶ καὶ ἡ παλαιὰ Κρίμισσα περὶ τοὺς αὐτοὺς τόπους. Ἀπολλόδωρος δ' ἐν τοῖς περὶ Νεῶν τοῦ Φιλοκτήτου μνησθεὶς λέγειν τινάς φησιν, ὡς εἰς τὴν Κροτωνιᾶτιν ἀφικόμενος Κρίμισσαν ἄκραν οἰκίσαι καὶ Χώνην πόλιν ὑπὲρ αὐτῆς, ἀφ' ἧς οἱ ταύτῃ Χῶνες ἐκλήθησαν, παρ' αὐτοῦ δέ τινες σταλέντες εἰς Σικελίαν περὶ Ἔρυκα μετὰ Αἰγέστου τοῦ Τρωὸς Αἴγεσταν τειχίσαιεν.[1] καὶ Γρουμεντὸν δὲ καὶ Οὐερτῖναι τῆς μεσογαίας εἰσὶ καὶ Καλάσαρνα καὶ ἄλλαι μικραὶ κατοικίαι μέχρι Οὐενουσίας, πόλεως ἀξιολόγου· ταύτην δ' οἶμαι καὶ τὰς ἐφεξῆς ἐπὶ Καμπανίαν ἰόντι Σαυνίτιδας εἶναι. ὑπὲρ δὲ τῶν Θουρίων καὶ ἡ Ταυριανὴ χώρα λεγομένη ἵδρυται. οἱ δὲ Λευκανοὶ τὸ μὲν γένος εἰσὶ Σαυνῖται, Ποσειδωνιατῶν δὲ καὶ τῶν συμμάχων κρατήσαντες πολέμῳ κατέσχον τὰς πόλεις αὐτῶν. τὸν μὲν οὖν ἄλλον χρόνον ἐδημοκρατοῦντο, ἐν δὲ τοῖς πολέμοις ᾑρεῖτο βασιλεὺς ἀπὸ[2] τῶν νεμομένων ἀρχάς· νῦν δ' εἰσὶ Ῥωμαῖοι.

4. Τὴν δ' ἐξῆς παραλίαν Βρέττιοι μέχρι τοῦ Σικελικοῦ κατέχουσι πορθμοῦ, σταδίων πεντήκοντα καὶ τριακοσίων ἐπὶ τοῖς χιλίοις. φησὶ δ' Ἀντίοχος ἐν τῷ περὶ τῆς Ἰταλίας συγγράμματι ταύτην Ἰταλίαν κληθῆναι, καὶ περὶ ταύτης συγγράφειν, πρότερον δ' Οἰνωτρίαν προσαγορεύεσθαι. ὅριον δ' αὐτῆς ἀποφαίνει πρὸς μὲν τῷ Τυρρηνικῷ

---

[1] τειχίσαιεν, Kramer, for τειχίσαι; so the later editors.
[2] ἀπό, Corais, for ὑπό; so Meineke.

---

[1] That is, his work entitled "On the (Homeric) Catalogue of Ships" (cp. 1. 2. 24).

Crimissa, which is near the same regions, was also founded by Philoctetes. Apollodorus, in his work *On Ships*,[1] in mentioning Philoctetes, says that, according to some, when Philoctetes arrived at the territory of Croton, he colonised the promontory Crimissa, and, in the interior above it, the city Chone, from which the Chonians of that district took their name, and that some of his companions whom he had sent forth with Aegestes the Trojan to the region of Eryx in Sicily fortified Aegesta.[2] Moreover, Grumentum and Vertinae are in the interior, and so are Calasarna and some other small settlements, until we arrive at Venusia, a notable city; but I think that this city and those that follow in order after it as one goes towards Campania are Samnite cities. Beyond Thurii lies also the country that is called Tauriana. The Leucani are Samnite in race, but upon mastering the Poseidoniatae and their allies in war they took possession of their cities. At all other times, it is true, their government was democratic, but in times of war they were wont to choose a king from those who held magisterial offices. But now they are Romans.

4. The seaboard that comes next after Leucania, as far as the Sicilian Strait and for a distance of thirteen hundred and fifty stadia, is occupied by the Brettii. According to Antiochus, in his treatise *On Italy*, this territory (and this is the territory which he says he is describing) was once called Italy, although in earlier times it was called Oenotria. And he designates as its boundaries, first, on the Tyrrhenian Sea, the same boundary that I have

---

[2] Also spelled Segesta and Egesta.

πελάγει τὸ αὐτὸ ὅπερ καὶ τῆς Βρεττιανῆς [1] ἔφαμεν,
τὸν Λᾶον ποταμόν· πρὸς δὲ τῷ Σικελικῷ τὸ
Μεταπόντιον. τὴν δὲ Ταραντίνην, ἢ συνεχὴς τῷ
Μεταποντίῳ ἐστίν, ἐκτὸς τῆς Ἰταλίας ὀνομάζει,
Ἰάπυγας καλῶν. ἔτι δ᾽ ἀνώτερον Οἰνωτρούς τε
καὶ Ἰταλοὺς μόνους ἔφη καλεῖσθαι τοὺς ἐντὸς
τοῦ ἰσθμοῦ πρὸς τὸν Σικελικὸν κεκλιμένους
C 255 πορθμόν. ἔστι δ᾽ αὐτὸς ὁ ἰσθμὸς ἑκατὸν καὶ
ἑξήκοντα στάδιοι μεταξὺ δυεῖν κόλπων, τοῦ τε
Ἱππωνιάτου, ὃν Ἀντίοχος Ναπητῖνον εἴρηκε, καὶ
τοῦ Σκυλλητικοῦ. περίπλους δ᾽ ἐστὶ τῆς ἀπο-
λαμβανομένης χώρας πρὸς τὸν Πορθμὸν ἐντὸς
στάδιοι δισχίλιοι. μετὰ δὲ ταῦτα ἐπεκτείνεσθαί [2]
φησι τοὔνομα καὶ τὸ τῆς Ἰταλίας καὶ τὸ τῶν
Οἰνωτρῶν μέχρι τῆς Μεταποντίνης καὶ τῆς
Σειρίτιδος· οἰκῆσαι γὰρ τοὺς τόπους τούτους
Χῶνας, Οἰνωτρικὸν ἔθνος κατακοσμούμενον, καὶ
τὴν γῆν ὀνομάσαι Χώνην. οὗτος μὲν οὖν ἁπλουστέρως εἴρηκε καὶ ἀρχαϊκῶς, οὐδὲν διορίσας περὶ
τῶν Λευκανῶν καὶ τῶν Βρεττίων. ἔστι δ᾽ ἡ μὲν
Λευκανία μεταξὺ τῆς τε παραλίας τῆς Τυρρηνικῆς
καὶ τῆς Σικελικῆς, τῆς μὲν ἀπὸ τοῦ Σιλάριδος
μέχρι Λάου, τῆς δ᾽ ἀπὸ τοῦ Μεταποντίου μέχρι
Θουρίων· κατὰ δὲ τὴν ἤπειρον ἀπὸ Σαυνιτῶν
μέχρι τοῦ ἰσθμοῦ τοῦ ἀπὸ Θουρίων εἰς Κηρίλλους,
πλησίον Λάου· στάδιοι δ᾽ εἰσὶ τοῦ ἰσθμοῦ τριακόσιοι. ὑπὲρ δὲ τούτων Βρέττιοι, χερρόνησον
οἰκοῦντες, ἐν ταύτῃ δ᾽ ἄλλη περιείληπται χερ-

[1] Βρεττιανῆς, Madvig, for Βρεττανίας.
[2] ἐπεκτείνεσθαι, Groskurd, for ἐπεκτείνεται; so the later
editors.

assigned to the country of the Brettii—the River
Laüs; and secondly, on the Sicilian Sea, Metapontium. But as for the country of the Tarantini,
which borders on Metapontium, he names it as
outside of Italy, and calls its inhabitants Iapyges.
And at a time more remote, according to him, the
names "Italians" and "Oenotrians" were applied
only to the people who lived this side the isthmus
in the country that slopes toward the Sicilian
Strait The isthmus itself, one hundred and sixty
stadia in width, lies between two gulfs—the Hipponiate (which Antiochus has called Napetine) and
the Scylletic. The coasting-voyage round the
country comprised between the isthmus and the
Strait is two thousand stadia. But after that, he
says, the name of "Italy" and that of the "Oenotrians" was further extended as far as the territory
of Metapontium and that of Seiris, for, he adds, the
Chones, a well-regulated Oenotrian tribe, had taken
up their abode in these regions and had called the
land Chone. Now Antiochus had spoken only in a
rather simple and antiquated way, without making
any distinctions between the Leucani and the
Brettii. In the first place, Leucania lies between
the Tyrrhenian and Sicilian coast-lines,[1] the former
coast-line from the River Silaris as far as Laüs, and
the latter, from Metapontium as far as Thurii; in
the second place, on the mainland, from the country
of the Samnitae as far as the isthmus which extends
from Thurii to Cerilli (a city near Laüs), the isthmus
is three hundred stadia in width. But the Brettii
are situated beyond the Leucani; they live on

[1] Between the coast-lines on the Tyrrhenian and Sicilian
Seas.

13

ρόνησος ἡ τὸν ἰσθμὸν ἔχουσα τὸν ἀπὸ Σκυλλητίου
ἐπὶ τὸν Ἱππωνιάτην κόλπον. ὠνόμασται δὲ τὸ
ἔθνος ὑπὸ Λευκανῶν· Βρεττίους γὰρ καλοῦσι τοὺς
ἀποστάτας· ἀπέστησαν δ᾽, ὥς φασι, ποιμαίνοντες
αὐτοῖς πρότερον, εἶθ᾽ ὑπὸ ἀνέσεως ἐλευθεριάσαντες,
ἡνίκα ἐπεστράτευσε Δίων Διονυσίῳ καὶ ἐξετάραξεν
ἅπαντας πρὸς ἅπαντας. τὰ καθόλου μὲν δὴ ταῦτα
περὶ Λευκανῶν καὶ Βρεττίων λέγομεν.

5. Ἀπὸ γὰρ Λάου πρώτη πόλις ἐστὶ τῆς
Βρεττίας Τεμέση, Τέμψαν δ᾽ οἱ νῦν καλοῦσιν,
Αὐσόνων κτίσμα, ὕστερον δὲ καὶ Αἰτωλῶν τῶν
μετὰ Θόαντος, οὓς ἐξέβαλον Βρέττιοι, Βρεττίους
δὲ ἐπέτριψαν Ἀννίβας τε καὶ Ῥωμαῖοι. ἔστι
δὲ πλησίον τῆς Τεμέσης ἡρῷον, ἀγριελαίοις
συνηρεφές, Πολίτου τῶν Ὀδυσσέως ἑταίρων,
ὃν δολοφονηθέντα ὑπὸ τῶν βαρβάρων γενέσθαι
βαρύμηνιν, ὥστε τοὺς περιοίκους δασμολογεῖν
αὐτῷ κατά τι λόγιον, καὶ παροιμίαν εἶναι πρὸς
τοὺς ἀνηλεεῖς,[1] τὸν ἥρωα τὸν ἐν Τεμέσῃ λεγόντων
ἐπικεῖσθαι αὐτοῖς. Λοκρῶν δὲ τῶν Ἐπιζεφυρίων
ἑλόντων τὴν πόλιν, Εὔθυμον μυθεύουσι τὸν
πύκτην καταβάντα ἐπ᾽ αὐτὸν κρατῆσαι τῇ μάχῃ
καὶ βιάσασθαι παραλῦσαι τοῦ δασμοῦ τοὺς

---

[1] τοὺς ἀνηλεεῖς, Kramer and Müller-Dübner, following
Buttmann, for αὐτοὺς μηδείς. Meineke, τοὺς ἀηδεῖς.

---

[1] According to Pausanias (6. 6. 2) the oracle bade the
people annually to give the hero to wife the fairest maiden
in Temesa.

[2] "Merciless" is an emendation. Some read "disagree-
able." According to Aelian (*Var. Hist.* 8. 18), the popular
saying was applied to those who in pursuit of profit over-
reached themselves (so Plutarch *Prov.* 31). But Eustathius

a peninsula, but this peninsula includes another
peninsula which has the isthmus that extends from
Scylletium to the Hipponiate Gulf. The name of
the tribe was given to it by the Leucani, for the
Leucani call all revolters "brettii." The Brettii
revolted, so it is said (at first they merely tended
flocks for the Leucani, and then, by reason of the
indulgence of their masters, began to act as free
men), at the time when Dio made his expedition
against Dionysius and aroused all peoples against all
others. So much, then, for my general description
of the Leucani and the Brettii.

5. The next city after Laüs belongs to Brettium,
and is named Temesa, though the men of to-day call
it Tempsa; it was founded by the Ausones, but later
on was settled also by the Aetolians under the
leadership of Thoas; but the Aetolians were ejected
by the Brettii, and then the Brettii were crushed by
Hannibal and by the Romans. Near Temesa, and
thickly shaded with wild olive-trees, is the hero-
temple of Polites, one of the companions of Odysseus,
who was treacherously slain by the barbarians, and
for that reason became so exceedingly wroth against
the country that, in accordance with an oracle, the
people of the neighbourhood collected tribute [1] for
him; and hence, also, the popular saying applied to
those who are merciless,[2] that they are "beset by
the hero of Temesa." But when the Epizephyrian
Locrians captured the city, Euthymus, the pugilist,
so the story goes, entered the lists against Polites,
defeated him in the fight and forced him to release the

(note on *Iliad* 1. 185) quotes "the geographer" (*i.e.* Strabo;
see note 1, p. 320) as making the saying apply to "those who
are unduly wroth, or very severe when they should not be."

ἐπιχωρίους. ταύτης δὲ τῆς Τεμέσης φασὶ μεμνῆσθαι τὸν ποιητήν, οὐ τῆς ἐν Κύπρῳ Ταμασσοῦ (λέγεται γὰρ ἀμφοτέρως) τῷ[1]

ἐς Τεμέσην μετὰ χαλκόν,

C 256 καὶ δείκνυται χαλκουργεῖα πλησίον, ἃ νῦν ἐκλέλειπται. ταύτης δὴ συνεχὴς Τερίνα, ἣν Ἀννίβας καθεῖλεν, οὐ δυνάμενος φυλάττειν, ὅτε δὴ εἰς αὐτὴν καταπεφεύγει τὴν Βρεττίαν. εἶτα Κωσεντία μητρόπολις Βρεττίων. μικρὸν δ᾽ ὑπὲρ ταύτης Πανδοσία φρούριον ἐρυμνόν, περὶ ἣν Ἀλέξανδρος ὁ Μολοττὸς διεφθάρη. ἐξηπάτησε δὲ καὶ τοῦτον ὁ ἐκ Δωδώνης χρησμός, φυλάττεσθαι κελεύων τὸν Ἀχέροντα καὶ Πανδοσίαν· δεικνυμένων γὰρ ἐν τῇ Θεσπρωτίᾳ ὁμωνύμων τούτοις, ἐνταῦθα κατέστρεψε τὸν βίον. τρικόρυφον δ᾽ ἐστὶ τὸ φρούριον, καὶ παραρρεῖ ποταμὸς Ἀχέρων. προσηπάτησε δὲ καὶ ἄλλο λόγιον,

Πανδοσία τρικόλωνε, πολύν ποτε λαὸν ὀλέσσεις·

ἔδοξε γὰρ πολεμίων φθοράν, οὐκ οἰκείων δηλοῦσθαι. φασὶ δὲ καὶ βασίλειόν ποτε γενέσθαι τῶν Οἰνωτρικῶν βασιλέων τὴν Πανδοσίαν. μετὰ δὲ τὴν Κωσεντίαν Ἱππώνιον, Λοκρῶν κτίσμα· Βρεττίους δὲ κατέχοντας ἀφείλοντο Ῥωμαῖοι καὶ μετωνόμασαν Οὐιβῶνα Οὐαλεντίαν. διὰ δὲ τὸ εὐλεί-

---

[1] τῷ, Müller-Dübner. for τό. Meineke relegates τὸ . . . χαλκόν to the foot of the page.

---

[1] Odyssey 1. 184.
[2] Cp. 6. 3. 4 and footnote.

natives from the tribute. People say that Homer
has in mind this Temesa, not the Tamassus in Cyprus
(the name is spelled both ways), when he says "to
Temesa, in quest of copper."[1] And in fact copper
mines are to be seen in the neighbourhood, although
now they have been abandoned. Near Temesa is
Terina, which Hannibal destroyed, because he was
unable to guard it, at the time when he had taken
refuge in Brettium itself. Then comes Consentia,
the metropolis of the Brettii ; and a little above this
city is Pandosia, a strong fortress, near which
Alexander the Molossian[2] was killed. He, too, was
deceived by the oracle[3] at Dodona, which bade him
be on his guard against Acheron and Pandosia ; for
places which bore these names were pointed out to
him in Thesprotia, but he came to his end here in
Brettium. Now the fortress has three summits, and
the River Acheron flows past it. And there was
another oracle that helped to deceive him : "Three-
hilled Pandosia, much people shalt thou kill one day";
for he thought that the oracle clearly meant the
destruction of the enemy, not of his own people. It
is said that Pandosia was once the capital of the
Oenotrian Kings. After Consentia comes Hipponium,
which was founded by the Locrians. Later on, the
Brettii were in possession of Hipponium, but the
Romans took it away from them and changed its
name to Vibo Valentia. And because the country

---

[3] The oracle, quoted by Casaubon from some source unknown to subsequent editors was :

Αἰακίδη, προφύλαξο μολεῖν 'Αχερούσιον ὕδωρ
Πανδοσίην δ' ὅθι τοι θάνατος πεπρωμένος ἐστί.

"Son of Aeacus, beware to go to the Acherusian water and
Pandosia, where 'tis fated thou shalt die."

17

μωνα εἶναι τὰ περικείμενα χωρία καὶ ἀνθηρὰ τὴν
Κόρην ἐκ Σικελίας πεπιστεύκασιν ἀφικνεῖσθαι
δεῦρο ἀνθολογήσουσαν· ἐκ δὲ τούτου ταῖς γυναιξὶν
ἐν ἔθει γέγονεν ἀνθολογεῖν τε καὶ στεφανηπλοκεῖν,
ὥστε ταῖς ἑορταῖς αἰσχρὸν εἶναι στεφάνους ὠνη-
τοὺς φορεῖν. ἔχει δ' ἐπίνειον, ὃ κατεσκεύασέ
ποτε Ἀγαθοκλῆς ὁ τύραννος τῶν Σικελιωτῶν,
κρατήσας τῆς πόλεως. ἐντεῦθεν δ' ἐπὶ τὸν Ἡρακλέους λιμένα πλεύσασιν ἀρχὴ τοῦ ἐπιστρέφειν
τὰ ἄκρα τῆς Ἰταλίας τὰ πρὸς τῷ Πορθμῷ πρὸς
τὴν ἑσπέραν. ἐν δὲ τῷ παράπλῳ τούτῳ Μέδμα,
πόλις Λοκρῶν τῶν αὐτῶν ὁμώνυμος κρήνη μεγάλη,
πλησίον ἔχουσα ἐπίνειον καλούμενον Ἐμπόριον·
ἐγγὺς δὲ καὶ Μέταυρος ποταμός, καὶ ὕφορμος
ὁμώνυμος. πρόκεινται δὲ τῆς ἠιόνος ταύτης αἱ
τῶν Λιπαραίων νῆσοι, διέχουσαι τοῦ Πορθμοῦ
σταδίους διακοσίους. οἱ δ' Αἰόλου φασίν, οὗ καὶ
τὸν ποιητὴν μεμνῆσθαι κατὰ τὴν Ὀδύσσειαν· εἰσὶ
δ' ἑπτὰ τὸν ἀριθμὸν ἐν ἀπόψει πᾶσαι καὶ τοῖς ἐκ
τῆς Σικελίας καὶ τοῖς ἐκ τῆς ἠπείρου τοῖς κατὰ
τὴν Μέδμαν ἀφορῶσι· περὶ ὧν ἐροῦμεν, ὅταν περὶ
τῆς Σικελίας λέγωμεν. ἀπὸ δὲ τοῦ Μεταύρου
ποταμοῦ, Μέταυρος [1] ἕτερος· ἐκδέχεται δ' ἐντεῦθεν

[1] Μέταυρος, Kramer emends to ποταμός, and Meineke deletes.

[1] i.e. Persephone.
[2] The "Siciliotes" were Sicilian Greeks, as distinguished from native Sicilians.
[3] Now Tropea. But in fact the turn towards the west begins immediately after Hipponium.
[4] Odyssey 10. 2 ff.
[5] Strabo's "Metaurus" and "second Metaurus" are confusing. Kramer, Meineke, and others wish to emend the text so as to make the "second" river refer to the Crataeis or some other river. But we should have expected Strabo

round about Hipponium has luxuriant meadows
abounding in flowers, people have believed that Core[1]
used to come hither from Sicily to gather flowers;
and consequently it has become the custom among the
women of Hipponium to gather flowers and to weave
them into garlands, so that on festival days it is
disgraceful to wear bought garlands. Hipponium
has also a naval station, which was built long ago by
Agathocles, the tyrant of the Siciliotes,[2] when he made
himself master of the city. Thence one sails to the
Harbour of Heracles,[3] which is the point where the
headlands of Italy near the Strait begin to turn
towards the west. And on this voyage one passes
Medma, a city of the same Locrians aforementioned,
which has the same name as a great fountain there,
and possesses a naval station near by, called Emporium. Near it is also the Metaurus River, and
a mooring-place bearing the same name. Off this
coast lie the islands of the Liparaei, at a distance of
two hundred stadia from the Strait. According to
some, they are the islands of Aeolus, of whom the
Poet makes mention in the *Odyssey*.[4] They are
seven in number and are all within view both from
Sicily and from the continent near Medma. But I
shall tell about them when I discuss Sicily. After
the Metaurus River comes a second Metaurus.[5]

to mention first the Medma (now the Mesima), which was
much closer to Medma than the Metaurus (now the Marro),
and to which he does not refer at all. Possibly he thought
both rivers were called Metaurus (cp. Müller, *Ind. Var. Lectionis*, p. 975), in which case "the second Metaurus" is the
Metaurus proper. The present translator, however, believes
that Strabo, when he says "second Metaurus," alludes to the
Umbrian Metaurus (5. 2. 10) as the first, and that the copyist,
unaware of this fact, deliberately changed "Medma" to
"Metaurus" in the two previous instances.

τὸ Σκύλλαιον, πέτρα χερρονησίζουσα ὑψηλή, τὸν
C 257 ἰσθμὸν ἀμφίδυμον καὶ ταπεινὸν ἔχουσα, ὃν ᾿Αναξί-
λαος ὁ τύραννος τῶν ῾Ρηγίνων ἐπετείχισε τοῖς
Τυρρηνοῖς, κατασκευάσας ναύσταθμον, καὶ ἀφεί-
λετο τοὺς λῃστὰς τὸν διὰ τοῦ Πορθμοῦ διάπλουν.
πλησίον γάρ ἐστι καὶ ἡ Καῖνυς, διέχουσα τῆς
Μέδμης σταδίους πεντήκοντα καὶ διακοσίους, ἡ
τελευταία ἄκρα ποιοῦσα τὰ στενὰ τοῦ Πορθμοῦ
πρὸς τὴν ἐκ τῆς Σικελίας ἄκραν τὴν Πελωριάδα·
ἔστι δ᾿ αὕτη μία τῶν τριῶν ποιουσῶν τρίγωνον
τὴν νῆσον, νεύει δὲ ἐπὶ θερινὰς ἀνατολάς, καθάπερ
ἡ Καῖνυς πρὸς τὴν ἑσπέραν, ἀνταποστροφήν τινα
ἀπ᾿ ἀλλήλων ποιουμένων αὐτῶν. ἀπὸ δὲ Καίνυος
μέχρι τοῦ Ποσειδωνίου ἢ[1] τῆς ῾Ρηγίνων στυλίδος
τοῦ Πορθμοῦ διήκει στενωπὸς ὅσον ἑξαστάδιος,
μικρῷ δὲ πλέον τὸ ἐλάχιστον διαπέραμα, ἀπὸ δὲ
στυλίδος ἑκατὸν εἰς ῾Ρήγιον, ἤδη τοῦ Πορθμοῦ
πλατυνομένου, προϊοῦσι πρὸς τὴν ἔξω καὶ πρὸς
ἕω θάλατταν τὴν τοῦ Σικελικοῦ καλουμένου
πελάγους.

6. Κτίσμα δ᾿ ἐστὶ τὸ ῾Ρήγιον Χαλκιδέων, οὓς
κατὰ χρησμὸν δεκατευθέντας τῷ ᾿Απόλλωνι δι᾿
ἀφορίαν, ὕστερον ἐκ Δελφῶν ἀποικῆσαι δεῦρό
φασι, παραλαβόντας καὶ ἄλλους τῶν οἴκοθεν· ὡς
δ᾿ ᾿Αντίοχός φησι, Ζαγκλαῖοι μετεπέμψαντο τοὺς
Χαλκιδέας καὶ οἰκιστὴν ᾿Αντίμνηστον συνέστησαν

---

[1] ἤ, Jones inserts ; Corais and others insert καί.

---

[1] Now Cape Cavallo.
[2] North-east (cp. 1. 2. 21).
[3] Altar or temple of Poseidon.
[4] Cp. 6. 1. 9.

Next after this river comes Scyllaeum, a lofty rock which forms a peninsula, its isthmus being low and affording access to ships on both sides. This isthmus Anaxilaüs, the tyrant of the Rhegini, fortified against the Tyrrheni, building a naval station there, and thus deprived the pirates of their passage through the strait. For Caenys,[1] too, is near by, being two hundred and fifty stadia distant from Medma; it is the last cape, and with the cape on the Sicilian side, Pelorias, forms the narrows of the Strait. Cape Pelorias is one of the three capes that make the island triangular, and it bends towards the summer sunrise,[2] just as Caenys bends towards the west, each one thus turning away from the other in the opposite direction. Now the length of the narrow passage of the Strait from Caenys as far as the Poseidonium,[3] or the Columna Rheginorum, is about six stadia, while the shortest passage across is slightly more; and the distance is one hundred stadia from the Columna to Rhegium, where the Strait begins to widen out, as one proceeds towards the east, towards the outer sea, the sea which is called the Sicilian Sea.

6. Rhegium was founded by the Chalcidians who, it is said, in accordance with an oracle, were dedicated, one man out of every ten Chalcidians, to Apollo,[4] because of a dearth of crops, but later on emigrated hither from Delphi, taking with them still others from their home. But according to Antiochus, the Zanclaeans sent for the Chalcidians and appointed Antimnestus their founder-in-chief.[5] To this colony

[5] Zancle was the original name of Messana (now Messina) in Sicily. It was colonised and named Messana by the Peloponnesian Messenians (6. 2. 3).

STRABO

ἐκείνων. ἦσαν δὲ τῆς ἀποικίας καὶ οἱ Μεσσηνίων
φυγάδες τῶν ἐν Πελοποννήσῳ κατασταστιασθέντες
ὑπὸ τῶν μὴ βουλομένων δοῦναι δίκας ὑπὲρ τῆς
φθορᾶς τῶν παρθένων τῆς ἐν Λίμναις γενομένης τοῖς Λακεδαιμονίοις, ἃς καὶ αὐτοὶ[1] ἐβιά-
σαντο, πεμφθείσας ἐπὶ τὴν ἱερουργίαν, καὶ τοὺς
ἐπιβοηθοῦντας ἀπέκτειναν. παραχωρήσαντες
οὖν εἰς Μάκιστον οἱ φυγάδες πέμπουσιν εἰς
θεοῦ, μεμφόμενοι τὸν Ἀπόλλω καὶ τὴν Ἄρ-
τεμιν, εἰ τοιούτου τυγχάνοιεν ἀνθ' ὧν ἐτιμώρουν
αὑτοῖς, καὶ πυνθανόμενοι, πῶς ἂν σωθεῖεν ἀπο-
λωλότες. ὁ δ' Ἀπόλλων ἐκέλευσε στέλλεσθαι
μετὰ Χαλκιδέων εἰς τὸ Ῥήγιον καὶ τῇ ἀδελφῇ
αὐτοῦ χάριν ἔχειν· οὐ γὰρ ἀπολωλέναι αὐτούς,
ἀλλὰ σεσῶσθαι, μέλλοντάς γε δὴ μὴ συναφανι-
σθήσεσθαι τῇ πατρίδι, ἁλωσομένῃ μικρὸν ὕστερον
ὑπὸ Σπαρτιατῶν· οἱ δ' ὑπήκουσαν. διόπερ οἱ τῶν
Ῥηγίνων ἡγεμόνες μέχρι Ἀναξίλα τοῦ Μεσσηνίων
γένους ἀεὶ καθίσταντο. Ἀντίοχος δὲ τὸ παλαιὸν
ἅπαντα τὸν τόπον τοῦτον οἰκῆσαί φησι Σικελοὺς
καὶ Μόργητας· διᾶραι δὲ εἰς τὴν Σικελίαν ὕστερον,
ἐκβληθέντας ὑπὸ τῶν Οἰνωτρῶν. φασὶ δέ τινες
καὶ τὸ Μοργάντιον ἐντεῦθεν τὴν προσηγορίαν ἀπὸ
C 258 τῶν Μοργήτων ἔχειν. ἴσχυσε δὲ μέγιστον ἡ τῶν
Ῥηγίνων πόλις καὶ περιοικίδας ἔσχε συχνάς, ἐπι-
τείχισμά τε ὑπῆρξεν ἀεὶ τῇ νήσῳ καὶ πάλαι
καὶ νεωστὶ ἐφ' ἡμῶν, ἡνίκα Σέξτος Πομπήιος

[1] αὐτοί, the reading of the MSS., Jones restores; for
αὐτάς, the reading of the editors since Corais.

[1] Cp 6. 3. 3. and 8. 4. 9.   [2] Cp. Pausanias, 4. 4. 1.
[3] Anaxilas (also spelled Anaxilaüs) was ruler of Rhegium
from 494 to 476 B.C. (Diodorus Siculus 11. 48).
22

also belonged the refugees of the Peloponnesian
Messenians who had been defeated by the men of
the opposing faction.   These men were unwilling to
be punished by the Lacedaemonians for the violation
of the maidens [1] which took place at Limnae, though
they were themselves guilty of the outrage done to
the maidens, who had been sent there for a religious
rite and had also killed those who came to their aid.[2]
So the refugees, after withdrawing to Macistus, sent
a deputation to the oracle of the god to find fault
with Apollo and Artemis if such was to be their fate
in return for their trying to avenge those gods, and
also to enquire how they, now utterly ruined, might
be saved.   Apollo bade them go forth with the
Chalcidians to Rhegium, and to be grateful to his
sister; for, he added, they were not ruined, but saved,
inasmuch as they were surely not to perish along
with their native land, which would be captured a
little later by the Spartans.   They obeyed; and
therefore the rulers of the Rhegini down to Anaxilas [3]
were always appointed from the stock of the
Messenians.   According to Antiochus, the Siceli and
Morgetes had in early times inhabited the whole of
this region, but later on, being ejected by the
Oenotrians, had crossed over into Sicily.   According
to some, Morgantium also took its name from the
Morgetes of Rhegium.[4]   The city of Rhegium was
once very powerful and had many dependencies in
the neighbourhood; and it was always a fortified
outpost threatening the island, not only in earlier
times but also recently, in our own times, when Sextus

[4] Cp. 6. 2. 4.   The Latin name of this Sicilian city was
"Murgantia."   Livy (10. 17) refers to another Murgantia in
Samnium.

ἀπέστησε τὴν Σικελίαν. ὠνομάσθη δὲ Ῥήγιον, εἶθ', ὥς φησιν Αἰσχύλος, διὰ τὸ συμβὰν πάθος τῇ χώρᾳ ταύτῃ· ἀπορραγῆναι γὰρ ἀπὸ τῆς ἠπείρου τὴν Σικελίαν ὑπὸ σεισμῶν, ἄλλοι τε κἀκεῖνος εἴρηκεν·

ἀφ' οὗ δὴ Ῥήγιον κικλήσκεται.

τεκμαίρονται δ' ἀπὸ τῶν περὶ τὴν Αἴτνην συμπτωμάτων καὶ τῶν κατ' ἄλλα μέρη τῆς Σικελίας καὶ τῶν κατὰ Λιπάραν καὶ τὰς περὶ αὐτὴν νήσους, ἔτι δὲ τῶν κατὰ τὰς Πιθηκούσσας καὶ τὴν προσεχῆ περαίαν ἅπασαν οὐκ ἀπεικὸς ὑπάρχειν καὶ τοῦτο συμβῆναι. νυνὶ μὲν οὖν ἀνεῳγμένων τούτων τῶν στομάτων, δι' ὧν τὸ πῦρ ἀναφυσᾶται καὶ μύδροι καὶ ὕδατα ἐκπίπτει, σπάνιόν τι σείεσθαί φασι τὴν περὶ τὸν Πορθμὸν γῆν, τότε δὲ πάντων ἐμπεφραγμένων τῶν εἰς τὴν ἐπιφάνειαν πόρων, ὑπὸ γῆς σμυχόμενον τὸ πῦρ καὶ τὸ πνεῦμα σεισμοὺς ἀπειργάζετο σφοδρούς, μοχλευόμενοι δ' οἱ τόποι πρὸς τὴν βίαν τῶν ἀνέμων ὑπεῖξάν ποτε καὶ ἀναρραγέντες ἐδέξαντο τὴν ἑκατέρωθεν θάλατταν καὶ ταύτην καὶ τὴν μεταξὺ τῶν ἄλλων τῶν ταύτῃ νήσων. καὶ γὰρ ἡ Προχύτη καὶ Πιθηκοῦσσαι ἀποσπάσματα τῆς ἠπείρου καὶ αἱ Καπρίαι καὶ ἡ Λευκωσία καὶ Σειρῆνες καὶ αἱ Οἰνωτρίδες. αἱ δὲ καὶ ἐκ τοῦ πελάγους ἀνέδυσαν, καθάπερ καὶ νῦν πολλαχοῦ συμβαίνει· τὰς μὲν γὰρ πελαγίας ἐκ βυθοῦ μᾶλλον ἀνενεχθῆναι πιθανόν, τὰς δὲ προκειμένας τῶν ἀκρωτηρίων καὶ πορθμῷ διῃρημένας ἐντεῦθεν ἀπερρωγέναι δοκεῖν

---

[1] Cp. 1. 3. 19 and the footnote on "rent."

GEOGRAPHY, 6. 1. 6

Pompeius caused Sicily to revolt. It was named Rhegium, either, as Aeschylus says, because of the calamity that had befallen this region, for, as both he and others state, Sicily was once "rent"[1] from the continent by earthquakes, "and so from this fact," he adds, "it is called Rhegium." They infer from the occurrences about Aetna and in other parts of Sicily, and in Lipara and in the islands about it, and also in the Pithecussae and the whole of the coast of the adjacent continent, that it is not unreasonable to suppose that the rending actually took place. Now at the present time the earth about the Strait, they say, is but seldom shaken by earthquakes, because the orifices there, through which the fire is blown up and the red-hot masses and the waters are ejected, are open. At that time, however, the fire that was smouldering beneath the earth, together with the wind, produced violent earthquakes, because the passages to the surface were all blocked up, and the regions thus heaved up yielded at last to the force of the blasts of wind, were rent asunder, and then received the sea that was on either side, both here[2] and between the other islands in that region.[3] And, in fact, Prochyte and the Pithecussae are fragments broken off from the continent, as also Capreae, Leucosia, the Sirenes, and the Oenotrides. Again, there are islands which have arisen from the high seas, a thing that even now happens in many places; for it is more plausible that the islands in the high seas were heaved up from the deeps, whereas it is more reasonable to think that those lying off the promontories and separated merely by a strait from the mainland have been

[2] At the Strait.   [3] Cp. 1. 3. 10 and the footnote.

εὐλογώτερον. πλὴν εἴτε διὰ ταῦτα τοὔνομα τῇ
πόλει γέγονεν, εἴτε διὰ τὴν ἐπιφάνειαν τῆς πόλεως,
ὡς ἂν βασίλειον τῇ Λατίνῃ φωνῇ προσαγορευ-
σάντων Σαυνιτῶν διὰ τὸ τοὺς ἀρχηγέτας αὐτῶν
κοινωνῆσαι Ῥωμαίοις τῆς πολιτείας καὶ ἐπὶ πολὺ
χρήσασθαι τῇ Λατίνῃ διαλέκτῳ, πάρεστι σκοπεῖν,
ὁποτέρως ἔχει τἀληθές. ἐπιφανῆ δ᾽ οὖν πόλιν
οὖσαν καὶ πολλὰς μὲν πόλεις οἰκίσασαν, πολλοὺς
δ᾽ ἄνδρας παρασχομένην ἀξίους λόγου, τοὺς μὲν
κατὰ πολιτικὴν ἀρετήν, τοὺς δὲ κατὰ παιδείαν,
κατασκάψαι Διονύσιον αἰτιασάμενον, ὅτι αἰτη-
σαμένῳ κόρην πρὸς γάμον τὴν τοῦ δημίου θυγα-
τέρα προὔτειναν· ὁ δ᾽ υἱὸς αὐτοῦ μέρος τι τοῦ
κτίσματος ἀναλαβὼν Φοιβίαν ἐκάλεσεν. ἐπὶ δὲ
Πύρρου ἡ τῶν Καμπανῶν φρουρὰ παρασπονδη-
θέντας διέφθειρε τοὺς πλείστους· μικρὸν δὲ πρὸ
τῶν Μαρσικῶν καὶ σεισμοὶ κατήρειψαν πολὺ τῆς
C 259 κατοικίας. Πομπήιον δ᾽ ἐκβαλὼν τῆς Σικελίας ὁ
Σεβαστὸς Καῖσαρ, ὁρῶν λειπανδροῦσαν τὴν πόλιν,
συνοίκους ἔδωκεν αὐτῇ τῶν ἐκ τοῦ στόλου τινάς,
καὶ νῦν ἱκανῶς εὐανδρεῖ.

7. Ἀπὸ δὲ τοῦ Ῥηγίου πλέοντι πρὸς ἕω
Λευκοπέτραν καλοῦσιν ἄκραν ἀπὸ τῆς χρόας
ἐν πεντήκοντα σταδίοις, εἰς ἣν τελευτᾶν φασι τὸ
Ἀπέννινον ὄρος. ἐντεῦθεν δ᾽ Ἡράκλειον, ὃ δὴ
τελευταῖον ἀκρωτήριον ὂν νεύει πρὸς μεσημβρίαν·

---

[1] Regium.

[2] Dionysius the Elder (b. about 432 B.C., d. 367 B.C.)

[3] Diodorus Siculus (14. 44) merely says that the Assembly
of the Rhegini refused him a wife.

[4] Apparently in honour of Phoebus (Apollo); for, accord-

rent therefrom. However, the question which of the two explanations is true, whether Rhegium got its name on account of this or on account of its fame (for the Samnitae might have called it by the Latin word for "royal," [1] because their progenitors had shared in the government with the Romans and used the Latin language to a considerable extent), is open to investigation. Be this as it may, it was a famous city, and not only founded many cities but also produced many notable men, some notable for their excellence as statesmen and others for their learning; nevertheless, Dionysius [2] demolished it, they say, on the charge that when he asked for a girl in marriage they proffered the daughter of the public executioner; [3] but his son restored a part of the old city and called it Phoebia. [4] Now in the time of Pyrrhus the garrison of the Campani broke the treaty and destroyed most of the inhabitants, and shortly before the Marsic war much of the settlement was laid in ruins by earthquakes; but Augustus Caesar, after ejecting Pompeius from Sicily, seeing that the city was in want of population, gave it some men from his expeditionary forces as new settlers, and it is now fairly populous.

7. As one sails from Rhegium towards the east, and at a distance of fifty stadia, one comes to Cape Leucopetra [5] (so called from its colour), in which, it is said, the Apennine Mountain terminates. Then comes Heracleium, which is the last cape of Italy and inclines towards the south; for on doubling it

ing to Plutarch (*De Alexandri Virtute* 338 B), Dionysius the Younger called himself the son of Apollo, "offspring of his mother Doris by Phoebus."

[5] Literally, " White Rock."

κάμψαντι γὰρ εὐθὺς ὁ πλοῦς Λιβὶ μέχρι πρὸς ἄκραν Ἰαπυγίαν· εἶτ᾽ ἐκκλίνει πρὸς ἄρκτον ἀεὶ καὶ μᾶλλον καὶ πρὸς τὴν ἑσπέραν ἐπὶ τὸν κόλπον τὸν Ἰόνιον. μετὰ δὲ τὸ Ἡράκλειον ἄκρα τῆς Λοκρίδος, ἣ καλεῖται Ζεφύριον, ἔχουσα προσεχῆ[1] τοῖς ἑσπερίοις ἀνέμοις λιμένα, ἐξ οὗ καὶ τοὔνομα. εἶθ᾽ ἡ πόλις οἱ Λοκροὶ οἱ Ἐπιζεφύριοι, Λοκρῶν ἄποικοι τῶν ἐν τῷ Κρισαίῳ κόλπῳ, μικρὸν ὕστερον τῆς[2] Κρότωνος καὶ Συρακουσσῶν κτίσεως ἀποικισθέντες ὑπὸ Εὐάνθους· Ἔφορος δ᾽ οὐκ εὖ, τῶν Ὀπουντίων Λοκρῶν ἀποίκους φήσας. ἔτη μὲν οὖν τρία ἢ τέτταρα ᾤκουν ἐπὶ τῷ Ζεφυρίῳ· εἶτα μετήνεγκαν τὴν πόλιν, συμπραξάντων καὶ Συρακουσσίων· ἅμα γὰρ οὗτοι ἐν οἷς·[3] καὶ ἔστιν ἐκεῖ κρήνη Λοκρία, ὅπου οἱ Λοκροὶ ἐστρατοπεδεύσαντο. εἰσὶ δ᾽ ἀπὸ Ῥηγίου μέχρι Λοκρῶν ἑξακόσιοι στάδιοι. ἵδρυται δ᾽ ἡ πόλις ἐπ᾽ ὀφρύος, ἣν Ἐπῶπιν[4] καλοῦσι.

---

[1] προσεχῆ (cp. προσεχής 4. 6. 2, 5. 3. 6, 5. 4. 4), Jones inserts.

[2] ἀπό, after τῆς, the editors either bracket or delete.

[3] ἅμα γὰρ οὗτοι ἐν οἷς, except ἅμα, is corrupt. The conjectures are: ἅμα τούτοις (Corais), ἅμα γὰρ οὗτοι ἐνῴκουν (Casaubon), ἅμα γὰρ οὗτοι ἐνῳκίσαντο αὐτοῖς (Groskurd), and ἅμα Ταραντίνοις (C. Müller). Kramer and Meineke give the passage up as hopeless. Jones inclines strongly to ἅμα Ταραντίνοις.

[4] Ἐπῶπιν, Meineke, for Ἐσῶπιν.

---

[1] The "Ionian Gulf" was the southern "part of what is now called the Adriatic Sea" (2. 5. 20); see 7. 5. 8-9.

[2] Literally, the "Western Locrians," both city and inhabitants having the same name.

[3] Now the Gulf of Salona in the Gulf of Corinth.

one immediately sails with the southwest wind as far as Cape Iapygia, and then veers off, always more and more, towards the northwest in the direction of the Ionian Gulf.[1] After Heracleium comes a cape belonging to Locris, which is called Zephyrium; its harbour is exposed to the winds that blow from the west, and hence the name. Then comes the city Locri Epizephyrii,[2] a colony of the Locri who live on the Crisaean Gulf,[3] which was led out by Evanthes only a little while after the founding of Croton and Syracuse.[4] Ephorus is wrong in calling it a colony of the Locri Opuntii. However, they lived only three or four years at Zephyrium, and then moved the city to its present site, with the co-operation of Syracusans [for at the same time the latter, among whom . . .][5] And at Zephyrium there is a spring, called Locria, where the Locri first pitched camp. The distance from Rhegium to Locri is six hundred stadia. The city is situated on the brow of a hill called Epopis.

[4] Croton and Syracuse were founded, respectively, in 710 and 734 B.C. According to Diodorus Siculus (4. 24), Heracles had unintentionally killed Croton and had foretold the founding of a famous city on the site, the same to be named after Croton.

[5] The Greek text, here translated as it stands, is corrupt. The emendations thus far offered yield (instead of the nine English words of the above rendering) either (1) "for the latter were living" (or "had taken up their abode") "there at the same time" or (2) "together with the Tarantini." There seems to be no definite corroborative evidence for either interpretation; but according to Pausanias, "colonies were sent to Croton, and to Locri at Cape Zephyrium, by the Lacedaemonians" (3. 3); and "Tarentum is a Lacedaemonian colony" (10. 10). Cp. the reference to the Tarantini in Strabo's next paragraph.

STRABO

8. Πρῶτοι δὲ νόμοις ἐγγραπτοῖς χρήσασθαι πεπιστευμένοι εἰσί· καὶ πλεῖστον χρόνον εὐνομηθέντας Διονύσιος ἐκπεσὼν ἐκ τῆς Συρακουσσίων ἀνομώτατα πάντων διεχρήσατο, ὅς γε προεγάμει μὲν παρεισιὼν εἰς τὸ δωμάτιον τὰς νυμφοστο-λισθείσας,[1] συναγαγὼν δὲ τὰς ὡραίας παρθένους περιστερὰς κολοπτέρους[2] ἐν τοῖς συμποσίοις ἠφίει, κἀκείνας ἐκέλευε[3] γυρεύειν γυμνάς, τινὰς δὲ καὶ σανδάλια ὑποδουμένας ἄζυγα, τὸ μὲν ὑψηλόν, τὸ δὲ ταπεινόν, περιδιώκειν τὰς φάσσας[4] τοῦ ἀπρεποῦς χάριν· δίκας μέντοι ἔτισεν, ἐπειδὴ πάλιν εἰς τὴν Σικελίαν ἐπανῆλθεν, ἀναληψόμενος τὴν ἀρχήν· καταλύσαντες γὰρ οἱ Λοκροὶ τὴν φρουρὰν ἠλευθέρωσαν σφᾶς καὶ τῆς γυναικὸς αὐτοῦ καὶ τῶν παιδίων κύριοι κατέστησαν· δύο δ᾽ ἦσαν αἱ θυγατέρες καὶ τῶν υἱῶν ὁ νεώτερος ἤδη μειράκιον· ἅτερος γὰρ Ἀπολλοκράτης συνε-στρατήγει τῷ πατρὶ τὴν κάθοδον. πολλὰ δὲ δεομένῳ τῷ Διονυσίῳ καὑτῷ καὶ Ταραντίνοις ὑπὲρ αὐτοῦ, προέσθαι τὰ σώματα ἐφ᾽[5] οἷς ἂν ἐθελήσωσιν, οὐκ ἔδοσαν, ἀλλὰ πολιορκίαν ὑπέ-
C 260 μειναν καὶ πόρθησιν τῆς χώρας, τὸν δὲ θυμὸν εἰς τὰς θυγατέρας τὸν πλεῖστον ἐξέχεαν· κατα-πορνευθείσας γὰρ ἐστραγγάλησαν, εἶτα καύ-σαντες τὰ σώματα κατήλεσαν τὰ ὀστᾶ καὶ

---

[1] νυμφοστολισθείσας, Jones, with Kramer and Müller-Dübner, restores the reading of the MSS., as against the *Epit.*, the early editors, and Meineke.
[2] κολοπτέρους, Meineke, for ὁλοπτέρους.
[3] ἐκέλευε, the reading of *n o*, for ἐκέλευσε ; so the editors before Kramer.
[4] τὰς φάσσας, Groskurd, for ἔφασαν.
[5] ἐφ᾽, Xylander, for ἐν ; so the later editors.

8. The Locri Epizephyrii are believed to have been the first people to use written laws. After they had lived under good laws for a very long time, Dionysius, on being banished from the country of the Syracusans,[1] abused them most lawlessly of all men. For he would sneak into the bed-chambers of the girls after they had been dressed up for their wedding, and lie with them before their marriage; and he would gather together the girls who were ripe for marriage, let loose doves with cropped wings upon them in the midst of the banquets, and then bid the girls waltz around unclad, and also bid some of them, shod with sandals that were not mates (one high and the other low), chase the doves around—all for the sheer indecency of it. However, he paid the penalty after he went back to Sicily again to resume his government; for the Locri broke up his garrison, set themselves free, and thus became masters of his wife and children. These children were his two daughters, and the younger of his two sons (who was already a lad), for the other, Apollocrates, was helping his father to effect his return to Sicily by force of arms. And although Dionysius—both himself and the Tarantini on his behalf—earnestly begged the Locri to release the prisoners on any terms they wished, they would not give them up; instead, they endured a siege and a devastation of their country. But they poured out most of their wrath upon his daughters, for they first made them prostitutes and then strangled them, and then, after burning their bodies, ground up the bones and sank them in the sea. Now

---

[1] Dionysius the Younger was banished thence in 357 B.C.

STRABO

κατεπόντωσαν. τῆς δὲ τῶν Λοκρῶν νομογραφίας
μνησθεὶς Ἔφορος, ἣν Ζάλευκος συνέταξεν ἔκ τε
τῶν Κρητικῶν νομίμων καὶ Λακωνικῶν καὶ ἐκ
τῶν Ἀρεοπαγιτικῶν, φησὶν ἐν τοῖς πρώτοις και-
νίσαι τοῦτο τὸν Ζάλευκον, ὅτι, τῶν πρότερον τὰς
ζημίας τοῖς δικασταῖς ἐπιτρεψάντων ὁρίζειν ἐφ᾿
ἑκάστοις τοῖς ἀδικήμασιν, ἐκεῖνος ἐν τοῖς νόμοις
διώρισεν, ἡγούμενος τὰς μὲν γνώμας τῶν δικαστῶν
οὐχὶ τὰς αὐτὰς εἶναι περὶ τῶν αὐτῶν, δεῖν δὲ τὰς
αὐτὰς εἶναι·[1] ἐπαινεῖ δὲ[2] καὶ τὸ ἁπλουστέρως
περὶ τῶν[3] συμβολαίων διατάξαι. Θουρίους δ᾿
ὕστερον ἀκριβοῦν θέλοντας πέρα[4] τῶν Λοκρῶν
ἐνδοξοτέρους μὲν γενέσθαι, χείρονας δέ· εὐνομεῖ-
σθαι γὰρ οὐ τοὺς ἐν τοῖς νόμοις ἅπαντα φυλαττο-
μένους τὰ τῶν συκοφαντῶν, ἀλλὰ τοὺς ἐμμένοντας
τοῖς ἁπλῶς κειμένοις. τοῦτο δὲ καὶ Πλάτων
εἴρηκεν, ὅτι παρ᾿ οἷς πλεῖστοι νόμοι καὶ δίκαι
παρὰ τούτοις καὶ βίοι μοχθηροί, καθάπερ καὶ
παρ᾿ οἷς ἰατροὶ πολλοί, καὶ νόσους εἰκὸς εἶναι
πολλάς.

9. Τοῦ δὲ Ἄληκος ποταμοῦ τοῦ διορίζοντος
τὴν Ῥηγίνην ἀπὸ τῆς Λοκρίδος βαθεῖαν φάραγγα
διεξιόντος, ἴδιόν τι συμβαίνει τὸ περὶ τοὺς τέττι-
γας· οἱ μὲν γὰρ ἐν τῇ τῶν Λοκρῶν περαίᾳ φθέγ-
γονται, τοῖς δ᾿ ἀφώνοις εἶναι συμβαίνει· τὸ δ᾿
αἴτιον εἰκάζουσιν, ὅτι τοῖς μὲν παλίνσκιόν ἐστι τὸ

[1] εἶναι, Corais inserts. Meineke reads: τὰς δὲ ζημίας δεῖν
εἶναι τὰς αὐτάς.
[2] ἐπαινεῖ δέ, Corais, for ἐπαινεῖν ; so the later editors.
[3] αὐτῶν, after τῶν, Meineke deletes ; so Kramer and Groskurd, who would insert αὐτόν before περί.
[4] πέρα (o) for παρά (A B C l) ; so the other editors.

32

Ephorus, in his mention of the written legislation of the Locri, which was drawn up by Zaleucus from the Cretan, the Laconian, and the Areopagite usages, says that Zaleucus was among the first to make the following innovation—that whereas before his time it had been left to the judges to determine the penalties for the several crimes, he defined them in the laws, because he held that the opinions of the judges about the same crimes would not be the same, although they ought to be the same. And Ephorus goes on to commend Zaleucus for drawing up the laws on contracts in simpler language. And he says that the Thurii, who later on wished to excel the Locri in precision, became more famous, to be sure, but morally inferior; for, he adds, it is not those who in their laws guard against all the wiles of false accusers that have good laws, but those who abide by laws that are laid down in simple language. And Plato has said as much—that where there are very many laws, there are also very many law-suits and corrupt practices, just as where there are many physicians, there are also likely to be many diseases.[1]

9. The Halex River, which marks the boundary between the Rhegian and the Locrian territories, passes out through a deep ravine; and a peculiar thing happens there in connection with the grasshoppers, that although those on the Locrian bank sing, the others remain mute. As for the cause of this, it is conjectured that on the latter side the

---

[1] This appears to be an exact quotation, but the translator has been unable to find the reference in extant works. Plato utters a somewhat similar sentiment, however, in the *Republic* 404 E–405 A.

χωρίον, ὥστ᾿ ἐνδρόσους ὄντας μὴ διαστέλλειν τοὺς
ὑμένας, τοὺς δ᾿ ἡλιαζομένους ξηροὺς καὶ κερατώ-
δεις ἔχειν, ὥστ᾿ ἀπ᾿ αὐτῶν εὐφυῶς ἐκπέμπεσθαι
τὸν φθόγγον. ἐδείκνυτο δ᾿ ἀνδριὰς ἐν Λοκροῖς Εὐνόμου τοῦ κιθαρῳδοῦ, τέττιγα ἐπὶ τὴν κιθάραν
καθήμενον ἔχων. φησὶ δὲ Τίμαιος, Πυθίοις ποτὲ
ἀγωνιζομένους τοῦτόν τε καὶ Ἀρίστωνα Ῥηγῖνον
ἐρίσαι περὶ τοῦ κλήρου· τὸν μὲν δὴ Ἀρίστωνα
δεῖσθαι τῶν Δελφῶν ἑαυτῷ συμπράττειν· ἱεροὺς
γὰρ εἶναι τοῦ θεοῦ τοὺς προγόνους αὐτοῦ καὶ
τὴν ἀποικίαν ἐνθένδε ἐστάλθαι· τοῦ δ᾿ Εὐνόμου
φήσαντος, ἀρχὴν μηδὲ μετεῖναι ἐκείνοις τῶν περὶ
φωνὴν ἀγωνισμάτων, παρ᾿ οἷς καὶ οἱ τέττιγες
εἶεν ἄφωνοι, τὰ εὐφθογγότατα τῶν ζῴων, ὅμως
εὐδοκιμεῖν μηδὲν ἧττον τὸν Ἀρίστωνα καὶ ἐν
ἐλπίδι τὴν νίκην ἔχειν, νικῆσαι μέντοι τὸν
Εὔνομον καὶ ἀναθεῖναι τὴν λεχθεῖσαν εἰκόνα ἐν
τῇ πατρίδι, ἐπειδὴ κατὰ τὸν ἀγῶνα, μιᾶς τῶν
χορδῶν ῥαγείσης ἐπιστὰς τέττιξ ἐκπληρώσειε τὸν
C 261 φθόγγον. τὴν δ᾿ ὑπὲρ τῶν πόλεων τούτων μεσόγαιαν Βρέττιοι κατέχουσι· καὶ πόλις ἐνταῦθα
Μαμέρτιον καὶ ὁ δρυμὸς ὁ φέρων τὴν ἀρίστην
πίτταν τὴν Βρεττίαν, ὃν Σίλαν[1] καλοῦσιν, εὔδεν-
δρός τε καὶ εὔυδρος, μῆκος ἑπτακοσίων σταδίων.

10. Μετὰ δὲ Λοκροὺς Σάγρα, ὃν θηλυκῶς
ὀνομάζουσιν, ἐφ᾿ οὗ βωμοὶ Διοσκούρων, περὶ
οὓς Λοκροὶ μύριοι μετὰ Ῥηγίνων πρὸς δεκατρεῖς

---

[1] τὴν Βρεττίαν, ὃν Σίλαν, Palmer, for ἣν Βρεττιάνιον σίλαν;
so the other editors.

---

[1] Apparently as to which should perform first.

region is so densely shaded that the grasshoppers, being wet with dew, cannot expand their membranes, whereas those on the sunny side have dry and horn-like membranes and therefore can easily produce their song. And people used to show in Locri a statue of Eunomus, the cithara-bard, with a locust seated on the cithara. Timaeus says that Eunomus and Ariston of Rhegium were once contesting with each other at the Pythian games and fell to quarrelling about the casting of the lots [1]; so Ariston begged the Delphians to co-operate with him, for the reason that his ancestors belonged [2] to the god and that the colony had been sent forth from there; [3] and although Eunomus said that the Rhegini had absolutely no right even to participate in the vocal contests, since in their country even the grass-hoppers, the sweetest-voiced of all creatures, were mute, Ariston was none the less held in favour and hoped for the victory; and yet Eunomus gained the victory and set up the aforesaid image in his native land, because during the contest, when one of the chords broke, a grasshopper lit on his cithara and supplied the missing sound. The interior above these cities is held by the Brettii; here is the city Mamertium, and also the forest that produces the best pitch, the Brettian. This forest is called Sila, is both well wooded and well watered, and is seven hundred stadia in length.

10. After Locri comes the Sagra, a river which has a feminine name. On its banks are the altars of the Dioscuri, near which ten thousand Locri,

[2] Cp. 6. 1. 6.
[3] From Delphi to Rhegium.

μυριάδας Κροτωνιατῶν συμβαλόντες ἐνίκησαν·
ἀφ' οὗ τὴν παροιμίαν πρὸς τοὺς ἀπιστοῦντας
ἐκπεσεῖν φασιν, ἀληθέστερα τῶν ἐπὶ Σάγρᾳ.
προσμεμυθεύκασι δ' ἔνιοι καὶ διότι αὐθημερὸν
τοῦ ἀγῶνος ἐνεστῶτος Ὀλυμπίασιν ἀπαγγελθείη
τοῖς ἐκεῖ τὸ συμβὰν καὶ εὑρεθείη τὸ τάχος τῆς
ἀγγελίας ἀληθές. ταύτην δὲ τὴν συμφορὰν
αἰτίαν τοῖς Κροτωνιάταις φασὶ τοῦ μὴ πολὺν
ἔτι συμμεῖναι χρόνον διὰ τὸ πλῆθος τῶν τότε
πεσόντων ἀνδρῶν. μετὰ δὲ τὴν Σάγραν Ἀχαιῶν
κτίσμα Καυλωνία, πρότερον δ' Αὐλωνία λεγομένη,
διὰ τὸν προκείμενον αὐλῶνα. ἔστι δ' ἔρημος· οἱ
γὰρ ἔχοντες εἰς Σικελίαν[1] ὑπὸ τῶν βαρβάρων
ἐξέπεσον καὶ τὴν ἐκεῖ Καυλωνίαν ἔκτισαν. μετὰ
δὲ ταύτην Σκυλλήτιον, ἄποικος Ἀθηναίων τῶν
μετὰ Μενεσθέως, νῦν δὲ Σκυλάκιον καλεῖται·
Κροτωνιατῶν δ' ἐχόντων, Διονύσιος Λοκροῖς
προσώρισεν.[2] ἀπὸ δὲ τῆς πόλεως καὶ ὁ κόλπος
Σκυλλητικὸς ὠνόμασται, ποιῶν τὸν εἰρημένον
ἰσθμὸν πρὸς τὸν Ἱππωνιάτην κόλπον. ἐπεχεί-
ρησε δ' ὁ Διονύσιος καὶ διατειχίζειν τὸν ἰσθμόν,
στρατεύσας ἐπὶ Λευκανούς, λόγῳ μὲν ὡς ἀσφά-
λειαν παρέξων ἀπὸ τῶν ἐκτὸς βαρβάρων τοῖς
ἐντὸς ἰσθμοῦ, τὸ δ' ἀληθὲς λῦσαι τὴν πρὸς

---

[1] εἰς Σικελίαν, Corais, for ἐν Σικελίᾳ ; as later editors.
[2] προσώρισεν, Meineke, for μέρος ὥρισεν.

---

[1] The Greek, as the English, leaves one uncertain whether
merely the Locrian or the combined army amounted to
10,000 men. Justin (20. 3) gives the number of the Locrian
army as 15,000, not mentioning the Rhegini ; hence one
might infer that there were 5,000 Rhegini, and Strabo might

with Rhegini,[1] clashed with one hundred and thirty thousand Crotoniates and gained the victory—an occurrence which gave rise, it is said, to the proverb we use with incredulous people, "Truer than the result at Sagra." And some have gone on to add the fable that the news of the result was reported on the same day[2] to the people at the Olympia when the games were in progress, and that the speed with which the news had come was afterwards verified. This misfortune of the Crotoniates is said to be the reason why their city did not endure much longer, so great was the multitude of men who fell in the battle. After the Sagra comes a city founded by the Achaeans, Caulonia, formerly called Aulonia, because of the glen[3] which lies in front of it. It is deserted, however, for those who held it were driven out by the barbarians to Sicily and founded the Caulonia there. After this city comes Scylletium, a colony of the Athenians who were with Menestheus (and now called Scylacium).[4] Though the Crotoniates held it, Dionysius included it within the boundaries of the Locri. The Scylletic Gulf, which, with the Hipponiate Gulf forms the aforementioned isthmus,[5] is named after the city. Dionysius undertook also to build a wall across the isthmus when he made war upon the Leucani, on the pretext, indeed, that it would afford security to the people inside the isthmus from the barbarians outside, but in truth because he wished to break the alliance which the

---

have so written, for the Greek symbol for 5,000 ($_1\epsilon$), might have fallen out of the text.

[2] Cicero (*De Natura Deorum* 2. 2.) refers to this tradition.

[3] "Aulon."

[4] Cp. Vergil, *Aeneid* 3. 552.   [5] 6 1. 4.

STRABO

ἀλλήλους κοινωνίαν τῶν Ἑλλήνων βουλόμενος,
ὥστ' ἄρχειν ἀδεῶς τῶν ἐντός· ἀλλ' ἐκώλυσαν
οἱ ἐκτὸς εἰσελθόντες.

11. Μετὰ δὲ τὸ Σκυλλήτιον ἡ Κροτωνιᾶτις
χώρα καὶ τῶν Ἰαπύγων ἄκραι τρεῖς. μετὰ δὲ
ταύτας τὸ Λακίνιον, Ἥρας ἱερόν, πλούσιόν ποτε
ὑπάρξαν καὶ πολλῶν ἀναθημάτων μεστόν. τὰ
διάρματα δ' οὐκ εὐκρινῶς λέγεται· πλὴν ὥς γε
ἐπὶ τὸ πολὺ σταδίους ἀπὸ Πορθμοῦ μέχρι
Λακινίου Πολύβιος ἀποδίδωσι δισχιλίους[1] καὶ
τριακοσίους, ἐντεῦθεν δὲ καὶ δίαρμα εἰς ἄκραν
Ἰαπυγίαν ἑπτακοσίους. τοῦτο μὲν οὖν στόμα
λέγουσι τοῦ Ταραντίνου κόλπου. αὐτὸς δ' ὁ
κόλπος ἔχει περίπλουν ἀξιόλογον μιλίων διακοσίων τεσσαράκοντα, ὡς ὁ χωρογράφος φησί·
C 262 τριακοσίων[2] ὀγδοήκοντα εὐζώνῳ, Ἀρτεμίδωρος·
τοσούτοις δὲ καὶ λείπων τοῦ πλάτους τοῦ στό-

---

[1] Following Mannert, many of the editors, perhaps rightly,
emend δισχιλίους to χιλίους.

[2] τριακοσίων . . . κόλπου: the MSS. read as above except
that B C contain ττ instead of τριακοσίων ὀγδοήκοντα, and that
only two MSS., B n (the latter *pr. m.*), have εὐζώνῳ rather
than ἀζώνῳ. Groskurd reads: [τὴν πεζῇ δὲ περιοδείαν δώδεκα
ἡμερῶν] εὐζώνῳ Ἀρτεμίδωρος [λέγει· πλέοντι δὲ σταδίων δισχι-
λίων]· τοσούτους δὲ καὶ λείπων [τῷ στόματι ὅσους καὶ Πολύβιος
εἴρηκε] τοῦ πλάτους τοῦ στόματος τοῦ κόλπου. C. Müller reads:
[οἱ δ' ἐλάττονα ποιοῦσι, σταδίων λέγοντες χιλίων] τριακοσίων
ὀγδοήκοντα, μείζονα δ' ὁ Ἀρτεμίδωρος τοσούτους, ἔτι δὲ καὶ λ',
εἰπὼν τοῦ πλάτους τοῦ στόματος τοῦ κόλπου. Meineke indicates
three lacunae—after φησί, ὀγδοήκοντα, and λείπων, and reads
ἀζώνῳ; but there are no lacunae in the MSS. Jones proposes: [σταδίων δὲ] ὀγδοήκοντα μείζονα κτλ. with the MSS.
See note on opposite page.

---

[1] The Lacinium derived its name from Cape Lacinium (now

38

Greeks had with one another, and thus command with impunity the people inside; but the people outside came in and prevented the undertaking.

11. After Scylletium comes the territory of the Crotoniates, and three capes of the Iapyges; and after these, the Lacinium,[1] a temple of Hera, which at one time was rich and full of dedicated offerings. As for the distances by sea, writers give them without satisfactory clearness, except that, in a general way, Polybius gives the distance from the strait to Lacinium as two thousand three hundred stadia,[2] and the distance thence across to Cape Iapygia as seven hundred. This point is called the mouth of the Tarantine Gulf. As for the gulf itself, the distance around it by sea is of considerable length, two hundred and forty miles,[3] as the Chorographer [4] says, but Artemidorus says three hundred and eighty for a man well-girded, although he falls short of the real breadth of the mouth of the gulf by as much.[5]

Cape Nao), on which it was situated.   According to Diodorus Siculus (4. 24), Heracles, when in this region, put to death a cattle-thief named Lacinius.   Hence the name of the cape.

[2] Strabo probably wrote "two thousand" and not "one thousand" (see Mannert, t. 9. 9, p. 202), and so read Gosselin, Groskurd, Forbiger, Müller-Dübner and Meineke.   Compare Strabo's other quotation (5. 1. 3) from Polybius on this subject.   There, as here, unfortunately, the figures ascribed to Polybius cannot be compared with his original statement, which is now lost.

[3] 240 Roman miles=1,920, or 2,000 (see 7. 7. 4), stadia.

[4] See 5. 2. 7, and the footnote.

[5] This passage ("although . . . much") is merely an attempt to translate the Greek of the manuscripts.   The only variant in the manuscripts is that of "ungirded" for "well-girded."   If Strabo wrote either, which is extremely doubtful, we must infer that Artemidorus' figure, whatever it was,

ματος τοῦ κόλπου. βλέπει δὲ πρὸς ἀνατολὰς
χειμερινάς, ἀρχὴ δ' αὐτοῦ τὸ Λακίνιον· κάμψαντι
γὰρ εὐθὺς αἱ τῶν Ἀχαιῶν πόλεις,[1] αἱ νῦν οὐκ
εἰσὶ πλὴν τῆς Ταραντίνων. ἀλλὰ διὰ τὴν δόξαν
τινῶν ἄξιον καὶ ἐπὶ πλέον αὐτῶν μνησθῆναι.

12. Πρώτη δ' ἐστὶ Κρότων ἐν ἑκατὸν καὶ
πεντήκοντα σταδίοις ἀπὸ τοῦ Λακινίου καὶ
ποταμὸς Αἴσαρος καὶ λιμὴν καὶ ἄλλος ποταμὸς
Νέαιθος, ᾧ[2] τὴν ἐπωνυμίαν γενέσθαι φασὶν ἀπὸ
τοῦ συμβεβηκότος. καταχθέντας γάρ τινας τῶν
ἀπὸ τοῦ Ἰλιακοῦ στόλου πλανηθέντων Ἀχαιῶν
ἐκβῆναι λέγουσιν ἐπὶ τὴν κατάσκεψιν τῶν χωρίων,
τὰς δὲ συμπλεούσας αὐταῖς Τρωάδας καταμα-
θούσας ἔρημα ἀνδρῶν τὰ πλοῖα ἐμπρῆσαι, βαρυνο-
μένας τὸν πλοῦν, ὥστ' ἀναγκασθῆναι μένειν
ἐκείνους, ἅμα καὶ τὴν γῆν σπουδαίαν ὁρῶντας·
εὐθὺς δὲ καὶ ἄλλων πλειόνων εἰσαφικνουμένων
καὶ ζηλούντων ἐκείνους κατὰ τὸ ὁμόφυλον, πολλὰς
κατοικίας γενέσθαι, ὧν αἱ πλείους ἐπώνυμοι τῶν

---

[1] ἦσαν, after πόλεις, Jones deletes.
[2] ᾧ, Meineke, for ὦν ; Corais reads οὗ.

---

pertained to the number of days it would take a pedestrian,
at the rate, say, of 160 stadia (20 Roman miles) per day, to
make the journey around the gulf by land. Most of the
editors (including Meineke) dismiss the passage as hopeless
by merely indicating gaps in the text. Groskurd and C. Müller
not only emend words of the text but also fill in the supposed
gaps with seventeen and nine words, respectively. Groskurd
makes Artemidorus say that a well-girded pedestrian can
complete the journey around the gulf in twelve days, that
the coasting-voyage around it is 2,000 stadia, and that
he leaves for the mouth the same number (700) of stadia
assigned by Polybius to the breadth of the mouth of the
gulf. But C. Müller writes : "Some make it less, saying

The gulf faces the winter-sunrise;[1] and it begins at Cape Lacinium, for, on doubling it, one immediately comes to the cities[2] of the Achaeans, which, except that of the Tarantini, no longer exist, and yet, because of the fame of some of them, are worthy of rather extended mention.

12. The first city is Croton, within one hundred and fifty stadia from the Lacinium; and then comes the River Aesarus, and a harbour, and another river, the Neaethus. The Neaethus got its name, it is said, from what occurred there: Certain of the Achaeans who had strayed from the Trojan fleet put in there and disembarked for an inspection of the region, and when the Trojan women who were sailing with them learned that the boats were empty of men, they set fire to the boats, for they were weary of the voyage, so that the men remained there of necessity, although they at the same time noticed that the soil was very fertile. And immediately several other groups, on the strength of their racial kinship, came and imitated them, and thus arose many settlements, most of which took their

---

[1] *i.e.* south-east.
[2] As often Strabo refers to *sites* of perished cities as *cities*.

1,380 stadia, whereas Artemidorus makes it as many plus 30 (1,410), in speaking of the breadth of the mouth of the gulf." But the present translator, by making very simple emendations (see critical note 2 on page 38), arrives at the following : Artemidorus says eighty stadia longer (*i.e.* 2,000) although he falls short of the breadth of the mouth of the gulf by as much (*i.e.* 700 − 80 = 620). It should be noted that Artemidorus, as quoted by Strabo, always gives distances in terms of stadia, not miles (*e. g.* 3. 2. 11, 8. 2. 1, 14. 2. 29, *et passim*), and that his figures at times differ considerably from those of the Chorographer (cp. 6. 3. 10).

Τρώων ἐγένοντο, καὶ ποταμὸς δὲ ὁ Νέαιθος ἀπὸ
τοῦ πάθους τὴν προσωνυμίαν ἔσχε. φησὶ δ᾽
Ἀντίοχος, τοῦ θεοῦ φήσαντος Ἀχαιοῖς Κρότωνα
κτίζειν, ἀπελθεῖν Μύσκελλον κατασκεψόμενον
τὸν τόπον, ἰδόντα δ᾽ ἐκτισμένην ἤδη Σύβαριν,
ποταμῷ τῷ πλησίον ὁμώνυμον, κρῖναι ταύτην
ἀμείνω· ἐπανερέσθαι δ᾽ οὖν ἀπιόντα τὸν θεόν, εἰ
λῶον[1] εἴη ταύτην ἀντ᾽ ἐκείνης κτίζειν, τὸν δὲ
ἀνειπεῖν (ἐτύγχανε δὲ ὑπόκυφος ὢν ὁ Μύσκελλος)·

Μύσκελλε βραχύνωτε, παρὲκ σέθεν[2] ἄλλο
    ματεύων
κλάσματα[3] θηρεύεις· ὀρθὸν[4] δ᾽ ὅ τι δῷ τις
    ἐπαινεῖν.

ἐπανελθόντα δὲ κτίσαι τὸν Κρότωνα, συμπρά-
ξαντος καὶ Ἀρχίου τοῦ τὰς Συρακούσας οἰκί-
σαντος, προσπλεύσαντος κατὰ τύχην, ἡνίκα
ὥρμητο ἐπὶ τὸν τῶν Συρακουσῶν οἰκισμόν. ᾤκουν
δὲ Ἰάπυγες τὸν Κρότωνα πρότερον, ὡς Ἔφορός
φησι. δοκεῖ δ᾽ ἡ πόλις τά τε πολέμια ἀσκῆσαι
καὶ τὰ περὶ τὴν ἄθλησιν· ἐν μιᾷ γοῦν Ὀλυμπιάδι
οἱ τῶν ἄλλων προτερήσαντες τῷ σταδίῳ ἑπτὰ
ἄνδρες ἅπαντες ὑπῆρξαν Κροτωνιᾶται, ὥστ᾽

---

[1] λῶον (A pr. m.), for δοτόν ; so the editors.

[2] παρὲκ σέθεν, Toup, Siebenkees, Kramer, and Müller-
Dübner, for παρὲς σέθεν ; παρεξέλθ᾽, Epit. ; παρὲκ θεόν, Corais,
and Meineke, following the versions of Zenobius (3. 42) and
Diod. Sic. (8. 17).

[3] For κλάσματα (all MSS.) Corais, Meineke, and Müller-
Dübner read κλαύματα ("tears"), following the versions of
Zenob. and Diod. Sic.

[4] For ὀρθόν (all MSS.) Corais, Meineke, and Müller-
Dübner read δῶρον, following Epit., Zenob., and Diod. Sic.

names from the Trojans; and also a river, the Neaethus, took its appellation from the aforementioned occurrence.[1] According to Antiochus, when the god told the Achaeans to found Croton, Myscellus departed to inspect the place, but when he saw that Sybaris was already founded—having the same name as the river near by—he judged that Sybaris was better; at all events, he questioned the god again when he returned whether it would be better to found this instead of Croton, and the god replied to him (Myscellus[2] was a hunchback as it happened): " Myscellus, short of back, in searching else outside thy track, thou hunt'st for morsels only; 'tis right that what one giveth thee thou do approve;"[3] and Myscellus came back and founded Croton, having as an associate Archias, the founder of Syracuse, who happened to sail up while on his way to found Syracuse.[4] The Iapyges used to live at Croton in earlier times, as Ephorus says. And the city is reputed to have cultivated warfare and athletics; at any rate, in one Olympian festival the seven men who took the lead over all others in the stadium-race were all Crotoniates, and therefore the

---

[1] The Greek " Nēas aethein " means " to burn ships."

[2] Ovid (*Metamorphoses* 15. 20) spells the name " Myscelus," and perhaps rightly; that is, " Mouse-leg " (?).

[3] For a fuller account, see Diodorus Siculus 8. 17. His version of the oracle is: " Myscellus, short of back, in searching other things apart from god, thou searchest only after tears; what gift god giveth thee, do thou approve."

[4] The generally accepted dates for the founding of Croton and Syracuse are, respectively, 710 B.C. and 734 B.C. But Strabo's account here seems to mean that Syracuse was founded immediately after Croton (cp. 6. 2. 4). Cp. also Thucydides 6. 3. 2.

εἰκότως εἰρῆσθαι δοκεῖ, διότι Κροτωνιατῶν ὁ
ἔσχατος πρῶτος ἦν τῶν ἄλλων Ἑλλήνων, καὶ
τὴν παροιμίαν δὲ ὑγιέστερον Κρότωνος λέγουσαν
ἐντεῦθεν εἰρῆσθαί φασιν, ὡς τοῦ τόπου πρὸς
ὑγείαν καὶ εὐεξίαν ἔχοντός τι φορὸν διὰ τὸ πλῆθος
τῶν ἀθλητῶν. πλείστους οὖν Ὀλυμπιονίκας
ἔσχε, καίπερ οὐ πολὺν χρόνον οἰκηθεῖσα διὰ τὸν
C 263 φθόρον τῶν ἐπὶ Σάγρᾳ πεσόντων ἀνδρῶν τοσούτων
τὸ πλῆθος· προσέλαβε δὲ τῇ δόξῃ καὶ τὸ τῶν
Πυθαγορείων πλῆθος καὶ Μίλων, ἐπιφανέστατος
μὲν τῶν ἀθλητῶν γεγονώς, ὁμιλητὴς δὲ Πυθαγόρου,
διατρίψαντος ἐν τῇ πόλει πολὺν χρόνον. φασὶ δ᾽
ἐν τῷ συσσιτίῳ ποτὲ τῶν φιλοσόφων πονήσαντος
στύλου τὸν Μίλωνα ὑποδύντα σῶσαι ἅπαντας,
ὑποσπάσαι δὲ καὶ ἑαυτόν· τῇ δ᾽ αὐτῇ ῥώμῃ
πεποιθότα εἰκὸς καὶ τὴν ἱστορουμένην ὑπό τινων
εὑρέσθαι καταστροφὴν τοῦ βίου. λέγεται γοῦν
ὁδοιπορῶν ποτε δι᾽ ὕλης βαθείας παραβῆναι τὴν
ὁδὸν ἐπὶ πλέον, εἶθ᾽ εὑρὼν ξύλον μέγα ἐσφηνω-
μένον, ἐμβαλὼν χεῖρας ἅμα καὶ πόδας εἰς τὴν
διάστασιν βιάζεσθαι πρὸς τὸ διαστῆσαι τελέως·
τοσοῦτον δ᾽ ἴσχυσε μόνον, ὥστ᾽ ἐκπεσεῖν τοὺς
σφῆνας, εἶτ᾽ εὐθὺς ἐπισυμπεσεῖν τὰ μέρη τοῦ
ξύλου, ἀποληφθέντα[1] δ᾽ αὐτὸν ἐν τῇ τοιαύτῃ
πάγῃ θηρόβρωτον γενέσθαι.

13. Ἐφεξῆς δ᾽ ἐστὶν ἐν διακοσίοις σταδίοις
Ἀχαιῶν κτίσμα ἡ Σύβαρις δυεῖν ποταμῶν μεταξύ,

---

[1] ἀποληφθέντα, the reading of the Epit. (ἀπολειφθέντα,
A B C l); so Corais, Meineke and others (cp. ἀποληφθείς,
7. 3. 14).

---

[1] Cp. 6. 1. 10.

saying " The last of the Crotoniates was the first among all other Greeks" seems reasonable. And this, it is said, is what gave rise to the other proverb, " more healthful than Croton," the belief being that the place contains something that tends to health and bodily vigour, to judge by the multitude of its athletes. Accordingly, it had a very large number of Olympic victors, although it did not remain inhabited a long time, on account of the ruinous loss of its citizens who fell in such great numbers [1] at the River Sagra. And its fame was increased by the large number of its Pythagorean philosophers, and by Milo, who was the most illustrious of athletes, and also a companion of Pythagoras, who spent a long time in the city. It is said that once, at the common mess of the philosophers, when a pillar began to give way, Milo slipped in under the burden and saved them all, and then drew himself from under it and escaped. And it is probably because he relied upon this same strength that he brought on himself the end of his life as reported by some writers; at any rate, the story is told that once, when he was travelling through a deep forest, he strayed rather far from the road, and then, on finding a large log cleft with wedges, thrust his hands and feet at the same time into the cleft and strained to split the log completely asunder; but he was only strong enough to make the wedges fall out, whereupon the two parts of the log instantly snapped together; and caught in such a trap as that, he became food for wild beasts.

13. Next in order, at a distance of two hundred stadia, comes Sybaris, founded by the Achaeans;

45

Κράθιδος καὶ Συβάριδος· οἰκιστὴς δ᾽ αὐτῆς ὁ ᾽Ις[1]
Ἑλικεύς. τοσοῦτον δ᾽ εὐτυχίᾳ διήνεγκεν ἡ πόλις
αὕτη τὸ παλαιόν, ὡς τεττάρων μὲν ἐθνῶν τῶν
πλησίον ἐπῆρξε,[2] πέντε δὲ καὶ εἴκοσι πόλεις
ὑπηκόους ἔσχε, τριάκοντα δὲ μυριάσιν ἀνδρῶν
ἐπὶ Κροτωνιάτας ἐστράτευσεν, πεντήκοντα δὲ
σταδίων κύκλον συνεπλήρουν οἱ[3] οἰκοῦντες ἐπὶ
τῷ Κράθιδι. ὑπὸ μέντοι τρυφῆς καὶ ὕβρεως
ἅπασαν τὴν εὐδαιμονίαν ἀφῃρέθησαν ὑπὸ Κροτωνιατῶν ἐν ἡμέραις ἑβδομήκοντα·[4] ἑλόντες γὰρ
τὴν πόλιν ἐπήγαγον τὸν ποταμὸν καὶ κατέκλυσαν.
ὕστερον δ᾽ οἱ περιγενόμενοι συνελθόντες ἐπῴκουν
ὀλίγοι· χρόνῳ δὲ καὶ οὗτοι διεφθάρησαν ὑπὸ
Ἀθηναίων καὶ ἄλλων Ἑλλήνων, οἳ συνοικήσοντες
μὲν ἐκείνοις ἀφίκοντο, καταφρονήσαντες δὲ αὐτῶν
τοὺς μὲν διεχειρίσαντο, τὴν δὲ πόλιν εἰς ἕτερον
τόπον μετέθηκαν πλησίον καὶ Θουρίους προσηγόρευσαν ἀπὸ κρήνης ὁμωνύμου. ὁ μὲν οὖν
Σύβαρις τοὺς πίνοντας ἵππους ἀπ᾽ αὐτοῦ πτυρ-
τικοὺς ποιεῖ· διὸ καὶ τὰς ἀγέλας ἀπείργουσιν ἀπ᾽
αὐτοῦ· ὁ δὲ Κρᾶθις τοὺς ἀνθρώπους ξανθοτριχεῖν
καὶ λευκοτριχεῖν ποιεῖ λουομένους καὶ ἄλλα
πολλὰ πάθη ἰᾶται. Θούριοι δ᾽ εὐτυχήσαντες
πολὺν χρόνον ὑπὸ Λευκανῶν ἠνδραποδίσθησαν,
Ταραντίνων δ᾽ ἀφελομένων ἐκείνους ἐπὶ Ῥωμαίους
κατέφυγον, οἱ δὲ πέμψαντες συνοίκους ὀλιγαν-
δροῦσι μετωνόμασαν Κωπιὰς τὴν πόλιν.

---

[1] The MSS. read ὁ ᾽Ισελικεύς; Οἷς . . . Ἑλικεύς (Corais);
ὁ ᾽Ισ[ος] Ἑλικεύς (Meineke); but C. Müller, ὁ ῎Ις.
[2] ἐπῆρξε, Meineke, for ὑπῆρξε.
[3] οἱ, before οἰκοῦντες, Jones inserts.
[4] For ἑβδομήκοντα (ο᾽), the *Epit.* reads ἐννέα (θ).

it is between two rivers, the Crathis and the Sybaris. Its founder was Is of Helice.[1] In early times this city was so superior in its good fortune that it ruled over four tribes in the neighbourhood, had twenty-five subject cities, made the campaign against the Crotoniates with three hundred thousand men, and its inhabitants on the Crathis alone completely filled up a circuit of fifty stadia. However, by reason of luxury [2] and insolence they were deprived of all their felicity by the Crotoniates within seventy days; for on taking the city these conducted the river over it and submerged it. Later on, the survivors, only a few, came together and were making it their home again, but in time these too were destroyed by Athenians and other Greeks, who, although they came there to live with them, conceived such a contempt for them that they not only slew them but removed the city to another place near by and named it Thurii, after a spring of that name. Now the Sybaris River makes the horses that drink from it timid, and therefore all herds are kept away from it; whereas the Crathis makes the hair of persons who bathe in it yellow or white, and besides it cures many afflictions. Now after the Thurii had prospered for a long time, they were enslaved by the Leucani, and when they were taken away from the Leucani by the Tarantini, they took refuge in Rome, and the Romans sent colonists to supplement them, since their population was reduced, and changed the name of the city to Copiae.

[1] The reading, "Is of Helice," is doubtful. On Helice, see 1. 3. 18 and 8. 7. 2.
[2] Cp. "Sybarite."

14. Μετὰ δὲ Θουρίους Λαγαρία φρούριον, Ἐπειοῦ καὶ Φωκέων κτίσμα, ὅθεν καὶ ὁ Λαγαριτανὸς οἶνος, γλυκὺς καὶ ἁπαλὸς καὶ παρὰ τοῖς C 264 ἰατροῖς σφόδρα εὐδοκιμῶν· καὶ ὁ Θουρῖνος δὲ τῶν ἐν ὀνόματι οἴνων ἐστίν. εἶθ' Ἡράκλεια πόλις μικρὸν ὑπὲρ τῆς θαλάττης, καὶ ποταμοὶ δύο πλωτοὶ Ἄκιρις καὶ Σῖρις, ἐφ' οὗ πόλις ἦν ὁμώνυμος Τρωική· χρόνῳ δὲ τῆς Ἡρακλείας ἐντεῦθεν οἰκισθείσης ὑπὸ Ταραντίνων, ἐπίνειον αὕτη τῶν Ἡρακλεωτῶν ὑπῆρξε. διεῖχε δ' Ἡρακλείας μὲν τέτταρας καὶ εἴκοσι σταδίους, Θουρίων δὲ περὶ τριακοσίους τριάκοντα· τῆς δὲ τῶν Τρώων κατοικίας τεκμήριον ποιοῦνται τὸ τῆς Ἀθηνᾶς τῆς Ἰλιάδος ξόανον ἱδρυμένον αὐτόθι, ὅπερ καταμῦσαι μυθεύουσιν ἀποσπωμένων τῶν ἱκετῶν ὑπὸ Ἰώνων τῶν ἑλόντων τὴν πόλιν· τούτους γὰρ ἐπελθεῖν οἰκήτορας, φεύγοντας τὴν Λυδῶν ἀρχήν, καὶ βίᾳ λαβεῖν τὴν πόλιν Χώνων οὖσαν, καλέσαι δὲ αὐτὴν Πολίειον· δείκνυσθαι δὲ καὶ νῦν καταμῦον [1] τὸ ξόανον. ἰταμὸν μὲν οὖν καὶ τὸ οὕτω μυθεύειν, ὥστε μὴ καταμῦσαι φάναι μόνον,[2] καθάπερ καὶ τὸ [3] ἐν Ἰλίῳ ἀποστραφῆναι κατὰ τὸν Κασάνδρας βιασμόν, ἀλλὰ καὶ καταμῦον δείκνυσθαι. πολὺ δὲ ἰταμώτερον τὸ τοσαῦτα [4] ποιεῖν ἐξ Ἰλίου κεκομισμένα ξόανα, ὅσα φασὶν οἱ συγγραφεῖς· καὶ γὰρ ἐν Ῥώμῃ καὶ ἐν Λαουινίῳ καὶ ἐν Λουκερίᾳ

---

[1] νῦν καταμῦον (k n o and corr. in B), for νύκτα μῦον (A B C l); so the editors.
[2] φάναι μόνον, Kramer, for φαινόμενον. Corais: φανῆναι μόνον; Meineke: ἀναινόμενον.
[3] τό, Meineke omits, without cause.
[4] τοσαῦτα, Tyrwhitt, for τοιαῦτα; so the editors.

14. After Thurii comes Lagaria, a stronghold, founded by Epeius and the Phocaeans; thence comes the Lagaritan wine, which is sweet, mild, and extremely well thought of among physicians. That of Thurii, too, is one of the famous wines. Then comes the city Heracleia, a short distance above the sea; and two navigable rivers, the Aciris and the Siris. On the Siris there used to be a Trojan city of the same name, but in time, when Heracleia was colonised thence by the Tarantini, it became the port of the Heracleotes. It is twenty-four stadia distant from Heracleia and about three hundred and thirty from Thurii. Writers produce as proof of its settlement by the Trojans the wooden image of the Trojan Athene which is set up there—the image that closed its eyes, the fable goes, when the suppliants were dragged away by the Ionians who captured the city; for these Ionians came there as colonists when in flight from the dominion of the Lydians, and by force took the city, which belonged to the Chones,[1] and called it Polieium; and the image even now can be seen closing its eyes. It is a bold thing, to be sure, to tell such a fable and to say that the image not only closed its eyes (just as they say the image in Troy turned away at the time Cassandra was violated) but can also be seen closing its eyes; and yet it is much bolder to represent as brought from Troy all those images which the historians say were brought from there; for not only in the territory of Siris, but also at Rome, at Lavinium, and at Luceria,

[1] Cp. 6. 1. 2.

καὶ ἐν Σιρίτιδι Ἰλιὰς Ἀθηνᾶ καλεῖται, ὡς ἐκεῖθεν κομισθεῖσα. καὶ τὸ τῶν Τρωάδων δὲ τόλμημα περιφέρεται πολλαχοῦ καὶ ἄπιστον φαίνεται, καίπερ δυνατὸν ὄν. τινὲς δὲ καὶ Ῥοδίων κτίσμα φασὶ καὶ Σιρῖτιν καὶ τὴν ἐπὶ Τεύθραντος[1] Σύβαριν. φησὶ δ᾽ Ἀντίοχος τοὺς Ταραντίνους Θουρίοις καὶ Κλεανδρίδᾳ[2] τῷ στρατηγῷ φυγάδι ἐκ Λακεδαίμονος πολεμοῦντας περὶ τῆς Σιρίτιδος συμβῆναι καὶ συνοικῆσαι μὲν κοινῇ, τὴν δ᾽ ἀποικίαν κριθῆναι Ταραντίνων· Ἡράκλειαν δ᾽ ὕστερον κληθῆναι, μεταβαλοῦσαν καὶ τοὔνομα καὶ τὸν τόπον.

15. Ἑξῆς δ᾽ ἐστὶ Μεταπόντιον, εἰς ἣν ἀπὸ τοῦ ἐπινείου τῆς Ἡρακλείας εἰσὶ στάδιοι τετταράκοντα πρὸς τοῖς ἑκατόν. Πυλίων δὲ λέγεται κτίσμα τῶν ἐξ Ἰλίου πλευσάντων μετὰ Νέστορος, οὓς οὕτως ἀπὸ γεωργίας εὐτυχῆσαί φασιν, ὥστε θέρος χρυσοῦν ἐν Δελφοῖς ἀναθεῖναι. σημεῖον δὲ ποιοῦνται τῆς κτίσεως τὸν τῶν Νηληιδῶν ἐναγισμόν· ἠφανίσθη δ᾽ ὑπὸ Σαυνιτῶν. Ἀντίοχος δέ φησιν ἐκλειφθέντα τὸν τόπον ἐποικῆσαι τῶν Ἀχαιῶν τινας μεταπεμφθέντας ὑπὸ τῶν ἐν Συβάρει Ἀχαιῶν, μεταπεμφθῆναι δὲ κατὰ μῖσος τὸ πρὸς Ταραντίνους τῶν Ἀχαιῶν, τῶν ἐκπεσόντων ἐκ

---

[1] Τεύθραντος is the reading of all the MSS. Groskurd conj. Τράεντος, and so reads Meineke. See note to translation.

[2] Κλεανδρίδᾳ, Corais, for Κλεανδρίᾳ; so the later editors.

---

[1] The "Teuthras" is otherwise unknown, except that there was a small river of that name, which cannot be identified, near Cumae (see Propertius 1. 11. 11 and Silius Italicus 11. 288). The river was probably named after Teuthras, king of Teuthrania in Mysia (see 12. 8. 2). But there seems to be no evidence of Sybarites in that region.

Athene is called "Trojan Athena," as though brought from Troy. And further, the daring deed of the Trojan women is current in numerous places, and appears incredible, although it is possible. According to some, however, both Siris and the Sybaris which is on the Teuthras[1] were founded by the Rhodians. According to Antiochus, when the Tarantini were at war with the Thurii and their general Cleandridas, an exile from Lacedaemon, for the possession of the territory of Siris, they made a compromise and peopled Siris jointly, although it was adjudged the colony of the Tarantini; but later on it was called Heracleia, its site as well as its name being changed.

15. Next in order comes Metapontium, which is one hundred and forty stadia from the naval station of Heracleia. It is said to have been founded by the Pylians who sailed from Troy with Nestor; and they so prospered from farming, it is said, that they dedicated a golden harvest[2] at Delphi. And writers produce as a sign of its having been founded by the Pylians the sacrifice to the shades of the sons of Neleus.[3] However, the city was wiped out by the Samnitae. According to Antiochus: Certain of the Achaeans were sent for by the Achaeans in Sybaris and re-settled the place, then forsaken, but they were summoned only because of a hatred which the Achaeans who had

Meineke and others are probably right in emending to the "Trais" (now the Trionto), on which, according to Diodorus Siculus (12. 22), certain Sybarites took up their abode in 445 B.C.

[2] An ear, or sheaf, of grain made of gold, apparently.

[3] Neleus had twelve sons, including Nestor. All but Nestor were slain by Heracles.

τῆς Λακωνικῆς, ἵνα μὴ Ταραντῖνοι γειτνιῶντες
ἐπιπηδήσαιεν τῷ τόπῳ. δυεῖν δ' οὐσῶν πόλεων,
τοῦ δὲ[1] Μεταποντίου ἐγγυτέρω τοῦ Τάραντος,
πεισθῆναι τοὺς ἀφιγμένους ὑπὸ τῶν Συβαριτῶν
C 265 τὸ Μεταπόντιον κατασχεῖν· τοῦτο μὲν γὰρ ἔχοντας
ἕξειν καὶ τὴν Σιρῖτιν, εἰ δ' ἐπὶ τὴν Σιρῖτιν τρά-
ποιντο, προσθήσειν τοῖς Ταραντίνοις τὸ Μεταπόντιον ἐν πλευραῖς οὖσι. πολεμοῦντας δ' ὕστερον πρὸς
τοὺς Ταραντίνους καὶ τοὺς ὑπερκειμένους Οἰνωτροὺς ἐπὶ μέρει διαλυθῆναι τῆς γῆς, ὅπερ γενέσθαι
τῆς τότε Ἰταλίας ὅριον καὶ τῆς Ἰαπυγίας. ἐνταῦθα
δὲ καὶ τὸν Μετάποντον μυθεύουσι καὶ τὴν Μελανίππην τὴν δεσμῶτιν καὶ τὸν ἐξ αὐτῆς Βοιωτόν.
δοκεῖ δ' Ἀντίοχος τὴν πόλιν Μεταπόντιον εἰρῆσθαι πρότερον Μέταβον, παρωνομάσθαι δ' ὕστερον·
τήν τε Μελανίππην οὐ πρὸς τοῦτον, ἀλλὰ πρὸς
Δίον κομισθῆναι ἐλέγχειν ἡρῷον τοῦ Μετάβου
καὶ Ἄσιον τὸν ποιητὴν φήσαντα, ὅτι τὸν Βοιωτὸν

Δίου ἐνὶ μεγάροις τέκεν εὐειδὴς Μελανίππη,

ὡς πρὸς ἐκεῖνον ἀχθεῖσαν τὴν Μελανίππην, οὐ
πρὸς Μέταβον. οἰκιστὴς δὲ τοῦ Μεταποντίου
Δαύλιος ὁ Κρίσης τύραννος γεγένηται τῆς περὶ

---

[1] δέ, after τοῦ, Corais inserts; but instead, Meineke and
Müller-Dübner, following Groskurd, insert τῆς δὲ Σιρίτιδος
ἀπωτέρω after ἐγγυτέρω.

---

[1] The other, of course, was Siris.
[2] The old name of Tarentum.
[3] i.e. the Metapontians gained undisputed control of
their city and its territory, which Antiochus speaks of as
a "boundary" (cp. 6. 1. 4 and 6. 3. 1).

been banished from Laconia had for the Tarantini,
in order that the neighbouring Tarantini might not
pounce upon the place; there were two cities, but
since, of the two, Metapontium was nearer [1] to
Taras,[2] the new-comers were persuaded by the
Sybarites to take Metapontium and hold it, for,
if they held this, they would also hold the territory
of Siris, whereas, if they turned to the territory of
Siris, they would add Metapontium to the territory
of the Tarantini, which latter was on the very flank
of Metapontium; and when, later on, the Metapontians were at war with the Tarantini and the
Oenotrians of the interior, a reconciliation was
effected in regard to a portion of the land—that
portion, indeed, which marked the boundary between the Italy of that time and Iapygia.[3] Here,
too, the fabulous accounts place Metapontus,[4] and
also Melanippe the prisoner and her son Boeotus.[5]
In the opinion of Antiochus, the city Metapontium
was first called Metabum and later on its name was
slightly altered, and further, Melanippe was brought,
not to Metabus, but to Dius,[6] as is proved by a
hero-temple of Metabus, and also by Asius the
poet, when he says that Boeotus was brought forth
" in the halls of Dius by shapely Melanippe," meaning that Melanippe was brought to Dius, not to
Metabus. But, as Ephorus says, the coloniser of
Metapontium was Daulius, the tyrant of the Crisa

---

[4] The son of Sisyphus. His "barbarian name," according
to Stephanus Byzantinus and Eustathius, was Metabus.
[5] One of Euripides' tragedies was entitled *Melanippe the
Prisoner*; only fragments are preserved. She was the
mother of Boeotus by Poseidon.
[6] A Metapontian.

53

Δελφούς, ὥς φησιν Ἔφορος. ἔστι δ᾽ ἔτι[1] καὶ
οὗτος ὁ[2] λόγος, ὡς ὁ πεμφθεὶς ὑπὸ τῶν Ἀχαιῶν
ἐπὶ τὸν συνοικισμὸν Λεύκιππος εἴη, χρησάμενος
δὲ παρὰ τῶν Ταραντίνων τὸν τόπον εἰς ἡμέραν καὶ
νύκτα μὴ ἀποδοίη, μεθ᾽ ἡμέραν μὲν λέγων πρὸς
τοὺς ἀπαιτοῦντας, ὅτι καὶ εἰς τὴν ἐφεξῆς νύκτα
αἰτήσαιτο καὶ λάβοι, νύκτωρ δ᾽, ὅτι καὶ πρὸς τὴν
ἐξῆς ἡμέραν.

Ἐφεξῆς δ᾽ ἐστὶν ὁ Τάρας καὶ ἡ Ἰαπυγία, περὶ
ὧν ἐροῦμεν, ὅταν πρότερον τὰς προκειμένας τῆς
Ἰταλίας νήσους περιοδεύσωμεν κατὰ τὴν ἐξ
ἀρχῆς πρόθεσιν· ἀεὶ γὰρ τοῖς ἔθνεσιν ἑκάστοις
τὰς γειτνιώσας προσκαταλέγοντες νήσους καὶ νῦν,
ἐπειδὴ μέχρι τέλους ἐπεληλύθαμεν τὴν Οἰνωτρίαν,
ἥνπερ καὶ Ἰταλίαν μόνην ὠνόμαζον οἱ πρότεροι,
δίκαιοί ἐσμεν φυλάξαι τὴν αὐτὴν τάξιν, ἐπελθόντες τὴν Σικελίαν καὶ τὰς περὶ αὐτὴν νήσους.

II

Ἔστι δ᾽ ἡ Σικελία τρίγωνος τῷ σχήματι, καὶ
διὰ τοῦτο Τρινακρία[3] μὲν πρότερον, Θρινακὶς[4]
δ᾽ ὕστερον προσηγορεύθη, μετονομασθεῖσα εὐφω-
νότερον. τὸ δὲ σχῆμα διορίζουσι τρεῖς ἄκραι,
Πελωριὰς μὲν ἡ πρὸς τὴν Καῖνυν καὶ τὴν στυλίδα
τὴν Ῥηγίνων ποιοῦσα τὸν Πορθμόν, Πάχυνος δὲ
ἡ ἐκκειμένη πρὸς ἔω καὶ τῷ Σικελικῷ κλυζομένη
πελάγει, βλέπουσα πρὸς τὴν Πελοπόννησον καὶ

---

[1] δ᾽ ἔτι, Capps, for δέ τις.
[2] ὁ, before λόγος, Jones inserts.
[3] For Τρινακρία, Jones suspects that Strabo wrote Τρινακρίς.

which is near Delphi. And there is this further
account, that the man who was sent by the Achaeans
to help colonise it was Leucippus, and that after
procuring the use of the place from the Tarantini
for only a day and night he would not give it back,
replying by day to those who asked it back that he
had asked and taken it for the next night also, and
by night that he had taken and asked it also for
the next day.

Next in order comes Taras and Iapygia; but
before discussing them I shall, in accordance with
my original purpose, give a general description of
the islands that lie in front of Italy ; for as from
time to time I have named also the islands which
neighbour upon the several tribes, so now, since I
have traversed Oenotria from beginning to end,
which alone the people of earlier times called Italy,
it is right that I should preserve the same order in
traversing Sicily and the islands round about it.

II

1. Sicily is triangular in shape ; and for this reason
it was at first called " Trinacria," though later the
name was changed to the more euphonious " Thri-
nacis." Its shape is defined by three capes : Pelorias,
which with Caenys and Columna Rheginorum forms
the strait, and Pachynus, which lies out towards the
east and is washed by the Sicilian Sea, thus facing
towards the Peloponnesus and the sea-passage to

⁴ For Θρινακίς, Meineke reads Θρινακία, following E and
Eustath. *ad Dion.* 467. C (?) and the editors before Kramer
read Τρινακίς.

τὸν ἐπὶ Κρήτης πόρον· τρίτη δ' ἐστὶν ἡ προσεχὴς
τῇ Λιβύῃ, βλέπουσα πρὸς ταύτην ἅμα καὶ τὴν
χειμερινὴν δύσιν, Λιλύβαιον. τῶν δὲ πλευρῶν,
ἃς ἀφορίζουσιν αἱ τρεῖς ἄκραι, δύο μέν εἰσι κοῖλαι
C 266 μετρίως, ἡ δὲ τρίτη κυρτή, ἡ ἀπὸ τοῦ Λιλυβαίου
καθήκουσα πρὸς τὴν Πελωριάδα, ἥπερ μεγίστη
ἐστί, σταδίων χιλίων καὶ ἑπτακοσίων, ὡς Ποσειδώνιος εἴρηκε προσθεὶς καὶ εἴκοσι. τῶν δ' ἄλλων
ἥ τ' ἐπὶ Πάχυνον ἀπὸ τοῦ Λιλυβαίου μείζων τῆς
ἑτέρας· ἐλαχίστη δὲ ἡ τῷ Πορθμῷ καὶ τῇ Ἰταλίᾳ
προσεχής, ἡ ἀπὸ τῆς Πελωριάδος ἐπὶ τὸν Πάχυνον,
σταδίων ὅσον χιλίων καὶ ἑκατὸν καὶ τριάκοντα.
τὸν δὲ περίπλουν ὁ Ποσειδώνιος σταδίων τετρακοσίων ἐπὶ τοῖς τετρακισχιλίοις ἀποφαίνει. ἐν δὲ
τῇ χωρογραφίᾳ μείζω λέγεται τὰ διαστήματα, κατὰ
μέρος διῃρημένα μιλιασμῷ· ἐκ δὲ Πελωριάδος εἰς
Μύλας εἴκοσι πέντε· τοσαῦτα δὲ καὶ ἐκ Μυλῶν
εἰς Τυνδαρίδα· εἶτα εἰς Ἀγάθυρνον τριάκοντα καὶ
τὰ ἴσα εἰς Ἄλαισαν¹ καὶ πάλιν ἴσα εἰς Κεφα-
λοίδιον· ταῦτα μὲν πολίχνια· εἰς δ' Ἱμέραν
ποταμὸν δεκαοκτὼ διὰ μέσης ῥέοντα τῆς Σικελίας,
εἶτ' εἰς Πάνορμον τριάκοντα πέντε· δύο δὲ καὶ
τριάκοντα εἰς τὸ τῶν Αἰγεστέων ἐμπόριον· λοιπὰ
δὲ εἰς Λιχύβαιον τριάκοντα ὀκτώ. ἐντεῦθεν δὲ
κάμψαντι ἐπὶ τὸ συνεχὲς πλευρὸν εἰς μὲν τὸ
Ἡράκλειον ἑβδομήκοντα πέντε, ἐπὶ δὲ τὸ Ἀκρα-

---

¹ Ἄλαισαν, Corais, for Ἄλισα; so Meineke.

---

[1] South-west.
[2] See footnote 4 on page 39.

Crete, and, third, Lilybaeum, the cape that is next
to Libya, thus facing at the same time towards
Libya and the winter sunset.[1] As for the sides
which are marked off by the three capes, two of
them are moderately concave, whereas the third,
the one that reaches from Lilybaeum to Pelorias, is
convex; and this last is the longest, being one
thousand seven hundred stadia in length, as Poseidonius states, though he adds twenty stadia more.
Of the other two sides, the one from Lilybaeum to
Pachynus is longer than the other, and the one next
to the strait and Italy, from Pelorias to Pachynus,
is shortest, being about one thousand one hundred
and thirty stadia long. And the distance round the
island by sea, as declared by Poseidonius, is four
thousand four hundred stadia. But in the Choro-
graphy [2] the distances given are longer, marked off
in sections and given in miles: from Pelorias to
Mylae, twenty-five miles; the same from Mylae to
Tyndaris; then to Agathyrnum thirty, and the same
to Alaesa, and again the same to Cephaloedium,
these being small towns; and eighteen to the River
Himera,[3] which flows through the middle of Sicily;
then to Panormus thirty-five, and thirty-two to the
Emporium of the Aegestes,[4] and the rest of the way,
to Lilybaeum, thirty-eight. Thence, on doubling
Lilybaeum, to the adjacent side, to the Heracleium
seventy-five miles, and to the Emporium of the

---

[3] C. Müller (see Map V at the end of this volume)
assumes that Strabo exchanged the Chorographer's distances
between (1) Alaesa and Cephaloedium, and (2) Cephaloedium
and the River Himera (see C. Müller, *Ind. Var. Lect.*,
p. 977).

[4] In Latin, Emporium Segestanorum.

STRABO

γαντινων [1] ἐμπόριον εἴκοσι, καὶ ἄλλα εἴκοσι εἰς
Καμάριναν· εἶτ᾽ ἐπὶ Πάχυνον πεντήκοντα. ἔνθεν
πάλιν κατὰ τὸ τρίτον πλευρὸν εἰς μὲν Συρακούσσας τριάκοντα ἕξ,[2] εἰς δὲ Κατάνην ἑξήκοντα· εἶτ᾽
εἰς Ταυρομένιον τριάκοντα τρία· εἶτ᾽ εἰς Μεσσήνην
τριάκοντα. πεζῇ δὲ ἐκ μὲν Παχύνου εἰς Πελωριάδα
ἑκατὸν ἑξήκοντα ὀκτώ, ἐκ δὲ Μεσσήνης εἰς
Λιλύβαιον τῇ Οὐαλερίᾳ ὁδῷ διακόσια [3] τριάκοντα
πέντε. ἔνιοι δ᾽ ἁπλούστερον εἰρήκασιν, ὥσπερ
Ἔφορος, τόν γε περίπλουν ἡμερῶν καὶ νυκτῶν
πέντε. Ποσειδώνιός τε τοῖς κλίμασιν ἀφορίζων
τὴν νῆσον, καὶ πρὸς ἄρκτον μὲν τὴν Πελωριάδα,
πρὸς νότον δὲ Λιλύβαιον, πρὸς ἕω δὲ τὸν Πάχυνον
τίθησιν. ἀνάγκη δέ, τῶν κλιμάτων ἐν παραλλη-
λογράμμῳ σχήματι διαστελλομένων, τὰ ἐγγραφό-
μενα τρίγωνα, καὶ μάλιστα ὅσα σκαληνὰ καὶ ὧν
οὐδεμία πλευρὰ οὐδεμίᾳ[4] τῶν τοῦ παραλληλογράμμου ἐφαρμόττει, ἀναρμόστως ἔχειν πρὸς τὰ

[1] Ἀκραγαντίνων (k), for Ἀκραγαντῖνον (ABCl) ; so Müller-
Dübner and Meineke.
[2] For τριάκοντα ἕξ, Bl have εἴκοσι, but B sec. m. λς᾽.
[3] διακόσια (σ᾽), Cluver conj. ; so read the editors. See
Klotz Quellen u. Forschungen z. alt. Geschichte u. Geographen,
Heft 11, p. 55 ; also Detlefsen, Heft 13, p. 65.
[4] οὐδεμίᾳ, after πλευρά, Corais inserts ; so the later editors.

[1] In Latin, Emporium Agrigentinorum.
[2] This distance is in fact more than sixty miles. C. Müller
assumes in the Map (l.c.) that the copyist left out the interval
from Emporium to Gela and put down an extra distance of
twenty miles therefor. But elsewhere (Ind. Var. Lect., l.c.),
he believes (more plausibly) that two intervals were omitted
and assigns twenty stadia to each, viz., Emporium to the
Harbour of Phintias, and thence to Calvisiana.
[3] Note in connection with the next sentence that the text

Acragantini[1] twenty, and another twenty[2] to Camarina; and then to Pachynus fifty. Thence again along the third side: to Syracuse thirty-six, and to Catana sixty; then to Tauromenium thirty-three; and then to Messene thirty.[3] On foot, however, the distance from Pachynus to Pelorias is one hundred and sixty-eight miles, and from Messene to Lilybaeum by the Valerian Way two hundred and thirty-five. But some writers have spoken in a more general way, as, for example, Ephorus: "At any rate, the voyage round the island takes five days and nights." Further, Poseidonius, in marking off the boundaries of the island by means of the "climata,"[4] puts Pelorias towards the north, Lilybaeum towards the south, and Pachynus towards the east. But since the "climata" are each divided off into parallelograms, necessarily the triangles that are inscribed (particularly those which are scalene and of which no side fits on any one of the sides of the parallelogram) cannot, because of their slant, be fitted to the "climata."[5] However this may be, one

does not give the distance from Messene to Pelorias, which is about nine miles.

[4] On the "climata" (belts of latitude), see 1. 1. 12 and footnote 2).

[5] Though the works of Poseidonius are lost, it is obvious that he properly fixed the position of the three vertices of the triangle according to the method of his time by the "climata," i.e. he fixed their north-and-south positions (cp. "latitude") and their east-and-west position (cp. "longitude"). Strabo rightly, but rather captiously, remarks that Poseidonius cannot by means of the "climata" mark off the boundaries of Sicily, since the triangle is merely inscribed in the parallelogram and no side of it coincides with any side of the parallelogram; in other words, the result of Poseidonius is too indefinite.

κλίματα διὰ τὴν λόξωσιν. ὅμως δ' οὖν ἐν τοῖς
τῆς Σικελίας τῇ Ἰταλίᾳ πρὸς νότον κειμένης[1] ἡ
Πελωριὰς ἀρκτικωτάτη λέγοιτ' ἂν καλῶς τῶν
τριῶν γωνιῶν, ὥσθ' ἡ ἐπιζευγνυμένη[2] ἀπ' αὐτῆς
ἐπὶ τὸν Πάχυνον ἐκκείσεται[3] πρὸς ἔω μὲν[4] πρὸς
ἄρκτον βλέπουσα,[5] ποιήσει δὲ τὴν πλευρὰν τὴν[6]
πρὸς τὸν Πορθμόν. δεῖ δ' ἐπιστροφὴν μικρὰν
λαμβάνειν ἐπὶ χειμερινὰς ἀνατολάς· οὕτω γὰρ ἡ
ἠιὼν παρακλίνει προϊοῦσιν ἀπὸ τῆς Κατάνης ἐπὶ
τὰς Συρακούσσας καὶ τὸν Πάχυνον. δίαρμα δ'
ἐστὶν ἀπὸ τοῦ Παχύνου πρὸς τὸ στόμα τοῦ
C 267 Ἀλφειοῦ στάδιοι τετρακισχίλιοι. Ἀρτεμίδωρος
δ' ἀπὸ τοῦ Παχύνου φήσας ἐπὶ Ταίναρον εἶναι
τετρακισχιλίους καὶ ἑξακοσίους, ἀπὸ δ' Ἀλφειοῦ
ἐπὶ Παμισὸν χιλίους ἑκατὸν τριάκοντα, παρασχεῖν
ἂν δοκεῖ μοι λόγον, μὴ οὐχ ὁμολογούμενα λέγῃ τῷ
φήσαντι τετρακισχιλίους εἶναι τοὺς ἐπὶ τὸν
Ἀλφειὸν ἀπὸ τοῦ Παχύνου. ἡ δ' ἀπὸ Παχύνου
πρὸς Λιλύβαιον, ἑσπεριώτερον δὲ τῆς Πελωριάδος
ἱκανῶς[7] ἐστιν, ἱκανῶς ἂν καὐτὴ λοξοῖτο[8] ἀπὸ
τοῦ μεσημβρινοῦ σημείου πρὸς τὴν ἑσπέραν,
βλέποι δὲ ἂν ἅμα πρός τε τὴν ἔω καὶ πρὸς τὸν

---

[1] κειμένης, the reading of Bk; so Siebenkees, Corais, and
Müller-Dübner. Meineke follows the reading of the other
MSS., but stars the preceding ἐν τοῖς.

[2] For ἡ ἐπιζευγμένη, Bk read τὴν ἐπιζευγμένην; Meineke
and other editors read the former.

[3] ἐκκείσεται, Corais, for ἐκκεῖσθαι; so Kramer and Müller-
Dübner. Meineke retains the infinitive, inserting ὅν before it.

[4] πρὸς ἔω μὲν [καί], Corais (and so Kramer and Müller-
Dübner) for πρὸς ἔω φαμέν, though Jones omits the καί.

[5] βλέπουσα, Corais, for βλέπουσαν; so the later editors,
though Meineke inserts ἅμα before πρὸς ἄρκτον, and deletes
δὲ after ποιήσει.

might fairly say, in the case of the "climata" of Sicily, which is situated south of Italy, that Pelorias is the most northerly of the three corners; and therefore the side that joins Pelorias to Pachynus will lie out[1] towards the east, thus facing towards the north, and also will form the side that is on the strait. But this side must take a slight turn toward the winter sunrise,[2] for the shore bends aside in this direction as one proceeds from Catana to Syracuse and Pachynus. Now the distance from Pachynus across to the mouth of the Alpheius[3] is four thousand stadia; but when Artemidorus says that it is four thousand six hundred stadia from Pachynus to Taenarum[4] and one thousand one hundred and thirty from the Alpheius to the Pamisus, he seems to me to afford us reason for suspecting that his statement is not in agreement with that of the man who says that the distance to the Alpheius from Pachynus is four thousand stadia. Again, the side that extends from Pachynus to Lilybaeum, which is considerably farther west than Pelorias, should itself also be made to slant considerably from its southernmost point[5] towards the west, and should face at the same time towards the east and towards the south,[6] one part being washed

---

[1] That is, will point. [2] South-east.
[3] In the Peloponnesus; now the Ruphis.
[4] Cape Matapan.
[5] *i. e.* of the side; hence from Pachynus.
[6] That is, a line at right angles to the side would point south-east.

---

[6] τήν, before πρός, Corais, for καί.
[7] ἱκανῶς, Meineke omits, following C.
[8] λόξοιτο, conj. of Tyrwhitt, for δόξοιτο; so read the editors.

νότον, τῇ μὲν ὑπὸ τοῦ Σικελικοῦ πελάγους κλυζομένῃ, τῇ δ' ὑπὸ τοῦ Λιβυκοῦ τοῦ πρὸς τὰς Σύρτεις διήκοντος ἀπὸ τῆς Καρχηδονίας. ἔστι δὲ καὶ ἀπὸ Λιλυβαίου τοὐλάχιστον δίαρμα ἐπὶ Λιβύην χίλιοι καὶ πεντακόσιοι περὶ Καρχηδόνα· καθ'[1] ὃ δὴ λέγεταί τις τῶν ὀξυδορκούντων ἀπό τινος σκοπῆς ἀπαγγέλλειν τὸν ἀριθμὸν τῶν ἀναγομένων[2] ἐκ Καρχηδόνος σκαφῶν τοῖς ἐν Λιλυβαίῳ. ἀπὸ δὲ τοῦ Λιλυβαίου τὴν ἐπὶ Πελωριάδα πλευρὰν ἀνάγκη λοξοῦσθαι πρὸς ἔω καὶ βλέπειν πρὸς τὸ μεταξὺ τῆς ἑσπέρας καὶ τῆς ἄρκτου, πρὸς ἄρκτον μὲν ἔχουσαν τὴν Ἰταλίαν, πρὸς δύσιν δὲ τὸ Τυρρηνικὸν πέλαγος καὶ τὰς Αἰόλου νήσους.

2. Πόλεις δ' εἰσὶ κατὰ μὲν τὸ πλευρὸν τὸ ποιοῦν τὸν Πορθμὸν Μεσσήνη πρῶτον, ἔπειτα Ταυρομένιον καὶ Κατάνη καὶ Συράκουσσαι· αἱ δὲ μεταξὺ Κατάνης καὶ Συρακουσσῶν ἐκλελοίπασι, Νάξος καὶ Μέγαρα, ὅπου καὶ αἱ τῶν ποταμῶν ἐκβολαὶ Συμαίθου καὶ πάντων[3] καταρρεόντων ἐκ τῆς Αἴτνης εἰς εὐλίμενα στόματα· ἐνταῦθα δὲ καὶ τὸ

[1] καθ', Xylander, for καί; so the later editors.
[2] ἀναγομένων (n o); ἀγομένων (ABC*l*).
[3] Συμαίθου καὶ πάντων, Jones reads. The MSS. read: συνελθοῦσαι (συνῆλθον, n o) πάντων (καὶ πάντα, AB, though in B καί, sec. m., is indicated as wrong and πάντων is written for πάντα). Madvig, and C. Müller (independently) conj. Συμαίθου καὶ Παντακίου.

---

[1] Cp. 17. 3. 16.
[2] Lilybaeum when held by the Carthaginians (250 B.C.) was besieged by the Romans. Pliny (7. 21) says that Varro

by the Sicilian Sea and the other by the Libyan Sea that reaches from Carthaginia to the Syrtes. The shortest passage from Lilybaeum across to Libya in the neighbourhood of Carthage is one thousand five hundred stadia;[1] and on this passage, it is said, some man of sharp vision, from a look-out, used to report to the men in Lilybaeum the number of ships that were putting to sea from Carthage.[2] Again, the side that extends from Lilybaeum to Pelorias necessarily slants towards the east, and faces towards the region that is between the west and the north,[3] having Italy on the north and on the west the Tyrrhenian Sea and the Islands of Aeolus.

2. The cities along the side that forms the Strait are, first, Messene, and then Tauromenium, Catana, and Syracuse; but those that were between Catana and Syracuse have disappeared—Naxus[4] and Megara;[5] and on this coast are the outlets of the Symaethus and all rivers that flow down from Aetna and have good harbours at their mouths; and here

gave the man's name as Strabo; and quotes Cicero as authority for the tradition that the man was wont, in the Punic War, looking from the Lilybaean promontory, a distance of 135 miles, to tell the number of ships that put out from the harbour of Carthage. But, assuming the possibility of seeing small ships at a distance of 135 miles, the observer would have to be at an altitude of a little more than two miles!

[3] That is, a line at right angles to the side points towards the north-west.

[4] Founded about 734 B.C. and destroyed by Dionysius in 403 B.C. (see Diodorus Siculus 14. 14), but it is placed by the commentators and maps between Tauromenium and Catana.

[5] Founded about the same time as Naxus and destroyed about 214 B.C.

τῆς Ξιφωνίας ἀκρωτήριον. φησὶ δὲ ταύτας
Ἔφορος πρώτας κτισθῆναι πόλεις Ἑλληνίδας ἐν
Σικελίᾳ δεκάτῃ[1] γενεᾷ μετὰ τὰ Τρωικά· τοὺς γὰρ
πρότερον δεδιέναι τὰ ληστήρια τῶν Τυρρηνῶν καὶ
τὴν ὠμότητα τῶν ταύτῃ βαρβάρων, ὥστε μηδὲ
κατ' ἐμπορίαν πλεῖν. Θεοκλέα δ' Ἀθηναῖον
παρενεχθέντα ἀνέμοις εἰς τὴν Σικελίαν κατανοῆσαι
τήν τε οὐδένειαν τῶν ἀνθρώπων καὶ τὴν ἀρετὴν
τῆς γῆς, ἐπανελθόντα δὲ Ἀθηναίους μὲν μὴ πεῖσαι,
Χαλκιδέας δὲ τοὺς ἐν Εὐβοίᾳ συχνοὺς παραλα-
βόντα καὶ τῶν Ἰώνων τινάς, ἔτι δὲ Δωριέων, ὧν[2]
οἱ πλείους ἦσαν Μεγαρεῖς, πλεῦσαι· τοὺς μὲν οὖν
Χαλκιδέας κτίσαι Νάξον, τοὺς δὲ Δωριέας Μέγαρα,
τὴν Ὕβλαν πρότερον καλουμένην. αἱ μὲν οὖν
πόλεις οὐκέτ' εἰσί, τὸ δὲ τῆς Ὕβλης ὄνομα συμμένει διὰ τὴν ἀρετὴν τοῦ Ὑβλαίου μέλιτος.

3. Τῶν δὲ συμμενουσῶν κατὰ τὸ λεχθὲν πλευρὸν πόλεων ἡ μὲν Μεσσήνη τῆς Πελωριάδος ἐν
C 268 κόλπῳ κεῖται, καμπτομένης ἐπὶ πολὺ πρὸς ἔω καὶ
μασχάλην τινὰ ποιούσης· ἀπέχει δὲ τοῦ μὲν
Ῥηγίου δίαρμα ἑξηκοντάστάδιον, τῆς δὲ στυλίδος
πολὺ ἔλαττον. κτίσμα δ' ἐστὶ Μεσσηνίων τῶν
ἐν Πελοποννήσῳ, παρ' ὧν τοὔνομα μετήλλαξε,
καλουμένη Ζάγκλη πρότερον διὰ τὴν σκολιότητα
τῶν τόπων (ζάγκλιον γὰρ ἐκαλεῖτο τὸ σκολιόν),
Ναξίων οὖσα πρότερον κτίσμα τῶν πρὸς Κατάνην·
ἐπῴκησαν δ' ὕστερον Μαμερτῖνοι, Καμπανῶν τι

---

[1] δεκάτῃ, Scaliger, for καὶ τῇ ; so the editors.
[2] ὧν, Corais inserts ; so the later editors.

---

[1] The noun "zanclon" (corresponding to the adjective
"zanclion") was a native Sicilian word, according to Thucydides (6. 4).

too is the promontory of Xiphonia. According to
Ephorus, these were the earliest Greek cities to be
founded in Sicily, that is, in the tenth generation
after the Trojan war; for before that time men
were so afraid of the bands of Tyrrhenian pirates
and the savagery of the barbarians in this region
that they would not so much as sail thither for
trafficking; but though Theocles, the Athenian,
borne out of his course by the winds to Sicily,
clearly perceived both the weakness of the peoples
and the excellence of the soil, yet, when he went
back, he could not persuade the Athenians, and
hence took as partners a considerable number of
Euboean Chalcidians and some Ionians and also
some Dorians (most of whom were Megarians) and
made the voyage; so the Chalcidians founded
Naxus, whereas the Dorians founded Megara, which
in earlier times had been called Hybla. The cities
no longer exist, it is true, but the name of Hybla
still endures, because of the excellence of the
Hyblaean honey.

3. As for the cities that still endure along the
aforementioned side: Messene is situated in a gulf
of Pelorias, which bends considerably towards the
east and forms an armpit, so to speak; but though
the distance across to Messene from Rhegium is
only sixty stadia, it is much less from Columna.
Messene was founded by the Messenians of the Peio-
ponnesus, who named it after themselves, changing
its name; for formerly it was called Zancle, on
account of the crookedness of the coast (anything
crooked was called "zanclion"),[1] having been founded
formerly by the Naxians who lived near Catana.
But the Mamertini, a tribe of the Campani, joined

φῦλον· ἐχρήσαντο δ᾽ ὁρμητηρίῳ Ῥωμαῖοι πρὸς τὸν
Σικελικὸν πόλεμον τὸν πρὸς Καρχηδονίους, καὶ
μετὰ ταῦτα Πομπήιος ὁ Σέξτος ἐνταῦθα συνεῖχε
τὸ ναυτικόν, πολεμῶν πρὸς τὸν Σεβαστὸν Καί-
σαρα, ἐντεῦθεν δὲ καὶ τὴν φυγὴν ἐποιήσατο,
ἐκπεσὼν ἐκ τῆς νήσου. δείκνυται δὲ καὶ ἡ
Χάρυβδις μικρὸν πρὸ τῆς πόλεως ἐν τῷ πόρῳ,
βάθος ἐξαίσιον, εἰς ὃ αἱ παλίρροιαι τοῦ Πορθμοῦ
κατάγουσιν εὐφυῶς τὰ σκάφη τραχηλιζόμενα
μετὰ συστροφῆς καὶ δίνης μεγάλης· καταποθέντων
δὲ καὶ διαλυθέντων τὰ ναυάγια παρασύρεται πρὸς
ἠιόνα τῆς Ταυρομενίας, ἣν καλοῦσιν ἀπὸ τοῦ
συμπτώματος τούτου Κοπρίαν. τοσοῦτον δ᾽
ἐπεκράτησαν οἱ Μαμερτῖνοι παρὰ τοῖς Μεσσηνίοις,
ὥστ᾽ ἐπ᾽ ἐκείνοις ὑπῆρξεν ἡ πόλις, καλοῦσι δὲ Μα-
μερτίνους μᾶλλον ἅπαντες αὐτοὺς ἢ Μεσσηνίους,
εὐοίνου τε σφόδρα τῆς χώρας οὔσης, οὐ Μεσσήνιον
καλοῦσι τὸν οἶνον, ἀλλὰ Μαμερτῖνον, τοῖς ἀρίστοις
ἐνάμιλλον ὄντα τῶν Ἰταλικῶν. οἰκεῖται δ᾽ ἱκανῶς
ἡ πόλις, μᾶλλον δὲ Κατάνη, καὶ γὰρ οἰκήτορας
δέδεκται Ῥωμαίους· ἧττον δ᾽ ἀμφοῖν τὸ Ταυρομένιον. καὶ Κατάνη δ᾽ ἐστὶ Ναξίων τῶν αὐτῶν
κτίσμα, Ταυρομένιον δὲ τῶν ἐν Ὕβλῃ Ζαγκλαίων·
ἀπέβαλε δὲ τοὺς οἰκήτορας τοὺς ἐξ ἀρχῆς ἡ
Κατάνη, κατοικίσαντος ἑτέρους Ἱέρωνος τοῦ
Συρακουσσίων τυράννου καὶ προσαγορεύσαντος
αὐτὴν Αἴτνην ἀντὶ Κατάνης. ταύτης δὲ καὶ
Πίνδαρος κτίστορα λέγει αὐτόν, ὅταν φῇ·

ξύνες ὅ τοι[1] λέγω, ζαθέων ἱερῶν
ὁμώνυμε πάτερ, κτίστορ Αἴτνας.

[Bergk, Frag. 105.]

---

[1] ξύνες ὅ τοι, Meineke, and Bergk, for ξένεστοι.

the colony later on. Now the Romans used it as a base of operations for their Sicilian war against the Carthaginians; and afterwards Pompeius Sextus, when at war with Augustus Caesar, kept his fleet together there, and when ejected from the island also made his escape thence. And in the ship-channel, only a short distance off the city, is to be seen Charybdis,[1] a monstrous deep, into which the ships are easily drawn by the refluent currents of the strait and plunged prow-foremost along with a mighty eddying of the whirlpool; and when the ships are gulped down and broken to pieces, the wreckage is swept along to the Tauromenian shore, which, from this occurrence, is called Copria.[2] The Mamertini prevailed to such an extent among the Messenii that they got control of the city; and the people are by all called Mamertini rather than Messenii; and further, since the country is exceedingly productive of wine, the wine is called, not Messenian, but Mamertine, and it rivals the best of the Italian wines. The city is fairly populous, though Catana is still more so, and in fact has received Romans as inhabitants; but Tauromenium is less populous than either. Catana, moreover, was founded by the same Naxians, whereas Tauromenium was founded by the Zanclaeans of Hybla; but Catana lost its original inhabitants when Hiero, tyrant of Syracuse, established a different set of colonists there and called it Aetna instead of Catana.[3] And Pindar too calls him the founder of Aetna when he says: "Attend to what I say to thee, O Father, whose name is that of the holy sacrifices,[4] founder of Aetna." But at the death of

---

[1] Cp. 1. 2. 36.   [2] "Dunghill."   [3] 476 B.C.
[4] The Greek here for "sacrifices" is "hierōn."

κατὰ[1] δὲ τὴν τελευτὴν τοῦ Ἱέρωνος κατελθόντες
οἱ Καταναῖοι τούς τε ἐνοίκους ἐξέβαλον καὶ τὸν
τάφον ἀνέσκαψαν τοῦ τυράννου. οἱ δὲ Αἰτναῖοι
παραχωρήσαντες τὴν Ἵννησαν καλουμένην τῆς
Αἴτνης ὀρεινὴν ᾤκησαν καὶ προσηγόρευσαν τὸ
χωρίον Αἴτνην, διέχον τῆς Κατάνης σταδίους
ὀγδοήκοντα, καὶ τὸν Ἱέρωνα οἰκιστὴν ἀπέφηναν.
ὑπέρκειται δὲ μάλιστα τῆς Κατάνης ἡ Αἴτνη,
καὶ τῶν περὶ τοὺς κρατῆρας παθῶν πλεῖστον
C 269 κοινωνεῖ· καὶ γὰρ οἱ ῥύακες εἰς τὴν Καταναίαν
ἐγγυτάτω καταφέρονται, καὶ τὰ περὶ τοὺς εὐσεβεῖς ἐκεῖ τεθρύληται[2] τὸν Ἀμφίνομον καὶ τὸν
Ἀναπίαν, οἳ τοὺς γονέας ἐπὶ τῶν ὤμων ἀράμενοι
διέσωσαν ἐπιφερομένου τοῦ κακοῦ. ὅταν δ᾽, ὁ
Ποσειδώνιός φησί, γίνηται[3] τὰ περὶ τὸ ὄρος,
κατατεφροῦται πολλῷ βάθει τὰ Καταναίων χω-
ρία· ἡ μὲν οὖν σποδός, λυπήσασα πρὸς καιρόν,
εὐεργετεῖ τὴν χώραν χρόνοις ὕστερον, εὐάμπελον
γὰρ παρέχεται καὶ χρηστόκαρπον, τῆς ἄλλης
οὐχ ὁμοίως οὔσης εὐοίνου· τάς τε ῥίζας, ἃς[4]
ἐκφέρει τὰ κατατεφρωθέντα χωρία, πιαίνειν[5] ἐπὶ
τοσοῦτον τὰ πρόβατά φασιν, ὥστε πνίγεσθαι·
διόπερ ἐκ τῶν ὤτων ἀφαιροῦσιν αἷμα δι᾽ ἡμερῶν
τεσσάρων ἢ πέντε,[6] καθάπερ τοῦτο καὶ κατὰ τὴν
Ἐρύθειαν συμβαῖνον εἰρήκαμεν. ὁ δὲ ῥύαξ εἰς

---

[1] κατά, Corais and Meineke emend to μετά.
[2] ἐκεῖ τεθρύληται, Xylander, for ἐκτεθρύλλαται; so the later
editors.
[3] ὅταν δ᾽, ὁ Ποσειδώνιος φησί, γίνηται, Meineke, for ὅταν τῷ
Ποσειδῶνι φαίνηται.
[4] ἅς, Corais inserts; so the later editors.
[5] δ᾽, after πιαίνειν, Corais deletes; so the later editors.
[6] But k reads τεσσαράκοντα ἢ πεντήκοντα, "forty or fifty."

Hiero[1] the Catanaeans came back, ejected the inhabitants, and demolished the tomb of the tyrant.[2] And the Aetnaeans, on withdrawing, took up their abode in a hilly district of Aetna called Innesa, and called the place, which is eighty stadia from Catana, Aetna, and declared Hiero its founder. Now the city of Aetna is situated in the interior about over Catana, and shares most in the devastation caused by the action of the craters;[3] in fact the streams of lava rush down very nearly as far as the territory of Catana; and here is the scene of the act of filial piety, so often recounted, of Amphinomus and Anapias, who lifted their parents on their shoulders and saved them from the doom that was rushing upon them. According to Poseidonius, when the mountain is in action, the fields of the Catanaeans are covered with ash-dust to a great depth. Now although the ash is an affliction at the time, it benefits the country in later times, for it renders it fertile and suited to the vine, the rest of the country not being equally productive of good wine; further, the roots produced by the fields that have been covered with ash-dust make the sheep so fat, it is said, that they choke; and this is why blood is drawn from their ears every four or five days[4]—a thing of which I have spoken before[5] as occurring near Erytheia. But when the lava

---

[1] 467 B.C.   [2] 461 B.C.

[3] Groskurd, Müller-Dübner, Forbiger, Tardieu, and Tozer (*Selections*, p. 174) supply as subject of "shares" a pronoun referring to Catana, assuming that Aetna, the subject of the sentence, is the mountain, not the city.

[4] One of the later manuscripts reads "forty or fifty days."

[5] 3. 5. 4. (*q.v.*).

πῆξιν μεταβάλλων ἀπολιθοῖ τὴν ἐπιφάνειαν τῆς
γῆς ἐφ᾿ ἱκανὸν βάθος, ὥστε λατομίας εἶναι χρείαν
τοῖς ἀνακαλύψαι βουλομένοις τὴν ἐξ ἀρχῆς ἐπιφάνειαν. τακείσης γὰρ ἐν τοῖς κρατῆρσι τῆς
πέτρας, εἶτ᾿ ἀναβληθείσης, τὸ ὑπερχυθὲν τῆς
κορυφῆς ὑγρὸν πηλός ἐστι μέλας, ῥέων κατὰ τῆς
ὀρεινῆς· εἶτα πῆξιν λαβὼν γίνεται λίθος μυλίας,
τὴν αὐτὴν φυλάττων χρόαν, ἣν ῥέων εἶχε. καὶ ἡ
σποδὸς δὲ καιομένων τῶν λίθων ὡς ἀπὸ τῶν
ξύλων γίνεται· καθάπερ οὖν τὸ πήγανον τῇ
ξυλίνῃ σποδῷ τρέφεται, τοιοῦτον ἔχειν τι οἰκεί-
ωμα πρὸς τὴν ἄμπελον εἰκὸς τὴν Αἰτναίαν
σποδόν.

4. Τὰς δὲ Συρακούσσας Ἀρχίας μὲν ἔκτισεν
ἐκ Κορίνθου πλεύσας περὶ τοὺς αὐτοὺς χρόνους,
οἷς ᾠκίσθησαν ἥ τε Νάξος καὶ τὰ Μέγαρα. ἅμα
δὲ Μύσκελλόν τέ φασιν εἰς Δελφοὺς ἐλθεῖν καὶ
τὸν Ἀρχίαν· χρηστηριαζομένων δ᾿ [1] ἐρέσθαι τὸν
θεόν, πότερον αἱροῦνται πλοῦτον ἢ ὑγίειαν· τὸν
μὲν οὖν Ἀρχίαν ἑλέσθαι τὸν πλοῦτον, Μύσκελλον
δὲ τὴν ὑγίειαν· τῷ μὲν δὴ Συρακούσσας δοῦναι
κτίζειν, τῷ δὲ Κρότωνα. καὶ δὴ συμβῆναι Κροτωνιάτας μὲν οὕτως ὑγιεινὴν οἰκῆσαι πόλιν,
ὥσπερ εἰρήκαμεν, Συρακούσσας δὲ ἐπὶ τοσοῦτον
ἐκπεσεῖν πλοῦτον, ὥστε καὶ αὐτοὺς ἐν παροιμίᾳ
διαδοθῆναι, λεγόντων πρὸς τοὺς ἄγαν πολυτελεῖς,
ὡς οὐκ ἂν ἐξικνοῖτο [2] αὐτοῖς ἡ Συρακουσσίων
δεκάτη. πλέοντα δὲ τὸν Ἀρχίαν εἰς τὴν Σικελίαν
καταλιπεῖν μετὰ μέρους τῆς στρατιᾶς τοῦ τῶν
Ἡρακλειδῶν γένους Χερσικράτη συνοικιοῦντα

---

[1] χρηστηριαζομένων δ᾿, Meineke, for χρηστηριαζόμενον.

changes to a solid, it turns the surface of the earth into stone to a considerable depth, so that quarrying is necessary on the part of any who wish to uncover the original surface; for when the mass of rock in the craters melts and then is thrown up, the liquid that is poured out over the top is black mud and flows down the mountain, and then, solidifying, becomes mill-stone, keeping the same colour it had when in a liquid state. And ash is also produced when the stones are burnt, as from wood; therefore, just as wood-ashes nourish rue, so the ashes of Aetna, it is reasonable to suppose, have some quality that is peculiarly suited to the vine.

4. Syracuse was founded by Archias, who sailed from Corinth about the same time that Naxus and Megara were colonised. It is said that Archias went to Delphi at the same time as Myscellus, and when they were consulting the oracle, the god asked them whether they chose wealth or health; now Archias chose wealth, and Myscellus[1] health; accordingly, the god granted to the former to found Syracuse, and to the latter Croton. And it actually came to pass that the Crotoniates took up their abode in a city that was exceedingly healthful, as I have related,[2] and that Syracuse fell into such exceptional wealth that the name of the Syracusans was spread abroad in a proverb applied to the excessively extravagant—"the tithe of the Syracusans would not be sufficient for them." And when Archias, the story continues, was on his voyage to Sicily, he left Chersicrates, of the race of the Heracleidae,

---

[1] See 6. 1. 12.   [2] 6. 1. 12.

[2] ἐξίκνοῖτο, conj. Meineke, and Madvig independently, for ἐκγένοιτο; so Forbiger and A. Vogel.

τὴν νῦν Κέρκυραν καλουμένην, πρότερον δὲ
Σχερίαν. ἐκεῖνον μὲν οὖν ἐκβαλόντα Λιβυρνοὺς
C 270 κατέχοντας οἰκίσαι τὴν νῆσον, τὸν δ᾽ Ἀρχίαν
κατασχόντα πρὸς τὸ Ζεφύριον τῶν Δωριέων
εὑρόντα τινὰς δεῦρο ἀφιγμένους ἐκ τῆς Σικελίας
παρὰ τῶν τὰ Μέγαρα κτισάντων ἀπιόντας[1]
ἀναλαβεῖν αὐτούς, καὶ κοινῇ μετ᾽ αὐτῶν κτίσαι
τὰς Συρακούσσας. ηὐξήθη δὲ καὶ διὰ τὴν τῆς
χώρας εὐδαιμονίαν ἡ πόλις καὶ διὰ τὴν τῶν
λιμένων εὐφυΐαν. οἵ τε ἄνδρες ἡγεμονικοὶ κατέστησαν, καὶ συνέβη Συρακουσσίοις τυραννου-
μένοις τε[2] δεσπόζειν τῶν ἄλλων καὶ ἐλευθερω-
θεῖσιν ἐλευθεροῦν τοὺς ὑπὸ τῶν βαρβάρων
καταδυναστευομένους· ἦσαν γὰρ τῶν βαρβάρων
οἱ μὲν ἔνοικοι, τινὲς δ᾽ ἐκ τῆς περαίας ἐπῄεσαν,
οὐδένα δὲ τῆς παραλίας εἴων οἱ Ἕλληνες ἅπτε-
σθαι, τῆς δὲ μεσογαίας ἀπείργειν παντάπασιν
οὐκ ἴσχυον, ἀλλὰ διετέλεσαν μέχρι δεῦρο Σικελοὶ
καὶ Σικανοὶ καὶ Μόργητες καὶ ἄλλοι τινὲς νεμόμενοι τὴν νῆσον, ὧν ἦσαν καὶ Ἴβηρες, οὕσπερ
πρώτους φησὶ τῶν βαρβάρων Ἔφορος λέγεσθαι
τῆς Σικελίας οἰκιστάς. καὶ τὸ Μοργάντιον δὲ
εἰκὸς ὑπὸ τῶν Μοργήτων ᾠκίσθαι· πόλις δ᾽ ἦν
αὕτη, νῦν δ᾽ οὐκ ἔστιν. ἐπελθόντες δὲ Καρχηδόνιοι καὶ τούτους οὐκ ἐπαύσαντο κακοῦντες καὶ
τοὺς Ἕλληνας, ἀντεῖχον δ᾽ ὅμως οἱ Συρακούσσιοι.
Ῥωμαῖοι δ᾽ ὕστερον καὶ τοὺς Καρχηδονίους ἐξέβαλον καὶ τὰς Συρακούσσας ἐκ πολιορκίας εἷλον. ἐφ᾽

---

[1] ἀπιόντας, Groskurd transfers from position after Συρακούσσας (below) to position after κτισάντων; so Forbiger and
Tardieu; Kramer approving. no omit the word and
Meineke relegates it to the foot of the page.
[2] τε, the editors, for τό.

7 2

with a part of the expedition to help colonise what is now called Corcyra, but was formerly called Scheria; Chersicrates, however, ejected the Liburnians, who held possession of the island, and colonised it with new settlers, whereas Archias landed at Zephyrium,[1] found that some Dorians who had quit the company of the founders of Megara and were on their way back home had arrived there from Sicily, took them up and in common with them founded Syracuse. And the city grew, both on account of the fertility of the soil and on account of the natural excellence of its harbours. Furthermore, the men of Syracuse proved to have the gift of leadership, with the result that when the Syracusans were ruled by tyrants they lorded it over the rest, and when set free themselves they set free those who were oppressed by the barbarians. As for these barbarians, some were native inhabitants, whereas others came over from the mainland. The Greeks would permit none of them to lay hold of the seaboard, but were not strong enough to keep them altogether away from the interior; indeed, to this day the Siceli, the Sicani, the Morgetes, and certain others have continued to live in the island, among whom there used to be Iberians, who, according to Ephorus, were said to be the first barbarian settlers of Sicily. Morgantium, it is reasonable to suppose, was settled by the Morgetes; it used to be a city, but now it does not exist. When the Carthaginians came over they did not cease to abuse both these people and the Greeks, but the Syracusans nevertheless held out. But the Romans later on ejected the Carthaginians and took Syracuse by siege.

[1] Cape Bruzzano.

ἡμῶν δὲ Πομπηίου τάς τε ἄλλας κακώσαντος πόλεις
καὶ δὴ καὶ τὰς Συρακούσσας, πέμψας ἀποικίαν
ὁ Σεβαστὸς Καῖσαρ πολὺ μέρος τοῦ παλαιοῦ
κτίσματος ἀνέλαβε. πεντάπολις γὰρ ἦν τὸ
παλαιόν, ὀγδοήκοντα καὶ ἑκατὸν σταδίων ἔχουσα
τὸ τεῖχος. ἅπαντα μὲν δὴ τὸν κύκλον τοῦτον
ἐκπληροῦν οὐδὲν ἔδει, τὸ δὲ συνοικούμενον
τὸ πρὸς τῇ νήσῳ τῇ Ὀρτυγίᾳ μέρος ᾠήθη
δεῖν οἰκίσαι βέλτιον, ἀξιολόγου¹ πόλεως ἔχων
περίμετρον· ἡ δ' Ὀρτυγία συνάπτει γεφύρᾳ πρὸς
τὴν ἤπειρον πλησίον² οὖσα, κρήνην δ' ἔχει τὴν
Ἀρέθουσαν, ἐξιεῖσαν ποταμὸν εὐθὺς εἰς τὴν
θάλατταν.

Μυθεύουσι δὲ τὸν Ἀλφειὸν εἶναι τοῦτον, ἀρχό-
μενον μὲν ἐκ τῆς Πελοποννήσου, διὰ δὲ τοῦ
πελάγους ὑπὸ γῆς τὸ ῥεῖθρον ἔχοντα μέχρι πρὸς
τὴν Ἀρέθουσαν, εἶτ' ἐκδιδόντα ἐνθένδε πάλιν εἰς
τὴν θάλατταν. τεκμηριοῦνται δὲ τοιούτοις τισί·
καὶ γὰρ φιάλην τινὰ ἐκπεσοῦσαν εἰς τὸν ποταμὸν
ἐνόμισαν³ ἐν Ὀλυμπίᾳ δεῦρο ἀνενεχθῆναι εἰς τὴν
κρήνην, καὶ θολοῦσθαι ἀπὸ τῶν ἐν Ὀλυμπίᾳ
βουθυσιῶν. ὅ τε Πίνδαρος ἐπακολουθῶν τούτοις
εἴρηκε τάδε.

    ἄμπνευμα σεμνὸν Ἀλφεοῦ,
    κλεινᾶν⁴ Συρακοσσᾶν θάλος, Ὀρτυγία.

C 271 συναποφαίνεται δὲ τῷ Πινδάρῳ ταὐτὰ καὶ Τίμαιος
ὁ συγγραφεύς. εἰ μὲν οὖν πρὸ τοῦ συνάψαι τῇ
θαλάττῃ κατέπιπτεν ὁ Ἀλφειὸς εἴς τι βάραθρον,

¹ ἀξιολόγου, Casaubon, for ἀξιόλογον ; so later editors.
² πλησίον, Jones inserts. Meineke reads ὁμοροῦσα.
³ ἐνόμισαν, Corais deletes ; Meineke suspects.
⁴ κλεινᾶν, the editors, for κρήνας.

74

And in our own time, because Pompeius abused, not
only the other cities, but Syracuse in particular,
Augustus Caesar sent a colony and restored a considerable part of the old settlement; for in olden
times it was a city of five towns,[1] with a wall of one
hundred and eighty stadia. Now it was not at all
necessary to fill out the whole of this circuit, but it
was necessary, he thought, to build up in a better
way only the part that was settled—the part adjacent
to the Island of Ortygia—which had a sufficient circuit to make a notable city. Ortygia is connected
with the mainland, near which it lies, by a bridge,
and has the fountain of Arethusa, which sends
forth a river that empties immediately into the
sea.

People tell the mythical story that the river
Arethusa is the Alpheius, which latter, they say,
rises in the Peloponnesus, flows underground through
the sea as far as Arethusa, and then empties thence
once more into the sea. And the kind of evidence
they adduce is as follows : a certain cup, they think,
was thrown out into the river at Olympia and was
discharged into the fountain ; and again, the fountain
was discoloured as the result of the sacrifices of oxen
at Olympia. Pindar follows these reports when he
says : "O resting-place [2] august of Alpheius, Ortygia,[3]
scion of famous Syracuse." And in agreement with
Pindar Timaeus the historian also declares the same
thing. Now if the Alpheius fell into a pit before

---

[1] Nesos (the island Ortygia), Achradine, Tyche, Epipolai,
and Neapolis.

[2] Or more literally, "place to breathe again."

[3] *Nemean Odes*, 1. 1-2. Pindar further characterises
Ortygia (*l.* 3) as "the bed of Artemis."

STRABO

ἦν τις ἂν πιθανότης ἐντεῦθεν διήκειν κατὰ γῆς
ῥεῖθρον μέχρι τῆς Σικελίας, ἀμιγὲς τῇ θαλάττῃ
διασῶζον τὸ πότιμον ὕδωρ· ἐπειδὴ δὲ τὸ τοῦ
ποταμοῦ στόμα φανερόν ἐστιν εἰς τὴν θάλατταν
ἐκδιδόν, ἐγγὺς δὲ μηδὲν ἐν τῷ πύρῳ τῆς θαλάττης
φαινόμενον στόμα τὸ καταπῖνον τὸ ῥεῦμα τοῦ
ποταμοῦ (καίπερ οὐδ' οὕτως ἂν συμμεῖναι γλυκύ,
ὅμως τό γε ἐπὶ πλέον, εἰ καταδύνοι εἰς τὸ κατὰ
γῆς ῥεῖθρον),[1] παντάπασιν ἀμήχανόν ἐστι. τό
τε γὰρ τῆς Ἀρεθούσης ὕδωρ ἀντιμαρτυρεῖ, πότιμον
ὄν· τό τε διὰ τοσούτου πόρου συμμένειν τὸ ῥεῦμα
τοῦ ποταμοῦ, μὴ διαχεόμενον τῇ θαλάττῃ, μέχρι
ἂν εἰς τὸ πεπλασμένον ῥεῖθρον ἐμπέσῃ, παντελῶς
μυθῶδες. μόλις γὰρ ἐπὶ τοῦ Ῥοδανοῦ τοῦτο
πιστεύομεν, ᾧ συμμένει τὸ ῥεῦμα διὰ λίμνης ἰόν,
ὁρατὴν σῶζον τὴν ῥύσιν· ἀλλ' ἐκεῖ[2] μὲν καὶ
βραχὺ διάστημα καὶ οὐ κυμαινούσης τῆς λίμνης,
ἐνταῦθα δέ, ὅπου χειμῶνες ἐξαίσιοι καὶ κλυδασμοί,
πιθανότηνος οὐδεμιᾶς οἰκεῖος ὁ λόγος. ἐπιτείνει
δὲ τὸ ψεῦδος ἡ φιάλη παρατεθεῖσα· οὐδὲ γὰρ
αὐτὴ[3] ῥεύματι εὐπειθής, οὐχ ὅτι τῷ τοσούτῳ[4] τε
καὶ διὰ τοιούτων πόρων[5] φερομένῳ.

Φέρονται δ' ὑπὸ γῆς ποταμοὶ πολλοὶ καὶ πολλαχοῦ τῆς γῆς, ἀλλ' οὐκ ἐπὶ τοσοῦτον διάστημα·

---

[1] ὅμως . . . ῥεῖθρον, Meineke relegates to the foot of the
page ; C. Müller approving.
[2] ἐκεῖ, *Epit.*, for ἐκεῖνο (ABC*l*) ; so the editors in general.
[3] αὐτή, Corais, for αὕτη ; so the later editors.
[4] οὐχ ὅτι τῷ τοσούτῳ, Meineke, for οὐχὶ τῷ τότε οὕτω.
[5] πόρων, Corais, for ὅρῶν ; so the later editors.

[1] That is, whirlpool.

joining the sea, there would be some plausibility in the view that the stream extends underground from Olympia as far as Sicily, thereby preserving its potable water unmixed with the sea; but since the mouth of the river empties into the sea in full view, and since near this mouth, on the transit, there is no mouth [1] visible that swallows up the stream of the river (though even so the water could not remain fresh; yet it might, the greater part of it at least, if it sank into the underground channel),[2] the thing is absolutely impossible. For the water of Arethusa bears testimony against it, since it is potable; and that the stream of the river should hold together through so long a transit without being diffused with the sea-water, that is, until it falls into the fancied underground passage, is utterly mythical. Indeed, we can scarcely believe this in the case of the Rhodanus, although its stream does hold together when it passes through a lake,[3] keeping its course visible; in this case, however, the distance is short and the lake does not rise in waves, whereas in case of the sea in question, where there are prodigious storms and surging waves, the tale is foreign to all plausibility. And the citing of the story of the cup only magnifies the falsehood, for a cup does not of itself readily follow the current of any stream, to say nothing of a stream that flows so great a distance and through such passages.

Now there are many rivers in many parts of the world that flow underground, but not for such a distance; and even if this is possible, the stories

---

[2] The last clause is suspected; see critical note.

[3] Lake Lemenna, now the Lake of Geneva (see 4. 1. 11 and 4. 6. 6).

εἰ δὲ τοῦτο δυνατόν, τά γε προειρημένα ἀδύνατα
καὶ τὰ¹ περὶ τοῦ Ἰνάχου μύθῳ παραπλήσια·

ῥεῖ γὰρ ἀπ' ἄκρας
Πίνδου (φησὶν ὁ Σοφοκλῆς) Λάκμου
τ' ἀπὸ Περραιβῶν
ἐς Ἀμφιλόχους καὶ Ἀκαρνᾶνας,
μίσγει δ' ὕδασιν τοῖς Ἀχελῴου·

καὶ ὑποβάς,

ἐνθένδ' ἐς Ἄργος διὰ κῦμα τεμὼν
ἥκει δῆμον τὸν Λυρκείου,

ἐπιτείνουσι² δὲ τὴν τοιαύτην τερατολογίαν οἱ τὸν
Ἰνωπὸν εἰς Δῆλον ἐκ τοῦ Νείλου περαιοῦντες.
Ἀλφειὸν δὲ Ζωίλος ὁ ῥήτωρ ἐν τῷ Τενεδίων
ἐγκωμίῳ φησὶν ἐκ Τενέδου ῥεῖν, ὁ τὸν Ὅμηρον
ψέγων ὡς μυθογράφον. Ἴβυκος δὲ τὸν ἐν Σικυῶνι
Ἀσωπὸν ἐκ Φρυγίας ῥεῖν φησι. βελτίων δ'
Ἑκαταῖος, ὅς φησι τὸν ἐν τοῖς Ἀμφιλόχοις
Ἴναχον ἐκ τοῦ Λακμοῦ ῥέοντα, ἐξ οὗ καὶ ὁ Αἴας
ῥεῖ, ἕτερον εἶναι τοῦ Ἀργολικοῦ, ὠνομάσθαι δ'
ὑπὸ Ἀμφιλόχου τοῦ καὶ τὴν πόλιν Ἄργος
Ἀμφιλοχικὸν καλέσαντος· τοῦτον μὲν οὖν οὗτός
φησιν εἰς τὸν Ἀχελῷον ἐκβάλλειν, τὸν δὲ Αἴαντα
εἰς Ἀπολλωνίαν πρὸς δύσιν ῥεῖν.

Ἑκατέρωθεν δὲ τῆς νήσου λιμήν ἐστι μέγας,
ὧν ὁ μείζων καὶ ὀγδοήκοντα σταδίων ἐστί. ταύτην
C 272 δὲ τὴν πόλιν ἀνέλαβεν ὁ Καῖσαρ καὶ τὴν Κατάνην,
ὡς δ' αὕτως Κεντόριπα, συμβαλομένην πολλὰ
πρὸς τὴν Πομπηίου κατάλυσιν. κεῖνται δ' ὑπὲρ

¹ τά, Jones restores; Corais and later editors emend to τῷ.
² Meineke, without warrant, relegates to the foot of the
page the words ἐπιτείνουσι . . . ῥεῖν φησι.

aforesaid, at least, are impossible, and those concerning the river Inachus are like a myth : " For it flows from the heights of Pindus," says Sophocles, " and from Lacmus,[1] from the land of the Perrhaebians, into the lands of the Amphilochians and Acarnanians, and mingles with the waters of Acheloüs," and, a little below, he adds, " whence it cleaves the waves to Argos and comes to the people of Lyrceium." Marvellous tales of this sort are stretched still further by those who make the Inopus cross over from the Nile to Delos. And Zoïlus [2] the rhetorician says in his *Eulogy of the Tenedians* that the Alpheius rises in Tenedos—the man who finds fault with Homer as a writer of myths ! And Ibycus says that the Asopus in Sicyon rises in Phrygia. But the statement of Hecataeus is better, when he says that the Inachus among the Amphilochians, which flows from Lacmus, as does also the Aeas, is different from the river of Argos, and that it was named by Amphilochus, the man who called the city Argos Amphilochicum.[3] Now Hecataeus says that this river does empty into the Acheloüs, but that the Aeas [4] flows towards the west into Apollonia.

On either side of the island of Ortygia is a large harbour; the larger of the two is eighty stadia in circuit. Caesar restored this city and also Catana; and so, in the same way, Centoripa, because it contributed much to the overthrow of Pompeius.

---

[1] More often spelled Lacmon ; one of the heights of Pindus.
[2] Zoïlus (about 400–320 B.C.), the grammarian and rhetorician, of Amphipolis in Macedonia, is chiefly known for the bitterness of his attacks on Homer, which gained him the surname of "Homeromastix" ("scourge of Homer").
[3] Cp. 7. 7. 7.   [4] Cp. 7. 5. 8.

STRABO

Κατάνης τὰ Κεντόριπα, συνάπτοντα τοῖς Αἰτναίοις ὄρεσι καὶ τῷ Συμαίθῳ ποταμῷ ῥέοντι εἰς τὴν Καταναίαν.

5. Τῶν δὲ λοιπῶν τῆς Σικελίας πλευρῶν ἡ μὲν ἀπὸ τοῦ Παχύνου πρὸς Λιλύβαιον διήκουσα ἐκλέλειπται τελέως, ἴχνη τινὰ σώζουσα τῶν ἀρχαίων κατοικιῶν, ὧν ἦν καὶ Καμάρινα, ἄποικος Συρακουσσίων. Ἀκράγας δὲ Γελῴων οὖσα[1] καὶ τὸ ἐπίνειον καὶ Λιλύβαιον ἔτι συμμένει. τῇ γὰρ Καρχηδονίᾳ τούτων μάλιστα ὑποπιπτόντων τῶν μερῶν, μακροὶ καὶ συνεχεῖς οἱ πόλεμοι γενόμενοι τὰ πολλὰ κατέφθειραν. ἡ δὲ λοιπὴ καὶ μεγίστη πλευρά, καίπερ οὐδ᾽ αὐτὴ πολυάνθρωπος οὖσα, ὅμως ἱκανῶς συνοικεῖται. καὶ γὰρ Ἄλαισα καὶ Τυνδαρὶς καὶ τὸ τῶν Αἰγεστέων ἐμπόριον καὶ Κεφαλοιδὶς[2] πολίσματά ἐστι· Πάνορμος δὲ καὶ Ῥωμαίων ἔχει κατοικίαν. τὴν δὲ Αἰγεσταίαν κτισθῆναί φασιν ὑπὸ τῶν μετὰ Φιλοκτήτου διαβάντων εἰς τὴν Κροτωνιᾶτιν, καθάπερ ἐν τοῖς Ἰταλικοῖς εἴρηται, παρ᾽ αὐτοῦ σταλέντων εἰς τὴν Σικελίαν μετὰ Αἰγέστου τοῦ Τρωός.[3]

6. Ἐν δὲ τῇ μεσογαίᾳ τὴν μὲν Ἔνναν, ἐν ᾗ τὸ ἱερὸν τῆς Δήμητρος, ἔχουσιν ὀλίγοι, κειμένην ἐπὶ λόφῳ, περιειλημμένην πλάτεσιν ὀροπεδίοις ἀροσίμοις πᾶσαν.[4] ἐκάκωσαν δ᾽ αὐτὴν μάλιστα ἐμπολιορκηθέντες οἱ περὶ Εὔνουν δραπέται, καὶ

---

[1] δὲ Γελῴων οὖσα, Kramer, for δὲ λέγω ιωνουσα (sic); so the later editors. See Thucyd. 6. 4.

[2] Κεφαλοιδίς, Meineke, for Κεφαλοίδεις.

[3] Schleiermacher proposed that the passage οἰκεῖται . . . ἀξιόλογον (§ 6) be transferred to a position after Τρωός. Kramer is inclined to approve, C. Müller approves; and Meineke, Forbiger and Tardieu so read.

Centoripa lies above Catana, bordering on the Aetnaean mountains, and on the Symaethus River, which flows into the territory of Catana.

5. Of the remaining sides of Sicily, that which extends from Pachynus to Lilybaeum has been utterly deserted, although it preserves traces of the old settlements, among which was Camarina, a colony of the Syracusans; Acragas, however, which belongs to the Geloans, and its seaport, and also Lilybaeum still endure. For since this region was most exposed to attack on the part of Carthaginia, most of it was ruined by the long wars that arose one after another. The last and longest side is not populous either, but still it is fairly well peopled; in fact, Alaesa, Tyndaris, the Emporium of the Aegestes, and Cephaloedis[1] are all cities, and Panormus has also a Roman settlement. Aegestaea was founded, it is said, by those who crossed over with Philoctetes to the territory of Croton, as I have stated in my account of Italy;[2] they were sent to Sicily by him along with Aegestes the Trojan.

6. In the interior is Enna, where is the temple of Demeter, with only a few inhabitants; it is situated on a hill, and is wholly surrounded by broad plateaus that are tillable. It suffered most at the hands of Eunus[3] and his runaway slaves, who were besieged

---

[1] Another name for Cephaloedium (6. 2. 1).   [2] 6. 1. 3.

[3] Eunus was a native of Apameia in Syria, but became a slave of a certain Antigenes at Enna, and about 136 B.C. became the leader of the Sicilian slaves in the First Servile War. For a full account of his amazing activities as juggler, diviner, leader, and self-appointed king, as also of his great following see Diodorus Siculus 34. 2. 5–18.

---

[4] πᾶσαν, the reading of all MSS., Jones restores, for πᾶσιν (Corais and Meineke).

μόλις ἐξαιρεθέντες ὑπὸ Ῥωμαίων· ἔπαθον δὲ τὰ
αὐτὰ ταῦτα καὶ Καταναῖοι καὶ Ταυρομενῖται καὶ
ἄλλοι πλείους.

Οἰκεῖται δὲ καὶ ὁ Ἔρυξ λόφος ὑψηλός, ἱερὸν
ἔχων Ἀφροδίτης τιμώμενον διαφερόντως, ἱερο-
δούλων γυναικῶν πλῆρες τὸ παλαιόν, ἃς ἀνέθεσαν
κατ᾽ εὐχὴν οἵ τ᾽ ἐκ τῆς Σικελίας καὶ ἔξωθεν πολλοί·
νυνὶ δ᾽ ὥσπερ αὐτὴ ἡ κατοικία λειπανδρεῖ τὸ ἱερόν,[1]
καὶ τῶν ἱερῶν σωμάτων ἐκλέλοιπε τὸ πλῆθος.
ἀφίδρυμα δ᾽ ἐστὶ καὶ ἐν Ῥώμῃ τῆς θεοῦ ταύτης
τὸ πρὸ τῆς πύλης τῆς Κολλίνης ἱερὸν Ἀφροδίτης
Ἐρυκίνης λεγόμενον, ἔχον καὶ νεὼν καὶ στοὰν
περικειμένην ἀξιόλογον.

Ἡ δ᾽ ἄλλη κατοικία καὶ τῆς μεσογαίας ποιμένων
ἡ πλείστη γεγένηται· οὔτε γὰρ Ἱμέραν ἔτι συνοι-
κουμένην ἴσμεν οὔτε Γέλαν οὔτε Καλλίπολιν οὔτε
Σελινοῦντα οὔτ᾽ Εὔβοιαν οὔτ᾽ ἄλλας πλείους, ὧν
τὴν μὲν Ἱμέραν οἱ ἐν Μυλαῖς ἔκτισαν Ζαγκλαῖοι,[2]
Καλλίπολιν δὲ Νάξιοι, Σελινοῦντα δὲ οἱ αὐτόθι

---

[1] ἥ, before τὸ ἱερόν, Jones deletes (B *sec. m.* reads καί).
But other editors, following Corais, delete the whole
phrase.
[2] Meineke, without warrant, inserts Γέλαν δὲ Ῥόδιοι after
Ζαγκλαῖοι.

---

[1] Now Mt. San Giuliano. But Eryx is at the north-
western angle of Sicily, near the sea, not in the interior,
and for this reason some editors consider the passage out of
place.
[2] Also called Eryx. Hamilcar Barca transferred most of
the inhabitants to Drepanum (at the foot of the mountain) in
260 B.C. After that time the city was of no consequence,

there and only with difficulty were dislodged by the Romans. The inhabitants of Catana and Tauromenium and also several other peoples suffered this same fate.

Eryx, a lofty hill,[1] is also inhabited. It has a temple of Aphrodite that is held in exceptional honour, and in early times was full of female temple-slaves, who had been dedicated in fulfilment of vows not only by the people of Sicily but also by many people from abroad; but at the present time, just as the settlement itself,[2] so the temple is in want of men, and the multitude of temple-slaves has disappeared. In Rome, also, there is a reproduction of this goddess, I mean the temple before the Colline Gate[3] which is called that of Venus Erycina and is remarkable for its shrine and surrounding colonnade.

But the rest of the settlements[4] as well as most of the interior have come into the possession of shepherds; for I do not know of any settled population still living in either Himera, or Gela, or Callipolis or Selinus or Euboea or several other places. Of these cities Himera was founded by the Zanclaeans of Mylae, Callipolis by the Naxians, Selinus by the Megarians of the Sicilian Megara, and Euboea by

but the sacred precinct, with its strong walls, remained a strategic position of great importance.

[3] The temple of Venus Erycina on the Capitol was dedicated by Q. Fabius Maximus in 215 B.C., whereas the one here referred to, outside the Colline Gate, was dedicated by L. Portius Licinus in 181 B.C.

[4] *i.e.* the rest of the settlements on "the remaining sides" (mentioned at the beginning of § 5), as the subsequent clause shows.

C 273 Μεγαρεῖς, Εὔβοιαν δὲ οἱ Λεοντῖνοι.¹ καὶ τῶν
βαρβαρικῶν δ' ἐξηλείφθησαν² πολλαί, καθάπερ
οἱ Καμικοὶ³ τὸ Κωκάλου βασίλειον, παρ' ᾧ Μίνως
δολοφονηθῆναι λέγεται. τὴν οὖν ἐρημίαν κατανοή-
σαντες Ῥωμαῖοι, κατακτησάμενοι τά τε ὄρη καὶ
τῶν πεδίων τὰ πλεῖστα ἱπποφορβοῖς καὶ βου-
κόλοις καὶ ποιμέσι παρέδοσαν· ὑφ' ὧν πολλάκις
εἰς κινδύνους κατέστη μεγάλους ἡ νῆσος, τὸ μὲν
πρῶτον ἐπὶ λῃστείας τρεπομένων σποράδην τῶν
νομέων, εἶτα καὶ κατὰ πλήθη συνισταμένων καὶ
πορθούντων τὰς κατοικίας, καθάπερ ἡνίκα οἱ περὶ
Εὔνουν τὴν Ἔνναν κατέσχον. νεωστὶ δ' ἐφ'
ἡμῶν εἰς τὴν Ῥώμην ἀνεπέμφθη Σέλουρός τις,
Αἴτνης υἱὸς λεγόμενος, στρατιᾶς ἀφηγησάμενος
καὶ λεηλασίαις πυκναῖς καταδεδραμηκὼς τὰ κύκλῳ
τῆς Αἴτνης πολὺν χρόνον, ὃν ἐν τῇ ἀγορᾷ μονο-
μάχων ἀγῶνος συνεστῶτος εἴδομεν διασπασθέντα
ὑπὸ θηρίων· ἐπὶ πήγματος γάρ τινος ὑψηλοῦ
τεθεὶς ὡς ἂν ἐπὶ τῆς Αἴτνης, διαλυθέντος αἰφνιδίως
καὶ συμπεσόντος, κατηνέχθη καὶ αὐτὸς εἰς γαλε-
άγρας θηρίων εὐδιαλύτους, ἐπίτηδες παρεσκευασμένας ὑπὸ τῷ πήγματι.

7. Τὴν δὲ τῆς χώρας ἀρετὴν θρυλουμένην ὑπὸ
πάντων, οὐδὲν χείρω τῆς Ἰταλίας ἀποφαινομένων,
τί δεῖ λέγειν; σίτῳ δὲ καὶ μέλιτι καὶ κρόκῳ καὶ

---

¹ Following Siebenkees, Meineke and others transfer to a
position after Λεοντῖνοι the words κεκάκωται . . . ἀεί (at end
of § 7).
² ἐξηλείφθησαν, Meineke emends to ἐξελείφθησαν.
³ Καμικοί, Xylander, for Κωμικοί ; so the later editors.

---

¹ A number of the editors transfer to this point the sentence "The whole . . . fortunes," at the end of § 7 below.

the Leontines.[1]   Many of the barbarian cities, also, have been wiped out; for example Camici,[2] the royal residence of Cocalus,[3] at which Minos is said to have been murdered by treachery.   The Romans, therefore, taking notice that the country was deserted, took possession of the mountains and most of the plains and then gave them over to horseherds, cowherds, and shepherds; and by these herdsmen the island was many times put in great danger, because, although at first they only turned to brigandage in a sporadic way, later they both assembled in great numbers and plundered the settlements, as, for example, when Eunus and his men took possession of Enna.   And recently, in my own time, a certain Selurus, called the "son of Aetna," was sent up to Rome because he had put himself at the head of an army and for a long time had overrun the regions round about Aetna with frequent raids; I saw him torn to pieces by wild beasts at an appointed combat of gladiators in the Forum; for he was placed on a lofty scaffold, as though on Aetna, and the scaffold was made suddenly to break up and collapse, and he himself was carried down with it into cages of wild-beasts—fragile cages that had been prepared beneath the scaffold for that purpose.

7. As for the fertility of the country, why should I speak of it, since it is on the lips of all men, who declare that it is no whit inferior to that of Italy? And in the matter of grain, honey, saffron, and

---

[2] Camici (or Camicus) is supposed to have been on the site of what is Camastro.

[3] The mythical king who harboured Daedalus when he fled from Minos.

STRABO

ἄλλοις τισὶ κἂν ἀμείνω τις φαίη. πρόσεστι δὲ
καὶ τὸ ἐγγύθεν· ὡσανεὶ γὰρ μέρος τι τῆς Ἰταλίας
ἐστὶν ἡ νῆσος, καὶ ὑποχορηγεῖ τῇ Ῥώμῃ, καθάπερ
ἐκ τῶν Ἰταλικῶν ἀγρῶν, ἔκαστα εὐμαρῶς καὶ ἀτα-
λαιπώρως. καὶ δὴ καὶ καλοῦσιν αὐτὴν ταμεῖον
τῆς Ῥώμης· κομίζεται γὰρ τὰ γινόμενα πάντα
πλὴν ὀλίγων τῶν αὐτόθι ἀναλισκομένων δεῦρο.
ταῦτα δ᾽ ἐστὶν οὐχ οἱ καρποὶ μόνον, ἀλλὰ καὶ
βοσκήματα καὶ δέρματα καὶ ἔρια καὶ τὰ τοιαῦτα.
φησὶ δ᾽ ὁ Ποσειδώνιος οἷον ἀκροπόλεις ἐπὶ θαλάττης δύο τὰς Συρακούσσας ἱδρῦσθαι καὶ τὸν
Ἔρυκα, μέσην δὲ ἀμφοῖν ὑπερκεῖσθαι τῶν κύκλῳ
πεδίων τὴν Ἔνναν.

Κεκάκωται δὲ καὶ ἡ Λεοντίνη πᾶσα, Ναξίων
οὖσα καὶ αὐτὴ τῶν αὐτόθι· τῶν μὲν γὰρ ἀτυχη-
μάτων ἐκοινώνησαν ἀεὶ τοῖς Συρακουσσίοις, τῶν
δ᾽ εὐτυχημάτων οὐκ ἀεί.

8. Πλησίον δὲ τῶν Κεντορίπων ἐστὶ πόλισμα,
ἡ μικρὸν ἔμπροσθεν λεχθεῖσα Αἴτνη, τοὺς ἀνα-
βαίνοντας ἐπὶ τὸ ὄρος δεχομένη καὶ παραπέμ-
πουσα· ἐντεῦθεν γὰρ ἀρχὴ τῆς ἀκρωρείας. ἔστι
δὲ ψιλὰ τὰ ἄνω χωρία καὶ τεφρώδη καὶ χιόνος
μεστὰ τοῦ χειμῶνος, τὰ κάτω δὲ δρυμοῖς καὶ
φυτείαις διείληπται παντοδαπαῖς. ἔοικε δὲ λαμβάνειν μεταβολὰς πολλὰς τὰ ἄκρα τοῦ ὄρους διὰ
τὴν νομὴν τοῦ πυρός, τοτὲ μὲν εἰς ἕνα κρατῆρα
C 274 συμφερομένου, τοτὲ δὲ σχιζομένου, καὶ τοτὲ μὲν
ῥύακας ἀναπέμποντος, τοτὲ δὲ φλόγας καὶ λιγνῦς,
ἄλλοτε δὲ καὶ μύδρους ἀναφυσῶντος· ἀνάγκη δὲ
τοῖς πάθεσι τούτοις τούς τε ὑπὸ γῆν πόρους

---

[1] See footnote on Leontines, § 6.

certain other products, one might call it even
superior. There is, furthermore, its propinquity;
for the island is a part of Italy, as it were, and
readily and without great labour supplies Rome with
everything it has, as though from the fields of Italy.
And in fact it is called the storehouse of Rome,
for everything it produces is brought hither except
a few things that are consumed at home, and not
the fruits only, but also cattle, hides, wool, and the
like. Poseidonius says that Syracuse and Eryx are
each situated like an acropolis by the sea, whereas
Enna lies midway between the two above the
encircling plains.

The whole of the territory of Leontini, also, which
likewise belonged to the Naxians of Sicily, has been
devastated; for although they always shared with
the Syracusans in their misfortunes, it was not
always so with their good fortunes.[1]

8. Near Centoripa is the town of Aetna, which
was mentioned a little above, whose people entertain
and conduct those who ascend the mountain; for
the mountain-summit begins here. The upper districts are bare and ash-like and full of snow during
the winter, whereas the lower are divided up by
forests and plantations of every sort. The topmost
parts of the mountain appear to undergo many
changes because of the way the fire distributes
itself, for at one time the fire concentrates in one
crater, but at another time divides, while at one
time the mountain sends forth lava, at another,
flames and fiery smoke, and at still other times it
also emits red-hot masses; and the inevitable result of
these disturbances is that not only the underground
passages, but also the orifices, sometimes rather

συμμεταβάλλειν καὶ τὰ στόμια ἐνίοτε πλείω[1]
κατὰ τὴν ἐπιφάνειαν τὴν πέριξ. οἱ δ' οὖν νεωστὶ
ἀναβάντες διηγοῦντο ἡμῖν, ὅτι καταλάβοιεν ἄνω
πεδίον ὁμαλόν, ὅσον εἴκοσι σταδίων τὴν περίμετρον, κλειόμενον ὀφρύϊ τεφρώδει, τειχίου τὸ
ὕψος ἔχοντι, ὥστε δεῖν καθάλλεσθαι τοὺς εἰς
τὸ πεδίον προελθεῖν βουλομένους· ὁρᾶν τ' ἐν[2] τῷ
μέσῳ βουνὸν τεφρώδη τὴν χρόαν, οἵαπερ καὶ ἡ
ἐπιφάνεια καθεωρᾶτο τοῦ πεδίου, ὑπὲρ δὲ τοῦ
βουνοῦ νέφος ὄρθιον διανεστηκὸς εἰς ὕψος ὅσον
διακοσίων ποδῶν ἠρεμοῦν (εἶναι γὰρ καὶ νηνεμίαν),
εἰκάζειν δὲ καπνῷ· δύο δὲ τολμήσαντας προελθεῖν
εἰς τὸ πεδίον, ἐπειδὴ θερμοτέρας ἐπέβαινον τῆς
ψάμμου καὶ βαθυτέρας, ἀναστρέψαι, μηδὲν ἔχοντας περιττότερον φράζειν τῶν φαινομένων τοῖς
πόρρωθεν ἀφορῶσι. νομίζειν δ' ἐκ τῆς τοιαύτης
ὄψεως πολλὰ μυθεύεσθαι, καὶ μάλιστα οἷά φασί
τινες περὶ Ἐμπεδοκλέους, ὅτι καθάλοιτο εἰς τὸν
κρατῆρα καὶ καταλίποι τοῦ πάθους ἴχνος τῶν ἐμ-
βάδων τὴν ἑτέραν, ἃς ἐφόρει χαλκᾶς· εὑρεθῆναι
γὰρ ἔξω μικρὸν ἄπωθεν τοῦ χείλους τοῦ κρατῆρος,
ὡς ἀνερριμμένην ὑπὸ τῆς βίας τοῦ πυρός· οὔτε
γὰρ προσιτὸν εἶναι τὸν τόπον οὔθ' ὁρατόν, εἰκάζειν τε μηδὲ καταρριφῆναί τι δύνασθαι ἐκεῖσε
ὑπὸ τῆς ἀντιπνοίας τῶν ἐκ βάθους ἀνέμων καὶ
τῆς θερμότητος, ἣν προαπαντᾶν εὔλογον πόρρωθεν

---

[1] Meineke inserts ὄντα after πλείω ; Corais, ἵναι, before
τὴν πέριξ.
[2] ἐν is not found in ABC*l*.

---

[1] "This is the small cone of eruption, in the centre of the
wide semicircular crater" (Tozer, *Selections*, p. 175), which

numerous, which appear on the surface of the mountain all round, undergo changes at the same time. Be this as it may, those who recently made the ascent gave me the following account: They found at the top a level plain, about twenty stadia in circuit, enclosed by a rim of ashes the height of a house-wall, so that any who wished to proceed into the plain had to leap down from the wall; they saw in the centre of the plain a mound [1] of the colour of ashes, in this respect being like the surface of the plain as seen from above, and above the mound a perpendicular cloud rising straight up to a height of about two hundred feet, motionless (for it was a windless day) and resembling smoke; and two of the men had the hardihood to proceed into the plain, but because the sand they were walking on got hotter and deeper, they turned back, and so were unable to tell those who were observing from a distance anything more than what was already apparent. But they believed, from such a view as they had, that many of the current stories are mythical, and particularly those which some tell about Empedocles, that he leaped down into the crater and left behind, as a trace of the fate he suffered, one of the brazen sandals which he wore; for it was found, they say, a short distance outside the rim of the crater, as though it had been thrown up by the force of the fire. Indeed, the place is neither to be approached nor to be seen, according to my informants; and further, they surmised that nothing could be thrown down into it either, owing to the contrary blasts of the winds arising from the

the poem of *Aetna* (*l.* 182), ascribed to Lucilius Junior, describes as follows: "penitusque exaestuat ultra."

πρὶν ἢ τῷ στομίῳ τοῦ κρατῆρος προσπελάσαι·
εἰ δὲ καταρριφθείη, φθάνοι ἂν διαφθαρὲν πρὶν
ἀναρριφῆναι πάλιν, ὁποῖον παρελήφθη πρότερον.
τὸ μὲν οὖν ἐκλείπειν ποτὲ τὰ πνεύματα καὶ τὸ
πῦρ, ἐπιλειπούσης ποτὲ[1] τῆς ὕλης, οὐκ ἄλογον,
οὐ μὴν ἐπὶ τοσοῦτόν γε, ὥστ' ἀντὶ τῆς τοσαύτης
βίας ἐφικτὸν ἀνθρώπῳ γενέσθαι τὸν πλησιασμόν.
ὑπέρκειται δ' ἡ Αἴτνη μᾶλλον μὲν τῆς κατὰ τὸν
Πορθμὸν καὶ τὴν Καταναίαν παραλίας, ἀλλὰ καὶ
τῆς κατὰ τὸ Τυρρηνικὸν πέλαγος καὶ τὰς Λιπαραίων νήσους. νύκτωρ μὲν οὖν καὶ φέγγη φαίνεται λαμπρὰ ἐκ τῆς κορυφῆς, μεθ' ἡμέραν δὲ
καπνῷ καὶ ἀχλύϊ κατέχεται.

9. Ἀνταίρει δὲ τῇ Αἴτνῃ τὰ Νεβρώδη[2] ὄρη,
ταπεινότερα μέν, πλάτει δὲ πολὺ παραλλάτ-
τοντα. ἅπασα δ' ἡ νῆσος κοίλη κατὰ γῆς ἐστι,
ποταμῶν καὶ πυρὸς μεστή, καθάπερ τὸ Τυρρηνικὸν πέλαγος, ὡς εἰρήκαμεν, μέχρι τῆς Κυμαίας.
C 275 θερμῶν γοῦν ὑδάτων ἀναβολὰς κατὰ πολλοὺς
ἔχει τόπους ἡ νῆσος, ὧν τὰ μὲν Σελινούντια καὶ
τὰ Ἱμεραῖα[3] ἁλμυρά ἐστι, τὰ δὲ Αἰγεσταῖα
πότιμα. περὶ Ἀκράγαντα δὲ λίμναι τὴν μὲν
γεῦσιν ἔχουσαι θαλάττης, τὴν δὲ φύσιν διάφορον·
οὐδὲ γὰρ τοῖς ἀκολύμβοις βαπτίζεσθαι συμβαίνει, ξύλων τρόπον ἐπιπολάζουσιν. οἱ Παλι-

[1] ποτέ, after ἐπιλειπούσης (the reading of the MSS.), Jones
restores; Meineke deletes, following the *Epit*.
[2] Νεβρώδη, Corais, for Νευρώδη; so Meineke.
[3] καὶ τὰ Ἱμεραῖα, Meineke, for κατὰ Ἱμέραν; C. Müller
approving. Corais inserts καὶ τὰ before the κατὰ Ἱμέραν.

---

[1] Now the Nebrodici.   [2] 5. 4. 9.

depths, and also owing to the heat, which, it is reasonable to suppose, meets one long before one comes near the mouth of the crater; but even if something should be thrown down into it, it would be destroyed before it could be thrown up in anything like the shape it had when first received; and although it is not unreasonable to assume that at times the blasts of the fire die down when at times the fuel is deficient, yet surely this would not last long enough to make possible the approach of man against so great a force. Aetna dominates more especially the seaboard in the region of the Strait and the territory of Catana, but also that in the region of the Tyrrhenian Sea and the Liparaean Islands. Now although by night a brilliant light shines from the summit, by day it is covered with smoke and haze.

9. Over against Aetna rise the Nebrodes Mountains,[1] which, though lower than Aetna, exceed it considerably in breadth. The whole island is hollow down beneath the ground, and full of streams and of fire, as is the case with the Tyrrhenian Sea, as far as the Cumaean country, as I have said before.[2] At all events, the island has at many places springs of hot waters which spout up, of which those of Selinus and those of Himera are brackish, whereas those of Aegesta are potable. Near Acragas are lakes which, though they have the taste of sea-water, are different in nature; for even people who cannot swim do not sink, but float on the surface like wood. The territory of the Palici has craters[3]

[3] Strabo refers to what is now the Lago di Naftia, a small volcanic lake near the Eryces River and Leontini, and not far from the sea.

κοὶ δὲ κρατῆρας ἔχουσιν ἀναβάλλοντας ὕδωρ εἰς
θολοειδὲς ἀναφύσημα καὶ πάλιν εἰς τὸν αὐτὸν
δεχομένους μυχόν. τὸ δὲ περὶ Μάταυρον[1] σπή-
λαιον ἐντὸς ἔχει σύριγγα εὐμεγέθη καὶ ποταμὸν
δι' αὐτῆς ῥέοντα ἀφανῆ μέχρι πολλοῦ διαστήματος, εἶτ' ἀνακύπτοντα πρὸς τὴν ἐπιφάνειαν,
καθάπερ Ὀρόντης ἐν τῇ Συρίᾳ, καταδὺς εἰς τὸ
μεταξὺ χάσμα Ἀπαμείας καὶ Ἀντιοχείας, ὃ
καλοῦσι Χάρυβδιν, ἀνατέλλει πάλιν ἐν τετταράκοντα σταδίοις· τὰ δὲ παραπλήσια καὶ ὁ
Τίγρις ἐν τῇ Μεσοποταμίᾳ καὶ ὁ Νεῖλος ἐν τῇ
Λιβύῃ μικρὸν πρὸ τῶν πηγῶν. τὸ δὲ περὶ
Στύμφαλον ὕδωρ ἐπὶ διακοσίους σταδίους ὑπὸ
γῆν ἐνεχθὲν ἐν τῇ Ἀργείᾳ τὸν Ἐρασῖνον ἐκδίδωσι ποταμόν, καὶ πάλιν τὸ πρὸς τὴν Ἀρκαδικὴν
Ἀσέαν ὑποβρύχιον ὠσθὲν ὀψέ ποτε τόν τε
Εὐρώταν καὶ τὸν Ἀλφειὸν ἀναδίδωσιν, ὥστε
καὶ πεπιστεῦσθαι μυθῶδές τι, ὅτι τῶν ἐπιφη-
μισθέντων στεφάνων ἑκατέρῳ καὶ ἐρριφέντα[2] εἰς
τὸ κοινὸν ῥεῦμα ἀναφαίνεται κατὰ τὸν ἐπιφη-
μισμὸν ἑκάτερος ἐν τῷ οἰκείῳ ποταμῷ. εἴρηται
δὲ καὶ τὸ λεγόμενον περὶ τοῦ Τιμάυου.

10. Συγγενῆ δὲ καὶ τούτοις καὶ τοῖς κατὰ τὴν
Σικελίαν πάθεσι τὰ περὶ τὰς Λιπαραίων νήσους
καὶ αὐτὴν τὴν Λιπάραν δείκνυται. εἰσὶ δ' ἑπτὰ
μὲν τὸν ἀριθμόν. μεγίστη δὲ ἡ Λιπάρα, Κνιδίων

---

[1] For Μάταυρον, an unknown place, Cluver suggests Μάζα-
ρον, and others, Μάζαρα; the former is probably correct.
Corais' Μέταυρον and C. Müller's Ἰμάχαρον seem groundless.
[2] ἐρριφέντα, Jones, for ῥιφέντα, on a query of Dr. Rouse.

---

[1] The form "Mataurus" seems to be corrupt. At any
rate, it probably should be identified with Mazara (now

that spout up water in a dome-like jet and receive it back again into the same recess. The cavern near Mataurus [1] contains an immense gallery through which a river flows invisible for a considerable distance, and then emerges to the surface, as is the case with the Orontes in Syria,[2] which sinks into the chasm (called Charybdis) between Apameia and Antiocheia and rises again forty stadia away. Similar, too, are the cases both of the Tigris [3] in Mesopotamia and of the Nile in Libya, only a short distance from their sources. And the water in the territory of Stymphalus [4] first flows underground for two hundred stadia and then issues forth in Argeia as the Erasinus River; and again, the water near the Arcadian Asea is first forced below the surface and then, much later, emerges as both the Eurotas and the Alpheius; and hence the belief in a certain fabulous utterance, that if two wreaths be dedicated separately to each of the two rivers and thrown into the common stream, each will reappear, in accordance with the dedication, in the appropriate river. And I have already mentioned what is told about the Timavus River.[5]

10. Phenomena akin both to these and to those in Sicily are to be seen about the Liparaean Islands and Lipara itself. The islands are seven in number, but the largest is Lipara (a colony of the Cnidians), which,

Mazzara), near which there is now a small river flowing through a rocky district.

[2] Cp. 16 2. 7.

[3] So Pliny, *Nat. Hist.* 6. 31.

[4] Strabo refers to the lake of Stymphalus in Arcadia in the Peloponnesus. For a full description see Frazer's note on Pausanias, 8 22. 1, Vol. IV, p 268.

[5] 5. 1. 8.

ἄποικος, ἐγγυτάτω τῆς Σικελίας κειμένη, μετά γε
τὴν Θέρμεσσαν· ἐκαλεῖτο δὲ πρότερον Μελιγου-
νίς· ἡγήσατο δὲ καὶ στόλῳ καὶ πρὸς τὰς τῶν
Τυρρηνῶν ἐπιδρομὰς πολὺν χρόνον ἀντέσχεν,
ὑπηκόους ἔχουσα τὰς νῦν λεγομένας Λιπαραίων
νήσους ἃς Αἰόλου τινὲς προσαγορεύουσι. καὶ
δὴ καὶ τὸ ἱερὸν τοῦ Ἀπόλλωνος ἐκόσμησε
πολλάκις τὸ ἐν Δελφοῖς ἀπὸ τῶν ἀκροθινίων·
ἔχει δὲ καὶ τὴν γῆν εὔκαρπον καὶ στυπτηρίας
μέταλλον ἐμπρόσοδον [1] καὶ θερμὰ ὕδατα καὶ
πυρὸς ἀναπνοάς. ταύτης δὲ μεταξύ πώς ἐστι
καὶ τῆς Σικελίας ἡ Θέρμεσσα,[2] ἣν νῦν Ἱερὰν
Ἡφαίστου καλοῦσι, πετρώδης πᾶσα καὶ ἔρημος
καὶ [3] διάπυρος· ἔχει δὲ ἀναπνοὰς τρεῖς ὡς ἂν ἐκ
τριῶν κρατήρων. ἐκ δὲ τοῦ μεγίστου καὶ μύδρους
αἱ φλόγες ἀναφέρουσιν, οἳ προσκεχώκασιν ἤδη
πολὺ μέρος τοῦ πόρου. ἐκ δὲ τῆς τηρήσεως
πεπίστευται, διότι τοῖς ἀνέμοις συμπαροξύνονται
καὶ αἱ φλόγες αἵ τε ἐνταῦθα καὶ αἱ κατὰ τὴν
Αἴτνην, παυομένων δὲ παύονται καὶ αἱ φλόγες.
C 276 οὐκ ἄλογον δέ· καὶ γὰρ οἱ ἄνεμοι γεννῶνται καὶ
τρέφονται τὴν ἀρχὴν λαβόντες ἀπὸ τῶν ἐκ τῆς
θαλάττης ἀναθυμιάσεων, ὥστ' ἀπὸ συγγενοῦς
ὕλης καὶ πάθους καὶ τὸ πῦρ ἐξαπτόμενον οὐκ
ἐᾷ θαυμάζειν τοὺς ὁρῶντας ἀμωσγέπως [4] τὰ

---

[1] ἐμπρόσοδον (A, *Epit.*, Meineke); εὐπρόσοδον (*no*, Corais);
ἐν πρόσοδον (*Cl*).
[2] ἡ Θέρμεσσα, Corais inserts; so the later editors.
[3] καί, after ἔρημος, Corais inserts; so Müller-Dübner and
Meineke.
[4] ἀμωσγέπως, Corais, for ἄλλως γέ πως; so Meineke.

---

[1] Styptic earth (= Latin *alumen*) is discussed at length by

Thermessa excepted, lies nearest to Sicily. It was
formerly called Meligunis; and it not only com-
manded a fleet, but for a long time resisted the
incursions of the Tyrrheni, for it held in obedience
all the Liparaean Islands, as they are now called,
though by some they are called the Islands of
Aeolus. Furthermore, it often adorned the temple
of Apollo at Delphi with dedications from the
first fruits of victory. It has also a fruitful soil, and
a mine of styptic earth [1] that brings in revenues,[2]
and hot springs, and fireblasts. Between Lipara
and Sicily is Thermessa, which is now called
Hiera of Hephaestus [3]; the whole island is rocky,
desert, and fiery, and it has three fire blasts,
rising from three openings which one might call
craters. From the largest the flames carry up also
red-hot masses, which have already choked up a considerable part of the Strait. From observation it
has been believed that the flames, both here and on
Aetna, are stimulated along with the winds and that
when the winds cease the flames cease too. And this
is not unreasonable, for the winds are begotten by the
evaporations of the sea and after they have taken
their beginning are fed thereby; and therefore it is
not permissible for any who have any sort of insight
into such matters to marvel if the fire too is kindled

Pliny (35. 52). It was not our alum, but an iron sulphate,
or a mixture of an iron and an aluminium sulphate, used in
dyeing and in medicine.

[2] Diodorus Siculus (5. 10) says: "This island" (Lipara)
"has the far-famed mines of styptic earth, from which the
Liparaeans and Romans get great revenues."

[3] *i.e.* "Sacred" Isle of Hephaestus. The isle is now called
Vulcanello. It is supposed to be the island that rose from the
sea about 183 B.C. (see Nissen, *Italische Landeskunde* I. 251).

τοιάδε. Πολύβιος δὲ τῶν τριῶν κρατήρων τὸν
μὲν κατερρυηκέναι φησὶν ἐκ μέρους, τοὺς δὲ
συμμένειν, τὸν δὲ μέγιστον τὸ χεῖλος ἔχειν,
περιφερὲς ὄν, πέντε σταδίων, κατ᾽ ὀλίγον δὲ
συνάγεσθαι εἰς πεντήκοντα[1] ποδῶν διάμετρον·
καθ᾽ οὗ βάθος εἶναι τὸ μέχρι θαλάττης σταδιαῖον, ὥστε καθορᾶν ταῖς νηνεμίαις. εἰ δὲ ταῦτ᾽
ἐστὶ πιστά, οὐκ ἀπιστητέον ἴσως οὐδὲ τοῖς περὶ
Ἐμπεδοκλέους μυθολογηθεῖσιν.[2] ἐὰν μὲν οὖν
Νότος μέλλῃ πνεῖν, ἀχλὺν ὀμιχλώδη καταχεῖ-
σθαι κύκλῳ φησὶ τῆς νησῖδος, ὥστε μηδὲ τὴν
Σικελίαν ἄπωθεν φαίνεσθαι· ὅταν δὲ Βορέας,
φλόγας καθαρὰς ἀπὸ τοῦ λεχθέντος κρατῆρος
εἰς ὕψος ἐξαίρεσθαι καὶ βρόμους ἐκπέμπεσθαι
μείζους· τὸν δὲ Ζέφυρον μέσην τινὰ ἔχειν τάξιν.
τοὺς δ᾽ ἄλλους κρατῆρας ὁμοειδεῖς μὲν εἶναι, τῇ
δὲ βίᾳ λείπεσθαι τῶν ἀναφυσημάτων· ἔκ τε δὴ
τῆς διαφορᾶς τῶν βρόμων καὶ ἐκ τοῦ πόθεν
ἄρχεται τὰ ἀναφυσήματα καὶ αἱ φλόγες καὶ
αἱ λιγνύες προσημαίνεσθαι καὶ τὸν εἰς ἡμέραν
τρίτην πάλιν μέλλοντα ἄνεμον πνεῖν· τῶν[3] γοῦν
ἐν Λιπάραις γενομένης ἀπλοίας προειπεῖν τινάς
φησι τὸν ἐσόμενον[4] καὶ μὴ διαψεύσασθαι. ἀφ᾽
οὗ δὴ τὸ μυθωδέστατον δοκοῦν εἰρῆσθαι τῷ
ποιητῇ οὐ μάτην φαίνεσθαι λεχθέν, ἀλλ᾽ αἰνι-
ξαμένου τὴν ἀλήθειαν, ὅταν φῇ ταμίαν τῶν
ἀνέμων τὸν Αἴολον· περὶ ὧν ἐμνήσθημεν καὶ

---

[1] For πεντήκοντα (νʹ), the *Epit.* reads τριάκοντα (λʹ).

[2] εἰ . . . . μυθολογηθεῖσιν, Meineke regards as an inter-
polation and relegates to foot of page ; C. Müller approving.

[3] For τῶν C. Müller suggests ἑαυτῷ (Polybius) ; perhaps
rightly.

by a cognate fuel or disturbance. According to
Polybius, one of the three craters has partially fallen
in, whereas the others remain whole; and the largest
has a circular rim five stadia in circuit, but it grad-
ually contracts to a diameter of fifty feet; and the
altitude of this crater above the level of the sea is a
stadium, so that the crater is visible on windless days.[1]
But if all this is to be believed, perhaps one should also
believe the mythical story about Empedocles.[2] Now
if the south wind is about to blow, Polybius continues,
a cloud-like mist pours down all round the island, so
that not even Sicily is visible in the distance; and
when the north wind is about to blow, pure flames
rise aloft from the aforesaid crater and louder
rumblings are sent forth; but the west wind holds a
middle position, so to speak, between the two; but
though the two other craters are like the first in
kind, they fall short in the violence of their
spoutings; accordingly, both the difference in the
rumblings, and the place whence the spoutings and
the flames and the fiery smoke begin, signify before-
hand the wind that is going to blow again three days
afterward[3]; at all events, certain of the men in
Liparae, when the weather made sailing impossible,
predicted, he says, the wind that was to blow, and
they were not mistaken; from this fact, then, it is
clear that that saying of the Poet which is regarded
as most mythical of all was not idly spoken, but that
he hinted at the truth when he called Aeolus

[1] *i.e.* from the sea. Or perhaps, "so that the sea is
visible from it."
[2] See 6. 2. 8.   [3] So Pliny 3. 14.

[4] After ἐσόμενον some of the editors, following the *Epit.*,
insert ἄνεμον.

πρότερον ἱκανῶς. ἔστιν ἡ ἐπίστασις τῆς ἐναργείας λέγοιτ' ἄν, . . . ἐπίσης τε γὰρ ἄμφω
πάρεστι, καὶ διαθέσει καὶ τῇ ἐναργείᾳ· ἥ γε
ἡδονὴ κοινὸν ἀμφοτέρων.[1] ἐπάνιμεν δ' ἐπὶ τὰ
ἑξῆς ἀφ' ὧν παρεξέβημεν.

11. Τὴν μὲν δὴ Λιπάραν καὶ τὴν Θέρμεσσαν
εἰρήκαμεν. ἡ δὲ Στρογγύλη καλεῖται μὲν ἀπὸ
τοῦ σχήματος, ἔστι δὲ καὶ αὐτὴ διάπυρος, βίᾳ
μὲν φλογὸς λειπομένη, τῷ δὲ φέγγει πλεονεκ-
τοῦσα· ἐνταῦθα δὲ τὸν Αἴολον οἰκῆσαί φασι.
τετάρτη δ' ἐστὶ Διδύμη, καὶ αὕτη δ' ἀπὸ τοῦ
σχήματος ὠνόμασται. τῶν δὲ λοιπῶν Ἐρικοῦσσα
μὲν καὶ Φοινικοῦσσα ἀπὸ τῶν φυτῶν κέκληνται,
ἀνεῖνται δὲ εἰς νομάς. ἑβδόμη δ' ἐστὶν Εὐώνυμος,
πελαγία μάλιστα καὶ ἔρημος· ὠνόμασται δ', ὅτι
μάλιστα τοῖς ἐκ Λιπάρας εἰς Σικελίαν πλέουσιν

---

[1] The words ἔστιν . . . . ἀμφοτέρων appear, without a
break, in the MSS., except that n and o have them in the
margin. The editors before Groskurd place the period before
ἱκανῶς, however, not before ἔστιν. Corais, Forbiger, Tardieu
and Meineke eject the words from the text. Groskurd alone
ventures to reconstitute the text, reading as follows:
[μεγάλη δέ] ἐστιν ἡ ἐπίστασις τῆς ἐνεργείας (for ἐναργείας, see 1.
2. 17) [ἤ] λέγοιτ' ἄν [μάλιστα παρασκευάζειν καὶ ἔκπληξιν καὶ
ἡδονήν·] ἐπίσης (deleting τε) γὰρ κ.τ.λ.

---

[1] *Odyssey* 10. 21.
[2] 1. 2 7–18, but especially §§ 15–18. Since Polybius, as
well as Strabo, discussed this subject at length, the sentence
"However, . . . sufficiently" might belong to the long
excerpt from Polybius (cp. 1. 2. 15–18). Here follows a sentence which, as it stands in the manuscripts, is incoherent,
and seems to be beyond restoration. But for the fact that
it is somewhat similiar to an accredited passage found elsewhere (1. 2. 17), one would hardly hesitate to regard it as a
marginal note and follow Meineke in ejecting it from the text.

"steward of the winds."[1] However, I have already discussed these matters sufficiently.[2] It is the close attention of the Poet to vivid description, one might call it, . . . for both[3] are equally present in rhetorical composition and vivid description; at any rate, pleasure is common to both. But I shall return to the topic which follows that at which I digressed.

11. Of Lipara, then, and Thermessa I have already spoken. As for Strongyle,[4] it is so called from its shape, and it too is fiery; it falls short in the violence of its flame, but excels in the brightness of its light; and this is where Aeolus lived, it is said. The fourth island is Didyme,[5] and it too is named after its shape. Of the remaining islands, Ericussa[6] and Phoenicussa[7] have been so called from their plants, and are given over to pasturage of flocks. The seventh is Euonymus,[8] which is farthest out in the high sea and is desert; it is so named because it is more to the left than the others, to those who sail from Lipara to Sicily.[9] Again, many times flames

[3] Perhaps (1) pleasure and (2) the excitement of amazement (see 1. 2. 17), as Groskurd thinks, or (1) the truthful element and (2) the mythical element (see also 1. 2. 19).

[4] *i.e.* "Round," the Stromboli of to-day.

[5] *i.e.* "Double." It is formed by two volcanic cones ; the Salina of to-day.

[6] *i.e.* "Heather" (cp. the botanical term "Ericaceae ") ; now called Alicudi.

[7] *i.e.* "Palm" (cp. the botanical term "Phoenicaceae") ; or perhaps "Rye-grass" (*Lolium perenne*), the sense in which Theophrastus (*Hist. Plant.* 2. 6. 11) uses the Greek word "phoenix"; now called Felicudi.

[8] *i.e.* "Left"; now called Panaria.

[9] This would not be true if one sailed the shortest way to Sicily, but Strabo obviously has in mind the voyage from the *city* of Lipara to Cape Pelorias.

εὐώνυμός ἐστι. πολλάκις δὲ καὶ φλόγες εἰς τὴν
ἐπιφάνειαν τοῦ πελάγους τοῦ περὶ τὰς νήσους
ὤφθησαν ἐπιδραμοῦσαι, τῶν κατὰ βάθους κοιλιῶν[1] ἀναστομωθέντος πόρου τινός, καὶ τοῦ πυρὸς
C 277 βιασαμένου πρὸς τὸ ἐκτός. Ποσειδώνιος δὲ κατὰ
τὴν ἑαυτοῦ μνήμην φησὶ περὶ τροπὰς θερινὰς
ἅμα τῇ ἔῳ μεταξὺ τῆς Ἱερᾶς καὶ τῆς Εὐωνύμου
πρὸς ὕψος ἀρθεῖσαν ἐξαίσιον τὴν θάλατταν ὁρα-
θῆναι, καὶ συμμεῖναί τινα χρόνον ἀναφυσωμένην
συνεχῶς, εἶτα παύσασθαι· τοὺς δὲ τολμήσαντας
προσπλεῖν, ἰδόντας νεκροὺς ἰχθύας ἐλαυνομένους
ὑπὸ τοῦ ῥοῦ (τοὺς δὲ καὶ θέρμῃ καὶ δυσωδίᾳ
πληγέντας) φυγεῖν, ἐν δὲ τῶν πλοιαρίων τὸ
μᾶλλον πλησιάσαν τοὺς μὲν τῶν ἐνόντων ἀπο-
βαλεῖν, τοὺς δ' εἰς Λιπάραν μόλις σῶσαι, τοτὲ
μὲν ἔκφρονας γινομένους ὁμοίως τοῖς ἐπιληπτικοῖς,
τοτὲ δὲ ἀνατρέχοντας εἰς τοὺς οἰκείους λογισμούς·
πολλαῖς δ' ἡμέραις ὕστερον ὁρᾶσθαι πηλὸν
ἐπανθοῦντα τῇ θαλάττῃ, πολλαχοῦ δὲ καὶ
φλόγας ἐκπιπτούσας καὶ καπνοὺς καὶ λιγνύας,
ὕστερον δὲ παγῆναι καὶ γενέσθαι τοῖς μιλίαις[2]
λίθοις ἐοικότα τὸν πάγον· τὸν δὲ τῆς Σικελίας
στρατηγόν, Τίτον Φλαμίνιον,[3] δηλῶσαι τῇ συγ-
κλήτῳ, τὴν δὲ πέμψασαν ἐκθύσασθαι ἔν τε τῷ
νησιδίῳ καὶ ἐν Λιπάραις τοῖς τε καταχθονίοις

---

[1] τοῦ πυρός, Kramer transposes from a position after
κοιλιῶν to a position before βιασαμένου ; so the later editors.
[2] μιλίαις, the *Epit* , for μιλίταις (cp. 10 5. 16) ; so Meineke.
[3] For Φλομίνιον, Du Theil, Corais (C. Müller approving),
read Φλαμινῖνον.

---

[1] Poseidonius was born about 130 B.C.

have been observed running over the surface of the
sea round about the islands when some passage had
been opened up from the cavities down in the
depths of the earth and the fire had forced its way
to the outside. Poseidonius says that within his
own recollection,[1] one morning at daybreak about
the time of the summer solstice, the sea between
Hiera and Euonymus was seen raised to an enor-
mous height, and by a sustained blast remained
puffed up for a considerable time, and then sub-
sided; and when those who had the hardihood to
sail up to it saw dead fish driven by the current, and
some of the men were stricken ill because of the
heat and stench, they took flight; one of the boats,
however, approaching more closely, lost some of its
occupants and barely escaped to Lipara with the
rest, who would at times become senseless like
epileptics, and then afterwards would recur to their
proper reasoning faculties; and many days later
mud was seen forming on the surface of the sea,
and in many places flames, smoke, and murky fire
broke forth, but later the scum hardened and
became as hard as mill-stone; and the governor of
Sicily, Titus Flaminius,[2] reported the event to the
Senate, and the Senate sent a deputation to offer
propitiatory sacrifices, both in the islet[3] and in
Liparae, to the gods both of the underworld and of

[2] This Titus Flaminius, who must have lived "within the
recollection" of Poseidonius, is otherwise unknown. If the
text is correct, he was governor of Sicily about 90 B.C.
Cp. Nissen, *op. cit.* II. 251. But Du Theil, Corais and
C. Müller emend to Titus "Flamininus," who was governor
in 123 B.C., trying to connect this eruption with that which
is generally put at 126 B.C. (cp. Pliny 2. 88 [89]).

[3] The islet just created.

θεοῖς καὶ τοῖς θαλαττίοις. ἀπὸ μὲν οὖν Ἐρι-
κώδους εἰς Φοινικώδη δέκα μίλιά φησιν ὁ χωρογράφος, ἔνθεν δ᾽ εἰς Διδύμην τριάκοντα, ἔνθεν
δ᾽ εἰς Λιπάραν πρὸς ἄρκτον ἐννέα καὶ εἴκοσι,
ἔνθεν δ᾽ εἰς Σικελίαν ἐννεακαίδεκα· ἑκκαίδεκα
δ᾽ ἐκ τῆς Στρογγύλης. πρόκειται δὲ τοῦ Παχύνου
Μελίτη, ὅθεν τὰ κυνίδια, ἃ καλοῦσι Μελιταῖα,
καὶ Γαῦδος, ὀγδοήκοντα καὶ ὀκτὼ μίλια τῆς
ἄκρας[1] ἀμφότεραι διέχουσαι· Κόσσουρα δὲ πρὸ
τοῦ Λιλυβαίου καὶ πρὸ τῆς Ἀσπίδος, Καρχη-
δονιακῆς πόλεως, ἣν Κλυπέαν καλοῦσι, μέση
ἀμφοῖν κειμένη καὶ τὸ λεχθὲν διάστημα ἀφ᾽
ἑκατέρας ἀπέχουσα· καὶ ἡ Αἰγίμουρος δὲ πρὸ
τῆς Σικελίας καὶ τῆς Λιβύης ἐστὶ καὶ ἄλλα
μικρὰ νησίδια. ταῦτα μὲν περὶ τῶν νήσων.

III

Ἐπεληλυθόσι δ᾽ ἡμῖν τὰ περὶ τὴν ἀρχαίαν
Ἰταλίαν μέχρι Μεταποντίου τὰ συνεχῆ λεκτέον.
συνεχὴς δ᾽ ἐστὶν ἡ Ἰαπυγία· ταύτην δὲ καὶ
Μεσσαπίαν καλοῦσιν οἱ Ἕλληνες, οἱ δ᾽ ἐπιχώριοι
κατὰ μέρη τὸ μέν τι Σαλεντίνους καλοῦσι, τὸ
περὶ τὴν ἄκραν τὴν Ἰαπυγίαν, τὸ δὲ Καλαβρούς.
ὑπὲρ τούτους πρόσβορροι Πευκέτιοί τέ εἰσι καὶ
Δαύνιοι κατὰ τὴν Ἑλλάδα διάλεκτον προσα-
γορευόμενοι, οἱ δ᾽ ἐπιχώριοι πᾶσαν τὴν μετὰ
τοὺς Καλαβροὺς Ἀπουλίαν καλοῦσι, τινὲς δ᾽

---

[1] τῆς ἄκρας, Cluver, for ἑκατέρας ; so the editors.

[1] See footnote 3 in Vol. II, p. 358.

the sea. Now, according to the Chorographer,[1] the distance from Ericodes to Phoenicodes[2] is ten miles, and thence to Didyme thirty, and thence to the northern part of Lipara twenty-nine, and thence to Sicily nineteen, but from Strongyle sixteen. Off Pachynus lie Melita,[3] whence come the little dogs called Melitaean, and Gaudos, both eighty-eight miles distant from the Cape. Cossura[4] lies off Lilybaeum, and off Aspis,[5] a Carthaginian city whose Latin name is Clupea; it lies midway between the two, and is the aforesaid distance[6] from either. Aegimurus,[7] also, and other small islands lie off Sicily and Libya. So much for the islands.

III

1. Now that I have traversed the regions of Old Italy[8] as far as Metapontium, I must speak of those that border on them. And Iapygia borders on them. The Greeks call it Messapia, also, but the natives, dividing it into two parts, call one part (that about the Iapygian Cape)[9] the country of the Salentini, and the other the country of the Calabri. Above these latter, on the north, are the Peucetii and also those people who in the Greek language are called Daunii, but the natives give the name Apulia to the whole country that comes after that of the Calabri, though some of them, particularly

---

[2] *i.e.* Ericussa and Phoenicussa.
[3] Now Malta.   [4] Now Pantellaria.
[5] So called from the resemblance of the hill (see 17. 3. 16), where it is situated, to a shield (*aspis*, Lat. *clupeus*).
[6] Eighty-eight miles.   [7] Now Al Djamur.
[8] *i.e.* Oenotria (see 6. 1. 15 and 5. 1. 1).   [9] Cape Leuca.

αὐτῶν καὶ Ποίδικλοι λέγονται, καὶ μάλιστα οἱ
Πευκέτιοι. ἔστι δέ τι [1] χερρονησιάζουσα ἡ Μεσ-
σαπία, τῷ ἀπὸ Βρεντεσίου μέχρι Τάραντος ἰσθμῷ
κλειομένη σταδίων δέκα καὶ τριακοσίων. ὅ τ'
ἐπίπλους [2] ἐστὶ περὶ τὴν ἄκραν Ἰαπυγίαν σταδίων
ὁμοῦ τι [3] τετρακοσίων. τοῦ δὲ Μεταποντίου μὲν
C 278 διέχει σταδίους περὶ διακοσίους καὶ εἴκοσιν,[4] ὁ δὲ
πλοῦς ἐπ' αὐτὸν πρὸς τὰς ἀνατολάς. τοῦ δὲ
κόλπου παντὸς τοῦ Ταραντίνου τὸ πλέον ἀλιμένου
ὄντος, ἐνταῦθα δὴ λιμήν [5] ἐστι μέγιστος καὶ κάλ-
λιστος, γεφύρᾳ κλειόμενος μεγάλῃ, σταδίων δ' ἐστὶν
ἑκατὸν τὴν περίμετρον. ἐκ δὲ τοῦ πρὸς τὸν μυχὸν
μέρους ἰσθμὸν ποιεῖ πρὸς τὴν ἔξω θάλατταν, ὥστ'
ἐπὶ χερρονήσῳ κεῖσθαι τὴν πόλιν, καὶ τὰ πλοῖα
ὑπερνεωλκεῖσθαι ῥᾳδίως ἑκατέρωθεν, ταπεινοῦ
ὄντος τοῦ αὐχένος. ταπεινὸν δὲ καὶ τὸ τῆς
πόλεως ἔδαφος, μικρὸν δ' ὅμως ἐπῆρται κατὰ
τὴν ἀκρόπολιν. τὸ μὲν οὖν παλαιὸν τεῖχος
κύκλον ἔχει μέγαν, νυνὶ δ' ἐκλέλειπται τὸ πλέον
τὸ πρὸς τῷ ἰσθμῷ, τὸ δὲ πρὸς τῷ στόματι τοῦ
λιμένος, καθ' ὃ καὶ ἡ ἀκρόπολις, συμμένει μέγεθος

---

[1] δέ τι, Corais, for δ' ἐπι; Meineke writes δ' ἐπιχερ-
ρονησιάζουσα, but stars it; T. G. Tucker conjectures
ὑποχερρονησιάζουσα.

[2] For ἐπίπλους, Meineke, following the conj. of Kramer,
reads περίπλους, but this is unnecessary.

[3] Before τετρακοσίων, Groskurd inserts χιλίων; but com-
paring the distances in 6. 3. 5, we should expect here
χίλιων διακοσίων (͵ασ'); and if περί (before τὴν ἄκραν) is
emended to ἐπί (Corais), the τετρακοσίων would be too
small.

[4] εἴκοσιν (κ'), after καί, Meineke inserts, following i; but
Meineke also inserts ὁ Τάρας after εἴκοσιν. In A there is a
lacuna of seven or eight letters.

the Peucetii, are called Poedicli also. Messapia forms a sort of peninsula, since it is enclosed by the isthmus that extends from Brentesium[1] as far as Taras, three hundred and ten stadia. And the voyage thither[2] around the Iapygian Cape is, all told, about four hundred[3] stadia. The distance from Metapontium[4] is about two hundred and twenty stadia, and the voyage to it is towards the rising sun. But though the whole Tarantine Gulf, generally speaking, is harbourless, yet at the city there is a very large and beautiful harbour,[5] which is enclosed by a large bridge and is one hundred stadia in circumference. In that part of the harbour which lies towards the innermost recess,[6] the harbour, with the outer sea, forms an isthmus, and therefore the city is situated on a peninsula; and since the neck of land is low-lying, the ships are easily hauled overland from either side. The ground of the city, too, is low-lying, but still it is slightly elevated where the acropolis is. The old wall has a large circuit, but at the present time the greater part of the city—the part that is near the isthmus—has been forsaken, but the part that is near the mouth of the harbour, where the acropolis is, still endures

[1] See 5. 3. 6 and footnote.
[2] From Brentesium to Taras.
[3] This figure is wrong. Strabo probably wrote 1,200; Groskurd thinks that he wrote 1,400, but in § 5 (below) the figures for the intervals of the same voyage total 1,220 stadia.
[4] To Taras.   [5] Mare Piccolo.
[6] *i.e.* the part that is immediately to the east of the city, as Tozer (*op. cit.*, p. 183) points out.

---

[5] ἐνταῦθα δὴ λιμήν, Corais, for ἐντεῦθεν. There is a lacuna of about seven letters in A, and *i* reads λιμήν.

ἀξιολόγου πόλεως ἐκπληροῦν. ἔχει δὲ γυμνάσιόν
τε κάλλιστον καὶ ἀγορὰν εὐμεγέθη, ἐν ᾗ καὶ ὁ
τοῦ Διὸς ἵδρυται κολοσσὸς χαλκοῦς, μέγιστος
μετὰ τὸν Ῥοδίων. μεταξὺ δὲ τῆς ἀγορᾶς καὶ τοῦ
στόματος ἡ ἀκρόπολις, μικρὰ λείψανα ἔχουσα
τοῦ παλαιοῦ κόσμου τῶν ἀναθημάτων· τὰ γὰρ
πολλὰ τὰ μὲν κατέφθειραν Καρχηδόνιοι, λαβόντες τὴν πόλιν, τὰ δ᾽ ἐλαφυραγώγησαν
Ῥωμαῖοι, κρατήσαντες βιαίως· ὧν ἐστι καὶ ὁ
Ἡρακλῆς ἐν τῷ Καπετωλίῳ χαλκοῦς κολοσσικός,
Λυσίππου ἔργον, ἀνάθημα Μαξίμου Φαβίου τοῦ
ἑλόντος τὴν πόλιν.

2. Περὶ δὲ τῆς κτίσεως Ἀντίοχος λέγων φησὶν
ὅτι τοῦ Μεσσηνιακοῦ πολέμου γενηθέντος οἱ μὴ
μετασχόντες Λακεδαιμονίων τῆς στρατείας ἐκρί-
θησαν δοῦλοι καὶ ὠνομάσθησαν Εἵλωτες, ὅσοις[1]
δὲ κατὰ τὴν στρατείαν παῖδες ἐγένοντο, Παρθενίας
ἐκάλουν καὶ ἀτίμους ἔκριναν· οἱ δ᾽ οὐκ ἀνασχό-
μενοι (πολλοὶ δ᾽ ἦσαν) ἐπεβούλευσαν τοῖς τοῦ
δήμου. αἰσθόμενοι δ᾽ ὑπέπεμψάν τινας, οἳ προσ-
ποιήσει φιλίας ἔμελλον ἐξαγγέλλειν τὸν τρόπον
τῆς ἐπιβουλῆς. τούτων δ᾽ ἦν καὶ Φάλανθος,
ὅσπερ ἐδόκει προστάτης ὑπάρχειν αὐτῶν, οὐκ
ἠρέσκετο δ᾽ ἁπλῶς τοῖς περὶ τῆς βουλῆς[2] ὀνο-

---

[1] For ὅσοις, no read ὅσοι, but the meaning of the sentence
can, and must, be the same in either case.
[2] For βουλῆς Müller-Dübner and Meineke read ἐπιβουλῆς.

---

[1] Tarentum revolted from Rome to Hannibal during the
Second Punic War, but was recaptured (209 B.C.) and severely
dealt with.
[2] 743–723 B.C.

and makes up a city of noteworthy size. And it has
a very beautiful gymnasium, and also a spacious
market-place, in which is situated the bronze
colossus of Zeus, the largest in the world except the
one that belongs to the Rhodians. Between the
market-place and the mouth of the harbour is
the acropolis, which has but few remnants of the
dedicated objects that in early times adorned it,
for most of them were either destroyed by the
Carthaginians when they took the city or carried off
as booty by the Romans when they took the place
by storm.[1] Among this booty is the Heracles in the
Capitol, a colossal bronze statue, the work of Lysippus, dedicated by Maximus Fabius, who captured
the city.

2. In speaking of the founding of Taras, Antiochus
says: After the Messenian war[2] broke out, those
of the Lacedaemonians who did not take part in the
expedition were adjudged slaves and were named
Helots,[3] and all children who were born in the
time of the expedition were called Partheniae[4] and
judicially deprived of the rights of citizenship, but
they would not tolerate this, and since they were
numerous formed a plot against the free citizens;
and when the latter learned of the plot they sent
secretly certain men who, through a pretence of
friendship, were to report what manner of plot it
was; among these was Phalanthus, who was reputed
to be their champion, but he was not pleased, in
general, with those who had been named to take
part in the council. It was agreed, however, that

[3] On the name and its origin, see 8. 5. 4; also Pauly-
Wissowa, *Real-Encycl. s.v.* "Heloten."
[4] "Children of Virgins."

μασθεῖσι.[1] συνέκειτο μὲν δὴ τοῖς Ὑακινθίοις ἐν
τῷ Ἀμυκλαίῳ συντελουμένου τοῦ ἀγῶνος, ἡνίκ᾽
ἂν τὴν κυνῆν περίθηται ὁ Φάλανθος, ποιεῖσθαι
τὴν ἐπίθεσιν· γνώριμοι δ᾽ ἦσαν ἀπὸ τῆς κόμης οἱ
τοῦ δήμου. ἐξαγγειλάντων[2] δὲ λάθρᾳ τὰ συγκείμενα τῶν περὶ Φάλανθον, καὶ τοῦ ἀγῶνος ἐνεστῶτος, προελθὼν ὁ κῆρυξ εἶπε, μὴ περιθέσθαι[3]
κυνῆν Φάλανθον. οἱ δ᾽ αἰσθόμενοι, ὡς μεμηνύκασι[4] τὴν ἐπιβουλήν, οἱ μὲν διεδίδρασκον, οἱ δὲ
ἱκέτευον. κελεύσαντες δ᾽ αὐτοὺς θαρρεῖν φυλακῇ
παρέδοσαν, τὸν δὲ Φάλανθον ἔπεμψαν εἰς θεοῦ
περὶ ἀποικίας· ὁ δ᾽ ἔχρησε·

C 279   Σατύριόν τοι δῶκα, Τάραντά τε πίονα δῆμον
οἰκῆσαι καὶ πῆμα Ἰαπύγεσσι γενέσθαι.

ἦκον οὖν σὺν Φαλάνθῳ οἱ Παρθενίαι, καὶ ἐδέξαντο
αὐτοὺς οἵ τε βάρβαροι καὶ οἱ Κρῆτες οἱ προκατα-
σχόντες τὸν τόπον. τούτους δ᾽ εἶναί φασι τοὺς
μετὰ Μίνω πλεύσαντας εἰς Σικελίαν, καὶ μετὰ
τὴν ἐκείνου τελευτὴν τὴν ἐν Καμικοῖς παρὰ
Κωκάλῳ συμβᾶσαν ἀπάραντας ἐκ Σικελίας, κατὰ
δὲ τὸν ἀνάπλουν δεῦρο παρωσθέντας, ὧν τινας
ὕστερον πεζῇ περιελθόντας τὸν Ἀδρίαν μέχρι

---

[1] For ὀνομασθεῖσι, Corais reads νομισθεῖσι, and so read
Müller-Dübner ; Meineke conj. ἐτοιμασθεῖσι or ὁμολογηθεῖσι,
but reads (with asterisk) ὀνομασθεῖσι.

[2] ἐξαγγειλάντων, Meineke, following Bκ, for ἐξαγγείλαντες.

[3] ἄν, before περιθέσθαι, Corais, following the Epit., deletes ;
so Meineke ; περιθέσθαι is the reading of the Epit., περιθῆναι
of B, and περιθεῖναι of the other MSS.

[4] μεμηνύκασι, Müller-Dübner emend to μεμήνυται ; Meineke
suspects μεμηνύκασι.

---

[1] The temple of Amyclaean Apollo.

the attack should be made at the Hyacinthian
festival in the Amyclaeum[1] when the games were
being celebrated, at the moment when Phalanthus
should put on his leather cap (the free citizens were
recognizable by their hair[2]); but when Phalanthus
and his men had secretly reported the agreement,
and when the games were in progress, the herald
came forward and forbade Phalanthus to put on a
leather cap; and when the plotters perceived that
the plot had been revealed, some of them began to
run away and others to beg for mercy; but they
were bidden to be of good cheer and were given
over to custody; Phalanthus, however, was sent
to the temple of the god[3] to consult with reference
to founding a colony; and the god responded, "I
give to thee Satyrium, both to take up thine abode
in the rich land of Taras and to become a bane to
the Iapygians." Accordingly, the Partheniae went
thither with Phalanthus, and they were welcomed
by both the barbarians and the Cretans who had
previously taken possession of the place. These
latter, it is said, are the people who sailed with
Minos to Sicily, and, after his death, which occurred
at the home of Cocalus in Camici,[4] set sail from
Sicily; but on the voyage back[5] they were driven
out of their course to Taras, although later some
of them went afoot around the Adrias[6] as far as

---

[2] *i.e.* by the length of it. According to Plutarch (*Lysander*
1) the wearing of long hair by the Spartans dated back to
Lycurgus (the ninth century B.C.), but according to Herodotus
(1. 82) they wore their hair short till the battle of Thyrea (in
the sixth century B.C.), when by legal enactment they began
to wear it long.

[3] At Delphi.
[5] Back to Crete.
[4] Cp. 6. 2. 6.
[6] The Adriatic.

STRABO

Μακεδονίας Βοττιαίους[1] προσαγορευθῆναι. Ἰάπυγας δὲ λεχθῆναι πάντας φασὶ μέχρι τῆς Δαυνίας ἀπὸ Ἰάπυγος, ὃν ἐκ Κρήσσης γυναικὸς Δαιδάλῳ γενέσθαι φασὶ καὶ ἡγήσασθαι τῶν Κρητῶν· Τάραντα δ' ὠνόμασαν ἀπὸ ἥρωός τινος τὴν πόλιν.

3. Ἔφορος δ' οὕτω λέγει περὶ τῆς κτίσεως· ἐπολέμουν Λακεδαιμόνιοι Μεσσηνίοις, ἀποκτείνασι τὸν βασιλέα Τήλεκλον εἰς Μεσσήνην ἀφικόμενον ἐπὶ θυσίαν, ὁμόσαντες μὴ πρότερον ἐπανήξειν οἴκαδε, πρὶν ἢ Μεσσήνην ἀνελεῖν ἢ πάντας ἀποθανεῖν· φύλακας δὲ τῆς πόλεως κατέλιπον στρατεύοντες τούς τε νεωτάτους καὶ πρεσβυτάτους τῶν πολιτῶν. δεκάτῳ δ' ὕστερον ἔτει[2] τοῦ πολέμου τὰς γυναῖκας τῶν Λακεδαιμονίων συνελθούσας ἐξ ἑαυτῶν πέμψαι τινὰς παρὰ τοὺς ἄνδρας τὰς μεμψαμένας, ὡς οὐκ ἐπ' ἴσοις πολεμοῖεν πρὸς τοὺς Μεσσηνίους· οἱ μὲν γὰρ μένοντες τεκνοποιοῦνται, οἱ δὲ χήρας ἀφέντες τὰς γυναῖκας ἐν τῇ πολεμίᾳ ἐστρατοπέδευον· καὶ κίνδυνος εἴη λειπανδρῆσαι τὴν πατρίδα. οἱ δ' ἅμα καὶ τὸν ὅρκον φυλάττοντες καὶ τὸν τῶν γυναικῶν λόγον ἐν νῷ θέμενοι πέμπουσι τῆς στρατιᾶς τοὺς εὐρωστοτάτους ἅμα καὶ νεωτάτους, οὓς ᾔδεσαν οὐ μετασχόντας τῶν ὅρκων διὰ τὸ παῖδας ἔτι ὄντας συνεξελθεῖν τοῖς ἐν ἡλικίᾳ· προσέταξαν δὲ συγγίγνεσθαι ταῖς παρθένοις ἀπάσαις ἅπαντας, ἡγού-

---

[1] Βοττιαίους, all the editors, for βουγείους (ABl), βουκείους (C); cp. Βοττιαίαν (6. 3. 6).
[2] ἔτει, after ὕστερον, is omitted in ABCl.

Macedonia and were called Bottiaeans. But all the people as far as Daunia, it is said, were called Iapyges, after Iapyx, who is said to have been the son of Daedalus by a Cretan woman and to have been the leader of the Cretans. The city of Taras, however, was named after some hero.

3. But Ephorus describes the founding of the city thus: The Lacedaemonians were at war with the Messenians because the latter had killed their king Teleclus when he went to Messene to offer sacrifice, and they swore that they would not return home again until they either destroyed Messene or were all killed; and when they set out on the expedition, they left behind the youngest and the oldest of the citizens to guard the city; but later on, in the tenth year of the war, the Lacedaemonian women met together and sent certain of their own number to make complaint to their husbands that they were carrying on the war with the Messenians on unequal terms, for the Messenians, staying in their own country, were begetting children, whereas they, having abandoned their wives to widowhood, were on an expedition in the country of the enemy, and they complained that the fatherland was in danger of being in want of men; and the Lacedaemonians, both keeping their oath and at the same time bearing in mind the argument of the women, sent the men who were most vigorous and at the same time youngest, for they knew that these had not taken part in the oaths, because they were still children when they went out to war along with the men who were of military age; and they ordered them to cohabit with the maidens, every man with every maiden, thinking that thus the maidens would

STRABO

μενοι πολυτεκνήσειν μᾶλλον· γενομένων δὲ τούτων,
οἱ μὲν παῖδες ὠνομάσθησαν Παρθενίαι. Μεσσήνη
δὲ ἑάλω πολεμηθεῖσα ἐννεακαίδεκα ἔτη, καθάπερ
καὶ Τυρταῖός φησιν·

> ἀμφ᾽ αὐτὴν[1] δ᾽ ἐμάχοντ᾽ ἐννεακαίδεκ᾽ ἔτη,
> νωλεμέως αἰεὶ ταλασίφρονα θυμὸν ἔχοντες,
> αἰχμηταὶ πατέρων ἡμετέρων πατέρες.
> εἰκοστῷ δ᾽ οἱ μὲν κατὰ πίονα ἔργα λιπόντες
> φεῦγον Ἰθωμαίων ἐκ μεγάλων ὀρέων.

C 280 τὴν μὲν οὖν Μεσσηνίαν κατενείμαντο, ἐπανελ-
θόντες δ᾽ οἴκαδε τοὺς Παρθενίας οὐχ ὁμοίως τοῖς
ἄλλοις ἐτίμων, ὡς οὐκ ἐκ γάμου γεγονότας· οἱ
συνιστάμενοι μετὰ τῶν Εἰλώτων ἐπεβούλευσαν
τοῖς Λακεδαιμονίοις καὶ συνέθεντο ἆραι σύσσημον
ἐν τῇ ἀγορᾷ πῖλον Λακωνικόν, ἐπειδὰν ἐγχειρῶσι.
τῶν δὲ Εἰλώτων τινὲς ἐξαγγείλαντες, τὸ μὲν
ἀντεπιτίθεσθαι χαλεπὸν ἔγνωσαν· καὶ γὰρ πολλοὺς εἶναι καὶ πάντας ὁμόφρονας, ὡς ἂν ἀλλήλων
ἀδελφοὺς νομιζομένους· τοὺς μέλλοντας δ᾽ αἴρειν
τὸ σύσσημον ἐκ τῆς ἀγορᾶς ἀπιέναι προσέταξαν.
οἱ μὲν δὴ μεμηνυμένην αἰσθόμενοι τὴν πρᾶξιν
ἐπέσχον, οἱ δὲ διὰ τῶν πατέρων ἔπεισαν αὐτοὺς
εἰς ἀποικίαν ἐξελθεῖν· κἂν μὲν κατάσχωσιν
ἀρκοῦντα τὸν τόπον, μένειν, εἰ δὲ μή, τῆς
Μεσσηνίας τὸ πέμπτον κατανείμασθαι μέρος
ἐπανιόντας. οἱ δὲ σταλέντες κατέλαβον[2] τοὺς
Ἀχαιοὺς πολεμοῦντας τοῖς βαρβάροις, μετασχόντες δὲ τῶν κινδύνων κτίζουσι τὴν Τάραντα.
4. Ἴσχυσαν δέ ποτε οἱ Ταραντῖνοι καθ᾽ ὑπερβο-

---

[1] ἀμφ᾽ αὐτήν, Kramer, for ἄμφω τώδε; so the later editors.
[2] κατέλαβον (marg. B sec. m.) for κατελάβοντο (ACl),
κατεβάλοντο (B); so the other editors.

112

bear many more children; and when this was done, the children were named Partheniae. But as for Messene, it was captured after a war of nineteen years, as Tyrtaeus says: "About it they fought for nineteen years, relentlessly, with heart ever steadfast, did the fathers of our fathers, spearmen they; and in the twentieth the people forsook their fertile farms and fled from the great mountains of Ithome." Now the Lacedaemonians divided up Messenia among themselves, but when they came on back home they would not honour the Partheniae with civic rights like the rest, on the ground that they had been born out of wedlock; and the Partheniae, leaguing with the Helots, formed a plot against the Lacedaemonians and agreed to raise a Laconian cap in the market-place as a signal for the attack. But though some of the Helots had revealed the plot, the Lacedaemonians decided that it would be difficult to make a counter-attack against them, for the Helots were not only numerous but were all of one mind, regarding themselves as virtually brothers of one another, and merely charged those who were about to raise the signal to go away from the market-place. So the plotters, on learning that the undertaking had been betrayed, held back, and the Lacedaemonians persuaded them, through the influence of their fathers, to go forth and found a colony, and if the place they took possession of sufficed them, to stay there, but if not, to come on back and divide among themselves the fifth part of Messenia. And they, thus sent forth, found the Achaeans at war with the barbarians, took part in their perils, and founded Taras.

4 At one time the Tarantini were exceedingly

STRABO

λήν, πολιτευόμενοι δημοκρατικῶς· καὶ γὰρ ναυτικὸν
ἐκέκτηντο μέγιστον τῶν ταύτῃ καὶ πεζοὺς ἔστελλον
τρισμυρίους, ἱππέας δὲ τρισχιλίους, ἱππάρχους
δὲ χιλίους. ἀπεδέξαντο δὲ καὶ τὴν Πυθαγόρειον
φιλοσοφίαν, διαφερόντως δ' Ἀρχύτας, ὃς καὶ
προέστη τῆς πόλεως πολὺν χρόνον. ἐξίσχυσε δ'
ἡ ὕστερον τρυφὴ διὰ τὴν εὐδαιμονίαν, ὥστε τὰς
πανδήμους ἑορτὰς πλείους ἄγεσθαι κατ' ἔτος παρ'
αὐτοῖς ἢ τὰς ἡμέρας· ἐκ δὲ τούτου καὶ χεῖρον ἐπολι-
τεύοντο. ἐν δὲ τῶν φαύλων πολιτευμάτων τεκμή-
ριόν ἐστι τὸ ξενικοῖς στρατηγοῖς χρῆσθαι· καὶ γὰρ
τὸν Μολοττὸν Ἀλέξανδρον μετεπέμψαντο ἐπὶ
Μεσσαπίους καὶ Λευκανούς, καὶ ἔτι πρότερον Ἀρχί-
δαμον τὸν Ἀγησιλάου καὶ ὕστερον Κλεώνυμον καὶ
Ἀγαθοκλέα, εἶτα Πύρρον, ἡνίκα συνέστησαν πρὸς
Ῥωμαίους. οὐδ' ἐκείνοις δ' εὐπειθεῖν ἠδύναντο
οὓς ἐπεκαλοῦντο, ἀλλ' εἰς ἔχθραν αὐτοὺς καθί-
στασαν. ὁ γοῦν Ἀλέξανδρος τὴν κοινὴν Ἑλλήνων τῶν ταύτῃ πανήγυριν, ἣν ἔθος ἦν ἐν Ἡρακλείᾳ
συντελεῖν τῆς Ταραντίνης, μετάγειν ἐπειρᾶτο εἰς
τὴν Θουρίαν κατὰ ἔχθος, ἐκέλευέ τε κατὰ τὸν

---

[1] Archytas (about 427-347 B.C.), besides being chosen
seven times as chief magistrate ("strategus") of Tarentum,
was famous as general, Pythagorean philosopher, mathema-
tician, and author. Aristotle and Aristoxenus wrote works
on his life and writings, but both of these works are now
lost.

[2] Alexander I was appointed king of Epeirus by Philip of
Macedonia about 342 B.C., and was killed by a Leucanian
about 330 B.C. (cp. 6. 1. 5).

[3] Archidamus III, king of Sparta, was born about 400 B.C.
and lost his life in 338 B.C. in this war.

[4] Little is known of this Cleonymus, save that he was the
son of Cleomenes II, who reigned at Sparta 370-309 B.C.

114

powerful, that is, when they enjoyed a democratic government; for they not only had acquired the largest fleet of all peoples in that part of the world but were wont to send forth an army of thirty thousand infantry, three thousand cavalry, and one thousand commanders of cavalry. Morever, the Pythagorean philosophy was embraced by them, but especially by Archytas,[1] who presided over the city for a considerable time. But later, because of their prosperity, luxury prevailed to such an extent that the public festivals celebrated among them every year were more in number than the days of the year; and in consequence of this they also were poorly governed. One evidence of their bad policies is the fact that they employed foreign generals; for they sent for Alexander[2] the Molossian to lead them in their war against the Messapians and Leucanians, and, still before that, for Archidamus,[3] the son of Agesilaüs, and, later on, for Cleonymus,[4] and Agathocles,[5] and then for Pyrrhus,[6] at the time when they formed a league with him against the Romans. And yet even to those whom they called in they could not yield a ready obedience, and would set them at enmity. At all events, it was out of enmity that Alexander tried to transfer to Thurian territory the general festival assembly of all Greek peoples in that part of the world—the assembly which was wont to meet at Heracleia in Tarantine territory, and that he began to urge that a place for

[5] Agathocles (b. about 361 B.C.–d. 289 B.C.) was a tyrant of Syracuse. He appears to have led the Tarantini about 300 B.C.

[6] Pyrrhus (about 318–272 B.C.), king of Epeirus, accepted the invitation of Tarentum in 281 B.C.

'Ακάλανδρον ποταμὸν τειχίζειν τόπον, ὅπου
ἔσοιντο αἱ σύνοδοι· καὶ δὴ καὶ ἡ συμβᾶσα αὐτῷ
κακοπραγία διὰ τὴν ἐκείνων ἀγνωμοσύνην ἀπαν-
C 281 τῆσαι λέγεται. περί[1] τε τὰ 'Αννίβεια καὶ τὴν
ἐλευθερίαν ἀφῃρέθησαν, ὕστερον δ' ἀποικίαν
'Ρωμαίων δεξάμενοι καθ' ἡσυχίαν ζῶσι καὶ βέλτιον
ἢ πρότερον· πρὸς δὲ Μεσσαπίους ἐπολέμησαν περὶ
'Ηρακλείας, ἔχοντες συνεργοὺς τόν τε τῶν Δαυνίων
καὶ τὸν τῶν Πευκετίων βασιλέα.

5. Ἡ δ' ἑξῆς τῶν 'Ιαπύγων χώρα παραδόξως
ἐστὶν ἀστεία· ἐπιπολῆς γὰρ φαινομένη τραχεῖα
εὑρίσκεται βαθύγειος σχιζομένη, ἀνυδροτέρα δ'
οὖσα εὔβοτος οὐδὲν ἧσσον καὶ εὔδενδρος ὁρᾶται.
εὐάνδρησε δέ ποτε καὶ τοῦτο σφόδρα τὸ χωρίον
σύμπαν καὶ ἔσχε πόλεις τρισκαίδεκα, ἀλλὰ νῦν
πλὴν Τάραντος καὶ Βρεντεσίου τἆλλα πολισ-
μάτιά[2] ἐστιν, οὕτως ἐκπεπόνηνται. τοὺς δὲ
Σαλεντίνους Κρητῶν ἀποίκους φασίν· ἐνταῦθα
δ' ἐστὶ καὶ τὸ τῆς 'Αθηνᾶς ἱερὸν πλούσιόν ποτε
ὑπάρξαν καὶ ὁ σκόπελος, ὃν καλοῦσιν ἄκραν
'Ιαπυγίαν, πολὺς ἐκκείμενος εἰς τὸ πέλαγος κατὰ[3]
τὰς χειμερινὰς ἀνατολάς, ἐπιστρέφων δέ πως ἐπὶ
τὸ Λακίνιον, ἀνταῖρον ἀπὸ τῆς ἑσπέρας αὐτῷ,
καὶ κλεῖον τὸ στόμα τοῦ Ταραντίνου κόλπου πρὸς
αὐτόν. καὶ τὰ Κεραύνια δ' ὁμοίως ὄρη κλείει
πρὸς αὐτὸν τὸ στόμα τοῦ 'Ιονίου κόλπου, καὶ
ἔστι τὸ δίαρμα ὅσον ἑπτακοσίων σταδίων ἀπ'
αὐτοῦ πρός τε τὰ Κεραύνια καὶ πρὸς τὸ Λακίνιον.

---

[1] Meineke transposes περί τε ... πρότερον to a position
after πρὸς δὲ ... βασιλέα.
[2] πολισμάτια, Kramer, for πολίσματα; so the later editors.
[3] κατά, after πέλαγος, Meineke emends to καί.

the meetings be fortified on the Acalandrus River. Furthermore, it is said that the unhappy end which befell him[1] was the result of their ingratitude. Again, about the time of the wars with Hannibal, they were deprived of their freedom, although later they received a colony of Romans, and are now living at peace and better than before. In their war against the Messapians for the possession of Heracleia, they had the co-operation of the king of the Daunians and the king of the Peucetians.

5. That part of the country of the Iapygians which comes next is fine, though in an unexpected way; for although on the surface it appears rough, it is found to be deep-soiled when ploughed, and although it is rather lacking in water, it is manifestly none the less good for pasturage and for trees. The whole of this district was once extremely populous; and it also had thirteen cities; but now, with the exception of Taras and Brentesium, all of them are so worn out by war that they are merely small towns. The Salentini are said to be a colony of the Cretans. The temple of Athene, once so rich, is in their territory, as also the look-out-rock called Cape Iapygia, a huge rock which extends out into the sea towards the winter sunrise,[2] though it bends approximately towards the Lacinium, which rises opposite to it on the west and with it bars the mouth of the Tarantine Gulf. And with it the Ceraunian Mountains, likewise, bar the mouth of the Ionian Gulf; the passage across from it both to the Ceraunian Mountains and to the Lacinium is about seven hundred stadia. But the distance by sea from Taras around to

[1] 6. 1. 5.   [2] *i.e.* south-east.

περίπλους δ᾽ ἐκ[1] Τάραντός ἐστιν εἰς[2] Βρεντέσιον
μέχρι μὲν Βάριδος[3] πολίχνης ἑξακόσιοι στάδιοι.
καλοῦσι δὲ Βᾶριν οἱ νῦν Οὐερητόν, κεῖται δ᾽ ἐπὶ
τοῖς ἄκροις τῆς Σαλεντίνης, καὶ τὸ πολὺ πεζῇ
μᾶλλον ἢ κατὰ πλοῦν εἰς αὐτὴν ἐκ τοῦ Τάραντος
εὐμαρὴς ἡ ἄφιξίς ἐστιν. ἔνθεν εἰς τὰ Λευκὰ
στάδιοι ὀγδοήκοντα, πολίχνιον καὶ τοῦτο, ἐν ᾧ
δείκνυται πηγὴ δυσώδους ὕδατος· μυθεύουσι δ᾽
ὅτι τοὺς περιλειφθέντας τῶν Γιγάντων ἐν τῇ
κατὰ Καμπανίαν Φλέγρᾳ, Λευτερνίους καλουμένους, Ἡρακλῆς ἐξελάσειε, καταφυγόντες δὲ[4]
δεῦρο ὑπὸ Γῆς περισταλεῖν, ἐκ δὲ ἰχώρων τοιοῦτον
ἴσχει[5] ῥεῦμα ἡ πηγή· διὰ τοῦτο δὲ καὶ τὴν
παραλίαν ταύτην Λευτερνίαν προσαγορεύουσιν.
ἐκ δὲ τῶν Λευκῶν εἰς Ὑδροῦντα πολίχνην ἑκατὸν
πεντήκοντα· ἐντεῦθεν δ᾽ εἰς Βρεντέσιον τετρα-
κόσιοι. οἱ δ᾽ ἴσοι καὶ εἰς Σάσωνα τὴν νῆσον,
ἥτις μέση πως ἵδρυται τοῦ διάρματος τοῦ ἐκ
τῆς Ἠπείρου πρὸς τὸ Βρεντέσιον· διόπερ οἱ μὴ
δυνάμενοι κρατεῖν τῆς εὐθυπλοίας καταίρουσιν
ἐν ἀριστερᾷ ἐκ τοῦ Σάσωνος πρὸς τὸν Ὑδροῦντα,
ἐντεῦθεν δὲ τηρήσαντες φορὸν πνεῦμα προσέχουσι
τοῖς μὲν Βρεντεσίνων λιμέσιν, ἐκβάντες δὲ πεζεύ-
ουσι συντομώτερον ἐπὶ Ῥοδιῶν, πόλεως Ἑλλη-
C 282 νίδος, ἐξ ἧς ἦν ὁ ποιητὴς Ἔννιος. ἔοικεν οὖν
χερρονήσῳ τὸ περιπλεόμενον χωρίον ἐκ Τάραντος
εἰς Βρεντέσιον· ἡ δ᾽ ἐκ Βρεντεσίου πεζευομένη

---

[1] δ᾽ ἐκ (hi), for δέ; so all editors. [2] εἰς, Meineke, for ἐς.
[3] Βάριδος, Corais, for Βάριτος (Bl), Βάρητος (AC); so the later editors.
[4] καταφυγόντες δέ, Corais, for καταφυγόντας; so the later editors.

118

Brentesium is as follows: First, to the small town of Baris, six hundred stadia; Baris is called by the people of to-day Veretum, is situated at the edge of the Salentine territory, and the trip thither from Taras is for the most part easier to make on foot than by sailing. Thence to Leuca eighty stadia; this, too, is a small town, and in it is to be seen a fountain of malodorous water; the mythical story is told that those of the Giants who survived at the Campanian Phlegra[1] and are called the Leuternian Giants were driven out by Heracles, and on fleeing hither for refuge were shrouded by Mother Earth, and the fountain gets its malodorous stream from the ichor of their bodies; and for this reason, also, the seaboard here is called Leuternia. Again, from Leuca to Hydrus,[2] a small town, one hundred and fifty stadia. Thence to Brentesium four hundred; and it is an equal distance to the island Sason,[3] which is situated about midway of the distance across from Epeirus to Brentesium. And therefore those who cannot accomplish the straight voyage sail to the left of Sason and put in at Hydrus; and then, watching for a favourable wind, they hold their course towards the harbours of the Brentesini, although if they disembark, they go afoot by a shorter route by way of Rodiae,[4] a Greek city, where the poet Ennius was born. So then, the district one sails around in going from Taras to Brentesium resembles a peninsula, and the overland

[1] See 5. 4. 4 and 5. 4. 6.
[2] Also called Hydruntum; now Otranto.
[3] Now Sasena.   [4] Also called Rudiae; now Rugge.

---

[5] ἴσχει, Jones restores, for ἴσχοι.

ὁδὸς εἰς τὸν Τάραντα, εὐζώνῳ μιᾶς οὖσα ἡμέρας, τὸν ἰσθμὸν ποιεῖ τῆς εἰρημένης χερρονήσου, ἣν Μεσσαπίαν τε καὶ Ἰαπυγίαν καὶ Καλαβρίαν καὶ Σαλεντίνην κοινῶς οἱ πολλοὶ προσαγορεύουσι· τινὲς δὲ διαιροῦσιν, ὡς ἐλέγομεν πρότερον. τὰ μὲν οὖν ἐν τῷ παράπλῳ πολίχνια εἴρηται.

6. Ἐν δὲ τῇ μεσογαίᾳ Ῥοδίαι τέ εἰσι καὶ Λουπίαι καὶ μικρὸν ὑπὲρ τῆς θαλάττης Ἀλητία· ἐπὶ δὲ τῷ ἰσθμῷ μέσῳ Οὐρία,[1] ἐν ᾗ[2] βασίλειον ἔτι δείκνυται τῶν δυναστῶν[3] τινος. εἰρηκότος δ᾽ Ἡροδότου Ὑρίαν[4] εἶναι ἐν τῇ Ἰαπυγίᾳ, κτίσμα Κρητῶν τῶν πλανηθέντων ἐκ τοῦ Μίνω στόλου τοῦ εἰς Σικελίαν, ἤτοι αὐτὴν δεῖ δέχεσθαι ἢ τὸ Οὐερητόν. Βρεντέσιον δ᾽ ἐποικῆσαι μὲν λέγονται Κρῆτες, οἱ μετὰ Θησέως ἐπελθόντες ἐκ Κνωσσοῦ, εἶθ᾽ οἱ ἐκ τῆς Σικελίας ἀπηρκότες μετὰ τοῦ Ἰάπυγος (λέγεται γὰρ ἀμφοτέρως), οὐ συμμεῖναι δέ φασιν αὐτούς, ἀλλὰ ἀπελθεῖν εἰς τὴν Βοττιαίαν. ὕστερον δὲ ἡ πόλις βασιλευομένη πολλὴν ἀπέβαλε τῆς χώρας ὑπὸ τῶν μετὰ Φαλάνθου Λακεδαιμονίων, ὅμως δ᾽ ἐκπεσόντα αὐτὸν ἐκ τοῦ Τάραντος ἐδέξαντο οἱ Βρεντεσῖνοι, καὶ τελευτήσαντα ἠξίωσαν λαμπρᾶς ταφῆς. χώραν δ᾽ ἔχουσι βελτίω τῆς Ταραντίνων· λεπτόγεως γὰρ ἐκείνη, χρηστόκαρπος δέ, μέλι δὲ καὶ ἔρια τῶν σφόδρα ἐπαινουμένων ἐστί. καὶ εὐλίμενον δὲ μᾶλλον τὸ Βρεντέσιον·

[1] Οὐρία, Cluver, for Θυρέαι (AC), Θυραῖαι (Bl); so the editors.

[2] ᾗ, Siebenkees, for ᾧ; so the later editors.

[3] δυναστῶν (Bl), for δυνατῶν; so Siebenkees, Corais, and Meineke.

[4] Ὑρίαν, Cluver, for Οὐρίαν; so the later editors.

journey from Brentesium to Taras, which is only a one
day's journey for a man well-girt, forms the isthmus
of the aforesaid peninsula;[1] and this peninsula most
people call by one general name Messapia, or
Iapygia, or Calabria, or Salentina, although some
divide it up, as I have said before.[2] So much, then,
for the towns on the sea-coast.

6. In the interior are Rodiae and Lupiae, and,
slightly above the sea, Aletia; and at the middle
of the isthmus, Uria, in which is still to be seen
the palace of one of the chieftains. When Herodotus[3] states that Hyria is in Iapygia and was
founded by the Cretans who strayed from the
fleet of Minos when on its way to Sicily,[4] we must
understand Hyria to be either Uria or Veretum.
Brentesium, they say, was further colonised by the
Cretans, whether by those who came over with
Theseus from Cnossus or by those who set sail from
Sicily with Iapyx (the story is told both ways),
although they did not stay together there, it is said,
but went off to Bottiaea.[5] Later on, however, when
ruled by kings, the city lost much of its country
to the Lacedaemonians who were under the leadership of Phalanthus; but still, when he was ejected
from Taras, he was admitted by the Brentesini, and
when he died was counted by them worthy of a
splendid burial. Their country is better than that
of the Tarantini, for, though the soil is thin, it
produces good fruits, and its honey and wool are
among those that are strongly commended. Brentesium is also better supplied with harbours; for

[1] 6. 3. 1.   [2] 6. 3. 1.   [3] 7. 170.   [4] Cp. 6. 3. 2.
[5] Cp. 6. 3. 2, where Antiochus says that some of them
went to Bottiaea.

ἑνὶ γὰρ στόματι πολλοὶ κλείονται λιμένες ἄκλι-
στοι, κόλπων ἀπολαμβανομένων ἐντός, ὥστ᾽
ἐοικέναι κέρασιν ἐλάφου τὸ σχῆμα, ἀφ᾽ οὗ καὶ
τοὔνομα· σὺν γὰρ τῇ πόλει κεφαλῇ μάλιστα
ἐλάφου προσέοικεν ὁ τόπος, τῇ δὲ Μεσσαπίᾳ
γλώττῃ βρεντέσιον¹ ἡ κεφαλὴ τοῦ ἐλάφου
καλεῖται. ὁ δὲ Ταραντῖνος οὐ παντελῶς ἐστιν
ἄκλυστος διὰ τὸ ἀναπεπτάσθαι, καί τινα καὶ
προσβραχῆ ἔχει τὰ περὶ τὸν μυχόν.

7. Ἐν² δὲ τοῖς ἀπὸ τῆς Ἑλλάδος καὶ τῆς
Ἀσίας διαίρουσιν εὐθύπλοια μᾶλλόν ἐστι ἐπὶ
τὸ Βρεντέσιον, καὶ δὴ καὶ δεῦρο πάντες καταίρουσιν, οἷς εἰς τὴν Ῥώμην πρόκειται ὁδός. δύο
δέ εἰσι, μία μὲν ἡμιονικὴ διὰ Πευκετίων, οὓς
Ποιδίκλους καλοῦσι, καὶ Δαυνίων καὶ Σαυνιτῶν
μέχρι Βενεουεντοῦ,³ ἐφ᾽ ᾗ ὁδῷ Ἐγνατία⁴ πόλις,
εἶτα Κελία⁵ καὶ Νήτιον καὶ Κανύσιον καὶ
C 283 Ἑρδωνία·⁶ ἡ δὲ διὰ Τάραντος, μικρὸν ἐν ἀριστερᾷ,
ὅσον δὲ⁷ μιᾶς ἡμέρας περίοδον κυκλεύσαντι, ἡ

¹ βρεντέσιον, Cluver emends to βρέντιον; so Corais and
Meineke. See Steph. Byz. and *Etym. M.*, but also Eustath.
ad Od., p. 1409.
² ἐν (the reading of all MSS.), Jones restores, for ἔτι, the
emendation of Xylander and subsequent editors.
³ Βενεουεντοῦ, all editors, for Οὐενουεντοῦ.
⁴ Ἰγνατία (B*l*).
⁵ For Κελία, Meineke writes Καιλία.
⁶ Ἑρδωνία, Meineke, for Κερδωνία.
⁷ δέ (the reading of all MSS.), Jones restores, for δή, the
emendation of Kramer and subsequent editors.

---

¹ So, too, the gulf, or bay, at Byzantium resembles a
stag's horn (7. 6. 2).
² Stephanus Byzantinus says: "According to Seleucus,

here many harbours are closed in by one mouth; and they are sheltered from the waves, because bays are formed inside in such a way as to resemble in shape a stag's horns;[1] and hence the name, for, along with the city, the place very much resembles a stag's head, and in the Messapian language the head of the stag is called "brentesium."[2] But the Tarantine harbour, because of its wide expanse, is not wholly sheltered from the waves; and besides there are some shallows in the innermost part of it.[3]

7. In the case of those who sail across from Greece or Asia, the more direct route is to Brentesium, and, in fact, all who propose to go to Rome by land put into port here. There are two roads[4] from here: one, a mule-road through the countries of the Peucetii (who are called Poedicli),[5] the Daunii, and the Samnitae as far as Beneventum; on this road is the city of Egnatia,[6] and then, Celia,[7] Netium,[8] Canusium,[9] and Herdonia.[10] But the road by way of Taras, lying slightly to the left of the other, though as much as one day's journey

in his second book on *Languages*, *brentium* is the Messapian word for *the head of the stag.*" Hence the editors who emend "brentesium" to "brentium" are almost certainly correct.

[3] Here, as in 6. 3. 1., Strabo is speaking of the inner harbour (Mare Piccolo), not the outer, of which, as Tozer (p. 184) says, Strabo takes no account.

[4] On these roads see Ashby and Gardner, *The Via Trajana*, Papers of the British School at Rome, 1916, Vol. VIII, No. 5, pp. 107 ff.

[5] Cp. 6. 3. 1.

[6] Also spelled Gnathia, Gnatia, and Ignatia; now Torre d'Agnazzo.

[7] Also spelled Caelia; now Ceglie di Bari.

[8] Now Noja.   [9] Now Canosa.   [10] Now Ordona.

'Αππία λεγομένη, ἁμαξήλατος μᾶλλον· ἐν ταύτῃ
δὲ πόλις Οὐρία τε καὶ Οὐενουσία, ἡ μὲν μεταξὺ
Τάραντος καὶ Βρεντεσίου, ἡ δ' ἐν¹ μεθορίοις
Σαυνιτῶν καὶ Λευκανῶν. συμβάλλουσι δὲ ἄμφω
κατὰ Βενεουεντὸν² καὶ τὴν Καμπανίαν ἐκ τοῦ
Βρεντεσίου. τοὐντεῦθεν δ' ἤδη μέχρι τῆς Ῥώμης
'Αππία καλεῖται, διὰ Καυδίου καὶ Καλατίας καὶ
Καπύης καὶ Κασιλίνου μέχρι Σινοέσσης.³ τὰ δ'
ἐνθένδε εἴρηται. ἡ δὲ πᾶσά ἐστιν ἐκ Ῥώμης εἰς
Βρεντέσιον μίλια τριακόσια ἑξήκοντα. τρίτη δ'
ἐστὶν ἐκ Ῥηγίου διὰ Βρεττίων καὶ Λευκανῶν καὶ
τῆς Σαυνίτιδος εἰς τὴν Καμπανίαν, συνάπτουσα
εἰς τὴν 'Αππίαν, μακροτέρα τῆς ἐκ Βρεντεσίου
τρισὶν ἢ τέτρασιν ἡμέραις διὰ τῶν 'Απεννίνων
ὀρῶν.

8. Ὁ δ' εἰς τὴν περαίαν ἐκ τοῦ Βρεντεσίου
πλοῦς⁴ ἐστιν, ὁ μὲν ἐπὶ τὰ Κεραύνια καὶ τὴν ἑξῆς
παραλίαν τῆς τε Ἠπείρου καὶ τῆς Ἑλλάδος, ὁ δ'
εἰς Ἐπίδαμνον, μείζων τοῦ προτέρου· χιλίων γάρ
ἐστι⁵ καὶ ὀκτακοσίων σταδίων· τέτριπται δὲ καὶ

---

¹ δ' ἐν, Corais, for δέ; so the later editors.
² Βενεουεντόν, all editors, for Οὐενουεντόν (ABC).
³ μέχρι Σινοέσσης, Tyrwhitt, for μέχρις Ὀνέσσης (ABCl),
μέχρις Οὐενουσίας (correction in t); so the editors.
⁴ The *Epit.* inserts διπλοῦς after πλοῦς; so Kramer and
Müller-Dübner.
⁵ For ἐστι καί, C. Müller proposes ἐστιν, ἐκεῖνος δέ; see
note on opposite page.

---

¹ *i.e.* to the point where it meets the other road, near
Beneventum.
² Now Montesarchio.   ³ Now Galazze.
⁴ The old Santa Maria di Capua, now in ruins ; not the
Capua of to-day, which is on the site of Casilinum.
⁵ Now Mondragone.

out of the way when one has made the circuit,[1] what is called the Appian Way, is better for carriages. On this road are the cities of Uria and Venusia, the former between Taras and Brentesium and the latter on the confines of the Samnitae and the Leucani. Both the roads from Brentesium meet near Beneventum and Campania. And the common road from here on, as far as Rome, is called the Appian Way, and passes through Caudium,[2] Calatia,[3] Capua,[4] and Casilinum to Sinuessa.[5] And the places from there on I have already mentioned. The total length of the road from Rome to Brentesium is three hundred and sixty miles. But there is also a third road, which runs from Rhegium through the countries of the Brettii, the Leucani, and the Samnitae into Campania, where it joins the Appian Way; it passes through the Apennine Mountains and it requires three or four days more than the road from Brentesium.

8. The voyage from Brentesium to the opposite mainland is made either to the Ceraunian Mountains and those parts of the seaboard of Epeirus and of Greece which come next to them, or else to Epidamnus; the latter is longer than the former, for it is one thousand eight hundred stadia.[6] And yet the latter is the usual route, because the city has

[6] Strabo has already said that the voyage from Brentesium to Epeirus by way of Sason (Saseno) was about 800 stadia (6. 3. 5). But Sason was much out of the way, and apparently was not on the regular route. Again, Epidamnus (now Durazzo) is in fact only about 800 stadia distant, not 1,800 as the text makes Strabo say. It is probable, therefore, that Strabo said either simply "for it is 800 stadia," or "for it is 1,000 stadia, while the former is 800."

οὗτος διὰ τὸ τὴν πόλιν εὐφυῶς κεῖσθαι πρός τε τὰ
τῶν Ἰλλυριῶν ἔθνη καὶ τὰ τῶν Μακεδόνων. παρα-
πλέοντι δ' ἐκ τοῦ Βρεντεσίου τὴν Ἀδριατικὴν
παραλίαν πόλις ἐστὶν ἡ Ἐγνατία,[1] οὖσα κοινὴ
καταγωγὴ πλέοντί τε καὶ πεζεύοντι εἰς Βάριον·
ὁ δὲ πλοῦς Νότῳ. μέχρι δεῦρο μὲν Πευκέτιοι[2]
κατὰ θάλατταν, ἐν[3] τῇ μεσογαίᾳ δὲ μέχρι
Σιλουίου. πᾶσα δὲ τραχεῖα καὶ ὀρεινή, πολὺ τῶν
Ἀπεννίνων ὀρῶν κοινωνοῦσα, ἀποίκους δ' Ἀρκά-
δας δέξασθαι δοκεῖ. εἰσὶ δ' ἐκ Βρεντεσίου εἰς
Βάριον ἑπτακόσιοί που στάδιοι· σχεδὸν δ' ἴσον
ἑκατέρας Τάρας[4] διέχει· τὴν δὲ συνεχῆ Δαύνιοι[5]
νέμονται, εἶτα Ἄπουλοι μέχρι Φρεντανῶν. ἀνάγκη
δέ, Πευκετίων καὶ Δαυνίων μηδ' ὅλως λεγομένων
ὑπὸ τῶν ἐπιχωρίων, πλὴν εἰ τὸ παλαιόν, ἁπάσης
δὲ ταύτης τῆς χώρας Ἀπουλίας λεγομένης νυνί,
μηδὲ τοὺς ὅρους ἐπ' ἀκριβὲς λέγεσθαι τῶν ἐθνῶν
τούτων· διόπερ οὐδ' ἡμῖν διισχυριστέον περὶ
αὐτῶν.

9. Ἐκ δὲ Βαρίου πρὸς τὸν ποταμὸν Αὔφιδον,
ἐφ' ᾧ τὸ ἐμπόριον τῶν Καννυσιτῶν, τετρακόσιοι·
ὁ δ' ἀνάπλους ἐπὶ τὸ ἐμπόριον ἐνενήκοντα. πλησίον
δὲ καὶ Σαλαπία, τὸ τῶν Ἀργυριππινῶν ἐπίνειον.
οὐ πολὺ γὰρ δὴ τῆς θαλάττης ὑπέρκεινται δύο

---

[1] Ἐγνατία, Xylander, for Στεγνατία; so the later editors.
[2] Πευκέτιοι, Xylander, for Πευκετίου; so the later editors.
[3] ἐν, before τῇ, Kramer inserts; so the later editors.
[4] Τάρας, after ἑκατέρας, Xylander inserts; so the later editors.
[5] Δαύνιοι (corrected in B sec. m.), for Καύνιοι; so the editors.

---

[1] Now Bari.   [2] To Barium.

a good position with reference both to the tribes of the Illyrians and to those of the Macedonians. As one sails from Brentesium along the Adriatic seaboard, one comes to the city of Egnatia, which is the common stopping-place for people who are travelling either by sea or land to Barium;[1] and the voyage is made with the south wind. The country of the Peucetii extends only thus far[2] on the sea, but in the interior as far as Silvium.[3] All of it is rugged and mountainous, since it embraces a large portion of the Apennine Mountains; and it is thought to have admitted Arcadians as colonists. From Brentesium to Barium is about seven hundred stadia, and Taras is about an equal distance from each. The adjacent country is inhabited by the Daunii; and then come the Apuli, whose country extends as far as that of the Frentani. But since the terms "Peucetii" and "Daunii" are not at all used by the native inhabitants, except in early times, and since this country as a whole is now called Apulia, necessarily the boundaries of these tribes cannot be told to a nicety either, and for this reason neither should I myself make positive assertions about them.

9. From Barium to the Aufidus River, on which is the Emporium of the Canusitae[4] is four hundred stadia and the voyage inland to Emporium is ninety. Near by is also Salapia,[5] the seaport of the Argyrippini. For not far above the sea (in the plain, at

---

[3] Silvium appears to have been on the site of what is now Garagone.

[4] This Emporium should probably be identified with the Canne of to-day (see Ashby and Gardner, *op. cit.*, p. 156).

[5] Now Salpi.

πόλεις, ἔν γε τῷ πεδίῳ, μέγισται τῶν Ἰταλιωτίδων
γεγονυῖαι πρότερον, ὡς ἐκ τῶν περιβόλων δῆλον,
τό τε Κανύσιον καὶ ἡ Ἀργυρίππα. ἀλλὰ νῦν
ἐλάττων[1] ἐστίν· ἐκαλεῖτο δ' ἐξ ἀρχῆς Ἄργος
Ἵππιον, εἶτ' Ἀργυρίππα, εἶτα νῦν Ἄρποι. λέγονται
C 284 δ' ἀμφότεραι Διομήδους κτίσματα, καὶ τὸ πεδίον
καὶ ἄλλα πολλὰ δείκνυται τῆς Διομήδους ἐν
τούτοις τοῖς τόποις δυναστείας σημεῖα. ἐν μὲν τῷ
τῆς Ἀθηνᾶς ἱερῷ τῆς ἐν Λουκερίᾳ παλαιὰ ἀναθή-
ματα· καὶ αὕτη δ' ὑπῆρξε πόλις ἀρχαία Δαυνίων,
νῦν δὲ τεταπείνωται. ἐν δὲ τῇ πλησίον θαλάττῃ
δύο νῆσοι Διομήδειαι προσαγορευόμεναι, ὧν ἡ μὲν
οἰκεῖται, τὴν δ' ἐρήμην φασὶν εἶναι· ἐν ᾗ καὶ τὸν
Διομήδη μυθεύουσιν ἀφανισθῆναί τινες καὶ τοὺς
ἑταίρους ἀπορνιθωθῆναι, καὶ δὴ καὶ νῦν διαμένειν
ἡμέρους καὶ βίον τινὰ ζῆν ἀνθρώπινον τάξει τε
διαίτης καὶ τῇ πρὸς ἀνθρώπους ἡμερότητι τοὺς
ἐπιεικεῖς, ἀπὸ δὲ τῶν κακούργων καὶ μιαρῶν φυγῇ.
εἴρηται δὲ καὶ τὰ παρὰ τοῖς Ἑνετοῖς διατεθρυλη-
μένα περὶ τοῦ ἥρωος τούτου καὶ αἱ νομισθεῖσαι
τιμαί. δοκεῖ δὲ καὶ ὁ Σιποῦς[2] Διομήδους εἶναι
κτίσμα, διέχων τῆς Σαλαπίας ὅσον τετταράκοντα
καὶ ἑκατὸν σταδίους, καὶ ὠνομάζετό γε Σηπιοῦς
Ἑλληνικῶς ἀπὸ τῶν ἐκκυματιζομένων σηπιῶν.
μεταξὺ δὲ τῆς Σαλαπίας καὶ τοῦ Σιποῦντος ποταμός τε πλωτὸς καὶ στομαλίμνη μεγάλη. δι' ἀμφοῖν
δὲ τὰ ἐκ Σιποῦντος κατάγεται, καὶ μάλιστα ὁ

---

[1] ἐλάττων, Meineke, for ἐλάττω.   [2] Σιπιοῦς (AC).

---

[1] Now Canosa.   [2] Now Arpino.   [3] Cp. 5. 1. 9.
[4] In Latin, Sipontum; now in ruins, near Santa Maria di
Siponto.

all events) are situated two cities, Canusium [1] and Argyrippa, [2] which in earlier times were the largest of the Italiote cities, as is clear from the circuits of their walls. Now, however, Argyrippa is smaller; it was called Argos Hippium at first, then Argyrippa, and then by the present name Arpi. Both are said to have been founded by Diomedes. [3] And as signs of the dominion of Diomedes in these regions are to be seen the Plain of Diomedes and many other things, among which are the old votive offerings in the temple of Athene at Luceria—a place which likewise was in ancient times a city of the Daunii, but is now reduced—and, in the sea near by, two islands that are called the Islands of Diomedes, of which one is inhabited, while the other, it is said, is desert; on the latter, according to certain narrators of myths, Diomedes was caused to disappear, and his companions were changed to birds, and to this day, in fact, remain tame and live a sort of human life, not only in their orderly ways but also in their tameness towards honourable men and in their flight from wicked and knavish men. But I have already mentioned the stories constantly told among the Heneti about this hero and the rites which are observed in his honour. [3] It is thought that Sipus [4] also was founded by Diomedes, which is about one hundred and forty stadia distant from Salapia; at any rate it was named "Sepius" in Greek after the "sepia" [5] that are cast ashore by the waves. Between Salapia and Sipus is a navigable river, and also a large lake that opens into the sea; and the merchandise from Sipus, particularly grain, is brought

[5] Cuttle-fish.

σῖτος. δείκνυται δὲ τῆς Δαυνίας περὶ λόφον, ᾧ
ὄνομα Δρίον, ἡρῷα, τὸ μὲν Κάλχαντος ἐπ' ἄκρᾳ
τῇ κορυφῇ· ἐναγίζουσι δ' αὐτῷ μέλανα κριὸν οἱ
μαντευόμενοι, ἐγκοιμώμενοι ἐν τῷ δέρματι· τὸ
δὲ Ποδαλειρίου κάτω πρὸς τῇ ῥίζῃ, διέχον τῆς
θαλάττης ὅσον σταδίους ἑκατόν· ῥεῖ δ' ἐξ αὐτοῦ
ποτάμιον πάνακες πρὸς τὰς τῶν θρεμμάτων νόσους.
πρόκειται δὲ τοῦ κόλπου τούτου πελάγιον ἀκρωτήριον ἐπὶ τριακοσίους ἀνατεῖνον σταδίους πρὸς
τὰς ἀνατολάς, τὸ Γάργανον, κάμπτοντι δὲ τὴν
ἄκραν πολισμάτιον Οὔριον, καὶ πρὸ τῆς ἄκρας αἱ
Διομήδειαι νῆσοι. ἔστι δὲ πᾶσα ἡ χώρα αὕτη
πάμφορός τε καὶ πολυφόρος, ἵπποις δὲ καὶ προβά-
τοις ἀρίστη· ἡ δ' ἐρέα μαλακωτέρα μὲν τῆς
Ταραντίνης ἐστί, λαμπρὰ δὲ ἧττον. ἡ δὲ χώρα
εὐδινὴ διὰ τὴν κοιλότητα τῶν πεδίων· οἱ δὲ καὶ
διώρυγα τεμεῖν ἐπιχειρῆσαί φασι τὸν Διομήδη
μέχρι τῆς θαλάττης, καταλιπεῖν δ' ἡμιτελῆ καὶ
ταύτην καὶ τὰς ἄλλας πράξεις μετάπεμπτον
οἴκαδε γενόμενον, κἀκεῖ καταστρέψαι τὸν βίον.
εἷς μὲν οὗτος ὁ λόγος περὶ αὐτοῦ, δεύτερος δ', ὡς
αὐτόθι μείνειε μέχρι καταστροφῆς τοῦ βίου, τρίτος
δ' ὁ μυθώδης, ὃν προεῖπον, τὸν ἐν τῇ νήσῳ λέγων
ἀφανισμόν, τέταρτον δὲ θείη τις ἂν τὸν τῶν
Ἐνετῶν· καὶ γὰρ ἐκεῖνοι παρά σφισί πως τὴν
καταστροφὴν αὐτοῦ μυθεύουσιν, ἣν ἀποθέωσιν
καλοῦσι.

10. Ταῦτα μὲν οὖν κατ' Ἀρτεμίδωρον κεῖται τὰ
C 285 διαστήματα. φησὶ δ' ὁ χωρογράφος τὰ ἀπὸ τοῦ

---

[1] Artemidorus (flourished about 100 B.C.), of Ephesus, was
an extensive traveller and a geographer of great importance.
He wrote a geography of the inhabited world in eleven

down on both. In Daunia, on a hill by the name of Drium, are to be seen two hero-temples: one, to Calchas, on the very summit, where those who consult the oracle sacrifice to his shade a black ram and sleep in the hide, and the other, to Podaleirius, down near the base of the hill, this temple being about one hundred stadia distant from the sea; and from it flows a stream which is a cure-all for diseases of animals. In front of this gulf is a promontory, Garganum, which extends towards the east for a distance of three hundred stadia into the high sea; doubling the headland, one comes to a small town, Urium, and off the headland are to be seen the Islands of Diomedes. This whole country produces everything in great quantity, and is excellent for horses and sheep; but though the wool is softer than the Tarantine, it is not so glossy. And the country is well sheltered, because the plains lie in hollows. According to some, Diomedes even tried to cut a canal as far as the sea, but left behind both this and the rest of his undertakings only half-finished, because he was summoned home and there ended his life. This is one account of him; but there is also a second, that he stayed here till the end of his life; and a third, the aforesaid mythical account, which tells of his disappearance in the island; and as a fourth one might set down the account of the Heneti, for they too tell a mythical story of how he in some way came to his end in their country, and they call it his apotheosis.

10. Now the above distances are put down in accordance with the data of Artemidorus[1]; but

books, a *Periplus* of the Mediterranean, and *Ionian Historical Sketches*. But his works, except numerous fragments preserved in other authors, are now lost.

STRABO

Βρεντεσίου μέχρι Γαργάνου μιλίων ἑκατὸν ἑξήκοντα πέντε, πλεονάζει δὲ αὐτὰ Ἀρτεμίδωρος·
ἐντεῦθεν δ' εἰς Ἀγκῶνα διακόσια πεντήκοντα
τέσσαρα μίλιά φησιν ἐκεῖνος, ὁ δ' Ἀρτεμίδωρος
εἰς Αἶσιν πλησίον ὄντα[1] τοῦ Ἀγκῶνος σταδίους
εἴρηκε χιλίους διακοσίους πεντήκοντα, πολὺ
ἐνδεέστερον ἐκείνου· Πολύβιος δ' ἀπὸ τῆς Ἰαπυγίας μεμιλιᾶσθαί φησι καὶ εἶναι μίλια πεντακόσια
ἑξήκοντα δύο εἰς Σήναν[2] πόλιν, ἐντεῦθεν δ' εἰς
Ἀκυληίαν ἑκατὸν ἑβδομήκοντα ὀκτώ. οὐχ ὁμολο-
γοῦντες τῷ φερομένῳ διαστήματι τῆς Ἰλλυρικῆς
παραλίας ἀπὸ τῶν Κεραυνίων ὀρῶν ἐπὶ τὸν τοῦ
Ἀδρίου μυχόν, ὑπὲρ ἑξακισχιλίων τοῦτον τὸν
παράπλουν[3] ἀποφαίνοντες καὶ μείζω καθιστάντες
ἐκείνου πολὺ ἐλάττονα ὄντα. καὶ πάντες δὲ πρὸς
ἅπαντας μάλιστα περὶ τῶν διαστημάτων οὐχ
ὁμολογοῦσι πρὸς ἀλλήλους, ὡς πολλάκις λέγομεν,[4]
ἡμεῖς δ' ὅπου μὲν ἐπικρίνειν δυνατόν, ἐκφέρομεν
τὸ δοκοῦν ἡμῖν, ὅπου δὲ μή, τὰ ἐκείνων εἰς μέσον
οἰόμεθα δεῖν τιθέναι. ἐὰν δὲ μηδὲν παρ' ἐκείνων
ἔχωμεν, οὐδὲν θαυμαστόν, οὐδ' εἰ παρελείψαμέν
τι καὶ ἡμεῖς, ἐν τοιαύτῃ καὶ ταῦθ' ὑποθέσει· τῶν
μὲν γὰρ μεγάλων οὐδὲν ἂν παραλίποιμεν, τὰ δὲ

---

[1] ὄντα, after πλησίον, Corais, for τά ; so the later editors.
[2] Σήναν, Meineke (from conj. of Cluver), for the corrupt
Σίλα.
[3] τὸν παράπλουν, Jones inserts, following conj. of Groskurd.
[4] λέγομεν, Meineke needlessly emends to ἐλέγομεν, from
conj. of Kramer.

---

[1] See 5. 2. 7 and footnote. [2] Monte Gargano.
[3] Sena Gallica ; now Sinigaglia. [4] The Adriatic.
[5] Polybius here gives the total length of the coast-line on

according to the Chorographer,[1] the distances from
Brentesium as far as Garganum [2] amount to one
hundred and sixty-five miles, whereas according to
Artemidorus they amount to more; and thence to
Ancona two hundred and fifty-four miles according
to the former, whereas according to Artemidorus the
distance to the Aesis River, which is near Ancona, is
one thousand two hundred and fifty stadia, a much
shorter distance. Polybius states that the distance
from Iapygia has been marked out by miles, and that
the distance to the city of Sena [3] is five hundred and
sixty-two miles, and thence to Aquileia one hundred
and seventy-eight. And they do not agree with the
commonly accepted distance along the Illyrian coast-
line, from the Ceraunian Mountains to the recess of
the Adrias,[4] since they represent this latter coasting-
voyage as over six thousand stadia,[5] thus making it
even longer than the former, although it is much
shorter. However, every writer does not agree with
every other, particularly about the distances, as I
often say.[6] As for myself, where it is possible to
reach a decision, I set forth my opinion, but where it
is not, I think that I should make known the opinions
of others. And when I have no opinion of theirs,
there is no occasion for surprise if I too have passed
something by, especially when one considers the
character of my subject; for I would not pass by
anything important, while as for little things, not

the Italian side as 740 miles, or 6,166 stadia (8⅓ stadia to
the mile; see 7. 7. 4), and elsewhere (2. 4. 3) Strabo quotes
him as reckoning the length of the Illyrian coast-line from
the Ceraunian Mts. only to Iapygia (not including Istria)
as 6,150 stadia. Cp. also 7. 5. 3, 4, 10.
  [6] Cp. 1. 2. 13; 2. 1. 7-8, and 2. 4. 3.

μικρὰ καὶ γνωρισθέντα μικρὸν ὤνησε καὶ παρα-
πεμφθέντα ἔλαθε καὶ οὐδὲν ἢ οὐ[1] πολὺ τοῦ
παντελοῦς ἔργου παρέλυσε.

11. Μεταξὺ δ' εὐθὺς ἀπὸ τοῦ Γαργάνου κόλπος
ὑποδέχεται βαθύς· οἱ δὲ περιοικοῦντες ἰδίως
Ἄπουλοι προσαγορεύονται, εἰσὶ δὲ ὁμόγλωττοι
μὲν τοῖς Δαυνίοις καὶ Πευκετίοις,[2] οὐδὲ τἆλλα δὲ
διαφέρουσιν ἐκείνων τό γε νῦν, τὸ δὲ πάλαι δια-
φέρειν εἰκός, ὅθενπερ καὶ τὰ ὀνόματα ἐναντία
πάντων ἐπικρατεῖν. πρότερον μὲν οὖν εὐτύχει
αὕτη πᾶσα ἡ γῆ, Ἀννίβας δὲ καὶ οἱ ὕστερον
πόλεμοι ἠρήμωσαν αὐτήν· ἐνταῦθα δὲ καὶ τὰ
περὶ Κάννας συνέβη, ὅπου πλεῖστος ὄλεθρος
σωμάτων Ῥωμαίοις καὶ τοῖς συμμάχοις ἐγένετο.
ἐν δὲ τῷ κόλπῳ λίμνη ἐστίν, ὑπὲρ δὲ τῆς λίμνης
ἐν μεσογαίᾳ τὸ Ἄπουλον Τέανον, ὁμώνυμον τῷ
Σιδικίνῳ· καθ' ὃ δοκεῖ συνάγεσθαι τὸ τῆς Ἰταλίας
πλάτος ἐφ' ἱκανὸν πρὸς τοὺς περὶ Δικαιαρχίαν
τόπους, ἐλαττόνων ἢ χιλίων σταδίων ἀπὸ θαλάττης ἐπὶ θάλατταν ἰσθμὸν καταλεῖπον. μετὰ δὲ
τὴν λίμνην ἐπὶ τοὺς Φρεντανοὺς καὶ τὴν Βοῦκαν[3]
παράπλους ἐστί· διακόσιοι δ' εἰσὶν ἐφ' ἑκάτερα
στάδιοι τῆς λίμνης ἐπί τε τὴν Βοῦκαν καὶ τὸ
Γάργανον. τὰ δ' ἑξῆς τοῖς περὶ Βοῦκαν εἴρηται
πρότερον.

---

[1] οὐ, before πολύ, the editors insert, as added, sec. m., in Bn.
[2] Πευκετίοις, Xylander, for Πευκίοις; so the later editors.
[3] Βοῦκαν, Xylander, for Βούκανον; so the later editors.

only do they profit one but slightly if known, but
their omission escapes unnoticed, and detracts not at
all, or else not much, from the completeness of the
work.[1]

11. The intervening space, immediately after Cape
Garganum, is taken up by a deep gulf; the people
who live around it are called by the special name
of Apuli, although they speak the same language
as the Daunii and the Peucetii, and do not differ
from them in any other respect either, at the
present time at least, although it is reasonable to
suppose that in early times they differed and that
this is the source of the three diverse names for
them that are now prevalent. In earlier times this
whole country was prosperous, but it was laid waste
by Hannibal and the later wars. And here too
occurred the battle of Cannae, in which the Romans
and their allies suffered a very great loss of life.
On the gulf is a lake; and above the lake, in the
interior, is Teanum Apulum,[2] which has the same
name as Teanum Sidicinum. At this point the
breadth of Italy seems to be considerably contracted,
since from here to the region of Dicaearcheia[3] an
isthmus is left of less than one thousand stadia from
sea to sea. After the lake comes the voyage along
the coast to the country of the Frentani and to
Buca;[4] and the distance from the lake either to
Buca or to Cape Garganum is two hundred stadia.
As for the places that come next after Buca, I have
already mentioned them.[5]

[1] Cp. 1. 1. 23.   [2] Passo di Civita.   [3] Puteoli.
[4] Now Termoli.   [5] 5. 4. 2.

IV

1. Τοσαύτη μέντοι καὶ τοιαύτη τις ἡ Ἰταλία.
πολλὰ δ᾽ εἰρηκότων, τὰ μέγιστα νῦν ἐπισημα-
νούμεθα, ὑφ᾽ ὧν νῦν[1] εἰς τοσοῦτον ὕψος ἐξήρθησαν
C 286 Ῥωμαῖοι. ἓν μέν, ὅτι νήσου δίκην ἀσφαλῶς
φρουρεῖται τοῖς πελάγεσι κύκλῳ πλὴν ὀλίγων
μερῶν ἃ[2] καὶ αὐτὰ τετείχισται τοῖς ὄρεσι δυσβά-
τοις οὖσι. δεύτερον δὲ τὸ ἀλίμενον κατὰ τὸ
πλεῖστον καὶ τὸ τοὺς ὄντας λιμένας μεγάλους
εἶναι καὶ θαυμαστούς, ὧν τὸ μὲν πρὸς τὰς ἔξωθεν
ἐπιχειρήσεις χρήσιμον, τὸ δὲ πρὸς τὰς ἀντεπι-
χειρήσεις καὶ τὴν τῶν ἐμποριῶν ἀφθονίαν συν-
εργόν. τρίτον δὲ τὸ πολλαῖς ὑποπεπτωκέναι
διαφοραῖς ἀέρων τε καὶ κράσεων, παρ᾽ ἃς καὶ
ζῷα καὶ φυτὰ καὶ πάνθ᾽ ἁπλῶς τὰ πρὸς τὸν
βίον χρήσιμα πλείστην ἐξάλλαξιν ἔχει πρός τε
τὸ βέλτιον καὶ τὸ χεῖρον. ἐκτέταται δὲ τὸ
μῆκος αὐτῆς ἐπὶ μεσημβρίαν ἀπὸ τῶν ἄρκτων
τὸ πλέον, προσθήκη δ᾽ ἐστὶν ἡ Σικελία τῷ μήκει
τοσαύτη οὖσα καὶ τοσούτῳ καθάπερ μέρος. εὐ-
κρασία δ᾽ ἀέρων καὶ δυσκρασία κρίνεται παρὰ τὰ
ψύχη καὶ τὰ θάλπη καὶ τὰ μεταξὺ τούτων, ὥστ᾽
ἐκ[3] τούτων ἀνάγκη τὴν νῦν Ἰταλίαν ἐν μέσῳ τῶν
ὑπερβολῶν ἀμφοτέρων κειμένην, τοσαύτην τῷ
μήκει, πλεῖστον τῆς εὐκράτου μετέχειν καὶ κατὰ
πλείστας ἰδέας. τοῦτο δὲ καὶ ἄλλως συμβέβη-

[1] νῦν, Meineke deletes.
[2] ἅ, Kramer inserts; so the later editors.
[3] ἐκ, Corais, for καί; so the later editors.

IV

1. Such, indeed, is the size and such the character of Italy. And while I have already mentioned many things which have caused the Romans at the present time to be exalted to so great a height, I shall now indicate the most important things. One is, that, like an island, Italy is securely guarded by the seas on all sides, except in a few regions, and even these are fortified by mountains that are hardly passable. A second is that along most of its coast it is harbourless and that the harbours it does have are large and admirable. The former is useful in meeting attacks from the outside, while the latter is helpful in making counter-attacks and in promoting an abundant commerce. A third is that it is characterised by many differences of air and temperature, on which depend the greater variation, whether for better or for worse, in animals, plants, and, in short, everything that is useful for the support of life.[1] Its length extends from north to south, generally speaking, and Sicily counts as an addition to its length, already so great. Now mild temperature and harsh temperature of the air are judged by heat, cold, and their intermediates;[2] and so from this it necessarily follows that what is now Italy, situated as it is between the two extremes and extending to such a length, shares very largely in the temperate zone and in a very large number of ways. And the following is still another advantage which has fallen to the lot of Italy; since the

[1] This statement is general and does not apply to Italy alone (cp. 2. 3. 1 and 2. 3. 7).   [2] Cp. 2. 3. 1.

STRABO

κεν αὐτῇ· τῶν γὰρ Ἀπεννίνων ὀρῶν δι' ὅλου τοῦ
μήκους διατεταμένων, ἐφ' ἑκάτερον δὲ τὸ πλευρὸν
πεδία καὶ γεωλοφίας καλλικάρπους ἀπολειπόντων,
οὐδὲν μέρος αὐτῆς ἐστιν, ὃ μὴ καὶ τῶν ὀρείων
ἀγαθῶν καὶ τῶν πεδινῶν[1] ἀπολαύον τυγχάνει.
καὶ προστίθει τὸ μέγεθος καὶ πλῆθος ποταμῶν
τε καὶ λιμνῶν, πρὸς δὲ τούτοις θερμῶν τε καὶ
ψυχρῶν ὑδάτων ἀναβολὰς πολλαχοῦ πρὸς ὑγείαν
φύσει παρεσκευασμένας, καὶ μὴν καὶ μετάλλων
εὐπορίας παντοδαπῶν. ὕλης τε καὶ τροφῆς ἀνθρώποις τε καὶ βοσκήμασιν οὐδ' ἀξίως ἔστιν
εἰπεῖν τὴν ἀφθονίαν, ὅσην παρέχεται, καὶ τὴν
χρηστοκαρπίαν. ἐν μέσῳ δὲ καὶ τῶν ἐθνῶν τῶν
μεγίστων οὖσα καὶ τῆς Ἑλλάδος καὶ τῶν ἀρίστων
τῆς Λιβύης[2] μερῶν, τῷ μὲν κρατιστεύειν ἐν ἀρετῇ
τε καὶ μεγέθει τὰ περιεστῶτα αὐτὴν πρὸς ἡγεμονίαν εὐφυῶς ἔχει, τῷ δ' ἐγγὺς εἶναι τὸ μετὰ
ῥαστώνης ὑπουργεῖσθαι πεπόρισται.

2. Εἰ δὲ δεῖ τῷ περὶ τῆς Ἰταλίας λόγῳ προσ-
θεῖναί τινα λόγον κεφαλαιώδη καὶ περὶ τῶν
Ῥωμαίων τῶν κατασχόντων αὐτὴν καὶ κατε-
σκευασμένων ὁρμητήριον πρὸς τὴν σύμπασαν
ἡγεμονίαν, προσειλήφθω καὶ ταῦτα· ὅτι Ῥωμαῖοι
μετὰ τὴν κτίσιν τῆς Ῥώμης βασιλευόμενοι διετέλεσαν σωφρόνως ἐπὶ πολλὰς γενεάς· ἔπειτα
τοῦ ἐσχάτου Ταρκυνίου μοχθηρῶς ἄρχοντος, τὸν
μὲν ἐξέβαλον, πολιτείαν δὲ συνεστήσαντο μικτὴν
ἔκ τε μοναρχίας καὶ ἀριστοκρατίας, κοινωνοῖς
C 287 δ' ἐχρήσαντο Σαβίνοις τε καὶ Λατίνοις· οὐκ
εὐγνωμόνων δ' οὔτε ἐκείνων ἀεὶ τυγχάνοντες

[1] πεδινῶν, Kramer, for πεδίων; so the later editors.

138

Apennine Mountains extend through the whole of
its length and leave on both sides plains and hills
which bear fine fruits, there is no part of it which
does not enjoy the blessings of both mountain and
plain. And add also to this the size and number of
its rivers and its lakes, and, besides these, the
fountains of water, both hot and cold, which in
many places nature has provided as an aid to health,
and then again its good supply of mines of all sorts.
Neither can one worthily describe Italy's abundant
supply of fuel, and of food both for men and beast,
and the excellence of its fruits. Further, since it
lies intermediate between the largest races [1] on the
one hand, and Greece and the best parts of Libya
on the other, it not only is naturally well-suited to
hegemony, because it surpasses the countries that
surround it both in the valour of its people and in
size, but also can easily avail itself of their services,
because it is close to them.

2. Now if I must add to my account of Italy a
summary account also of the Romans who took
possession of it and equipped it as a base of operations for the universal hegemony, let me add as
follows: After the founding of Rome, the Romans
wisely continued for many generations under the
rule of kings. Afterwards, because the last Tarquinius was a bad ruler, they ejected him, framed
a government which was a mixture of monarchy and
aristocracy, and dealt with the Sabini and Latini as
with partners. But since they did not always find
either them or the other neighbouring peoples well

---

[1] Iberians, Celts and Germans.

[2] Λιβύης, Pertz, for 'Ασίας; Müller-Dübner and Forbiger.

οὔτε τῶν ἄλλων τῶν πλησιοχώρων ἠναγκάζοντο
τρόπον τινὰ τῇ ἐκείνων καταλύσει τὴν σφετέραν
ἐπαύξειν. οὕτω δ᾽ αὐτοῖς κατ᾽ ὀλίγον προϊοῦσιν
εἰς ἐπίδοσιν συνέβη τὴν πόλιν αἰφνιδίως ἀπο-
βαλεῖν παρὰ τὴν ἁπάντων δόξαν, παρὰ δόξαν
δὲ καὶ ἀπολαβεῖν· ἐγένετο δὲ τοῦτο, ὥς φησι
Πολύβιος, ἔτει ἐννεακαιδεκάτῳ μετὰ τὴν ἐν Αἴγὸς
ποταμοῖς ναυμαχίαν, κατὰ¹ τὴν ἐπ᾽ Ἀνταλκί-
δου γενομένην εἰρήνην. διακρουσάμενοι δὲ τούτους
Ῥωμαῖοι, πρῶτον μὲν Λατίνους ἅπαντας ὑπηκόους ἐποιήσαντο, εἶτα Τυρρηνοὺς καὶ Κελτοὺς
τοὺς περὶ τὸν Πάδον ἔπαυσαν τῆς πολλῆς καὶ
ἀνέδην² ἐλευθερίας· εἶτα Σαυνίτας, μετὰ δὲ τούτους Ταραντίνους καὶ Πύρρον κατεπολέμησαν,
εἶτ᾽ ἤδη καὶ τὴν λοιπὴν τῆς νῦν Ἰταλίας πλὴν
τῆς περὶ τὸν Πάδον. ταύτης δ᾽ ἔτι καθεστώσης
ἐν πολέμῳ, διέβησαν εἰς τὴν Σικελίαν, ἀφελόμενοι
δὲ Καρχηδονίων αὐτὴν ἐπανῆλθον ἐπὶ τοὺς περὶ
τὸν Πάδον· συνεστῶτος δ᾽ ἔτι τούτου τοῦ πολέμου, παρῆν Ἀννίβας εἰς τὴν Ἰταλίαν, καὶ δεύτερος οὗτος πόλεμος πρὸς Καρχηδονίους συνέ-
πεσε, καὶ μετ᾽ οὐ πολὺ τρίτος, ἐν ᾧ κατεσκάφη
Καρχηδών· ἅμα δὲ τήν τε Λιβύην ἔσχον Ῥωμαῖοι
καὶ τῆς Ἰβηρίας ὅσον ἀφείλοντο τῶν Καρχηδονίων.
συνενεωτέρισαν δὲ τοῖς Καρχηδονίοις οἵ θ᾽ Ἕλληνες
καὶ Μακεδόνες καὶ τῆς Ἀσίας οἱ ἐντὸς Ἅλυος καὶ
τοῦ Ταύρου, καὶ τούτους οὖν ἅμα συγκατακτᾶσθαι

---

¹ κατά, Casaubon, for καί; so the later editors.
² ἀνέδην, Corais, for ἄδην (ABC*l*); ἀναίδην (*no*), so the
later editors. Cp. ἀνέδην, 4. 6. 9.

---

¹ To the Gauls, under Brennus.　　　　　² 1. 6.

intentioned, they were forced, in a way, to enlarge
their own country by the dismemberment of that
of the others. And in this way, while they were
advancing and increasing little by little, it came to
pass, contrary to the expectation of all, that they
suddenly lost their city,[1] although they also got
it back contrary to expectation. This took place,
as Polybius[2] says, in the nineteenth year after
the naval battle at Aegospotami, at the time of the
Peace of Antalcidas.[3] After having rid themselves
of these enemies, the Romans first made all the
Latini their subjects; then stopped the Tyrrheni
and the Celti who lived about the Padus from their
wide and unrestrained licence; then fought down
the Samnitae, and, after them, the Tarantini and
Pyrrhus; and then at last also the remainder of
what is now Italy, except the part that is about
the Padus. And while this part was still in a state
of war, the Romans crossed over to Sicily, and on
taking it away from the Carthaginians came back
again to attack the peoples who lived about the
Padus; and it was while that war was still in
progress that Hannibal invaded Italy. This latter
is the second war that occurred against the Carthaginians; and not long afterwards occurred the third,
in which Carthage was destroyed; and at the same
time the Romans acquired, not only Libya, but also
as much of Iberia as they had taken away from the
Carthaginians. But the Greeks, the Macedonians,
and those peoples in Asia who lived this side the
Halys River and the Taurus Mountains joined the
Carthaginians in a revolution, and therefore at

[3] Concluded at Sparta in the Spring of 386 B.C.

προήχθησαν, ὧν Ἀντίοχός τε ἦν ὁ βασιλεὺς καὶ
Φίλιππος καὶ Περσεύς. καὶ Ἰλλυριῶν δὲ καὶ
Θρᾳκῶν οἱ πλησιόχωροι τοῖς τε Ἕλλησι καὶ
Μακεδόσιν ἀρχὰς ἔλαβον τοῦ πρὸς Ῥωμαίους
πολέμου, καὶ διετέλεσαν πολεμοῦντες μέχρι κα-
ταλύσεως ἁπάντων τῶν ἐντὸς Ἴστρου καὶ τῶν
ἐντὸς Ἅλυος. τὰ δ' αὐτὰ ἔπαθον καὶ Ἴβηρες καὶ
Κελτοὶ καὶ ἅπαντες οἱ λοιποί, ὅσοι Ῥωμαίων
ἐπακούουσι·[1] τήν τε γὰρ Ἰβηρίαν οὐκ ἐπαύσαντο
ὑπαγόμενοι τοῖς ὅπλοις, ἕως ἅπασαν κατεστρέ-
ψαντο, Νομαντίνους τε ἐξελόντες καὶ Οὐρίαθον[2]
καὶ Σερτώριον ὕστερον διαφθείραντες, ὑστάτους
δὲ Καντάβρους, οὓς κατεστρέψατο[3] ὁ Σεβαστὸς
Καῖσαρ· τὴν δὲ Κελτικὴν ἅπασαν τήν τε ἐντὸς
καὶ τὴν ἐκτὸς σὺν τῇ Λιγυστικῇ πρότερον μὲν
κατὰ μέρος ἀεὶ προσήγοντο, ὕστερον δὲ Καῖσαρ
ὁ Θεός, καὶ μετὰ ταῦτα ὁ Σεβαστὸς κοινῷ πολέμῳ καὶ ἀθρόως κατεκτήσαντο, νυνὶ δὲ Γερμανοῖς
προσπολεμοῦσιν, ἀπὸ τούτων ὁρμώμενοι τῶν τόπων ὡς οἰκειοτάτων, καί τισιν ἤδη θριάμβοις
C 288 κεκοσμήκασιν ἀπ' αὐτῶν τὴν πατρίδα. τῆς δὲ
Λιβύης, ὅση μὴ Καρχηδονίων, βασιλεῦσιν ἐπετέ-
τραπτο ὑπηκόοις οὖσιν, ἀφιστάμενοι δὲ κατε-
λύοντο· νυνὶ δ' εἰς Ἰούβαν περιέστηκεν ἥ τε
Μαυρουσία καὶ πολλὰ μέρη τῆς ἄλλης Λιβύης

---

[1] ἐπακόυουσι (the reading of all MSS.), Jones restores, for
ὑπακόυουσι.
[2] Οὐρίαθον (as in 3. 4. 5) for Οὐρείεθον; so all editors.
[3] κατεστρέψατο, after οὕς, Jones inserts; others, following
Casaubon, insert κατέλυσεν.

---

[1] 134–133 B.C., under the leadership of Scipio Aemilianus.
[2] Cp. 3. 4. 5.

the same time the Romans were led on to a conquest
of these peoples, whose kings were Antiochus,
Philip, and Perseus. Further, those of the Illyrians
and Thracians who were neighbours to the Greeks
and the Macedonians began to carry on war against
the Romans and kept on warring until the Romans
had subdued all the tribes this side the Ister and this
side the Halys. And the Iberians, Celti, and all
the remaining peoples which now give ear to the
Romans had the same experience. As for Iberia,
the Romans did not stop reducing it by force of
arms until they had subdued the whole of it, first,
by driving out the Nomantini,[1] and, later on, by
destroying Viriathus [2] and Sertorius, and, last of all,
the Cantabri, who were subdued by Augustus Caesar.
As for Celtica (I mean Celtica as a whole, both the
Cisalpine and Transalpine, together with Liguria [3]),
the Romans at first brought it over to their side
only part by part, from time to time, but later the
Deified Caesar, and afterwards Caesar Augustus,
acquired it all at once in a general war. But at the
present time the Romans are carrying on war
against the Germans, setting out from the Celtic
regions as the most appropriate base of operations,
and have already glorified the fatherland with some
triumphs over them. As for Libya, so much of it
as did not belong to the Carthaginians was turned
over to kings who were subject to the Romans, and,
if they ever revolted, they were deposed. But at
the present time Juba has been invested with the
rule, not only of Maurusia, but also of many parts
of the rest of Libya, because of his loyalty and

[3] Literally, "Ligystica" (cp. 4. 6. 3, and 5. 2. 1).

διὰ τὴν πρὸς Ῥωμαίους εὔνοιάν τε καὶ φιλίαν.
τὰ δ' ὅμοια καὶ περὶ τὴν Ἀσίαν συνέβη· κατ'
ἀρχὰς μὲν διὰ τῶν βασιλέων διῳκεῖτο ὑπηκόων
ὄντων, ὕστερον δ' ἐκλιπόντων ἐκείνων, καθάπερ
τῶν Ἀτταλικῶν βασιλέων καὶ Σύρων καὶ Παφλαγόνων καὶ Καππαδόκων καὶ Αἰγυπτίων, ἢ [1]
ἀφισταμένων καὶ ἔπειτα καταλυομένων, καθάπερ
ἐπὶ Μιθριδάτου συνέβη τοῦ Εὐπάτορος καὶ τῆς
Αἰγυπτίας Κλεοπάτρας, ἅπαντα τὰ ἐντὸς Φάσιδος καὶ Εὐφράτου πλὴν Ἀράβων τινῶν ὑπὸ
Ῥωμαίοις ἐστὶ καὶ τοῖς ὑπ' ἐκείνων ἀποδειχθεῖσι
δυνάσταις. Ἀρμένιοι δὲ καὶ οἱ ὑπερκείμενοι τῆς
Κολχίδος, Ἀλβανοί τε καὶ Ἴβηρες, παρουσίας
δέονται μόνον τῶν ἡγησομένων, καλῶς δὲ κρα-
τοῦνται, νεωτερίζουσι δὲ διὰ τὰς τῶν Ῥωμαίων
ἀπασχολίας, καθάπερ καὶ οἱ πέραν τοῦ Ἴστρου
τὸν Εὔξεινον περιοικοῦντες πλὴν τοῦ Βοσπόρου
καὶ τῶν Νομάδων· τὸ μὲν γὰρ ὑπήκοον, τὸ δ'
ἄχρηστον εἰς πᾶν διὰ [2] τὸ ἀκοινώνητον, φυλακῆς
δὲ μόνον δεόμενον· καὶ τἆλλα δὲ τὰ πολλὰ
Σκηνιτῶν καὶ Νομάδων ἐστὶ πόρρω σφόδρα ὄντων. Παρθυαῖοι δέ, ὅμοροί τε ὄντες καὶ μέγιστον
δυνάμενοι, τοσοῦτον ὅμως ἐνέδοσαν πρὸς τὴν
Ῥωμαίων καὶ τῶν καθ' ἡμᾶς ἡγεμόνων ὑπεροχήν,
ὥστ' οὐ μόνον τὰ τρόπαια ἔπεμψαν εἰς Ῥώμην,

---

[1] ἤ, before ἀφισταμένων, Corais inserts; so the later
editors.
[2] διά, Groskurd inserts; so the later editors.

---

[1] Their country is to be identified with what is now
Chirwan and Daghestan (cp. 11. 1. 6).

his friendship for the Romans. And the case of
Asia was like that of Libya. At the outset it was
administered through the agency of kings who were
subject to the Romans, but from that time on, when
their line failed, as was the case with the Attalic,
Syrian, Paphlagonian, Cappadocian, and Egyptian
kings, or when they would revolt and afterwards
be deposed, as was the case with Mithridates
Eupator and the Egyptian Cleopatra, all parts of
it this side the Phasis and the Euphrates, except
certain parts of Arabia, have been subject to the
Romans and the rulers appointed by them. As for
the Armenians, and the peoples who are situated
above Colchis, both Albanians[1] and Iberians,[2] they
require the presence only of men to lead them, and
are excellent subjects, but because the Romans are
engrossed by other affairs, they make attempts at
revolution—as is the case with all the peoples who
live beyond the Ister in the neighbourhood of the
Euxine, except those in the region of the Bosporus[3]
and the Nomads,[4] for the people of the Bosporus
are in subjection, whereas the Nomads, on account
of their lack of intercourse with others, are of no
use for anything and only require watching. Also
the remaining parts of Asia, generally speaking,
belong to the Tent-dwellers and the Nomads, who
are very distant peoples. But as for the Parthians,
although they have a common border with the
Romans and also are very powerful, they have nevertheless yielded so far to the pre-eminence of the

---

[2] Their country is to be identified with what is now
Georgia (cp. 11. 1. 6).
[3] Cp. 7. 4. 4.
[4] Cp. 7. 3. 17.

ἃ κατὰ Ῥωμαίων ἀνέστησάν ποτε, ἀλλὰ καὶ
παῖδας ἐπίστευσε Φραάτης τῷ Σεβαστῷ Καίσαρι
καὶ παίδων παῖδας, ἐξομηρευσάμενος θεραπευ-
τικῶς τὴν φιλίαν· οἱ δὲ νῦν μετίασι ἐνθένδε
πολλάκις τὸν βασιλεύσοντα, καὶ σχεδόν τι πλησίον εἰσὶ τοῦ ἐπὶ Ῥωμαίοις ποιῆσαι τὴν σύμπασαν
ἐξουσίαν. καὶ αὐτὴν δὲ[1] τὴν Ἰταλίαν διαστᾶσαν
πολλάκις, ἀφ' οὗ γε ὑπὸ Ῥωμαίοις ἐστί, καὶ
αὐτὴν τὴν Ῥώμην ἡ τῆς πολιτείας ἀρετὴ καὶ
τῶν ἡγεμόνων ἐκώλυσεν ἐπὶ πλέον προελθεῖν
πλημμελείας καὶ διαφθορᾶς. χαλεπὸν δὲ ἄλλως
διοικεῖν[2] τὴν τηλικαύτην ἡγεμονίαν ἢ ἑνὶ ἐπι-
τρέψαντας ὡς πατρί. οὐδέποτε γοῦν εὐπορῆσαι
τοσαύτης εἰρήνης καὶ ἀφθονίας ἀγαθῶν ὑπῆρξε
Ῥωμαίοις καὶ τοῖς συμμάχοις αὐτῶν, ὅσην Καίσάρ
τε ὁ Σεβαστὸς παρέσχεν, ἀφ' οὗ παρέλαβε τὴν
ἐξουσίαν αὐτοτελῆ, καὶ νῦν ὁ διαδεξάμενος υἱὸς
ἐκεῖνον παρέχει Τιβέριος, κανόνα τῆς διοικήσεως
καὶ τῶν προσταγμάτων ποιούμενος ἐκεῖνον, καὶ
αὐτὸν οἱ παῖδες αὐτοῦ, Γερμανικός τε καὶ Δροῦσος,
ὑπουργοῦντες τῷ πατρί.

---

[1] δέ, Corais inserts; so the later editors.
[2] διοικεῖν, no, A (sec. m.), and the editors, for οἰκεῖν.

Romans and of the rulers of our time that they have sent to Rome the trophies which they once set up as a memorial of their victory over the Romans, and, what is more, Phraates has entrusted to Augustus Caesar his children and also his children's children, thus obsequiously making sure of Caesar's friendship by giving hostages; and the Parthians of to-day have often gone to Rome in quest of a man to be their king,[1] and are now about ready to put their entire authority into the hands of the Romans. As for Italy itself, though it has often been torn by factions, at least since it has been under the Romans, and as for Rome itself, they have been prevented by the excellence of their form of government and of their rulers from proceeding too far in the ways of error and corruption. But it were a difficult thing to administer so great a dominion otherwise than by turning it over to one man, as to a father; at all events, never have the Romans and their allies thrived in such peace and plenty as that which was afforded them by Augustus Caesar, from the time he assumed the absolute authority, and is now being afforded them by his son and successor, Tiberius, who is making Augustus the model of his administration and decrees, as are his children, Germanicus and Drusus, who are assisting their father.

[1] For example, Vonones.

BOOK VII

Z'

I

C 289   1. Εἰρηκόσι δ' ἡμῖν περὶ τῆς Ἰβηρίας καὶ τῶν
Κελτικῶν ἐθνῶν καὶ τῶν Ἰταλικῶν σὺν ταῖς
πλησίον νήσοις ἐφεξῆς ἂν εἴη λέγειν τὰ λειπόμενα
τῆς Εὐρώπης μέρη, διελοῦσι τὸν ἐνδεχόμενον
τρόπον. λείπεται δὲ τὰ πρὸς ἕω μὲν τὰ πέραν
τοῦ Ῥήνου[4] μέχρι τοῦ Τανάιδος[1] καὶ τοῦ στόματος
τῆς Μαιώτιδος[2] λίμνης, καὶ ὅσα μεταξὺ τοῦ
Ἀδρίου[3] καὶ τῶν ἀριστερῶν τῆς Ποντικῆς θαλάττης μερῶν ἀπολαμβάνει πρὸς νότον μέχρι τῆς
Ἑλλάδος καὶ τῆς Προποντίδος[5] ὁ Ἴστρος. διαιρεῖ
γὰρ οὗτος ἅπασαν ὡς ἐγγυτάτω δίχα τὴν λεχθεῖσαν
γῆν, μέγιστος τῶν κατὰ τὴν Εὐρώπην ποταμῶν,
ῥέων πρὸς νότον κατ' ἀρχάς, εἶτ' ἐπιστρέφων εὐθὺς
ἀπὸ τῆς δύσεως ἐπὶ τὴν ἀνατολὴν καὶ τὸν Πόντον.
ἄρχεται μὲν οὖν ἀπὸ τῶν Γερμανικῶν ἄκρων τῶν
ἑσπερίων, πλησίον δὲ καὶ τοῦ μυχοῦ τοῦ Ἀδριατικοῦ, διέχων αὐτοῦ περὶ χιλίους σταδίους· τελευτᾷ δ' εἰς τὸν Πόντον οὐ πολὺ ἄπωθεν τῶν τοῦ
Τύρα καὶ τοῦ Βορυσθένους ἐκβολῶν, ἐκκλίνων πως
πρὸς ἄρκτους.   Προσάρκτια μὲν οὖν ἐστι τῷ
Ἴστρῳ τὰ πέραν τοῦ Ῥήνου καὶ τῆς Κελτικῆς·

---

[1] The Don.   [2] The sea of Azof.
[3] The Adriatic.   [4] The Danube.
[5] The Sea of Marmora.

150

BOOK VII

I

1. Now that I have described Iberia and the Celtic and Italian tribes, along with the islands near by, it will be next in order to speak of the remaining parts of Europe, dividing them in the approved manner. The remaining parts are: first, those towards the east, being those which are across the Rhenus and extend as far as the Tanaïs[1] and the mouth of Lake Maeotis,[2] and also all those regions lying between the Adrias[3] and the regions on the left of the Pontic Sea that are shut off by the Ister[4] and extend towards the south as far as Greece and the Propontis;[5] for this river divides very nearly the whole of the aforesaid land into two parts. It is the largest of the European rivers, at the outset flowing towards the south and then turning straight from the west towards the east and the Pontus. It rises in the western limits of Germany, as also near the recess of the Adriatic (at a distance from it of about one thousand stadia), and comes to an end at the Pontus not very far from the outlets of the Tyras[6] and the Borysthenes,[7] bending from its easterly course approximately towards the north. Now the parts that are beyond the Rhenus and Celtica are to the north of the Ister; these are the

---

[6] The Dniester.   [7] The Dnieper.

ταῦτα δ' ἐστὶ τά τε Γαλατικὰ ἔθνη καὶ τὰ
Γερμανικὰ μέχρι Βασταρνῶν καὶ Τυρεγετῶν καὶ
τοῦ ποταμοῦ τοῦ Βορυσθένους, καὶ ὅσα μεταξὺ
τούτου καὶ Τανάιδος καὶ τοῦ στόματος τῆς
Μαιώτιδος εἴς τε τὴν μεσόγαιαν ἀνατείνει μέχρι
τοῦ ὠκεανοῦ καὶ τῇ Ποντικῇ κλύζεται θαλάττῃ·
μεσημβρινὰ δὲ τά τε Ἰλλυρικὰ καὶ τὰ Θρᾴκια,
καὶ ὅσα τούτοις ἀναμέμικται τῶν Κελτικῶν ἤ
τινων ἄλλων, μέχρι τῆς Ἑλλάδος. λέγωμεν δὲ
πρῶτον περὶ τῶν ἐκτὸς τοῦ Ἴστρου· πολὺ γὰρ
ἁπλούστερα τῶν ἐπὶ θάτερα μερῶν ἐστιν.

C 290 2. Εὐθὺς τοίνυν τὰ πέραν τοῦ Ῥήνου μετὰ τοὺς
Κελτοὺς πρὸς τὴν ἔω κεκλιμένα Γερμανοὶ νέμονται, μικρὸν ἐξαλλάττοντες τοῦ Κελτικοῦ φύλου
τῷ τε πλεονασμῷ τῆς ἀγριότητος καὶ τοῦ με-
γέθους καὶ τῆς ξανθότητος, τἆλλα δὲ παρα-
πλήσιοι, καὶ μορφαῖς καὶ ἤθεσι καὶ βίοις ὄντες
οἵους εἰρήκαμεν τοὺς Κελτούς. διὸ δὴ καί[1] μοι
δοκοῦσι Ῥωμαῖοι τοῦτο αὐτοῖς θέσθαι τοὔνομα,
ὡς ἂν γνησίους Γαλάτας φράζειν βουλόμενοι·
γνήσιοι γὰρ οἱ Γερμανοὶ κατὰ τὴν Ῥωμαίων
διάλεκτον.

3. Ἔστι δὲ τὰ μὲν πρῶτα μέρη τῆς χώρας
ταύτης τὰ πρὸς τῷ Ῥήνῳ μέχρι τῶν ἐκβολῶν
ἀπὸ τῆς πηγῆς ἀρξαμένοις· σχεδὸν δέ τι καὶ τοῦτ'

---

[1] δὴ καί, Meineke, for δίκαια ; so Müller-Dübner.

---

[1] Strabo here means the "exterior" or "Northern" ocean
(see 2. 5. 31 and the *Frontispiece*, Vol. I).
[2] 4. 4. 2–3.
[3] So also Julius Caesar, Tacitus, Pliny and the ancient
writers in general regarded the Germans as Celts (Gauls).

territories of the Galatic and the Germanic tribes, extending as far as the Bastarnians and the Tyregetans and the River Borysthenes. And the territories of all the tribes between this river and the Tanaïs and the mouth of Lake Maeotis extend up into the interior as far as the ocean[1] and are washed by the Pontic Sea. But both the Illyrian and the Thracian tribes, and all tribes of the Celtic or other peoples that are mingled with these, as far as Greece, are to the south of the Ister. But let me first describe the parts outside the Ister, for they are much simpler than those on the other side.

2. Now the parts beyond the Rhenus, immediately after the country of the Celti, slope towards the east and are occupied by the Germans, who, though they vary slightly from the Celtic stock in that they are wilder, taller, and have yellower hair, are in all other respects similar, for in build, habits, and modes of life they are such as I have said[2] the Celti are. And I also think that it was for this reason that the Romans assigned to them the name " Germani," as though they wished to indicate thereby that they were " genuine " Galatae, for in the language of the Romans " germani " means " genuine."[3]

3. The first parts of this country are those that are next to the Rhenus, beginning at its source and extending as far as its outlet; and this stretch of

Dr. Richard Braungart has recently published a large work in two volumes in which he ably defends his thesis that the Boii, Vindelici, Rhaeti, Norici, Taurisci, and other tribes, as shown by their agricultural implements and contrivances, were originally, not Celts, but Germans, and, in all probability, the ancestors of all Germans (*Sudgermanen*, Heidelberg, 1914).

STRABO

ἔστι τὸ ἑσπέριον τῆς χώρας πλάτος, ἡ ποταμία
πᾶσα. ταύτης δὲ τὰ μὲν εἰς τὴν Κελτικὴν μετή-
γαγον Ῥωμαῖοι, τὰ δ' ἔφθη μεταστάντα εἰς τὴν
ἐν βάθει χώραν, καθάπερ Μαρσοί· λοιποὶ δ'
εἰσὶν ὀλίγοι καὶ τῶν Σουγάμβρων μέρος· μετὰ
δὲ τοὺς παραποταμίους τἆλλά ἐστιν ἔθνη τὰ
μεταξὺ τοῦ Ῥήνου καὶ τοῦ Ἄλβιος ποταμοῦ, ὃς
παράλληλός πως ἐκείνῳ ῥεῖ πρὸς τὸν ὠκεανόν,
οὐκ ἐλάττω χώραν διεξιὼν ἥπερ ἐκεῖνος. εἰσὶ δὲ
μεταξὺ καὶ ἄλλοι ποταμοὶ πλωτοί (ὧν ἐν τῷ
Ἀμασίᾳ Δροῦσος Βρουκτέρους κατεναυμάχησε),
ῥέοντες ὡσαύτως ἀπὸ νότου πρὸς βορρᾶν καὶ τὸν
ὠκεανόν. ἐξῆρται[1] γὰρ ἡ χώρα πρὸς νότον καὶ
συνεχῆ ταῖς Ἄλπεσι ποιεῖ ῥάχιν τινὰ πρὸς ἕω
τεταμένην, ὡς ἂν μέρος οὖσαν[2] τῶν Ἄλπεων· καὶ
δὴ καὶ ἀπεφήναντό τινες οὕτως διά τε τὴν
λεχθεῖσαν θέσιν καὶ διὰ τὸ τὴν αὐτὴν ὕλην
ἐκφέρειν· οὐ μὴν ἐπὶ τοσοῦτό γε ὕψος ἀνίσχει τὰ
ταύτῃ μέρη.[3] ἐνταῦθα δ' ἐστὶ καὶ[4] ὁ Ἑρκύνιος
δρυμὸς καὶ τὰ τῶν Σοήβων ἔθνη, τὰ μὲν οἰκοῦντα
ἐντὸς τοῦ δρυμοῦ, καθάπερ τὰ τῶν Κολδούων,[5] ἐν

---

[1] ἐξῆρται, Casaubon, for ἐξήρτηται; so the later editors.
[2] οὖσαν, Xylander, for οὖσα; so the later editors
[3] μέρη, Meineke emends to ὄρη.
[4] καί, Kramer and Meineke omit; a typographical error,
apparently.
[5] καθάπερ . . . Κολδούων, Meineke relegates to the foot of
the page ; Κολδούων, Cluver emends to Κουάδων, Kramer to
Κοαδούων (perhaps rightly).

---

[1] e.g. the Ubii (see 4. 3. 4). [2] The Elbe. [3] The Ems.
[4] The chain of mountains that extends from northern
Switzerland to Mt. Krapak.
[5] Now called the "Black Forest," although the ancient
term, according to Elton (*Origins*, p. 51, quoted by Tozer),

river-land taken as a whole is approximately the
breadth of the country on its western side. Some
of the tribes of this river-land were transferred by
the Romans to Celtica, whereas the others antici-
pated the Romans by migrating deep into the
country, for instance, the Marsi; and only a few
people, including a part of the Sugambri,[1] are left.
After the people who live along the river come
the other tribes that live between the Rhenus and
the River Albis,[2] which latter flows approximately
parallel to the former, towards the ocean, and
traverses no less territory than the former. Between
the two are other navigable rivers also (among
them the Amasias,[3] on which Drusus won a naval
victory over the Bructeri), which likewise flow from
the south towards the north and the ocean; for the
country is elevated towards the south and forms a
mountain chain[4] that connects with the Alps and
extends towards the east as though it were a part
of the Alps; and in truth some declare that they
actually are a part of the Alps, both because of
their aforesaid position and of the fact that they
produce the same timber; however, the country in
this region does not rise to a sufficient height for
that. Here, too, is the Hercynian Forest,[5] and
also the tribes of the Suevi, some of which dwell
inside the forest, as, for instance, the tribes of the
Coldui,[6] in whose territory is Boihaemum,[7] the

embraced also "the forests of the Hartz, and the woods of
Westphalia and Nassau."
[6] Müller-Dübner and Forbiger, perhaps rightly, emend
"Coldui" to "Coadui." But as Tozer (p. 187) says, the
information Strabo here gives about Germany "is very
imperfect, and hardly extends at all beyond the Elbe."
[7] Hence the modern "Bohemia," "the home of the Boii."

οἷς ἐστι καὶ τὸ Βουίαιμον, τὸ τοῦ Μαροβόδου
βασίλειον, εἰς ὃν ἐκεῖνος τόπον ἄλλους τε μετα-
νέστησε πλείους καὶ δὴ καὶ τοὺς ὁμοεθνεῖς ἑαυτῷ
Μαρκομμάνους. ἐπέστη γὰρ τοῖς πράγμασιν
οὗτος ἐξ ἰδιώτου μετὰ τὴν ἐκ Ῥώμης ἐπάνοδον·
νέος γὰρ ἦν ἐνθάδε καὶ εὐεργετεῖτο ὑπὸ τοῦ Σεβαστοῦ, ἐπανελθὼν δὲ ἐδυνάστευσε καὶ κατεκτήσατο
πρὸς οἷς εἶπον Λουγίους[1] τε, μέγα ἔθνος, καὶ
Ζούμους καὶ Βούτωνας[2] καὶ Μουγίλωνας καὶ
Σιβινοὺς καὶ τῶν Σοήβων αὐτῶν μέγα ἔθνος,
Σέμνωνας. πλὴν τά γε τῶν Σοήβων, ὡς ἔφην,
ἔθνη τὰ μὲν ἐντὸς οἰκεῖ, τὰ δὲ ἐκτὸς τοῦ δρυμοῦ, ὅμορα τοῖς Γέταις. μέγιστον μὲν οὖν τὸ
τῶν Σοήβων ἔθνος· διήκει γὰρ ἀπὸ τοῦ Ῥήνου
μέχρι τοῦ Ἄλβιος· μέρος δέ τι αὐτῶν καὶ
πέραν τοῦ Ἄλβιος νέμεται, καθάπερ Ἑρμόν-
C 291 δοροι[3] καὶ Λαγκόβαρδοι, νυνὶ δὲ καὶ τελέως εἰς
τὴν περαίαν οὗτοί γε ἐκπεπτώκασι φεύγοντες.
κοινὸν δ᾽ ἐστὶν ἅπασι τοῖς ταύτῃ τὸ περὶ τὰς
μεταναστάσεις εὐμαρὲς διὰ τὴν λιτότητα τοῦ βίου
καὶ διὰ τὸ μὴ γεωργεῖν μηδὲ θησαυρίζειν, ἀλλ᾽ ἐν
καλυβίοις οἰκεῖν, ἐφήμερον ἔχουσι παρασκευήν·
τροφὴ δ᾽ ἀπὸ τῶν θρεμμάτων ἡ πλείστη, καθάπερ

---

[1] Λουγίους, Meineke, for Λουίους.

[2] For Βούτωνας, Kramer and Meineke read Γούτωνας (perhaps
rightly).

[3] Ἑρμόνδοροι, Casaubon, for Εὐμόνδοροι; so the later editors.

. [1] Scholars have suggested different emendations for
"Zumi," "Butones," "Mugilones," and "Sibini," since
all these seem to be corrupt (see C. Müller, *Ind. Var. Lect.*,

domain of Marabodus, the place whither he caused
to migrate, not only several other peoples, but in
particular the Marcomanni, his fellow-tribesmen;
for after his return from Rome this man, who before
had been only a private citizen, was placed in charge
of the affairs of state, for, as a youth he had been
at Rome and had enjoyed the favour of Augustus,
and on his return he took the rulership and acquired, in addition to the peoples aforementioned,
the Lugii (a large tribe), the Zumi, the Butones,
the Mugilones, the Sibini,[1] and also the Semnones,
a large tribe of the Suevi themselves. However,
while some of the tribes of the Suevi dwell inside
the forest, as I was saying, others dwell outside of
it, and have a common boundary with the Getae.[2]
Now as for the tribe of the Suevi,[3] it is the largest,
for it extends from the Rhenus to the Albis; and
a part of them even dwell on the far side of the
Albis, as, for instance, the Hermondori and the
Langobardi; and at the present time these latter,
at least, have, to the last man, been driven in flight
out of their country into the land on the far side
of the river. It is a common characteristic of all
the peoples in this part of the world[4] that they
migrate with ease, because of the meagreness of
their livelihood and because they do not till the
soil or even store up food, but live in small huts
that are merely temporary structures; and they live
for the most part off their flocks, as the Nomads do,

p. 981). For "Butones" it is fairly certain that Strabo
wrote "Gutones" (the Goths).

[2] The "Getae," also called "Daci," dwelt in what are
now Rumania and southern Hungary.

[3] Strabo now uses "tribe" in its broadest sense.

[4] Including the Galatae (see 4. 4. 2).

τοῖς Νομάσιν, ὥστ᾽ ἐκείνους μιμούμενοι τὰ οἰκεῖα
ταῖς ἁρμαμάξαις ἐπάραντες, ὅπη ἂν δόξῃ, τρέπον-
ται μετὰ τῶν βοσκημάτων. ἄλλα δ᾽ ἐνδεέστερά
ἐστιν ἔθνη Γερμανικὰ Χηροῦσκοί τε καὶ Χάττοι
καὶ Γαμαβριούιοι[1] καὶ Χαττουάριοι· πρὸς δὲ τῷ
ὠκεανῷ Σούγαμβροί τε καὶ Χαῦβοι καὶ Βρούκτε-
ροι καὶ Κίμβροι, Καῦκοί τε καὶ Καοῦλκοι καὶ
Καμψιανοὶ καὶ ἄλλοι πλείους. ἐπὶ ταὐτὰ δὲ τῷ
Ἀμασίᾳ φέρονται Βίσουργίς τε καὶ Λουπίας
ποταμός, διέχων Ῥήνου περὶ ἑξακοσίους σταδίους,
ῥέων διὰ Βρουκτέρων τῶν ἐλαττόνων. ἔστι δὲ
καὶ Σάλας ποταμός, οὗ μεταξὺ καὶ τοῦ Ῥήνου
πολεμῶν καὶ κατορθῶν Δροῦσος ἐτελεύτησεν ὁ
Γερμανικός. ἐχειρώσατο δ᾽ οὐ μόνον τῶν ἐθνῶν τὰ
πλεῖστα, ἀλλὰ καὶ τὰς ἐν τῷ παράπλῳ νήσους,
ὧν ἐστι καὶ ἡ Βυρχανίς, ἣν ἐκ πολιορκίας εἷλε.

4. Γνώριμα δὲ ταῦτα κατέστη τὰ ἔθνη πολε-
μοῦντα πρὸς Ῥωμαίους, εἶτ᾽ ἐνδιδόντα καὶ πάλιν
ἀφιστάμενα ἢ καὶ καταλείποντα τὰς κατοικίας·
κἂν πλείω δὲ γνώριμα ὑπῆρξεν, εἰ ἐπέτρεπε τοῖς
στρατηγοῖς ὁ Σεβαστὸς διαβαίνειν τὸν Ἄλβιν,
μετιοῦσι τοὺς ἐκεῖσε ἀπανισταμένους.[2] νυνὶ δ᾽
εὐπορώτερον ὑπέλαβε στρατηγεῖν τὸν ἐν χερσὶ
πόλεμον, εἰ τῶν ἔξω τοῦ Ἄλβιος καθ᾽ ἡσυχίαν

---

[1] Γαμαβριούιοι, Corais, for Γαμαβρίουοι ; so Meineke.
[2] ἀπανισταμένους, Corais, for ἐπανισταμένους ; so the later
editors.

---

[1] The Weser.   [2] The Lippe.
[3] The Lesser Bructeri appear to have lived south of the
Frisii and west of the Ems, while the Greater Bructeri lived
east of it and south of the Western Chauci (cp. Ptolemaeus
2. 11. 6–7).

so that, in imitation of the Nomads, they load their household belongings on their wagons and with their beasts turn whithersoever they think best. But other German tribes are still more indigent. I mean the Cherusci, the Chatti, the Gamabrivii and the Chattuarii, and also, near the ocean, the Sugambri, the Chaubi, the Bructeri, and the Cimbri, and also the Cauci, the Caülci, the Campsiani, and several others. Both the Visurgis[1] and the Lupias[2] Rivers run in the same direction as the Amasias, the Lupias being about six hundred stadia distant from the Rhenus and flowing through the country of the Lesser Bructeri.[3] Germany has also the Salas River[4]; and it was between the Salas and the Rhenus that Drusus Germanicus, while he was successfully carrying on the war, came to his end.[5] He had subjugated, not only most of the tribes, but also the islands along the coast, among which is Burchanis,[6] which he took by siege.

4. These tribes have become known through their wars with the Romans, in which they would either yield and then later revolt again, or else quit their settlements; and they would have been better known if Augustus had allowed his generals to cross the Albis in pursuit of those who emigrated thither. But as a matter of fact he supposed that he could conduct the war in hand more successfully if he should hold off from those outside the Albis, who

---

[4] The Thüringian Sasle.

[5] In his thirtieth year (9 A.D.) his horse fell on him and broke his leg (Livy, *Epitome* 140).

[6] Now Borkum. The Romans nicknamed it "Fabaria" ("Bean Island") because of the wild beans that grew there (Pliny 4. 27).

ὄντων ἀπέχοιτο, καὶ μὴ παροξύνοι πρὸς τὴν
κοινωνίαν τῆς ἔχθρας. ἤρξαντο δὲ τοῦ πολέμου
Σούγαμβροι πλησίον οἰκοῦντες τοῦ Ῥήνου, Μέ-
λωνα ἔχοντες ἡγεμόνα· κἀκεῖθεν ἤδη διεῖχον [1]
ἄλλοτ᾿ ἄλλοι, δυναστεύοντες καὶ καταλυόμενοι,,
πάλιν δ᾿ ἀφιστάμενοι, προδιδόντες καὶ τὰ ὅμηρα
καὶ τὰς πίστεις. πρὸς οὓς ἡ μὲν ἀπιστία μέγα
ὄφελος, οἱ δὲ πιστευθέντες τὰ μέγιστα κατέ-
βλαψαν, καθάπερ οἱ Χηροῦσκοι καὶ οἱ τούτοις
ὑπήκοοι, παρ᾿ οἷς τρία τάγματα Ῥωμαίων μετὰ
τοῦ στρατηγοῦ Οὐάρου Κοιντιλλίου παρα-
σπονδηθέντα ἀπώλετο ἐξ ἐνέδρας. ἔτισαν δὲ
δίκας ἅπαντες καὶ παρέσχον τῷ νεωτέρῳ Γερμα-
νικῷ λαμπρότατον θρίαμβον, ἐν ᾧ ἐθριαμβεύθη
τῶν ἐπιφανεστάτων ἀνδρῶν σώματα καὶ γυναικῶν,
Σεγιμοῦντός τε Σεγέστου υἱός, Χηρούσκων ἡγεμών,
καὶ ἀδελφὴ αὐτοῦ, γυνὴ δ᾿ Ἀρμενίου τοῦ πολε-
μαρχήσαντος ἐν τοῖς Χηρούσκοις ἐν τῇ πρὸς
C 292 Οὐάρον Κοιντίλλιον παρασπονδήσει καὶ νῦν ἔτι
συνέχοντος τὸν πόλεμον, ὄνομα Θουσνέλδα, καὶ
υἱὸς τριετὴς Θουμέλικος· ἔτι δὲ Σεσίθακος,
Σεγιμήρου [2] υἱὸς τῶν Χηρούσκων ἡγεμόνος, καὶ
γυνὴ τούτου Ῥαμίς, Οὐκρομίρου θυγάτηρ, ἡγεμόνος Χάττων,[3] καὶ Δευδόριξ, Βαιτόριγος τοῦ
Μέλωνος ἀδελφοῦ υἱός, Σούγαμβρος. Σεγέστης
δὲ ὁ πενθερὸς τοῦ Ἀρμενίου καὶ ἐξ ἀρχῆς διέστη

---

[1] διεῖχον, Corais emends to διεδέχοντο (cp. 4. 3. 4); Kramer
and Meineke following.
[2] Σεγιμήρου, Kramer, for Αἰγιμήρου; so the later editors.
[3] Χάττων, Cluver, for Βάττων; so the later editors.

---

[1] May 26, 17 A.D. (Tacitus, *Annals* 2. 41).

were living in peace, and should not incite them
to make common cause with the others in their
enmity against him. It was the Sugambri, who live
near the Rhenus, that began the war, Melo being
their leader; and from that time on different peoples
at different times would cause a breach, first growing
powerful and then being put down, and then
revolting again, betraying both the hostages they
had given and their pledges of good faith. In
dealing with these peoples distrust has been a great
advantage, whereas those who have been trusted
have done the greatest harm, as, for instance, the
Cherusci and their subjects, in whose country three
Roman legions, with their general Quintilius Varus,
were destroyed by ambush in violation of the treaty.
But they all paid the penalty, and afforded the
younger Germanicus a most brilliant triumph [1]—that
triumph in which their most famous men and women
were led captive, I mean Segimuntus, son of Segestes
and chieftain of the Cherusci, and his sister Thusnelda,
the wife of Armenius, the man who at the time of
the violation of the treaty against Quintilius Varus
was commander-in-chief of the Cheruscan army
and even to this day is keeping up the war, and
Thusnelda's three-year-old son Thumelicus; and
also Sesithacus, the son of Segimerus and chieftain
of the Cherusci, and Rhamis, his wife, and a daughter
of Ucromirus chieftain of the Chatti, and Deudorix,[2]
a Sugambrian, the son of Baetorix the brother of
Melo. But Segestes, the father-in-law of Armenius,
who even from the outset had opposed [3] the purpose
of Armenius, and, taking advantage of an opportune

[2] The same name as "Theodoric."

[3] So Tacitus, *Annals*, 1. 55 ; see also 1. 58, 71.

πρὸς τὴν γνώμην αὐτοῦ καὶ λαβὼν καιρὸν ηὐτο-
μόλησε καὶ τῷ θριάμβῳ παρῆν τῶν φιλτάτων, ἐν
τιμῇ ἀγόμενος· ἐπόμπευσε δὲ καὶ Λίβης τῶν
Χάττων ἱερεύς, καὶ ἄλλα δὲ σώματα ἐπομπεύθη
ἐκ τῶν πεπορθημένων ἐθνῶν, Καούλκων,[1] Καμψανῶν,[2] Βρουκτέρων, Οὐσίπων, Χηρούσκων, Χάττων,
Χαττουαρίων, Λανδῶν, Τουβαττίων.[3] διέχει δὲ τοῦ
Ἄλβιος ὁ Ῥῆνος περὶ τρισχιλίους σταδίους, εἴ τις
εὐθυπορούσας ἔχει τὰς ὁδούς· νυνὶ δὲ διὰ σκολιᾶς
καὶ ἑλώδους καὶ δρυμῶν κυκλοπορεῖν ἀνάγκη.

5. Ὁ δὲ Ἑρκύνιος δρυμὸς πυκνότερός τέ ἐστι
καὶ μεγαλόδενδρος, ἐν χωρίοις ἐρυμνοῖς κύκλον
περιλαμβάνων μέγαν, ἐν μέσῳ δὲ ἵδρυται χώρα
καλῶς οἰκεῖσθαι δυναμένη, περὶ ἧς εἰρήκαμεν.
ἔστι δὲ πλησίον αὐτῆς ἥ τε τοῦ Ἴστρου πηγὴ καὶ
ἡ τοῦ Ῥήνου, καὶ ἡ μεταξὺ ἀμφοῖν λίμνη καὶ τὰ
ἕλη τὰ ἐκ τοῦ Ῥήνου διαχεόμενα. ἔστι δ᾽ ἡ λίμνη
τὴν μὲν περίμετρον σταδίων πλειόνων ἢ τριακοσίων,[4] δίαρμα δὲ ἐγγὺς διακοσίων. ἔχει δὲ καὶ
νῆσον, ᾗ ἐχρήσατο ὁρμητηρίῳ Τιβέριος ναυμαχῶν
πρὸς Οὐινδολικούς. νοτιωτέρα δ᾽ ἐστὶ τῶν τοῦ
Ἴστρου πηγῶν καὶ αὕτη, καὶ ὁ Ἑρκύνιος δρυμός,

[1] Καούλκων, Meineke, for Καθούλκων.
[2] Καμψανῶν, Meineke, for καὶ Ἀμψανῶν.
[3] Τουβαττίων, Kramer, for Σουβαττίων ; so the later editors.
[4] For τριακοσίων (τ') Meineke writes πεντακοσίων (φ'). But
Jones conjectures ἑξακοσίων (χ'), which is almost certainly
what Strabo wrote.

---

[1] 4. 6. 9 and 7. 1. 3.
[2] Now the Lake of Constance ; also called the Bodensee.
Cp. 4. 3. 3 and 4. 6. 9.
[3] The Untersee. [4] Cp. 4. 3. 3.

time, had deserted him, was present as a guest of honour at the triumph over his loved ones. And Libes too, a priest of the Chatti, marched in the procession, as also other captives from the plundered tribes—the Caülci, Campsani, Bructeri, Usipi, Cherusci, Chatti, Chattuarii, Landi, Tubattii. Now the Rhenus is about three thousand stadia distant from the Albis, if one had straight roads to travel on, but as it is one must go by a circuitous route, which winds through a marshy country and forests.

5. The Hercynian Forest is not only rather dense, but also has large trees, and comprises a large circuit within regions that are fortified by nature; in the centre of it, however, lies a country (of which I have already spoken[1]) that is capable of affording an excellent livelihood. And near it are the sources of both the Ister and the Rhenus, as also the lake[2] between the two sources, and the marshes[3] into which the Rhenus spreads.[4] The perimeter of the lake is more than three hundred stadia, while the passage across it is nearly two hundred.[5] There is also an island in it which Tiberius used as a base of operations in his naval battle with the Vindelici. This lake is south of the sources of the Ister, as is also the Hercynian Forest, so that necessarily, in

---

[5] These figures, as they stand in the manuscripts, are, of course, relatively impossible, and Strabo could hardly have made such a glaring error. Meineke and others emend 300 to 500, leaving the 200 as it is; but on textual grounds, at least, 600 is far more probable. "Passage across" (in Strabo) means the usual boat-passage, but the terminal points of this passage are now unknown. According to W. A. B. Coolidge (*Encyclopedia Brittanica, s.v.* "Lake of Constance") the length of the lake is now 46½ miles (from Bregenz to Stein-am-Rhein), while its greatest width is 10½ miles.

ὥστ᾽ ἀνάγκη τῷ ἐκ τῆς Κελτικῆς ἐπὶ τὸν Ἑρκύνιον δρυμὸν ἰόντι πρῶτον μὲν διαπερᾶσαι τὴν λίμνην, ἔπειτα τὸν Ἴστρον, εἶτ᾽ ἤδη δι᾽ εὐπετεστέρων χωρίων ἐπὶ τὸν δρυμὸν τὰς προβάσεις ποιεῖσθαι δι᾽ ὀροπεδίων. ἡμερήσιον δ᾽ ἀπὸ τῆς λίμνης προελθὼν ὁδὸν Τιβέριος εἶδε τὰς τοῦ Ἴστρου πηγάς. προσάπτονται δὲ τῆς λίμνης ἐπ᾽ ὀλίγον μὲν οἱ Ῥαιτοί, τὸ δὲ πλέον Ἐλουήττιοι καὶ Οὐινδολικοὶ καὶ ἡ Βοΐων ἐρημία. μέχρι Παννονίων πάντες, τὸ πλέον δ᾽ Ἐλουήττιοι καὶ Οὐινδολικοί, οἰκοῦσιν ὀροπέδια. Ῥαιτοὶ δὲ καὶ Νωρικοὶ μέχρι τῶν Ἀλπίων ὑπερβολῶν ἀνίσχουσι καὶ πρὸς τὴν Ἰταλίαν περινεύουσιν, οἱ μὲν Ἰνσούβροις συνάπτοντες, οἱ δὲ Κάρνοις καὶ τοῖς περὶ τὴν Ἀκυληίαν χωρίοις. ἔστι δὲ καὶ ἄλλη ὕλη μεγάλη Γαβρῆτα ἐπὶ τάδε τῶν Σοήβων, ἐπέκεινα δ᾽ ὁ Ἑρκύνιος δρυμός, ἔχεται δὲ κἀκεῖνος ὑπ᾽ αὐτῶν.

II

1. Περὶ δὲ Κίμβρων τὰ μὲν οὐκ εὖ λέγεται, τὰ δ᾽ ἔχει ἀπιθανότητας[1] οὐ μετρίας. οὔτε γὰρ τὴν τοιαύτην αἰτίαν τοῦ πλάνητας γενέσθαι καὶ ληστρικοὺς ἀποδέξαιτ᾽ ἄν τις, ὅτι χερρόνησον οἰκοῦντες μεγάλῃ πλημμυρίδι ἐξελαθεῖεν ἐκ τῶν C 293 τόπων· καὶ γὰρ νῦν ἔχουσι τὴν χώραν, ἣν εἶχον πρότερον, καὶ ἔπεμψαν τῷ Σεβαστῷ δῶρον τὸν ἱερώτατον παρ᾽ αὐτοῖς λέβητα, αἰτούμενοι φιλίαν

---

[1] ἀπιθανότητας, Cobet, for πιθανότητας.

---

[1] The Forest of the Bohemians.

going from Celtica to the Hercynian Forest, one
first crosses the lake and then the Ister, and from
there on advances through more passable regions—
plateaus—to the forest. Tiberius had proceeded
only a day's journey from the lake when he saw the
sources of the Ister. The country of the Rhaeti
adjoins the lake for only a short distance, whereas
that of the Helvetii and the Vindelici, and also
the desert of the Boii, adjoin the greater part of it.
All the peoples as far as the Pannonii, but more
especially the Helvetii and the Vindelici, inhabit
plateaus. But the countries of the Rhaeti and the
Norici extend as far as the passes over the Alps
and verge toward Italy, a part thereof bordering on
the country of the Insubri and a part on that of the
Carni and the regions about Aquileia. And there is
also another large forest, Gabreta; [1] it is on this side
of the territory of the Suevi, whereas the Hercynian
Forest, which is also held by them, is on the far side.

II

1. As for the Cimbri, some things that are told
about them are incorrect and others are extremely
improbable. For instance, one could not accept
such a reason for their having become a wandering
and piratical folk as this—that while they were
dwelling on a peninsula they were driven out of
their habitations by a great flood-tide; for in fact
they still hold the country which they held in
earlier times; and they sent as a present to Augustus
the most sacred kettle [2] in their country, with a

[2] When the throats of prisoners of war were cut, the blood
was caught in huge brazen kettles (7. 2. 3).

καὶ ἀμνηστίαν τῶν ὑπηργμένων· τυχόντες δέ, ὧν
ἠξίουν, ἀπῆραν· γελοῖον δὲ τῷ φυσικῷ καὶ αἰωνίῳ
πάθει, δὶς ἑκάστης ἡμέρας συμβαίνοντι, προσ-
οργισθέντας ἀπελθεῖν ἐκ τοῦ τόπου. ἔοικε δὲ
πλάσματι τὸ συμβῆναί ποτε ὑπερβάλλουσαν
πλημμυρίδα· ἐπιτάσεις μὲν γὰρ καὶ ἀνέσεις δέχεται τεταγμένας δὲ καὶ περιοδιζούσας ὁ ὠκεανὸς ἐν
τοῖς τοιούτοις πάθεσιν. οὐκ εὖ δ' οὐδὲ ὁ φήσας
ὅπλα αἴρεσθαι πρὸς τὰς πλημμυρίδας τοὺς
Κίμβρους, οὐδ' ὅτι ἀφοβίαν οἱ Κελτοὶ ἀσκοῦντες
κατακλύζεσθαι τὰς οἰκίας ὑπομένουσιν, εἶτ'
ἀνοικοδομοῦσι, καὶ ὅτι πλείων αὐτοῖς συμβαίνει
φθόρος ἐξ ὕδατος ἢ πολέμου, ὅπερ Ἔφορός φησιν.
ἡ γὰρ τάξις ἡ τῶν πλημμυρίδων καὶ τὸ τὴν ἐπι-
κλυζομένην χώραν εἶναι γνώριμον οὐκ ἔμελλε
ταύτας[1] τὰς ἀτοπίας παρέξειν· δὶς γὰρ ἑκάστης
ἡμέρας τούτου συμβαίνοντος τὸ μηδ' ἅπαξ αἰ-
σθάνεσθαι φυσικὴν οὖσαν τὴν παλίρροιαν καὶ
ἀβλαβῆ, καὶ οὐ μόνοις τούτοις συμβαίνουσαν,
ἀλλὰ τοῖς παρωκεανίταις πᾶσι, πῶς οὐκ ἀπί-
θανον; οὐδὲ Κλείταρχος εὖ· φησὶ γὰρ τοὺς ἱππέας
ἰδόντας τὴν ἔφοδον τοῦ πελάγους ἀφιππάσασθαι
καὶ φεύγοντας ἐγγὺς γενέσθαι τοῦ περικαταλη-
φθῆναι. οὔτε δὲ τοσούτῳ τάχει τὴν ἐπίβασιν
ὁρμωμένην[2] ἱστοροῦμεν, ἀλλὰ λεληθότως προσι-
οῦσαν τὴν θάλατταν· οὔτε τὸ καθ' ἡμέραν γιγνό-
μενον καὶ πᾶσιν ἔναυλον ἤδη ὂν τοῖς πλησιάζειν

---

[1] ταύτας, Corais and Meineke emend to τοιαύτας.
[2] ὁρμωμένην, Corais, for ὁρωμένην; so the later editors.

---

[1] Cp. 3. 5. 9.

plea for his friendship and for an amnesty of their earlier offences, and when their petition was granted they set sail for home; and it is ridiculous to suppose that they departed from their homes because they were incensed on account of a phenomenon that is natural and eternal, occurring twice every day. And the assertion that an excessive flood-tide once occurred looks like a fabrication, for when the ocean is affected in this way it is subject to increases and diminutions, but these are regulated and periodical.[1] And the man who said that the Cimbri took up arms against the flood-tides was not right, either; nor yet the statement that the Celti, as a training in the virtue of fearlessness, meekly abide the destruction of their homes by the tides and then rebuild them, and that they suffer a greater loss of life as the result of water than of war, as Ephorus says. Indeed, the regularity of the flood-tides and the fact that the part of the country subject to inundations was known should have precluded such absurdities; for since this phenomenon occurs twice every day, it is of course improbable that the Cimbri did not so much as once perceive that the reflux was natural and harmless, and that it occurred, not in their country alone, but in every country that was on the ocean. Neither is Cleitarchus right; for he says that the horsemen, on seeing the onset of the sea, rode away, and though in full flight came very near being cut off by the water. Now we know, in the first place, that the invasion of the tide does not rush on with such speed as that, but that the sea advances imperceptibly; and, secondly, that what takes place daily and is audible to all who are about to draw near it, even before they

167

μέλλουσι, πρὶν ἢ θεάσασθαι, τοσοῦτον ἔμελλε παρέξεσθαι φόβον, ὥστε φεύγειν, ὡς ἂν εἰ ἐξ ἀδοκήτου προσέπεσε.

2. Ταῦτα δὲ¹ δικαίως ἐπιτιμᾷ τοῖς συγγραφεῦσι Ποσειδώνιος καὶ οὐ κακῶς εἰκάζει, διότι ληστρικοὶ ὄντες καὶ πλάνητες οἱ Κίμβροι καὶ μέχρι τῶν περὶ τὴν Μαιῶτιν ποιήσαιντο στρατείαν, ἀπ' ἐκείνων δὲ καὶ ἡ² Κιμμέριος κληθείη³ βόσπορος, οἷον Κιμβρικός, Κιμμερίους τοὺς Κίμβρους ὀνομασάντων τῶν Ἑλλήνων. φησὶ δὲ καὶ Βοίους τὸν Ἑρκύνιον δρυμὸν οἰκεῖν πρότερον, τοὺς δὲ Κίμβρους ὁρμήσαντας ἐπὶ τὸν τόπον τοῦτον, ἀποκρουσθέντας ὑπὸ τῶν Βοΐων ἐπὶ τὸν Ἴστρον καὶ τοὺς Σκορδίσκους Γαλάτας καταβῆναι, εἶτ' ἐπὶ Τευρίστας καὶ Ταυρίσκους, καὶ τούτους Γαλάτας, εἶτ' ἐπὶ Ἑλουηττίους, πολυχρύσους μὲν ἄνδρας, εἰρηναίους δέ· ὁρῶντας δὲ τὸν ἐκ τῶν ληστηρίων πλοῦτον ὑπερβάλλοντα τοῦ παρ' ἑαυτοῖς τοὺς Ἑλουηττίους ἐπαρθῆναι, μάλιστα δ' αὐτῶν Τιγυρηνούς τε καὶ Τωυγένους, C 294 ὥστε καὶ συνεξορμῆσαι. πάντες μέντοι κατελύθησαν ὑπὸ τῶν Ῥωμαίων, αὐτοί τε οἱ Κίμβροι καὶ οἱ συναράμενοι τούτοις, οἱ μὲν ὑπερβαλόντες τὰς Ἄλπεις εἰς τὴν Ἰταλίαν, οἱ δ' ἔξω τῶν Ἄλπεων.

3. Ἔθος δέ τι τῶν Κίμβρων διηγοῦνται τοιοῦτον, ὅτι ταῖς γυναιξὶν αὐτῶν συστρατευούσαις παρηκολούθουν προμάντεις ἱέρειαι πολιότριχες, λευχεί-

¹ δέ, Meineke emends to τε δή.
² ἡ, Meineke emends to ὁ, perhaps rightly.
³ κληθείη, Casaubon, for κληθείς; so the later editors.

¹ The Strait of Kerch (or Yenikale).

behold it, would not have been likely to prompt in them such terror that they would take to flight, as if it had occurred unexpectedly.

2. Poseidonius is right in censuring the historians for these assertions, and his conjecture is not a bad one, that the Cimbri, being a piratical and wandering folk, made an expedition even as far as the region of Lake Maeotis, and that also the "Cimmerian" Bosporus[1] was named after them, being equivalent to "Cimbrian," the Greeks naming the Cimbri "Cimmerii." And he goes on to say that in earlier times the Boii dwelt in the Hercynian Forest, and that the Cimbri made a sally against this place, but on being repulsed by the Boii, went down to the Ister and the country of the Scordiscan Galatae,[2] then to the country of the Teuristae[3] and Taurisci (these, too, Galatae), and then to the country of the Helvetii—men rich in gold but peaceable; however, when the Helvetii saw that the wealth which the Cimbri had got from their robberies surpassed that of their own country, they, and particularly their tribes of Tigyreni and of Toygeni, were so excited that they sallied forth with the Cimbri. All, however, were subdued by the Romans, both the Cimbri themselves and those who had joined their expeditions, in part after they had crossed the Alps into Italy and in part while still on the other side of the Alps.

3. Writers report a custom of the Cimbri to this effect: Their wives, who would accompany them on their expeditions, were attended by priestesses who

[2] These Galatae lived between the Ister (Danube) and Morava Rivers on the confines of Illyria.
[3] Cp. "Tauristae," 7. 3. 2.

μονες, καρπασίνας ἐφαπτίδας ἐπιπεπορπημέναι,
ζῶσμα χαλκοῦν ἔχουσαι, γυμνόποδες· τοῖς οὖν
αἰχμαλώτοις διὰ τοῦ στρατοπέδου συνήντων ξιφή-
ρεις, καταστέψασαι[1] δ᾽ αὐτοὺς ἦγον ἐπὶ κρατῆρα
χαλκοῦν ὅσον ἀμφορέων εἴκοσι· εἶχον δὲ ἀνα-
βάθραν, ἣν ἀναβᾶσα ὑπερπετὴς τοῦ λέβητος
ἐλαιμοτόμει ἕκαστον μετεωρισθέντα· ἐκ δὲ τοῦ
προχεομένου αἵματος εἰς τὸν κρατῆρα μαντείαν
τινὰ ἐποιοῦντο· ἄλλαι δὲ διασχίσασαι ἐσπλάγ-
χνευον ἀναφθεγγόμεναι νίκην τοῖς οἰκείοις. ἐν
δὲ τοῖς ἀγῶσιν ἔτυπτον τὰς βύρσας τὰς περιτε-
ταμένας τοῖς γέρροις τῶν ἁρμαμαξῶν, ὥστ᾽ ἀποτε-
λεῖσθαι ψόφον ἐξαίσιον.

4. Τῶν δὲ Γερμανῶν, ὡς εἶπον, οἱ μὲν προσάρ-
κτιοι παρήκουσι τῷ ὠκεανῷ, γνωρίζονται δ᾽ ἀπὸ
τῶν ἐκβολῶν τοῦ Ῥήνου λαβόντες τὴν ἀρχὴν
μέχρι τοῦ Ἄλβιος, τούτων δ᾽ εἰσὶ γνωριμώ-
τατοι Σούγαμβροί τε καὶ Κίμβροι, τὰ δὲ πέραν
τοῦ Ἄλβιος τὰ πρὸς τῷ ὠκεανῷ παντάπασιν
ἄγνωστα ἡμῖν ἐστιν. οὔτε γὰρ τῶν προτέρων
οὐδένα ἴσμεν τὸν παράπλουν τοῦτον πεποιη-
μένον πρὸς τὰ ἑωθινὰ μέρη τὰ μέχρι τοῦ στόματος τῆς Κασπίας θαλάττης, οὔθ᾽ οἱ Ῥωμαῖοί
πω προῆλθον εἰς τὰ περαιτέρω τοῦ Ἄλβιος· ὡς
δ᾽ αὕτως οὐδὲ πεζῇ παρωδεύκασιν οὐδένες. ἀλλ᾽
ὅτι μὲν κατὰ μῆκος ἰοῦσιν ἐπὶ τὴν ἕω τὰ κατὰ

---

[1] καταστρέψασαι (ACl).

---

[1] About 120 gallons.   [2] Cp. 7. 2. 1.   [3] 7. 1. 1.
[4] Cp. 7. 1. 1 and the footnote on "ocean."
[5] See the *Frontispiece*, Vol. I.
[6] On the "climata," see 1. 1. 12 and the footnote.

were seers; these were grey-haired, clad in white,
with flaxen cloaks fastened on with clasps, girt with
girdles of bronze, and bare-footed; now sword in
hand these priestesses would meet with the prisoners
of war throughout the camp, and having first crowned
them with wreaths would lead them to a brazen
vessel of about twenty amphorae;[1] and they had a
raised platform which the priestess would mount,
and then, bending over the kettle,[2] would cut the
throat of each prisoner after he had been lifted up;
and from the blood that poured forth into the vessel
some of the priestesses would draw a prophecy,
while still others would split open the body and
from an inspection of the entrails would utter a
prophecy of victory for their own people; and
during the battles they would beat on the hides
that were stretched over the wicker-bodies of the
wagons and in this way produce an unearthly noise.

4. Of the Germans, as I have said,[3] those towards
the north extend along the ocean;[4] and beginning
at the outlets of the Rhenus, they are known as far
as the Albis; and of these the best known are the
Sugambri and the Cimbri; but those parts of the
country beyond the Albis that are near the ocean
are wholly unknown to us. For of the men of
earlier times I know of no one who has made this
voyage along the coast to the eastern parts that
extend as far as the mouth[5] of the Caspian Sea;
and the Romans have not yet advanced into the
parts that are beyond the Albis; and likewise no
one has made the journey by land either. However,
it is clear from the "climata"[6] and the parallel
distances that if one travels longitudinally towards
the east, one encounters the regions that are about

τὸν Βορυσθένη καὶ τὰ πρὸς βορρᾶν[1] τοῦ Πόντου
χωρία ἅπαντα, δῆλον ἐκ τῶν κλιμάτων καὶ τῶν
παραλλήλων διαστημάτων· τί δ' ἐστὶ πέραν
τῆς Γερμανίας καὶ τί τῶν ἄλλων τῶν ἑξῆς, εἴτε
Βαστάρνας χρὴ λέγειν, ὡς οἱ πλείους ὑπονοοῦσιν,
εἴτ' ἄλλους μεταξὺ ἢ Ἰάζυγας ἢ Ῥωξολανοὺς ἤ
τινας ἄλλους τῶν Ἁμαξοίκων οὐ ῥᾴδιον εἰπεῖν·
οὐδ' εἰ μέχρι τοῦ ὠκεανοῦ παρήκουσι παρὰ πᾶν
τὸ μῆκος, ἢ ἐστί τι ἀοίκητον ὑπὸ ψύχους ἢ ἄλλης
αἰτίας, ἢ εἰ καὶ γένος ἀνθρώπων ἄλλο διαδέχεται
μεταξὺ τῆς θαλάττης καὶ τῶν ἑῴων Γερμανῶν
ἱδρυμένον. τοῦτο δὲ τὸ αὐτὸ ἀγνόημα καὶ περὶ
τῶν ἄλλων τῶν ἐφεξῆς προσαρκτίων ἐπέχει·[2]
οὔτε γὰρ τοὺς Βαστάρνας οὔτε τοὺς Σαυρομάτας
καὶ ἁπλῶς τοὺς ὑπὲρ τοῦ Πόντου οἰκοῦντας ἴσμεν,
οὔθ' ὁπόσον ἀπέχουσι τῆς Ἀτλαντικῆς θαλάττης,
οὔτ' εἰ συνάπτουσιν αὐτῇ.

III

1. Τὸ δὲ νότιον μέρος τῆς Γερμανίας τὸ πέραν
τοῦ Ἄλβιος τὸ μὲν συνεχὲς ἀκμὴν ὑπὸ τῶν
Σοήβων κατέχεται· εἶτ' εὐθὺς ἡ τῶν Γετῶν
συνάπτει γῆ, κατ' ἀρχὰς μὲν στενή, παρατετα-
C 295 μένη τῷ Ἴστρῳ κατὰ τὸ νότιον μέρος, κατὰ δὲ
τοὐναντίον τῇ παρωρείᾳ τοῦ Ἑρκυνίου δρυμοῦ,

---

[1] μέρη, after βορρᾶν, Corais deletes; so Meineke.
[2] ἐπέχει, conj. of Kramer, for ἔλεγεν; so the later editors
read.

---

[1] Cp. 2. 5. 7 and 7. 3. 17.

the Borysthenes and that are to the north of the
Pontus; but what is beyond Germany and what
beyond the countries which are next after Germany
—whether one should say the Bastarnae, as most
writers suspect, or say that others lie in between,
either the Iazyges, or the Roxolani,[1] or certain
other of the Wagon-dwellers[2]—it is not easy to say;
nor yet whether they extend as far as the ocean
along its entire length, or whether any part is
uninhabitable by reason of the cold or other cause,
or whether even a different race of people, succeeding the Germans, is situated between the sea and
the eastern Germans. And this same ignorance
prevails also in regard to the rest of the peoples
that come next in order on the north; for I know
neither the Bastarnae,[3] nor the Sauromatae, nor, in
a word, any of the peoples who dwell above the
Pontus, nor how far distant they are from the
Atlantic Sea,[4] nor whether their countries border
upon it.

III

1. As for the southern part of Germany beyond
the Albis, the portion which is just contiguous to
that river is occupied by the Suevi; then immediately
adjoining this is the land of the Getae, which,
though narrow at first, stretching as it does along
the Ister on its southern side and on the opposite
side along the mountain-side of the Hercynian Forest

---

[2] Cp. 2. 5. 26. [3] See 2. 5. 30.
[4] The same in Strabo as "the Atlantic Ocean," including
the "Northern Ocean."

μέρος τι τῶν ὀρῶν καὶ αὐτὴ κατέχουσα, εἶτα πλατύνεται πρὸς τὰς ἄρκτους μέχρι Τυρεγετῶν· τοὺς δὲ ἀκριβεῖς ὅρους οὐκ ἔχομεν φράζειν. διὰ δὲ τὴν ἄγνοιαν τῶν τόπων τούτων οἱ τὰ Ῥιπαῖα ὄρη καὶ τοὺς Ὑπερβορείους μυθοποιοῦντες λόγου ἠξίωνται, καὶ ἃ Πυθέας ὁ Μασσαλιώτης κατεψεύσατο ταῦτα τῆς παρωκεανίτιδος, προσχήματι χρώμενος τῇ περὶ τὰ οὐράνια καὶ τὰ μαθηματικὰ ἱστορία. ἐκεῖνοι μὲν οὖν ἐάσθωσαν· οὐδὲ γὰρ εἴ τινα Σοφοκλῆς τραγῳδεῖ περὶ τῆς Ὠρειθυίας λέγων, ὡς ἀναρπαγεῖσα ὑπὸ Βορέου κομισθείη

> ὑπέρ τε πόντον πάντ' ἐπ' ἔσχατα χθονὸς
> νυκτός τε πηγὰς οὐρανοῦ τ' ἀναπτυχὰς
> Φοίβου τε[1] παλαιὸν κῆπον,

οὐδὲν ἂν εἴη πρὸς τὰ νῦν, ἀλλ' ἐατέον, ὥσπερ καὶ ἐν τῷ Φαίδρῳ ὁ Σωκράτης. ἃ δὲ ἔκ τε τῆς παλαιᾶς ἱστορίας καὶ τῆς νῦν παρειλήφαμεν, ταῦτα λέγωμεν.

2. Οἱ τοίνυν Ἕλληνες τοὺς[2] Γέτας Θρᾷκας ὑπελάμβανον· ᾤκουν δ' ἐφ' ἑκάτερα τοῦ Ἴστρου καὶ οὗτοι καὶ οἱ Μυσοί, Θρᾷκες ὄντες καὶ αὐτοί, καὶ οὓς νῦν Μοισοὺς[3] καλοῦσιν· ἀφ' ὧν ὡρμήθησαν καὶ οἱ νῦν μεταξὺ Λυδῶν καὶ Φρυγῶν καὶ Τρώων

---

[1] τε, Meineke deletes.
[2] τε, before Γέτας, Meineke deletes.
[3] Μοισούς, Tyrwhitt, for Μυσούς; so the later editors read.

---

[1] Cp. Pliny 4. 26.   [2] Cp. 1. 3. 22.
[3] Cp. 1. 4. 3–5, 2. 3. 5 and 2. 4. 1–2.
[4] The daughter of Erechtheus, a mythical Attic king. The passage here quoted is a fragment (Nauck, *Fragmenta*, 870) of a play now lost. Cp. *Antigone*, 981 ff.
[5] The west.   [6] The east.

(for the land of the Getae also embraces a part of the mountains), afterwards broadens out towards the north as far as the Tyregetae; but I cannot tell the precise boundaries. It is because of men's ignorance of these regions that any heed has been given to those who created the mythical "Rhipaean Mountains"[1] and "Hyperboreans,"[2] and also to all those false statements made by Pytheas the Massalian regarding the country along the ocean, wherein he uses as a screen his scientific knowledge of astronomy and mathematics.[3] So then, those men should be disregarded; in fact, if even Sophocles, when in his rôle as a tragic poet he speaks of Oreithyia,[4] tells how she was snatched up by "Boreas" and carried "over the whole sea to the ends of the earth and to the sources of night[5] and to the unfoldings of heaven[6] and to the ancient garden of Phoebus,"[7] his story can have no bearing on the present inquiry, but should be disregarded, just as it is disregarded by Socrates in the *Phaedrus*.[8] But let us confine our narrative to what we have learned from history, both ancient and modern.

2. Now the Greeks used to suppose that the Getae were Thracians; and the Getae lived on either side the Ister, as did also the Mysi, these also being Thracians and identical with the people who are now called Moesi; from these Mysi sprang also the Mysi who now live between the Lydians and the

---

[7] The south, apparently; and thus Boreas would have carried her to the four ends of the earth. The home of Boreas (North Wind), according to the poets, was in the Haemus (Balkan), or Rhipaean, Mountains, on the "Sarpedonian Rock."

[8] Plato, *Phaedrus* 229.

οἰκοῦντες Μυσοί. καὶ αὐτοὶ δ᾽ οἱ Φρύγες Βρίγες
εἰσί, Θρᾳκιόν τι ἔθνος, καθάπερ καὶ Μυγδόνες
καὶ Βέβρυκες καὶ Μεδοβιθυνοὶ[1] καὶ Βιθυνοὶ καὶ
Θῦνοι, δοκῶ δὲ καὶ τοὺς Μαριανδυνούς. οὗτοι
μὲν οὖν τελέως ἐκλελοίπασι πάντες τὴν Εὐρώπην,
οἱ δὲ Μυσοὶ συνέμειναν. καὶ Ὅμηρον δ᾽[2] ὀρθῶς
εἰκάζειν μοι δοκεῖ Ποσειδώνιος[3] τοὺς ἐν τῇ Εὐρώπῃ
Μυσοὺς κατονομάζειν (λέγω δὲ τοὺς ἐν τῇ Θρᾴκῃ),
ὅταν φῇ·

αὐτὸς δὲ πάλιν τρέπεν ὄσσε φαεινώ,
νόσφιν ἐφ᾽ ἱπποπόλων Θρηκῶν καθορώμενος
αἶαν
Μυσῶν τ᾽ ἀγχεμάχων·

ἐπεὶ εἴ γε τοὺς κατὰ τὴν Ἀσίαν Μυσοὺς δέχοιτό
τις, ἀπηρτημένος ἂν εἴη ὁ λόγος. τὸ γὰρ ἀπὸ
τῶν Τρώων τρέψαντα τὴν ὅρασιν ἐπὶ τὴν Θρακῶν
γῆν συγκαταλέγειν ταύτῃ τὴν τῶν Μυσῶν, τῶν
οὐ νόσφιν ὄντων,[4] ἀλλ᾽ ὁμόρων τῇ Τρωάδι καὶ
ὄπισθεν αὐτῆς ἱδρυμένων καὶ ἑκατέρωθεν, διειργο-
μένων δ᾽ ἀπὸ τῆς Θρᾴκης πλατεῖ Ἑλλησπόντῳ,
συγχέοντος ἂν εἴη τὰς ἠπείρους καὶ ἅμα τῆς
φράσεως οὐκ ἀκούοντος. τὸ γὰρ πάλιν τρέπεν
μάλιστα μέν ἐστιν εἰς τοὐπίσω· ὁ δ᾽ ἀπὸ τῶν
Τρώων μεταφέρων τὴν ὄψιν ἐπὶ τοὺς ἢ[5] ὄπισθεν

---

[1] Μεδοβιθυνοί, Meineke, Müller-Dübner and others, following Tzschucke, emend to Μαιδοβιθυνοί, the correct spelling of
the word. But both here and in 7. 5. 12 (Μεδων) the MSS.
of Strabo are unanimous.
[2] δ᾽, after Ὅμηρον, Jones inserts; Kramer and the later
editors, δέ.
[3] δέ, after Ποσειδώνιος, Kramer deletes.
[4] ὄντων, Corais, for ἐόντων; so the later editors.

Phrygians and Trojans. And the Phrygians themselves are Brigians, a Thracian tribe, as are also the
Mygdonians, the Bebricians, the Medobithynians,[1]
the Bithynians, and the Thynians, and, I think, also
the Mariandynians. These peoples, to be sure,
have all utterly quitted Europe, but the Mysi have
remained there. And Poseidonius seems to me to
be correct in his conjecture that Homer designates
the Mysi in Europe (I mean those in Thrace) when
he says, " But back he turned his shining eyes, and
looked far away towards the land of the horse-
tending Thracians, and of the Mysi, hand-to-hand
fighters," [2] for surely, if one should take Homer to
mean the Mysi in Asia, the statement would not
hang together. Indeed, when Zeus turns his eyes
away from the Trojans towards the land of the
Thracians, it would be the act of a man who confuses
the continents and does not understand the poet's
phraseology to connect with Thrace the land of the
Asiatic Mysi, who are not "far away," but have a
common boundary with the Troad and are situated
behind it and on either side of it, and are separated
from Thrace by the broad Hellespont; for " back he
turned " generally [3] means "to the rear," and he
who transfers his gaze from the Trojans to the
people who are either in the rear of the Trojans or

---

[1] The correct spelling of the word is " Maedobithynians."
[2] *Iliad* 13. 3–5.
[3] The other meaning of the word in question (πάλιν) is
"again." Aristarchus, the great Homeric scholar (fl. about
155 B.C.), quoted by Hesychius (*s.v.*), says that "generally
the poet uses πάλιν in the place-sense and not, as we do, in
the time-sense."

---

[5] ἤ, Madvig, for μή.

C 296 αὐτῶν ἢ ἐκ πλαγίων ὄντας προσωτέρω μὲν μετα-
φέρει, εἰς τοὐπίσω δ' οὐ πάνυ. καὶ τὸ ἐπιφερό-
μενον δ' αὐτοῦ τούτου μαρτύριον, ὅτι τοὺς Ἱππημολγοὺς καὶ Γαλακτοφάγους καὶ Ἀβίους συνῆψεν
αὐτοῖς, οἵπερ εἰσὶν οἱ ἁμάξοικοι Σκύθαι καὶ
Σαρμάται. καὶ γὰρ νῦν ἀναμέμικται ταῦτα τὰ
ἔθνη τοῖς Θρᾳξὶ καὶ τὰ Βασταρνικά, μᾶλλον μὲν
τοῖς ἐκτὸς Ἴστρου, ἀλλὰ καὶ τοῖς ἐντός. τούτοις
δὲ καὶ τὰ Κελτικά, οἵ τε Βόιοι καὶ Σκορδίσκοι καὶ
Ταυρίσκοι. τοὺς δὲ Σκορδίσκους ἔνιοι Σκορδίστας
καλοῦσι καὶ τοὺς Ταυρίσκους δὲ Λιγυρίσκους[1] καὶ
Ταυρίστας φασί.

3. Λέγει δὲ τοὺς Μυσοὺς ὁ Ποσειδώνιος καὶ
ἐμψύχων ἀπέχεσθαι κατ' εὐσέβειαν, διὰ δὲ τοῦτο
καὶ θρεμμάτων· μέλιτι δὲ χρῆσθαι καὶ γάλακτι
καὶ τυρῷ ζῶντας καθ' ἡσυχίαν, διὰ δὲ τοῦτο
καλεῖσθαι θεοσεβεῖς τε καὶ καπνοβάτας· εἶναι δὲ
τινας τῶν Θρᾳκῶν, οἳ χωρὶς γυναικὸς ζῶσιν, οὓς
Κτίστας καλεῖσθαι, ἀνιερῶσθαί τε διὰ τιμὴν καὶ

---

[1] For Λιγυρίσκους, Meineke writes Τευρίσκους, perhaps
rightly.

---

[1] i.e. "to the rear" of himself.

[2] "And of the proud Hippemolgi (mare-milkers), Galactophagi (curd-eaters), and Abii (a resourceless folk), men most
just" (Iliad 1–3. 5–6). Cp. 1. 1. 6.

[3] "Ligurisci" is almost certainly corrupt. Meineke is
probably right in emending to "Teurisci."

[4] Cp. "Teuristae," 7. 2. 2.

[5] Scholars have suggested various emendations to "capnobatae," but there is no variation in the spelling of the
word in any of the manuscripts, either here or in § 4 below.
Its literal meaning is "smoke-treaders" (cp. ἀεροβάτης,

on their flanks, does indeed transfer his gaze rather far, but not at all "to the rear."[1] Again, the appended phrase[2] is testimony to this very view, because the poet connected with the Mysi the "Hippemolgi" and "Galactophagi" and "Abii," who are indeed the wagon-dwelling Scythians and Sarmatians. For at the present time these tribes, as well as the Bastarnian tribes, are mingled with the Thracians (more indeed with those outside the Ister, but also with those inside). And mingled with them are also the Celtic tribes—the Boii, the Scordisci, and the Taurisci. However, the Scordisci are by some called "Scordistae"; and the Taurisci are called also "Ligurisci"[3] and "Tauristae."[4]

3. Poseidonius goes on to say of the Mysians that in accordance with their religion they abstain from eating any living thing, and therefore from their flocks as well; and that they use as food honey and milk and cheese, living a peaceable life, and for this reason are called both "god-fearing" and "capnobatae";[5] and there are some of the Thracians who live apart from woman-kind; these are called "Ctistae,"[6] and because of the honour in which they are held, have been dedicated to the gods and live with freedom from every fear;

ἀεροβάτῳ Aristophanes, *Clouds* 225, 1503), and it seems to allude in some way to the smoke of sacrifice and the more or less ethereal existence of the people, or else (see Herodotus 1. 202 and 4. 75) to the custom of generating an intoxicating vapour by throwing hemp-seed upon red-hot stones. Berkel and Wakefield would emend, respectively, to "capnopatae" and "capnobotae" ("smoke-eaters," *i.e.* people who live on food of no value).

[6] Literally, "creators" or "founders." But, like "capnobatae," the force of the word here is unknown.

μετὰ ἀδείας ζῆν· τούτους δὴ συλλήβδην ἅπαντας
τὸν ποιητὴν εἰπεῖν ἀγαυοὺς Ἱππημολγούς, Γαλακτοφάγους Ἀβίους τε, δικαιοτάτους ἀνθρώπους.
Ἀβίους δὲ προσαγορεύειν μάλιστα, ὅτι χωρὶς
γυναικῶν, ἡγούμενον ἡμιτελῆ τινα βίον τὸν χῆρον,
καθάπερ καὶ τὸν οἶκον ἡμιτελῆ τὸν Πρωτεσιλάου,
διότι χῆρος· ἀγχεμάχους δὲ τοὺς Μυσούς, ὅτι
ἀπόρθητοι, καθὰ οἱ ἀγαθοὶ πολεμισταί· δεῖν δὲ
ἐν τῷ τρισκαιδεκάτῳ[1] ἐγγράφειν ἀντὶ τοῦ Μυσῶν
τ' ἀγχεμάχων Μοισῶν τ' ἀγχεμάχων.[2]

4. Τὸ μὲν οὖν τὴν γραφὴν κινεῖν ἐκ τοσούτων
ἐτῶν εὐδοκιμήσασαν περιττὸν ἴσως. πολὺ γὰρ
πιθανώτερον ὠνομάσθαι μὲν ἐξ ἀρχῆς Μυσούς,
μετωνομάσθαι δὲ καὶ[3] νῦν. τοὺς Ἀβίους δὲ
τοὺς χήρους οὐ μᾶλλον ἢ τοὺς ἀνεστίους καὶ
τοὺς ἁμαξοίκους δέξαιτ' ἄν τις· μάλιστα γὰρ
περὶ τὰ συμβόλαια καὶ τὴν τῶν χρημάτων
ἐκτίμησιν[4] συνισταμένων τῶν ἀδικημάτων, τοὺς
οὕτως ἀπ' ὀλίγων εὐτελῶς ζῶντας δικαιοτάτους
εὔλογον κληθῆναι· ἐπεὶ καὶ οἱ φιλόσοφοι τῇ
σωφροσύνῃ τὴν δικαιοσύνην ἐγγυτάτω τιθέντες
τὸ αὔταρκες καὶ τὸ λιτὸν ἐν τοῖς πρώτοις ἐζή-
λωσαν· ἀφ' οὗ καὶ προεκπτώσεις[5] τινὰς αὐτῶν
παρέωσαν ἐπὶ τὸν κυνισμόν. τὸ δὲ χήρους
γυναικῶν οἰκεῖν οὐδεμίαν τοιαύτην ἔμφασιν ὑπο-
γράφει, καὶ μάλιστα παρὰ τοῖς Θρᾳξί, καὶ τούτων

---

[1] τρισκαιδεκάτῳ, Corais, for δεκάτῳ; so the later editors.
[2] Μοισῶν τ' ἀγχεμάχων, Meineke inserts.
[3] καί, Meineke emends to ὡς.
[4] For ἐκτίμησιν, the reading of the MSS., Meineke writes κτῆσιν.
[5] προεκπτώσεις, Meineke and others, for προσεκπτώσεις.

accordingly, Homer speaks collectively of all these peoples as "proud Hippemolgi, Galactophagi and Abii, men most just," but he calls them "Abii" more especially for this reason, that they live apart from women, since he thinks that a life which is bereft of woman is only half-complete (just as he thinks the "house of Protesilaüs" is only "half complete," because it is so bereft [1]); and he speaks of the Mysians as "hand-to-hand fighters" because they were indomitable, as is the case with all brave warriors; and Poseidonius adds that in the Thirteenth Book [2] one should read "Moesi, hand-to-hand fighters" instead of "Mysi, hand-to-hand fighters."

4. However, it is perhaps superfluous to disturb the reading that has had approval for so many years; for it is much more credible that the people were called Mysi at first and that later their name was changed to what it is now. And as for the term "Abii," one might interpret it as meaning those who are "without hearths" and "live on wagons" quite as well as those who are "bereft"; for since, in general, injustices arise only in connection with contracts and a too high regard for property, so it is reasonable that those who, like the Abii, live cheaply, on slight resources, should have been called "most just." In fact, the philosophers who put justice next to self-restraint strive above all things for frugality and personal independence; and consequently extreme self-restraint diverts some of them to the Cynical mode of life. But as for the statement that they live "bereft of women," the poet suggests nothing of the sort, and particularly in the country of the Thracians and

---

[1] *Iliad* 2. 701.   [2] *Iliad* 13. 5.

τοῖς Γέταις. ὅρα δ' ἃ λέγει Μένανδρος περὶ
αὐτῶν, οὐ πλάσας, ὡς εἰκός, ἀλλ' ἐξ ἱστορίας
λαβών·

C 297   πάντες μὲν οἱ Θρᾷκες, μάλιστα δ' οἱ Γέται
   ἡμεῖς ἁπάντων (καὶ γὰρ αὐτὸς εὔχομαι
   ἐκεῖθεν εἶναι τὸ γένος) οὐ σφόδρ' ἐγκρατεῖς
   ἐσμέν,

καὶ ὑποβὰς μικρὸν τῆς περὶ τὰς γυναῖκας ἀκρασίας
τίθησι τὰ παραδείγματα·

   γαμεῖ γὰρ ἡμῶν οὐδὲ εἷς ὃς [1] οὐ δέκ' ἢ
   ἕνδεκα γυναῖκας δώδεκά τ' ἢ πλείους τινές·
   ἂν τέτταρας δ' ἢ πέντε γεγαμηκὼς τύχῃ
   καταστροφῆς τις, ἀνυμέναιος, ἄθλιος,
   ἄνυμφος οὗτος ἐπικαλεῖτ' ἐν τοῖς ἐκεῖ.

ταῦτα γὰρ ὁμολογεῖται μὲν καὶ παρὰ τῶν ἄλλων.
οὐκ εἰκὸς δὲ τοὺς αὐτοὺς ἅμα μὲν ἄθλιον νομίζειν
βίον τὸν μὴ μετὰ πολλῶν γυναικῶν, ἅμα δὲ
σπουδαῖον καὶ δίκαιον τὸν τῶν γυναικῶν χῆρον.
τὸ δὲ δὴ καὶ θεοσεβεῖς νομίζειν καὶ καπνοβάτας
τοὺς ἐρήμους γυναικῶν σφόδρα ἐναντιοῦται ταῖς
κοιναῖς ὑπολήψεσιν. ἅπαντες γὰρ τῆς δεισι-
δαιμονίας ἀρχηγοὺς οἴονται τὰς γυναῖκας· αὗται
δὲ καὶ τοὺς ἄνδρας προκαλοῦνται πρὸς τὰς ἐπὶ
πλέον θεραπείας τῶν θεῶν καὶ ἑορτὰς καὶ ποτνια-
σμούς· σπάνιον δ' εἴ τις ἀνὴρ καθ' αὑτὸν ζῶν
εὑρίσκεται τοιοῦτος. ὅρα δὲ πάλιν τὸν αὐτὸν
ποιητήν, ἃ λέγει εἰσάγων τὸν ἀχθόμενον ταῖς
περὶ τὰς θυσίας τῶν γυναικῶν δαπάναις [2] καὶ
λέγοντα·

---

[1] ὅς, before οὐ, Jones inserts. Pletho inserts ὁ, Tzschucke
ᾧ; but Corais, whom Müller-Dübner and Meineke follow,
deletes οὐ and inserts εἰ μή.

of those of their number who are Getae. And see the statement of Menander about them, which, as one may reasonably suppose, was not invented by him but taken from history : " All the Thracians, and most of all we Getae (for I too boast that I am of this stock) are not very continent" ;[1] and a little below he sets down the proofs of their incontinence in their relations with women : "For every man of us marries ten or eleven women, and some, twelve or more ; but if anyone meets death before he has married more than four or five, he is lamented among the people there as a wretch without bride and nuptial song." Indeed, these facts are confirmed by the other writers as well. Further, it is not reasonable to suppose that the same people regard as wretched a life without many women, and yet at the same time regard as pious and just a life that is wholly bereft of women. And of course to regard as "both god-fearing and capnobatae" those who are without women is very much opposed to the common notions on that subject ; for all agree in regarding the women as the chief founders of religion, and it is the women who provoke the men to the more attentive worship of the gods, to festivals, and to supplications, and it is a rare thing for a man who lives by himself to be found addicted to these things. See again what the same poet says when he introduces as speaker the man who is vexed by the money spent by the women in connection with

---

[1] This and the succeeding fragment are otherwise unknown (Kock, *Com. Attic. Frag.* 547–548).

---

[2] δαπάναις ("expenses"), Corais and the later editors, for ἀπάταις ("deceits").

ἐπιτρίβουσι δ' ἡμᾶς οἱ θεοί,
μάλιστα τοὺς γήμαντας· ἀεὶ γάρ τινα
ἄγειν ἑορτὴν ἔστ' ἀνάγκη·

τὸν δὲ μισογύνην, αὐτὰ ταῦτα αἰτιώμενον·

ἐθύομεν δὲ πεντάκις τῆς ἡμέρας,
ἐκυμβάλιζον δ' ἑπτὰ θεράπαιναι κύκλῳ,
αἱ δ' ὠλόλυζον.

τὸ μὲν οὖν ἰδίως τοὺς ἀγύνους τῶν Γετῶν εὐσεβεῖς νομίζεσθαι παράλογόν τι ἐμφαίνει· τὸ δ' ἰσχύειν ἐν τῷ ἔθνει τούτῳ τὴν περὶ τὸ θεῖον σπουδὴν ἐκ τε ὧν εἶπε Ποσειδώνιος οὐκ ἀπιστητέον (καὶ ἐμψύχων ἀπέχεσθαι δι' εὐσέβειαν[1]) καὶ ἐκ τῆς ἄλλης ἱστορίας.

5. Λέγεται γάρ τινα τῶν Γετῶν, ὄνομα Ζάμολξιν,[2] δουλεῦσαι Πυθαγόρᾳ, καί τινα τῶν οὐρανίων παρ' ἐκείνου μαθεῖν, τὰ δὲ καὶ παρ' Αἰγυπτίων, πλανηθέντα καὶ μέχρι δεῦρο· ἐπανελθόντα δ' εἰς τὴν οἰκείαν σπουδασθῆναι παρὰ τοῖς ἡγεμόσι καὶ τῷ ἔθνει, προλέγοντα τὰς ἐπισημασίας· τελευτῶντα δὲ πεῖσαι τὸν βασιλέα κοινωνὸν τῆς ἀρχῆς αὐτὸν λαβεῖν, ὡς τὰ παρὰ τῶν θεῶν ἐξαγγέλλειν ἱκανόν· καὶ κατ' ἀρχὰς μὲν ἱερέα κατασταθῆναι τοῦ μάλιστα τιμωμένου C 298 παρ' αὐτοῖς θεοῦ, μετὰ ταῦτα δὲ καὶ Θεὸν προσαγορευθῆναι, καὶ καταλαβόντα ἀντρῶδές τι

---

[1] καὶ . . . εὐσέβειαν, Meineke deletes as a marginal gloss.
[2] Ζάλμοξιν (C).

---

[1] A fragment from some play now lost (Kock, *fr.* 601).
[2] A fragment from the *Misogynes* (*Woman-Hater*). Kock, *fr.* 326.
[3] For another version of the story of Zamolxis, see Herod-

the sacrifices : " The gods are the undoing of us,
especially us married men, for we must always
be celebrating some festival " ; [1] and again when he
introduces the Woman-hater, who complains about
these very things : " we used to sacrifice five times
a day, and seven female attendants would beat the
cymbals all round us, while others would cry out to
the gods." [2] So, then, the interpretation that the
wifeless men of the Getae are in a special way
reverential towards the gods is clearly contrary
to reason, whereas the interpretation that zeal for
religion is strong in this tribe, and that because
of their reverence for the gods the people abstain
from eating any living thing, is one which, both
from what Poseidonius and from what the histories
in general tell us, should not be disbelieved.

5. In fact, it is said that a certain man of the
Getae, Zamolxis by name, had been a slave to
Pythagoras, and had learned some things about
the heavenly bodies from him,[3] as also certain other
things from the Egyptians, for in his wanderings
he had gone even as far as Egypt ; and when he
came on back to his home-land he was eagerly
courted by the rulers and the people of the tribe,
because he could make predictions from the celestial
signs ; and at last he persuaded the king to take
him as a partner in the government, on the ground
that he was competent to report the will of the
gods ; and although at the outset he was only made
a priest of the god who was most honoured in their
country, yet afterwards he was even addressed as

otus (4. 94-96), who doubts whether such a man ever existed,
but says that he was reputed to have been, for a time, a
slave of Pythagoras in Samos.

χωρίον ἄβατον τοῖς ἄλλοις ἐνταῦθα διαιτᾶσθαι,
σπάνιον ἐντυγχάνοντα τοῖς ἐκτός, πλὴν τοῦ
βασιλέως καὶ τῶν θεραπόντων· συμπράττειν δὲ
τὸν βασιλέα, ὁρῶντα τοὺς ἀνθρώπους προσέχοντας
ἑαυτῷ πολὺ πλέον ἢ πρότερον, ὡς ἐκφέροντι τὰ
προστάγματα κατὰ συμβουλὴν θεῶν. τουτὶ δὲ
τὸ ἔθος διέτεινεν ἄχρι καὶ εἰς ἡμᾶς, ἀεί τινος
εὑρισκομένου τοιούτου τὸ ἦθος, ὃς τῷ μὲν βασιλεῖ
σύμβουλος ὑπῆρχε, παρὰ δὲ τοῖς Γέταις ὠνομάζετο
Θεός· καὶ τὸ ὄρος ὑπελήφθη [1] ἱερόν, καὶ προσαγορεύουσιν οὕτως· ὄνομα δ' αὐτῷ Κωγαίονον,
ὁμώνυμον τῷ παραρρέοντι ποταμῷ. καὶ δὴ ὅτε
Βυρεβίστας [2] ἦρχε τῶν Γετῶν, ἐφ' ὃν ἤδη παρε-
σκευάσατο Καῖσαρ ὁ Θεὸς στρατεύειν, Δεκαίνεος
εἶχε ταύτην τὴν τιμήν· καί πως τὸ τῶν ἐμψύχων
ἀπέχεσθαι Πυθαγόρειον τοῦ Ζαμόλξιος ἔμεινε
παραδοθέν.

6. Τοιαῦτα μὲν οὖν καλῶς [3] ἄν τις διαποροίη
περὶ τῶν κειμένων παρὰ τῷ ποιητῇ, περί τε
Μυσῶν καὶ ἀγαυῶν Ἱππημολγῶν· ἃ δ' Ἀπολλόδωρος ἐν τῷ δευτέρῳ Περὶ Νεῶν προοιμιαζόμενος
εἴρηκεν, ἥκιστα λέγοιτ' ἄν. ἐπαινεῖ γὰρ Ἐρατοσθένους ἀπόφασιν, ὅτι φησὶν ἐκεῖνος καὶ Ὅμηρον

---

[1] ὑπελήφθη, all editors, for ὑπελείφθη.
[2] So the name is spelled here and in 16. 2. 39; but
Βοερεβίστας in 7. 3. 11 and 7. 3. 12.
[3] καλῶς, Jones (following *l*), for κακῶς. Others insert οὐ
before κακῶς.

---

[1] The " cavernous place " previously referred to.
[2] Some scholars identify this mountain with what is now
Mt. Gogany (near Mika) ; others, with Mt. Kaszon (on the
borders of Transylvania and Moldavia). The former is
more likely.

god, and having taken possession of a certain
cavernous place that was inaccessible to anyone
else he spent his life there, only rarely meeting
with any people outside except the king and his
own attendants ; and the king cooperated with him,
because he saw that the people paid much more
attention to himself than before, in the belief that
the decrees which he promulgated were in accordance with the counsel of the gods. This custom
persisted even down to our own time, because some
man of that character was always to be found, who,
though in fact only a counsellor to the king, was
called god among the Getae. And the people
took up the notion that the mountain [1] was sacred
and they so call it, but its name is Cogaeonum,[2]
like that of the river which flows past it. So, too,
at the time when Byrebistas,[3] against whom already [4]
the Deified Caesar had prepared to make an
expedition, was reigning over the Getae, the
office in question was held by Decaeneus, and
somehow or other the Pythagorean doctrine of
abstention from eating any living thing still
survived as taught by Zamolxis.

6. Now although such difficulties as these might
fairly be raised concerning what is found in the
text of Homer about the Mysians and the "proud
Hippemolgi," yet what Apollodorus states in the
preface to the Second Book of his work *On Ships* [5]
can by no means be asserted ; for he approves the
declaration of Eratosthenes, that although both

---

[3] Strabo also spells the name "Boerebistas (7. 3. 11, 12).
[4] Cp. 7. 3. 11.
[5] Or rather *On the Catalogue of Ships* (1. 2. 24).

STRABO

καὶ τοὺς ἄλλους τοὺς παλαιούς, τὰ μὲν Ἑλληνικὰ
εἰδέναι, τῶν δὲ πόρρω πολλὴν ἔχειν ἀπειρίαν,
ἀπείρους μὲν μακρῶν ὁδῶν ὄντας, ἀπείρους δὲ
τοῦ ναυτίλλεσθαι. συνηγορῶν δὲ τούτοις Ὅμηρόν
φησι τὴν μὲν Αὐλίδα καλεῖν πετρήεσσαν, ὥσπερ
καὶ ἔστι, πολύκνημον δὲ τὸν Ἐτεωνόν, πολυ-
τρήρωνα δὲ τὴν Θίσβην, ποιήεντα δὲ τὸν Ἁλί-
αρτον· τὰ δ' ἄπωθεν οὔτ' αὐτὸν εἰδέναι οὔτε
τοὺς ἄλλους. ποταμῶν γοῦν περὶ τετταράκοντα
ῥεόντων εἰς τὸν Πόντον, μηδὲ τῶν ἐνδοξοτάτων
μηδενὸς μεμνῆσθαι, οἷον Ἴστρου, Τανάιδος, Βορυσθένους, Ὑπάνιος, Φάσιδος, Θερμώδοντος, Ἅλυος·
ἔτι δὲ Σκυθῶν μὲν μὴ μεμνῆσθαι, πλάττειν [1] δὲ
ἀγαυούς τινας Ἱππημολγοὺς καὶ Γαλακτοφάγους
Ἀβίους τε. Παφλαγόνας τε τοὺς ἐν τῇ μεσογαίᾳ
ἱστορηκέναι παρὰ τῶν πεζῇ τοῖς τόποις πλησια-
σάντων, τὴν παραλίαν δὲ ἀγνοεῖν· καὶ εἰκότως
γε. ἄπλουν γὰρ εἶναι τότε τὴν θάλατταν ταύτην
καὶ καλεῖσθαι Ἄξενον διὰ τὸ δυσχείμερον καὶ
τὴν ἀγριότητα τῶν περιοικούντων ἐθνῶν, καὶ
μάλιστα τῶν Σκυθικῶν, ξενοθυτούντων καὶ
σαρκοφαγούντων καὶ τοῖς κρανίοις ἐκπώμασι
C 299 χρωμένων· ὕστερον δ' Εὔξεινον κεκλῆσθαι, τῶν
Ἰώνων ἐν τῇ παραλίᾳ πόλεις κτισάντων· ὁμοίως
δ' ἀγνοεῖν καὶ τὰ περὶ Αἴγυπτον καὶ Λιβύην,
οἷον τὰς ἀναβάσεις τοῦ Νείλου καὶ προσχώσεις

---

[1] πλάττειν, the editors (from conj. of Villebrun) for
πάντας.

[1] Iliad 2. 496.   [2] Iliad 2. 497.
[3] Iliad 2. 502.   [4] Iliad 2. 503.
[5] Now, respectively, the Danube, Don, Dnieper, Bog,
Rion, Termeh, and Kizil-Irmak.

188

Homer and the other early authors knew the Greek places, they were decidedly unacquainted with those that were far away, since they had no experience either in making long journeys by land or in making voyages by sea. And in support of this Apollodorus says that Homer calls Aulis "rocky"[1] (and so it is), and Eteonus "place of many ridges,"[2] and Thisbe "haunt of doves,"[3] and Haliartus "grassy,"[4] but, he says, neither Homer nor the others knew the places that were far away. At any rate, he says, although about forty rivers flow into the Pontus, Homer mentions not a single one of those that are the most famous, as, for example, the Ister, the Tanaïs, the Borysthenes, the Hypanis, the Phasis, the Thermodon, the Halys ;[5] and, besides, he does not mention the Scythians, but invents certain "proud Hippemolgi" and "Galactophagi" and "Abii"; and as for the Paphlagonians of the interior, he reports what he has learned from those who have approached the regions afoot, but he is ignorant of the seaboard,[6] and naturally so, for at that time this sea was not navigable, and was called Axine[7] because of its wintry storms and the ferocity of the tribes that lived around it, and particularly the Scythians, in that they sacrificed strangers, ate their flesh, and used their skulls as drinking-cups ; but later it was called "Euxine,"[8] when the Ionians founded cities on the seaboard. And, likewise, Homer is also ignorant of the facts about Egypt and Libya, as, for example, about the risings of the Nile and the silting up of the sea,[9]

[6] Cp. 12. 3. 26.   [7] That is "Inhospitable."
[8] "Hospitable," euphemistically.   [9] Cp. 1. 2. 29.

189

τοῦ πελάγους, ὧν οὐδαμοῦ μεμνῆσθαι, οὐδὲ τοῦ
ἰσθμοῦ τοῦ μεταξὺ τῆς Ἐρυθρᾶς καὶ τῆς Αἰγυπτίας θαλάττης, οὐδὲ τῶν κατὰ τὴν Ἀραβίαν καὶ
Αἰθιοπίαν καὶ τὸν ὠκεανόν, εἰ μὴ Ζήνωνι τῷ
φιλοσόφῳ προσεκτέον γράφοντι·

Αἰθίοπάς θ' ἱκόμην καὶ Σιδονίους Ἄραβάς τε.

οὐ θαυμαστὸν δ' εἶναι περὶ Ὁμήρου· καὶ γὰρ
τοὺς ἔτι νεωτέρους ἐκείνου πολλὰ ἀγνοεῖν καὶ
τερατολογεῖν· Ἡσίοδον μὲν Ἡμίκυνας λέγοντα
καὶ Μεγαλοκεφάλους καὶ Πυγμαίους, Ἀλκμᾶνα
δὲ Στεγανόποδας, Αἰσχύλον δὲ Κυνοκεφάλους
καὶ Στερνοφθάλμους καὶ Μονομμάτους (ἐν τῷ
Προμηθεῖ φασι[1]) καὶ ἄλλα μυρία. ἀπὸ δὲ τούτων
ἐπὶ τοὺς συγγραφέας βαδίζει Ῥιπαῖα ὄρη λέγοντας
καὶ τὸ Ὠγύιον[2] ὄρος καὶ τὴν τῶν Γοργόνων καὶ
Ἑσπερίδων κατοικίαν καὶ τὴν παρὰ Θεοπόμπῳ
Μεροπίδα γῆν, παρ' Ἑκαταίῳ δὲ Κιμμερίδα πόλιν,
παρ' Εὐημέρῳ δὲ τὴν Παγχαίαν γῆν, παρ' Ἀρισ-

---

[1] (ἐν . . . φασι), Corais and Meineke, following o, delete
as being a gloss.

[2] Ὠγύιον, the reading of the MSS. except C (Ὠγύιν), l
(Ὠγυεν), and ik (Ὠγύγιον) which last is followed, perhaps
rightly, by Xylander and Corais.

---

[1] Red.   [2] Mediterranean.

[3] Odyssey 4. 84. Zeno emended the Homeric text to read
as above (see 1. 2. 34).

[4] Cp. 1. 2. 35.

[5] Aeschylus refers to "one-eyed" men in Prometheus
Bound (l. 804). The other epithets (See Nauck, Frs. 431,
441) were taken from plays now lost.

[6] Cp. 7. 3. 1.

[7] "Mt. Ogyium" is otherwise unknown. The reading is
probably corrupt.

[8] Aelian (Var. Hist., 3. 18) says that Theopompus the

things which he nowhere mentions; neither does
he mention the isthmus between the Erythraean[1]
and the Egyptian[2] Seas, nor the regions of Arabia
and Ethiopia and the ocean, unless one should
give heed to Zeno the philosopher when he writes,
"And I came to the Ethiopians and Sidonians and
Arabians."[3]   But this ignorance in Homer's case is
not amazing, for those who have lived later than
he have been ignorant of many things and have
invented marvellous tales: Hesiod, when he speaks
of "men who are half-dog,"[4] of "long-headed men,"
and of "Pygmies"; and Alcman, when he speaks of
"web-footed men"; and Aeschylus, when he speaks
of "dog-headed men," of "men with eyes in their
breasts," and of "one-eyed men" (in his *Prometheus*,
it is said[5]); and a host of other tales.   From these
men he proceeds against the historians who speak
of the "Rhipaean Mountains,"[6] and of "Mt.
Ogyium,"[7] and of the settlement of the Gorgons
and Hesperides, and of the "Land of Meropis"[8]
in Theopompus,[9] and the "City of Cimmeris" in
Hecataeus,[10] and the "Land of Panchaea"[11] in

historian related a conversation between King Midas and
Silenus in which Silenus reported a race called "Meropians"
who inhabited a continent larger than Asia, Europe, and
Africa combined.

[9] Theopompus (b. about 380 B.C.) wrote, among other
works, two histories, (1) the *Hellenica*, in twelve books,
being a continuation of Thucydides and covering the period
from 411 to 394 B.C., and (2) the *Philippica*, in fifty-eight
books, being a history of the life and times of Philip of
Macedon (360–336 B.C.).   Only a few fragments of these
works remain.

[10] Hecataeus (b. about 540 B.C.) wrote both a geographical
and an historical treatise.   Only fragments remain.

[11] Cp. 2. 4. 2.

τοτέλει δὲ ποταμίους λίθους ἐξ ἄμμου, ἐκ δὲ τῶν
ὄμβρων τήκεσθαι· ἐν δὲ τῇ Λιβύῃ Διονύσου πόλιν
εἶναι, ταύτῃ δ' οὐκ ἐνδέχεσθαι δὶς τὸν αὐτὸν
ἐπιτυχεῖν.[1] ἐπιτιμᾷ δὲ καὶ τοῖς περὶ Σικελίαν
τὴν πλάνην λέγουσι καθ' Ὅμηρον τὴν Ὀδυσσέως·
εἰ γὰρ αὖ[2] χρῆναι τὴν μὲν πλάνην ἐκεῖ γεγονέναι
φάσκειν, τὸν δὲ ποιητὴν ἐξωκεανικέναι μυθολογίας
χάριν· καὶ τοῖς μὲν ἄλλοις συγγνώμην εἶναι,
Καλλιμάχῳ δὲ μὴ πάνυ, μεταποιουμένῳ γε γραμ-
ματικῆς· ὃς τὴν μὲν Γαῦδον Καλυψοῦς νῆσόν
φησι, τὴν δὲ Κόρκυραν Σχερίαν· ἄλλους δ'
αἰτιᾶται ψεύσασθαι περὶ Γερήνων καὶ τοῦ
Ἀκακησίου καὶ Δήμου ἐν Ἰθάκῃ, Πελεθρονίου δ'
ἐν Πηλίῳ, Γλαυκωπίου δ' ἐν Ἀθήναις. τούτοις
δὲ μικρά τινα προσθεὶς τοιαῦτα παύεται, τὰ

---

[1] ἐπιτυχεῖν, Jones, following conj. of Capps, for ἐπιτεῖναι.
Others emend to ἐξευρεῖν.

[2] αὖ, Corais emends to ἄν. Meineke rightly suspects that
εἰ γὰρ αὖ is corrupt.

---

[1] Euhemerus (fl. about 310 B.C.) wrote a work on *Sacred
History* (cp. 1. 3. 1).

[2] Such words as these have not been found in the extant
works of Aristotle.

[3] Cp. 1. 2. 17–19.

[4] Callimachus of Cyrene (fl. about 250 B.C.) is said to have
written about 800 works, in prose and verse. Only 6 hymns,
64 epigrams and some fragments are extant.

[5] Cp. 1. 2. 37.   [6] See footnote 2 on 1. 2. 37.

[7] Cp. 8. 3. 7, 29 and the *Odyssey* (the "Gerenian" Nestor).

[8] Strabo alludes to the wrong interpretation which some
put upon ἀκάκητα, the epithet of Hermes (*Iliad* 16. 185),
making it refer to a cavern in Arcadia, called "Acacesium,"
near Mt. Cyllene, where Hermes was born. Hesiod (*Theog.*

Euhemerus,[1] and in Aristotle "the river-stones, which are formed of sand but are melted by the rains."[2] And in Libya, Apollodorus continues, there is a "City of Dionysus" which it is impossible for the same man ever to find twice. He censures also those who speak of the Homeric wanderings of Odysseus as having been in the neighbourhood of Sicily; for in that case, says he, one should go on and say that, although the wanderings took place there, the poet, for the sake of mythology, placed them out in Oceanus.[3] And, he adds, the writers in general can be pardoned, but Callimachus[4] cannot be pardoned at all, because he makes a pretence of being a scholar;[5] for he calls Gaudos[6] the "Isle of Calypso" and Corcyra "Scheria." And others he charges with falsifying about "Gerena,"[7] and "Acacesium,"[8] and "Demus"[9] in Ithaca, and about "Pelethronium"[10] in Pelion, and about Glaucopium[11] in Athens. To these criticisms Apollodorus adds some petty ones of like sort and then stops, but he

614) gives the same epithet to Prometheus, who, according to the scholiast, was so called from "Mt. Acacesium" in Arcadia, where he was much revered.

[9] *Iliad* 3. 201. The critics in question maintained that "demus" ("deme," "people") was the name of a place in Ithaca.

[10] "Pelethronium" is not found in Homer or Hesiod. According to some it was a city of Thessaly; others, a mountain (or a part of Mt. Pelion) in Thessaly; and others, the cave where Cheiron trained Achilles.

[11] "Glaucopium" is not found in Homer or Hesiod. According to Eustathius it was applied by the ancients to the citadel of Athens, or to the temple of Athene, and was derived from Athene "Glaucopis" ("Flashing-eyed"); but Stephanus Byzantinus derives the word from Glaucopus, son of Alalcomeneus.

πλεῖστα μετενέγκας παρὰ τοῦ Ἐρατοσθένους,
ὡς καὶ πρότερον ἐμνήσθημεν, οὐκ εὖ εἰρημένα.
τὸ μὲν γὰρ τοὺς ὕστερον ἐμπειροτέρους γεγονέναι
τῶν πάλαι[1] περὶ τὰ τοιαῦτα καὶ Ἐρατοσθένει
καὶ τούτῳ δοτέον· τὸ δ' οὕτω πέρα τοῦ μετρίου
προάγειν, καὶ μάλιστα ἐφ' Ὁμήρου, δοκεῖ μοι
κἂν ἐπιπλῆξαί τις δικαίως, καὶ τοὐναντίον εἰπεῖν,
ὡς περὶ ὧν ἀγνοοῦσιν αὐτοί, περὶ τούτων. τῷ
C 300 ποιητῇ προφέρουσι. τὰ μὲν οὖν ἄλλα ἐν τοῖς
καθ' ἕκαστα οἰκείας μνήμης τυγχάνει, τὰ δ' ἐν
τοῖς καθόλου.

7. Νυνὶ δὲ περὶ Θρᾳκῶν ἐλέγομεν,

Μυσῶν τ' ἀγχεμάχων καὶ ἀγαυῶν Ἱππημολγῶν,

Γλακτοφάγων Ἀβίων τε, δικαιοτάτων ἀνθρώπων,

βουλόμενοι συγκρῖναι τά τε ὑφ' ἡμῶν καὶ τὰ ὑπὸ
Ποσειδωνίου λεχθέντα καὶ τὰ ὑπὸ τούτων· πρότερον δ' ὅτι τὴν ἐπιχείρησιν ὑπεναντίαν τοῖς
προτεθεῖσι πεποίηνται. προύθεντο μὲν γὰρ δι-
δάξαι, διότι τῶν πόρρω τῆς Ἑλλάδος πλείων ἦν
ἄγνοια τοῖς πρεσβυτέροις ἢ τοῖς νεωτέροις· ἔδειξαν[2] δὲ τἀναντία, καὶ οὐ κατὰ[3] τὰ πόρρω μόνον,
ἀλλὰ καὶ τὰ ἐν αὐτῇ τῇ Ἑλλάδι. ἀλλ', ὡς ἔφην,
τὰ ἄλλα μὲν ὑπερκείσθω· τὰ δὲ νῦν σκοπῶμεν.
Σκυθῶν μὲν γὰρ μὴ μεμνῆσθαι κατ' ἄγνοιάν φασι,

---

[1] τά, after πάλαι, the editors delete.
[2] ἔδειξαν, Xylander, for ἔδειξε; so the later editors.
[3] κατά, Groskurd inserts; so the later editors.

---

[1] 1. 2. 24. [2] For example, 12. 3. 26–27.
[3] The first and second books, passim.
[4] See 7. 3. 2 and the footnote.

borrowed most of them from Eratosthenes, and as I have remarked before[1] they are wrong. For while one must concede to Eratosthenes and Apollodorus that the later writers have shown themselves better acquainted with such matters than the men of early times, yet to proceed beyond all moderation as they do, and particularly in the case of Homer, is a thing for which, as it seems to me, one might justly rebuke them and make the reverse statement: that where they are ignorant themselves, there they reproach the poet with ignorance. However, what remains to be said on this subject meets with appropriate mention in my detailed descriptions of the several countries,[2] as also in my general description.[3]

7. Just now I was discussing the Thracians, and the " Mysians, hand-to-hand fighters, and the proud Hippemolgi, Galactophagi, and Abii, men most just,"[4] because I wished to make a comparison between the statements made by Poseidonius and myself and those made by the two men in question. Take first the fact that the argument which they have attempted is contrary to the proposition which they set out to prove; for although they set out to prove that the men of earlier times were more ignorant of regions remote from Greece than the men of more recent times, they showed the reverse, not only in regard to regions remote, but also in regard to places in Greece itself. However, as I was saying, let me put off everything else and look to what is now before me: they[5] say that the poet through ignorance fails to mention the Scythians, or their savage dealings with strangers, in that they

[5] Eratosthenes and Apollodorus.

μηδὲ τῆς περὶ τοὺς ξένους ὠμότητος αὐτῶν, κατα-
θυόντων καὶ σαρκοφαγούντων καὶ τοῖς κρανίοις
ἐκπώμασι χρωμένων, δι᾽ οὓς Ἄξενος ὠνομάζετο ὁ
πόντος, πλάττειν δ᾽ ἀγαυούς τινας Ἱππημολγούς,
Γαλακτοφάγους Ἀβίους τε, δικαιοτάτους ἀνθρώπους, τοὺς οὐδαμοῦ γῆς ὄντας. πῶς οὖν Ἄξενον
ὠνόμαζον, εἰ μὴ ᾔδεισαν τὴν ἀγριότητα, μηδ᾽
αὐτοὺς τοὺς μάλιστα τοιούτους; οὗτοι δ᾽ εἰσὶ
δήπου οἱ Σκύθαι. πότερον¹ δ᾽ οὐδ᾽ Ἱππημολγοὶ
ἦσαν οἱ ἐπέκεινα τῶν Μυσῶν καὶ Θρακῶν καὶ
Γετῶν, οὐδὲ Γαλακτοφάγοι καὶ Ἄβιοι; ἀλλὰ καὶ
νῦν εἰσιν Ἁμάξοικοι καὶ Νομάδες καλούμενοι,
ζῶντες ἀπὸ θρεμμάτων καὶ γάλακτος καὶ τυροῦ,
καὶ μάλιστα ἱππείου, θησαυρισμὸν δ᾽ οὐκ εἰδότες
οὐδὲ καπηλείαν, πλὴν ἢ² φόρτον ἀντὶ φόρτου. πῶς
οὖν ἠγνόει τοὺς Σκύθας ὁ ποιητής, Ἱππημολγοὺς
καὶ Γαλακτοφάγους τινὰς προσαγορεύων; ὅτι γὰρ
οἱ τότε τούτους Ἱππημολγοὺς ἐκάλουν, καὶ Ἡσίο-
δος μάρτυς ἐν τοῖς ὑπ᾽ Ἐρατοσθένους παρατεθεῖσιν
ἔπεσιν·

Αἰθίοπάς τε Λίγυς τε ἰδὲ³ Σκύθας ἱππημολγούς.

τί δὲ θαυμαστόν, εἰ διὰ τὸ πλεονάζειν παρ᾽ ἡμῖν
τὴν περὶ τὰ συμβόλαια ἀδικίαν, δικαιοτάτους
εἶπεν ἀγαυοὺς⁴ τοὺς ἥκιστα ἐν τοῖς συμβολαίοις
καὶ τῷ ἀργυρισμῷ ζῶντας, ἀλλὰ καὶ κοινὰ κεκτη-
μένους πάντα πλὴν ξίφους καὶ ποτηρίου, ἐν δὲ

---

¹ πότερον, conj. Kramer, for πρότερον; so the later editors.
² ἤ, Meineke emends to εἰ.
³ Λίγυς τε ἰδέ, Kramer, for Λιγυστὶ δέ; so the later editors.
⁴ ἀγαυούς, Meineke emends, without noting, to ἀνθρώπους.

"Mare-milkers."   ² "Curd-eaters."

sacrifice them, eat their flesh, and use their skulls as drinking-cups, although it was on account of the Scythians that the Pontus was called "Axine," but that he invents certain "proud Hippemolgi, Galactophagi, and Abii, men most just"—people that exist nowhere on earth, How, then, could they call the sea "Axine" if they did not know about the ferocity or about the people who were most ferocious? And these, of course, are the Scythians. And were the people who lived beyond the Mysians and Thracians and Getae not also "Hippemolgi,"[1] not also "Galactophagi"[2] and "Abii"?[3] In fact, even now[4] there are Wagon-dwellers and Nomads, so called, who live off their herds, and on milk and cheese, and particularly on cheese made from mare's milk, and know nothing about storing up food or about peddling merchandise either, except the exchange of wares for wares. How, then, could the poet be ignorant of the Scythians if he called certain people "Hippemolgi and Galactophagi"? For that the people of his time were wont to call the Scythians "Hippemolgi," Hesiod, too, is witness in the words cited by Eratosthenes: "The Ethiopians, the Ligurians, and also the Scythians, Hippemolgi."[5] Now wherein is it to be wondered at that, because of the widespread injustice connected with contracts in our country, Homer called "most just" and "proud" those who by no means spend their lives on contracts and money-getting but actually possess all things in common except sword and drinking-cup, and above all things have their

---

[3] "A resourceless folk."

[4] Cp. the similar words quoted from Ephorus, 7. 3. 9.

[5] A fragment otherwise unknown (*fr.* 232 ; Rzach, *fr.* 55).

τοῖς πρῶτον τὰς γυναῖκας Πλατωνικῶς ἔχοντας
κοινὰς καὶ τέκνα; καὶ Αἰσχύλος δ' ἐμφαίνει
συνηγορῶν τῷ ποιητῇ, φήσας περὶ τῶν Σκυθῶν,

C 301   ἀλλ' ἱππάκης βρωτῆρες εὔνομοι Σκύθαι.

αὕτη δ' ἡ ὑπόληψις καὶ νῦν ἔτι συμμένει παρὰ
τοῖς Ἕλλησιν· ἁπλουστάτους τε γὰρ αὐτοὺς
νομίζομεν καὶ ἥκιστα κακεντρεχεῖς εὐτελεστέρους
τε πολὺ ἡμῶν καὶ αὐταρκεστέρους· καίτοι ὅ γε
καθ' ἡμᾶς βίος εἰς πάντας σχεδόν τι διατέτακε
τὴν πρὸς τὸ χεῖρον μεταβολήν, τρυφὴν καὶ ἡδονὰς
καὶ κακοτεχνίας εἰς[1] πλεονεξίας μυρίας πρὸς ταῦτ'
εἰσάγων. πολὺ οὖν τῆς τοιαύτης κακίας καὶ εἰς
τοὺς βαρβάρους ἐμπέπτωκε τούς τε ἄλλους καὶ
τοὺς Νομάδας. καὶ γὰρ θαλάττης ἁψάμενοι
χείρους γεγόνασι, λῃστεύοντες καὶ ξενοκτονοῦντες,
καὶ ἐπιπλεκόμενοι πολλοῖς μεταλαμβάνουσι τῆς
ἐκείνων πολυτελείας καὶ καπηλείας· ἃ δοκεῖ μὲν
εἰς ἡμερότητα συντείνειν, διαφθείρει δὲ τὰ ἤθη καὶ
ποικιλίαν ἀντὶ τῆς ἁπλότητος τῆς ἄρτι λεχθείσης
εἰσάγει.
8. Οἱ μέντοι πρὸ ἡμῶν, καὶ μάλιστα οἱ ἐγγὺς
τοῖς Ὁμήρου χρόνοις, τοιοῦτοί τινες ἦσαν καὶ
ὑπελαμβάνοντο παρὰ τοῖς Ἕλλησιν, ὁποίους
Ὅμηρός φησιν. ὅρα δὲ ἃ λέγει Ἡρόδοτος περὶ
τοῦ τῶν Σκυθῶν βασιλέως, ἐφ' ὃν ἐστράτευσε
Δαρεῖος, καὶ τὰ ἐπεσταλμένα παρ' αὐτοῦ. ὅρα

---

[1] εἰς, Corais, Meineke and other editors emend to καί. See
πλεονεξίας, 7. 4. 6 (end of §).

---

[1] *Republic*, 457 D, 458 C–D, 460 B–D, 540, and 543.

wives and their children in common, in the Platonic way?[1]   Aeschylus, too, is clearly pleading the cause of the poet when he says about the Scythians: "But the Scythians, law-abiding, eaters of cheese made of mare's milk."[2]   And this assumption even now still persists among the Greeks; for we regard the Scythians the most straightforward of men and the least prone to mischief, as also far more frugal and independent of others than we are.   And yet our mode of life has spread its change for the worse to almost all peoples, introducing amongst them luxury and sensual pleasures and, to satisfy these vices, base artifices that lead to innumerable acts of greed.   So then, much wickedness of this sort has fallen on the barbarian peoples also, on the Nomads as well as the rest; for as the result of taking up a seafaring life they not only have become morally worse, indulging in the practice of piracy and of slaying strangers, but also, because of their intercourse with many peoples, have partaken of the luxury and the peddling habits of those peoples. But though these things seem to conduce strongly to gentleness of manner, they corrupt morals and introduce cunning instead of the straightforwardness which I just now mentioned.

8. Those, however, who lived before our times, and particularly those who lived near the time of Homer, were—and among the Greeks were assumed to be—some such people as Homer describes.   And see what Herodotus says concerning that king of the Scythians against whom Dareius made his expedition, and the message which the king sent

----

[2] From a play now lost (Nauck, *fr.* 198).

STRABO

δὲ καὶ ἃ λέγει Χρύσιππος περὶ τῶν τοῦ Βοσπόρου
βασιλέων τῶν περὶ Λεύκωνα. πλήρεις δὲ καὶ αἱ
Περσικαὶ ἐπιστολαὶ τῆς ἁπλότητος, ἧς λέγω, καὶ
τὰ ὑπὸ τῶν Αἰγυπτίων καὶ Βαβυλωνίων καὶ
Ἰνδῶν ἀπομνημονευόμενα. διὰ τοῦτο δὲ καὶ ὁ
Ἀνάχαρσις καὶ Ἄβαρις καί τινες ἄλλοι τοιοῦτοι
παρὰ τοῖς Ἕλλησιν εὐδοκίμουν, ὅτι ἐθνικόν τινα
χαρακτῆρα ἐπέφαινον εὐκολίας καὶ λιτότητος [1]
καὶ δικαιοσύνης. καὶ τί δεῖ τοὺς πάλαι λέγειν;
Ἀλέξανδρος γὰρ ὁ Φιλίππου κατὰ τὴν ἐπὶ Θρᾷκας
τοὺς ὑπὲρ τοῦ Αἵμου στρατείαν ἐμβαλὼν εἰς
Τριβαλλούς, ὁρῶν μέχρι τοῦ Ἴστρου καθήκοντας
καὶ τῆς ἐν αὐτῷ νήσου Πεύκης, τὰ πέραν δὲ
Γέτας ἔχοντας, ἀφῖχθαι λέγεται μέχρι δεῦρο, καὶ
εἰς μὲν τὴν νῆσον ἀποβῆναι μὴ δύνασθαι σπάνει
πλοίων· ἐκεῖσε γὰρ καταφυγόντα τὸν τῶν Τριβαλλῶν βασιλέα Σύρμον ἀντισχεῖν πρὸς τὴν
ἐπιχείρησιν· εἰς δὲ τοὺς Γέτας διαβάντα ἑλεῖν

---

[1] λιτότητος (conj. Casaubon), for λειότητος (ABC*l*), τελειό-
τητος (*g*); so the later editors.

---

[1] Cp. 7. 3. 14. Dareius sent a message to King Idanthyrsus
in which he reproached the latter for fleeing and not fighting.
Idanthyrsus replied that he was not fleeing because of fear,
but was merely doing what he was wont to do in time of
peace ; and if Dareius insisted on a fight, he might search
out and violate the ancestral tombs, and thus come to realize
whether or no the Scythians would fight ; "and in reply to
your assertion that you are my master, I say 'howl on'"
(Herodotus, 4. 127).

[2] Chrysippus of Soli (fl. about 230 B.C.), the Stoic philosopher, was a prolific writer, but with the exception of a
few fragments his works are lost. The present reference is
obviously to his treatise on *Modes of Life*, which is quoted by
Plutarch (*De Stoicorum Repugnantiis*, 20. 3 = 1043 B).

[3] Leuco, who succeeded his father Satyrus I, reigned from
393 to 353 B.C. (see 7. 4. 4).

200

back to him.[1]   See also what Chrysippus [2] says concerning the kings of the Bosporus, the house of
Leuco.[3]   And not only the Persian letters [4] are full
of references to that straightforwardness of which I
am speaking but also the memoirs written by the
Egyptians, Babylonians, and Indians.   And it was
on this account that Anacharsis,[5] Abaris,[6] and other
men of the sort were in fair repute among the
Greeks, because they displayed a nature character-
ized by complacency, frugality, and justice.   But
why should I speak of the men of olden times?
For when Alexander, the son of Philip, on his expedition against the Thracians beyond the Haemus,[7]
invaded the country of the Triballians [8] and saw that
it extended as far as the Ister and the island of
Peuce [9] in the Ister, and that the parts on the far
side were held by the Getae, he went as far as
that,[10] it is said, but could not disembark upon the
island because of scarcity of boats (for Syrmus, the
king of the Triballi had taken refuge there and
resisted his attempts) ; he did, however, cross over
to the country of the Getae, took their city, and

[4] *i.e.* the letters of the Persian kings, such as those quoted
by Herodotus.
[5] Anacharsis was a Scythian prince and philosopher, one
of the "Seven Sages," a traveller, long a resident of Athens
(about 590 B.C.), a friend of Solon, and (according to Ephorus)
an inventor (7. 3. 9).   See Herodotus, 4. 76.
[6] Abaris was called the "Hyperborean" priest and prophet
of Apollo, and is said to have visited Athens in the eighth
century, or perhaps much later.   According to the legend,
he healed the sick, travelled round the world, without once
eating, on a golden arrow given him by Apollo, and delivered
Sparta from a plague.
[7] The Balkan Mountains.   [8] A Thracian tribe.
[9] See 7. 3. 15 and footnote.   [10] *i.e.* as far as the island.

αὐτῶν πόλιν καὶ ἀναστρέψαι διὰ ταχέων εἰς τὴν
οἰκείαν, λαβόντα δῶρα παρὰ[1] τῶν ἐθνῶν καὶ
παρὰ τοῦ Σύρμου. φησὶ δὲ Πτολεμαῖος ὁ Λάγου
κατὰ ταύτην τὴν στρατείαν συμμῖξαι τῷ Ἀλε-
ξάνδρῳ Κελτοὺς τοὺς περὶ τὸν Ἀδρίαν φιλίας καὶ
C 302 ξενίας χάριν, δεξάμενον δὲ αὐτοὺς φιλοφρόνως τὸν
βασιλέα ἐρέσθαι παρὰ πότον, τί μάλιστα εἴη ὃ
φοβοῖντο, νομίζοντα αὐτὸν ἐρεῖν· αὐτοὺς δ᾽ ἀπο-
κρίνασθαι, ὅτι οὐδένα[2] πλὴν εἰ ἄρα μὴ ὁ οὐρανὸς
αὐτοῖς ἐπιπέσοι, φιλίαν γε μὴν ἀνδρὸς τοιούτου
περὶ παντὸς τίθεσθαι. ταῦτα δὲ ἁπλότητος τῆς
τῶν βαρβάρων ἐστὶ σημεῖα, τοῦ τε μὴ συγχωρή-
σαντος μὲν τὴν ἀπόβασιν τὴν εἰς τὴν νῆσον, δῶρα
δὲ πέμψαντος καὶ συνθεμένου φιλίαν, καὶ τῶν
φοβεῖσθαι μὲν οὐδένα φαμένων, φιλίαν δὲ περὶ
παντὸς τίθεσθαι μεγάλων ἀνδρῶν. ὅ τε Δρο-
μιχαίτης κατὰ τοὺς διαδόχους ἦν τοὺς Ἀλεξάνδρου[3] Γετῶν βασιλεύς· ἐκεῖνος τοίνυν λαβὼν
ζωγρίᾳ Λυσίμαχον ἐπιστρατεύσαντα αὐτῷ, δείξας
τὴν πενίαν τήν τε ἑαυτοῦ καὶ τοῦ ἔθνους, ὁμοίως
δὲ καὶ τὴν αὐτάρκειαν, ἐκέλευσε τοῖς τοιούτοις μὴ
πολεμεῖν, ἀλλὰ φίλοις χρῆσθαι· ταῦτα δ᾽ εἰπών,
ξενίσας καὶ συνθέμενος φιλίαν, ἀπέλυσεν αὐτόν.

---

[1] παρά, Corais inserts ; so the later editors.
[2] οὐδένα, Groskurd emends to οὐδέν, and so Meineke ; but
see οὐδένα in sixth line below.
[3] τοὺς Ἀλεξάνδρου is probably a gloss ; Meineke deletes.

---

[1] Ptolemaeus Soter, " whom the Macedonians believed to
be the son of Philip" of Macedon (Pausanias 1. 6), was
founder of the Egyptian dynasty and reigned 323–285 B.C.
[2] Lagus married Arsinoë, a concubine of Philip.

returned with all speed to his home-land, after
receiving gifts from the tribes in question and from
Syrmus. And Ptolemaeus,[1] the son of Lagus,[2] says
that on this expedition the Celti who lived about
the Adriatic joined Alexander for the sake of
establishing friendship and hospitality, and that the
king received them kindly and asked them when
drinking what it was that they most feared, thinking
they would say himself, but that they replied they
feared no one, unless it were that Heaven might
fall on them, although indeed they added that they
put above everything else the friendship of such a
man as he. And the following are signs of the
straightforwardness of the barbarians: first, the fact
that Syrmus refused to consent to the debarkation
upon the island and yet sent gifts and made a
compact of friendship; and, secondly, that the Celti
said that they feared no one, and yet valued above
everything else the friendship of great men. Again,
Dromichaetes was king of the Getae in the time
of the successors of Alexander. Now he, when he
captured Lysimachus[3] alive, who had made an
expedition against him, first pointed out the poverty
both of himself and of his tribe and likewise their
independence of others, and then bade him not to
carry on war with people of that sort but rather to
deal with them as friends; and after saying this
he first entertained him as a guest, and made a
compact of friendship, and then released him.

[3] Lysimachus, one of Alexander's generals and successors,
obtained Thrace as his portion in the division of the provinces
after Alexander's death (323 B.C.), assuming the title of
king 306 B.C. He was taken captive, and released, by
Dromichaetes 291 B.C.

καὶ Πλάτων δὲ ἐν τῇ Πολιτείᾳ τὴν θάλατταν ὡς
πονηροδιδάσκαλον φεύγειν οἴεται δεῖν ὅτι πορρω-
τάτω τοὺς εὖ πολιτευσομένους καὶ μὴ οἰκεῖν ἐπ᾽
αὐτῇ.[1]

9. Ἔφορος δ᾽ ἐν τῇ τετάρτῃ μὲν τῆς ἱστορίας,
Εὐρώπῃ δ᾽ ἐπιγραφομένῃ βίβλῳ, περιοδεύσας τὴν
Εὐρώπην μέχρι Σκυθῶν ἐπὶ τέλει φησὶν εἶναι
τῶν τε ἄλλων Σκυθῶν καὶ τῶν Σαυρομάτων τοὺς
βίους ἀνομοίους· τοὺς μὲν γὰρ εἶναι χαλεπούς,
ὥστε καὶ ἀνθρωποφαγεῖν, τοὺς δὲ καὶ τῶν ἄλλων
ζῴων ἀπέχεσθαι. οἱ μὲν οὖν ἄλλοι, φησί, τὰ
περὶ τῆς ὠμότητος αὐτῶν λέγουσιν, εἰδότες τὸ
δεινόν τε καὶ τὸ θαυμαστὸν ἐκπληκτικὸν ὄν·
δεῖν[2] δὲ τἀναντία καὶ λέγειν καὶ παραδείγματα
ποιεῖσθαι, καὶ αὐτὸς οὖν περὶ τῶν δικαιοτάτοις
ἤθεσι χρωμένων ποιήσεσθαι τοὺς λόγους· εἶναι
γάρ τινας τῶν Νομάδων Σκυθῶν γάλακτι τρεφομένους ἵππων, τῇ τε[3] δικαιοσύνῃ πάντων δια-
φέρειν, μεμνῆσθαι δ᾽ αὐτῶν τοὺς ποιητάς· Ὅμηρον
μὲν

Γλακτοφάγων Ἀβίων τε, δικαιοτάτων ἀνθρώπων,

φήσαντα τὴν γῆν καθορᾶν τὸν Δία,[4] Ἡσίοδον δ᾽
ἐν[5] τῇ καλουμένῃ Γῆς Περιόδῳ, τὸν Φινέα ὑπὸ
τῶν Ἁρπυιῶν ἄγεσθαι

Γλακτοφάγων εἰς γαῖαν, ἀπήναις[6] οἰκί᾽ ἐχόντων.

---

[1] καὶ Πλάτων . . . αὐτῇ, Meineke relegates to the foot of
the page ; Groskurd transfers back to end of § 7.
[2] δεῖν, Corais, for δεινόν ; so the later editors.
[3] τε, Corais inserts ; so the later editors.
[4] Δία, Tzschucke, for δέ ; so the later editors.
[5] δ᾽, before ἐν, Meineke inserts (δέ, Kramer).
[6] ἀπήναις, all editors, for ἀπηνές.

Moreover, Plato in his *Republic* thinks that those who would have a well-governed city should flee as far as possible from the sea, as being a thing that teaches wickedness, and should not live near it.[1]

9. Ephorus, in the fourth book of his history, the book entitled *Europe* (for he made the circuit[2] of Europe as far as the Scythians), says towards the end that the modes of life both of the Sauromatae and of the other Scythians are unlike, for, whereas some are so cruel that they even eat human beings, others abstain from eating any living creature whatever. Now the other writers, he says, tell only about their savagery, because they know that the terrible and the marvellous are startling, but one should tell the opposite facts too and make them patterns of conduct, and he himself, therefore, will tell only about those who follow "most just" habits, for there are some of the Scythian Nomads who feed only on mare's milk,[3] and excel all men in justice; and they are mentioned by the poets: by Homer, when he says that Zeus espies the land "of the Galactophagi and Abii, men most just," and by Hesiod, in what is called his *Circuit of the Earth*,[4] when he says that Phineus is carried by the Storm Winds "to the land of the Galactophagi, who have their dwellings in wagons." Then Ephorus reasons out

---

[1] Corais and Groskurd point out that the reference should have been, not to the *Republic*, but to the *Laws* (4. 704–705), where Plato discusses the proper place for founding a city; cp. Aristotle's *Politics* (7. 6) on the same subject.

[2] In his description, not literally.

[3] Cp. the similar statement in 7. 3. 7.

[4] This poem seems to have comprised the third book of the *Megalae Eoeae* (now lost). See Pauly-Wissowa, *s.v.* "Hesiodus," p. 1206.

εἶτ᾽ αἰτιολογεῖ, διότι ταῖς διαίταις εὐτελεῖς ὄντες
καὶ οὐ χρηματισταὶ πρός τε ἀλλήλους εὐνο-
μοῦνται, κοινὰ πάντα ἔχοντες τά τε ἄλλα καὶ τὰς
γυναῖκας καὶ τέκνα καὶ τὴν ὅλην συγγένειαν,
C 303 πρός τε τοὺς ἐκτὸς ἄμαχοί εἰσι καὶ ἀνίκητοι,
οὐδὲν ἔχοντες ὑπὲρ οὗ δουλεύσουσι. καλεῖ δὲ
καὶ Χοιρίλον, εἰπόντα ἐν τῇ διαβάσει τῆς σχεδίας,
ἣν ἔζευξε Δαρεῖος·

> μηλονόμοι τε Σάκαι, γενεᾷ Σκύθαι· αὐτὰρ
> ἔναιον
> Ἀσίδα πυροφόρον· Νομάδων γε μὲν ἦσαν
> ἄποικοι,
> ἀνθρώπων νομίμων.

καὶ τὸν Ἀνάχαρσιν δὲ σοφὸν καλῶν ὁ Ἔφορος
τούτου τοῦ γένους φησὶν εἶναι· νομισθῆναι δὲ
καὶ τῶν[1] ἑπτὰ σοφῶν ἕνα τελείᾳ[2] σωφροσύνῃ καὶ
συνέσει· εὑρήματά τε αὐτοῦ λέγει τά τε ζώπυρα
καὶ τὴν ἀμφίβολον ἄγκυραν καὶ τὸν κεραμικὸν
τροχόν. ταῦτα δὲ λέγω, σαφῶς μὲν εἰδὼς ὅτι καὶ
οὗτος αὐτὸς οὐ τἀληθέστατα[3] λέγει περὶ πάντων,
καὶ δὴ καὶ τὸ τοῦ Ἀναχάρσιδος (πῶς γὰρ ὁ
τροχὸς εὕρημα αὐτοῦ, ὃν οἶδεν Ὅμηρος πρεσβύ-
περος ὤν;

> ὡς δ᾽ ὅτε τις κεραμεὺς τροχὸν ἄρμενον ἐν παλά-
> μῃσι,

καὶ τὰ ἑξῆς)·[4] ἀλλ᾽ ἐκεῖνα διασημῆναι βουλό-

---

[1] τῶν, before ἑπτά, Corais inserts ; so Meineke.
[2] ἕνα τελείᾳ (the reading of the MSS.), Jones restores, for
ἐν εὐτελείᾳ (Kramer) ; ἐπ᾽ εὐτελείᾳ (Meineke).
[3] οὐ τἀληθέστατα, Corais. for οὔτε ἀληθέστατα ; so Meineke.
[4] ὡς δ᾽ ὅτε . . . ἑξῆς. Meineke relegates to the foot of the
page.

the cause as follows: since they are frugal in their
ways of living and not money-getters, they not only
are orderly towards one another, because they have
all things in common, their wives, children, the
whole of their kin and everything, but also remain
invincible and unconquered by outsiders, because
they have nothing to be enslaved for. And he cites
Choerilus[1] also, who, in his *The Crossing of the
Pontoon-Bridge* which was constructed by Dareius,[2]
says, "the sheep-tending Sacae, of Scythian stock;
but they used to live in wheat-producing Asia;
however, they were colonists from the Nomads, law-
abiding people." And when he calls Anacharsis
"wise," Ephorus says that he belongs to this race,
and that he was considered also one of Seven Wise
Men because of his perfect self-control and good
sense. And he goes on to tell the inventions of
Anarcharsis—the bellows, the two-fluked anchor and
the potter's wheel. These things I tell knowing
full well that Ephorus himself does not tell the
whole truth about everything; and particularly in
his account of Anacharsis (for how could the wheel
be his invention, if Homer, who lived in earlier
times, knew of it? "As when a potter his wheel
that fits in his hands,"[3] and so on); but as for those

---

[1] Not, apparently, the tragic poet, contemporary of
Aeschylus, but the epic poet of Samos (fl. towards the end
of the fifth century B.C.), who wrote, among other poems, an
epic poem (exact title uncertain) based on the Persian Wars.
The Crossing of the Pontoon-Bridge was probably a sub-title of
the epic. The same Choerilus is cited in 14. 5. 9.

[2] In his campaign against the Scythians, including the
Getae, as described by Herodotus (4. 83–93); see 7. 3. 15.

[3] *Iliad* 18. 600.

STRABO

μενος, ὅτι κοινῇ τινι φήμῃ καὶ ὑπὸ τῶν παλαιῶν
καὶ ὑπὸ τῶν ὕστερον[1] πεπιστεῦσθαι συνέβαινε
τὸ τῶν Νομάδων, τοὺς μάλιστα ἀπῳκισμένους
ἀπὸ τῶν ἄλλων ἀνθρώπων γαλακτοφάγους τε
εἶναι καὶ ἀβίους καὶ δικαιοτάτους, ἀλλ᾽ οὐχ ὑπὸ
Ὁμήρου πεπλάσθαι.

10. Περί τε τῶν Μυσῶν δίκαιός ἐστιν ὑποσχεῖν
λόγον τῶν ἐν τοῖς ἔπεσι λεγομένων Ἀπολλόδωρος, πότερ᾽ ἡγεῖται καὶ τούτους εἶναι πλάσματα,
ὅταν φῇ ὁ ποιητής·

Μυσῶν τ᾽ ἀγχεμάχων καὶ ἀγαυῶν Ἱππημολγῶν,

ἢ τοὺς ἐν τῇ Ἀσίᾳ δέχεται; τοὺς μὲν οὖν ἐν τῇ
Ἀσίᾳ δεχόμενος παρερμηνεύσει τὸν ποιητήν, ὡς
προείρηται, πλάσμα δὲ[2] λέγων, ὡς μὴ ὄντων ἐν
τῇ Θρᾴκῃ Μυσῶν, παρὰ τὰ ὄντα ἐρεῖ.[3] ἔτι γὰρ
ἐφ᾽ ἡμῶν γοῦν[4] Αἴλιος Κάτος μετῴκισεν ἐκ τῆς
περαίας τοῦ Ἴστρου πέντε μυριάδας σωμάτων
παρὰ τῶν Γετῶν, ὁμογλώττου τοῖς Θρᾳξὶν ἔθνους,
εἰς τὴν Θρᾴκην· καὶ νῦν οἰκοῦσιν αὐτόθι Μοισοὶ[5]
καλούμενοι, ἤτοι καὶ τῶν πρότερον οὕτω καλουμένων, ἐν δὲ τῇ Ἀσίᾳ Μυσῶν μετονομασθέντων,
ἤ, ὅπερ οἰκειότερόν ἐστι τῇ ἱστορίᾳ καὶ τῇ ἀπο-
φάσει τοῦ ποιητοῦ, τῶν ἐν τῇ Θρᾴκῃ Μυσῶν
καλουμένων πρότερον. περὶ μὲν δὴ τούτων ἅλις·
ἐπάνειμι δὲ ἐπὶ τὴν ἑξῆς περιήγησιν.

---

[1] For ὕστερον, Meineke reads ὑστέρων, following A.
[2] δέ, after πλάσμα, Corais inserts; so the later editors.
[3] ἐρεῖ, after ὄντα, Corais inserts; so the later editors.
[4] γοῦν, Meineke deletes, following no.
[5] Μοισοί, Tyrwhitt, for Μυσοί; so the later editors.

[1] Cp. 7. 3. C.   [2] 7. 3. 2.

208

other things, I tell them because I wish to make my point clear that there actually was a common report, which was believed by the men of both early and of later times, that a part of the Nomads, I mean those who had settled the farthest away from the rest of mankind, were "galactophagi," "abii," and "most just," and that they were not an invention of Homer.

10. It is but fair, too, to ask Apollodorus to account for the Mysians that are mentioned in the verses of Homer, whether he thinks that these too are inventions[1] (when the poet says, "and the Mysians, hand-to-hand fighters and the proud Hippemolgi"), or takes the poet to mean the Mysians in Asia. Now if he takes the poet to mean those in Asia, he will misinterpret him, as I have said before,[2] but if he calls them an invention, meaning that there were no Mysians in Thrace, he will contradict the facts; for at any rate, even in our own times, Aelius Catus[3] transplanted from the country on the far side of the Ister into Thrace[4] fifty thousand persons from among the Getae, a tribe with the same tongue as the Thracians.[5] And they live there in Thrace now and are called "Moesi"—whether it be that their people of earlier times were so called and that in Asia the name was changed to "Mysi,"[6] or (what is more apposite to history and the declaration of the poet) that in earlier times their people in Thrace were called "Mysi." Enough, however, on this subject. I shall now go back to the next topic in the general description.

[3] Perhaps as governor of Macedonia. He was consul with C. Sentius 4 A.D.   [4] Lower Moesia.
[5] Cp. 7. 3. 2.   [6] See 7. 3. 4.

11. Τῶν δὴ Γετῶν τὰ μὲν παλαιὰ ἀφείσθω, τὰ δ' εἰς ἡμᾶς ἤδη τοιαῦτα ὑπῆρξε. Βοιρεβίστας, ἀνὴρ Γέτης, ἐπιστὰς ἐπὶ τὴν τοῦ ἔθνους ἐπιστασίαν, ἀνέλαβε κεκακωμένους τοὺς ἀνθρώπους ὑπὸ συχνῶν πολέμων καὶ τοσοῦτον ἐπῆρεν ἀσκήσει καὶ νήψει καὶ τῷ προσέχειν τοῖς προστάγμασιν,[1]

C 304 ὥστ' ὀλίγων ἐτῶν μεγάλην ἀρχὴν κατεστήσατο, καὶ τῶν ὁμόρων τοὺς πλείστους ὑπέταξε τοῖς Γέταις· ἤδη δὲ καὶ Ῥωμαίοις φοβερὸς ἦν, διαβαίνων ἀδεῶς τὸν Ἴστρον καὶ τὴν Θρᾴκην λεηλατῶν μέχρι Μακεδονίας καὶ τῆς Ἰλλυρίδος, τούς τε Κελτοὺς τοὺς ἀναμεμιγμένους τοῖς τε Θρᾳξὶ καὶ τοῖς Ἰλλυριοῖς ἐξεπόρθησε, Βοΐους δὲ καὶ ἄρδην ἠφάνισε τοὺς ὑπὸ Κριτασίρῳ καὶ Ταυρίσκους. πρὸς δὲ τὴν εὐπείθειαν τοῦ ἔθνους συναγωνιστὴν ἔσχε Δεκαίνεον ἄνδρα γόητα, καὶ[2] πεπλανημένον κατὰ τὴν Αἴγυπτον καὶ προσημασίας ἐκμεμαθηκότα τινάς, δι' ὧν ὑπεκρίνετο τὰ θεῖα· καὶ δι' ὀλίγου καθίστατο θεός, καθάπερ ἔφαμεν περὶ τοῦ Ζαμόλξεως διηγούμενοι. τῆς δ' εὐπειθείας σημεῖον· ἐπείσθησαν γὰρ ἐκκόψαι τὴν ἄμπελον καὶ ζῆν οἴνου χωρίς. ὁ μὲν οὖν Βοιρεβίστας ἔφθη καταλυθεὶς ἐπαναστάντων αὐτῷ τινων, πρὶν ἢ Ῥωμαίους στεῖλαι στρατείαν ἐπ' αὐτόν· οἱ δὲ

[1] πράγμασιν (BCl).
[2] καί, Corais encloses in brackets ; Meineke deletes.

---

[1] Also spelled Byrebistas (see 7. 3. 5 and footnote).
[2] See 7. 3. 2 and 7. 5. 1.
[3] Also a Celtic tribe (7. 3. 2).   [4] 7. 5. 2.

11. As for the Getae, then, their early history must be left untold, but that which pertains to our own times is about as follows: Boerebistas [1] a Getan, on setting himself in authority over the tribe, restored the people, who had been reduced to an evil plight by numerous wars, and raised them to such a height through training, sobriety, and obedience to his commands that within only a few years he had established a great empire and subordinated to the Getae most of the neighbouring peoples. And he began to be formidable even to the Romans, because he would cross the Ister with impunity and plunder Thrace as far as Macedonia and the Illyrian country; and he not only laid waste the country of the Celti who were intermingled [2] with the Thracians and the Illyrians, but actually caused the complete disappearance of the Boii [3] who were under the rule of Critasirus, [4] and also of the Taurisci. [5] To help him secure the complete obedience of his tribe he had as his coadjutor Decaeneus, [6] a wizard, a man who not only had wandered through Egypt, but also had thoroughly learned certain prognostics through which he would pretend to tell the divine will; and within a short time he was set up as god (as I said when relating the story of Zamolxis). [7] The following is an indication of their complete obedience: they were persuaded to cut down their vines and to live without wine. However, certain men rose up against Boerebistas and he was deposed before the Romans sent an expedition against him; [8] and those who

[5] Also under the rule of Critasirus (7. 5. 2).
[6] See 7. 3. 5.   [7] 7. 3. 5.   [8] Cp. 7. 3. 5.

διαδεξάμενοι τὴν ἀρχὴν εἰς πλείω μέρη διέστησαν,
καὶ δὴ καὶ νῦν, ἡνίκα ἔπεμψεν ἐπ' αὐτοὺς στρατείαν ὁ Σεβαστὸς Καῖσαρ, εἰς πέντε μερίδας,[1]
τότε δὲ εἰς τέσσαρας διεστῶτες ἐτύγχανον· οἱ
μὲν οὖν τοιοῦτοι μερισμοὶ πρόσκαιροι καὶ ἄλλοτ'
ἄλλοι.

12. Γέγονε δὲ καὶ ἄλλος τῆς χώρας μερισμὸς
συμμένων ἐκ παλαιοῦ· τοὺς μὲν γὰρ Δακοὺς
προσαγορεύουσι, τοὺς δὲ Γέτας· Γέτας μὲν τοὺς
πρὸς τὸν Πόντον κεκλιμένους καὶ πρὸς τὴν ἕω,
Δακοὺς δὲ τοὺς εἰς τἀναντία πρὸς τὴν Γερμανίαν
καὶ τὰς τοῦ Ἴστρου πηγάς, οὓς οἶμαι Δάους
καλεῖσθαι τὸ παλαιόν· ἀφ' οὗ καὶ παρὰ τοῖς
Ἀττικοῖς ἐπεπόλασε τὰ τῶν οἰκετῶν ὀνόματα
Γέται καὶ Δᾶοι. τοῦτο γὰρ πιθανώτερον ἢ ἀπὸ
τῶν Σκυθῶν οὓς καλοῦσι Δάας· πόρρω γὰρ ἐκεῖνοι περὶ τὴν Ὑρκανίαν, καὶ οὐκ εἰκὸς ἐκεῖθεν
κομίζεσθαι ἀνδράποδα εἰς τὴν Ἀττικήν. ἐξ ὧν
γὰρ ἐκομίζετο, ἢ τοῖς ἔθνεσιν ἐκείνοις ὁμωνύμους
ἐκάλουν τοὺς οἰκέτας, ὡς Λυδὸν καὶ Σύρον, ἢ
τοῖς ἐπιπολάζουσιν ἐκεῖ ὀνόμασι προσηγόρευον,
ὡς Μάνην ἢ Μίδαν τὸν Φρύγα, Τίβιον δὲ τὸν
Παφλαγόνα. ἐπὶ τοσοῦτον δ'[2] ὑπὸ τοῦ Βοερι-
βίστα τὸ ἔθνος ἐξαρθὲν ἐταπεινώθη τελέως ὑπό
τε τῶν στάσεων καὶ τῶν Ῥωμαίων· ἱκανοὶ δ' ὅμως
εἰσὶν ἔτι καὶ νῦν στέλλειν τέτταρας μυριάδας.

---

[1] μερίδας, Casaubon, for μυρίαδας.
[2] δ' before ὑπό, Casaubon inserts; so the later editors.

succeeded him divided the empire into several parts. In fact, only recently, when Augustus Caesar sent an expedition against them, the number of parts into which the empire had been divided was five, though at the time of the insurrection it had been four. Such divisions, to be sure, are only temporary and vary with the times.

12. But there is also another division of the country which has endured from early times, for some of the people are called Daci, whereas others are called Getae—Getae, those who incline towards the Pontus and the east, and Daci, those who incline in the opposite direction towards Germany and the sources of the Ister. The Daci, I think, were called Daï in early times; whence the slave names " Geta " and " Daüs " [1] which prevailed among the Attic people; for this is more probable than that " Daüs " is from those Scythians who are called " Daae," [2] for they live far away in the neighbourhood of Hyrcania, and it is not reasonable to suppose that slaves were brought into Attica from there; for the Attic people were wont either to call their slaves by the same names as those of the nations from which they were brought (as " Lydus " or " Syrus "), or addressed them by names that were prevalent in their countries (as " Manes " or else " Midas " for the Phrygian, or " Tibius " for the Paphlagonian). But though the tribe was raised to such a height by Boerebistas, it has been completely humbled by its own seditions and by the Romans; nevertheless, they are capable, even to-day, of sending forth an army of forty thousand men.

[1] In Latin, "Davus."
[2] Cp. 11. 7. 1, 8. 2, 9. 2.

13. Ῥεῖ δὲ δι' αὐτῶν Μάρισος ποταμὸς εἰς τὸν
Δανούιον, ᾧ τὰς παρασκευὰς ἀνεκόμιζον οἱ Ῥωμαῖοι
τὰς πρὸς τὸν πόλεμον. καὶ γὰρ τοῦ ποταμοῦ
τὰ μὲν ἄνω καὶ πρὸς ταῖς πηγαῖς μέρη μέχρι
τῶν καταρακτῶν Δανούιον προσηγόρευον, ἃ μά-
C 305 λιστα διὰ τῶν Δακῶν φέρεται, τὰ δὲ κάτω μέχρι
τοῦ Πόντου τὰ παρὰ τοὺς Γέτας καλοῦσιν Ἴστρον·
ὁμόγλωττοι δ' εἰσὶν οἱ Δακοὶ τοῖς Γέταις. παρὰ
μὲν οὖν τοῖς Ἕλλησιν οἱ Γέται γνωρίζονται μᾶλλον διὰ τὸ συνεχεῖς τὰς μεταναστάσεις ἐφ' ἑκάτερα τοῦ Ἴστρου ποιεῖσθαι καὶ τοῖς Θραξὶ[1] καὶ
τοῖς Μυσοῖς[2] ἀναμεμῖχθαι· καὶ τὸ τῶν Τριβαλλῶν δ' ἔθνος, Θρακικὸν ὄν, τὸ αὐτὸ πέπονθε τοῦτο.
μεταναστάσεις γὰρ δέδεκται, τῶν πλησιοχώρων
εἰς τοὺς ἀσθενεστέρους ἐξανιστάντων,[3] τῶν μὲν ἐκ
τῆς περαίας Σκυθῶν καὶ Βαστάρνων καὶ Σαυρομάτων ἐπικρατούντων πολλάκις, ὥστε καὶ ἐπι-
διαβαίνειν τοῖς ἐξελαθεῖσι καὶ καταμένειν τινὰς
αὐτῶν ἢ ἐν ταῖς νήσοις ἢ ἐν τῇ Θρᾴκῃ· τῶν δ' ἐκ
θατέρου μέρους ὑπ' Ἰλλυριῶν μάλιστα κατισχυ-
μένων. αὐξηθέντες δ' οὖν ἐπὶ πλεῖστον οἵ τε
Γέται οἵ τε Δακοί, ὥστε καὶ εἴκοσι μυριάδας
ἐκπέμπειν στρατείας, νῦν ὅσον εἰς τέτταρας μυριάδας συνεσταλμένοι τυγχάνουσι καὶ ἐγγὺς μὲν
ἥκουσι τοῦ ὑπακούειν Ῥωμαίων· οὔπω δ' εἰσὶν

---

[1] καὶ τοῖς Θραξί, inadvertently omitted by Kramer and
Meineke.

[2] Μυσοῖς, Meineke emends to Μοισοῖς (unnecessarily here).

[3] ἐξανιστάντων (ABC), Jones restores; ἐξανιστώντων (E);
ἐξαναστάντων (Kramer, Müller-Dübner, Meineke).

---

[1] On the various names of the river, see Pauly-Wissowa,
s.v. "Danuvius."

13. The Marisus River flows through their country into the Danuvius,[1] on which the Romans used to convey their equipment for war; the "Danuvius" I say, for so they used to call the upper part of the river from near its sources on to the cataracts, I mean the part which in the main flows through the country of the Daci, although they give the name "Ister" to the lower part, from the cataracts on to the Pontus, the part which flows past the country of the Getae. The language of the Daci is the same as that of the Getae. Among the Greeks, however, the Getae are better known because the migrations they make to either side of the Ister are continuous, and because they are intermingled with the Thracians and Mysians. And also the tribe of the Triballi, likewise Thracian, has had this same experience, for it has admitted migrations into this country, because the neighbouring peoples force them[2] to emigrate into the country of those who are weaker; that is, the Scythians and Bastarnians and Sauromatians on the far side of the river often prevail to the extent that they actually cross over to attack those whom they have already driven out, and some of them remain there, either in the islands or in Thrace, whereas those[3] on the other side are generally overpowered by the Illyrians. Be that as it may, although the Getae and Daci once attained to very great power, so that they actually could send forth an expedition of two hundred thousand men, they now find themselves reduced to as few as forty thousand, and they have come close to the point of yielding obedience to the Romans, though as yet

---

[2] The Getae. [3] Getae.

ὑποχείριοι τελέως διὰ τὰς ἐκ τῶν Γερμανῶν
ἐλπίδας, πολεμίων ὄντων τοῖς Ῥωμαίοις.

14. Μεταξὺ δὲ[1] τῆς Ποντικῆς θαλάττης τῆς
ἀπὸ Ἴστρου ἐπὶ Τύραν καὶ ἡ τῶν Γετῶν ἐρημία
πρόκειται, πεδιὰς πᾶσα καὶ ἄνυδρος, ἐν ᾗ Δαρεῖος
ἀποληφθεὶς[2] ὁ Ὑστάσπεω, καθ᾽ ὃν καιρὸν διέβη
τὸν Ἴστρον ἐπὶ τοὺς Σκύθας, ἐκινδύνευσε παν-
στρατιᾷ δίψῃ διαλυθῆναι, συνῆκε δ᾽ ὀψὲ καὶ
ἀνέστρεψε. Λυσίμαχος δ᾽ ὕστερον στρατεύσας
ἐπὶ Γέτας καὶ τὸν βασιλέα Δρομιχαίτην οὐκ
ἐκινδύνευσε μόνον, ἀλλὰ καὶ ἑάλω ζωγρίᾳ· πάλιν
δ᾽ ἐσώθη, τυχὼν εὐγνώμονος τοῦ βαρβάρου, καθάπερ εἶπον πρότερον.

15. Πρὸς δὲ ταῖς ἐκβολαῖς μεγάλη νῆσός ἐστιν
ἡ Πεύκη· κατασχόντες δ᾽ αὐτὴν Βαστάρναι Πευκῖνοι προσηγορεύθησαν· εἰσὶ δὲ καὶ ἄλλαι νῆσοι
πολὺ ἐλάττους, αἱ μὲν ἀνωτέρω ταύτης, αἱ δὲ
πρὸς τῇ θαλάττῃ. ἑπτάστομος γάρ ἐστι· μέγιστον δὲ τὸ ἱερὸν στόμα καλούμενον, δι᾽ οὗ

---

[1] After μεταξὺ δέ, Meineke (following Groskurd) wrongly
inserts Γετῶν καί (cp. μεταξὺ δὲ κ.τ.λ., 6. 3. 11).
[2] ἀπολειφθείς (ABCl); cp. ἀποληφθείς and footnote, 6. 1. 12.

---

[1] The Dniester.
[2] As in a trap. Cp. the experience of Milo in 6. 1. 12
where the same Greek word is used.
[3] 7. 3. 8.
[4] Literally, "Pine" Island. The term "Peuce" was
applied also to what is now the St. George branch of the
delta, which branch was the southern boundary of the
island.
[5] Strabo seems to mean by "Sacred Mouth" what is now
the Dunavez branch of the delta, which turns off from the
St. George branch into a lagoon called Lake Ragim, which

they are not absolutely submissive, because of the hopes which they base on the Germans, who are enemies to the Romans.

14. In the intervening space, facing that part of the Pontic Sea which extends from the Ister to the Tyras,[1] lies the Desert of the Getae, wholly flat and waterless, in which Dareius the son of Hystaspis was caught[2] on the occasion when he crossed the Ister to attack the Scythians and ran the risk of perishing from thirst, army and all; however, he belatedly realised his error and turned back And, later on, Lysimachus, in his expedition against the Getae and King Dromichaetes, not only ran the risk but actually was captured alive; but he again came off safely, because he found the barbarian kind-hearted, as I said before.[3]

15 Near the outlets of the Ister River is a great island called Peuce;[4] and when the Bastarnians took possession of it they received the appellation of Peucini. There are still other islands which are much smaller; some of these are farther inland than Peuce, while others are near the sea, for the river has seven mouths. The largest of these mouths is what is called the Sacred Mouth,[5] on

opens into the sea at the Portidje mouth; for (1) the length of the Dunavez to the lake is about 120 stadia, and (2) what is known about the alluvial deposits and topographical changes in the delta clearly indicates that the lake once had a wide and deep opening into the sea. Ptolemaeus (3. 10. 2), in giving the names of the mouths, refers to what is now the St. George branch as "Sacred Mouth or Peuce," thus making the two identical; but Strabo forces a distinction by referring to the inland voyage of 120 stadia, since the branch (Peuce) is a boundary of the island (Peuce). Cp. M. Besnier, *Lexique de Géographie Ancienne, s.v.* "Peuce," and Pauly-Wissowa, *s.v.* "Danuvius," pp. 2117-20.

σταδίων ἀνάπλους ἐπὶ τὴν Πεύκην ἑκατὸν εἴκοσι,
ἧς κατὰ τὸ κάτω μέρος ἐποίησε τὸ ζεῦγμα
Δαρεῖος, δύναιτο δ' ἂν ζευχθῆναι καὶ κατὰ τὸ
ἄνω. τοῦτο δὲ καὶ πρῶτόν ἐστι στόμα ἐν
ἀριστερᾷ εἰσπλέοντι εἰς τὸν Πόντον· τὰ δ' ἑξῆς
ἐν παράπλῳ τῷ ἐπὶ τὸν Τύραν· διέχει δ' ἀπ'
αὐτοῦ τὸ ἕβδομον στόμα περὶ τριακοσίους σταδίους. γίνονται οὖν μεταξὺ τῶν στομάτων νησίδες.
τὰ μὲν δὴ τρία στόματα τὰ ἐφεξῆς τῷ ἱερῷ
στόματί ἐστι μικρά· τὰ δὲ λοιπὰ τοῦ μὲν πολὺ
ἐλάττονα, τῶν δὲ μείζονα· Ἔφορος δὲ πεντά-
στομον εἴρηκε τὸν Ἴστρον. ἐντεῦθεν δ' ἐπὶ Τύραν
C 306 ποταμὸν πλωτὸν ἐννακόσιοι στάδιοι· ἐν δὲ τῷ μεταξὺ δύο λίμναι μεγάλαι, ἡ μὲν ἀνεῳγμένη πρὸς
τὴν θάλατταν, ὥστε καὶ λιμένι χρῆσθαι, ἡ δ'
ἄστομος.

16. Ἐπὶ δὲ τῷ στόματι τοῦ Τύρα πύργος ἐστὶ
Νεοπτολέμου καλούμενος καὶ κώμη Ἑρμώνακτος
λεγομένη. ἀναπλεύσαντι δὲ ἑκατὸν τετταράκοντα
σταδίους ἐφ' ἑκάτερα πόλεις, ἡ μὲν Νικωνία, ἡ
δ' ἐν ἀριστερᾷ Ὀφιοῦσσα· οἱ δὲ προσοικοῦντες
τῷ ποταμῷ πόλιν φασὶν ἀνιόντι ἑκατὸν καὶ εἴκοσι
σταδίους. διέχει δὲ τοῦ στόματος ἡ νῆσος ἡ

---

[1] Cp. 7. 3. 9.
[2] From the Sea of Marmara through the Bosporus.
[3] Strabo and Ptolemaeus (3. 10. 7) agree in placing the
"mouth of the Tyras" at the outlet of the lake (into the
Pontus), not at what was the outlet proper (into the lake),
nor yet at the narrowest part of the lake where the city of
Tyras (now Akkerman) was situated.
[4] According to Forbiger (Strabo, Vol. II, p. 89, footnote)
this tower was "recently" (about 1850) discovered at the
end of the west coast of the lake. Cp. the Towers of
Caepio (3. 1. 9), Pelorus (3. 5. 5), and Pharos (17. 1. 6).

which one can sail inland a hundred and twenty
stadia to Peuce. It was at the lower part of Peuce
that Dareius made his pontoon-bridge,[1] although
the bridge could have been constructed at the upper
part also. The Sacred Mouth is the first mouth on
the left as one sails[2] into the Pontus; the others
come in order thereafter as one sails along the coast
towards the Tyras; and the distance from 1t to the
seventh mouth is about three hundred stadia. Accordingly, small islands are formed between the
mouths. Now the three mouths that come next
in order after the Sacred Mouth are small, but the
remaining mouths are much smaller than it, but
larger than any one of the three. According to
Ephorus, however, the Ister has only five mouths.
Thence to the Tyras, a navigable river, the distance
is nine hundred stadia. And in the interval are two
large lakes—one of them opening into the sea, so
that it can also be used as a harbour, but the other
mouthless.

16. At the mouth[3] of the Tyras is what is called
the Tower of Neoptolemus,[4] and also what is called
the village of Hermonax.[5] And on sailing inland
one hundred and forty stadia one comes to two
cities, one on each side, Niconia[6] on the right and
Ophiussa[7] on the left. But the people who live
near the river speak of a city one hundred and
twenty stadia inland.[8] Again, at a distance of five

[5] The exact site of the village is unknown, but Strabo
certainly places it at the mouth. Ptolemaeus (3. 10. 7),
places it 10 miles (in latitude) farther south than the mouth.
[6] Niconia was situated on the lake near what is now
Ovidiopol.
[7] According to Pliny (4. 26), the earlier name of Tyras
was Ophiussa; but this is doubtful.
[8] Tyras, on the site of what is now Akkerman.

Λευκὴ δίαρμα πεντακοσίων σταδίων, ἱερὰ τοῦ Ἀχιλλέως, πελαγία.

17. Εἶτα Βορυσθένης ποταμὸς πλωτὸς ἐφ' ἑξακοσίους σταδίους καὶ πλησίον ἄλλος ποταμὸς Ὕπανις καὶ νῆσος πρὸ τοῦ στόματος τοῦ Βορυσθένους, ἔχουσα λιμένα. πλεύσαντι δὲ τὸν Βορυσθένη σταδίους διακοσίους ὁμώνυμος τῷ ποταμῷ πόλις· ἡ δ' αὐτὴ καὶ Ὀλβία καλεῖται, μέγα ἐμπόριον, κτίσμα Μιλησίων. ἡ δὲ ὑπερκειμένη πᾶσα χώρα τοῦ λεχθέντος μεταξὺ Βορυσθένους καὶ Ἴστρου πρώτη μέν ἐστιν ἡ τῶν Γετῶν ἐρημία, ἔπειτα οἱ Τυρεγέται, μεθ' οὓς οἱ Ἰάζυγες Σαρμάται καὶ οἱ Βασίλειοι λεγόμενοι καὶ Οὖργοι,[1] τὸ μὲν πλέον νομάδες, ὀλίγοι δὲ καὶ γεωργίας ἐπιμελούμενοι· τούτους φασὶ καὶ παρὰ τὸν Ἴστρον οἰκεῖν, ἐφ' ἑκάτερα πολλάκις. ἐν δὲ τῇ μεσογαίᾳ Βαστάρναι μὲν τοῖς Τυρεγέταις ὅμοροι καὶ Γερμανοῖς, σχεδόν τι καὶ αὐτοὶ τοῦ Γερμανικοῦ γένους ὄντες, εἰς πλείω φῦλα διῃρημένοι. καὶ γὰρ Ἄτμονοι λέγονταί τινες καὶ Σιδόνες, οἱ δὲ τὴν

---

[1] For Οὖργοι, Mannert conjectures Γεωργοί, and C. Müller, Ἀγάθυρσοι. But in the margin of A, pr. m., is found Οὔγγροι νῦν, οἱ δὲ αὐτοὶ καὶ Τοῦρκοι λέγονται. See Theoph. on Photius, 64, and Suidas, s.v. Βόσπορος.

---

[1] "White" Island (now Ilan-Adassi); known as "Isle of the Blest" (Pliny 4. 27); where the shade of Achilles was united to that of Helen.

[2] The Dnieper.   [3] The Bog.

[4] Now Berezan (see C. Müller, *Ptolemaeus*, Didot edition, note on 3. 10. 9, p. 471).

[5] Now in ruins, near Nickolaiev.   [6] Now Bessarabia.

[7] The city and territory of Tyras.

hundred stadia from the mouth is the island called
Leuce,[1] which lies in the high sea and is sacred to
Achilles.

17. Then comes the Borysthenes River,[2] which is
navigable for a distance of six hundred stadia; and,
near it, another river, the Hypanis,[3] and off the
mouth of the Borysthenes, an island [4] with a harbour.
On sailing up the Borysthenes two hundred stadia
one comes to a city of the same name as the river,
but the same city is also called Olbia;[5] it is a great
trading centre and was founded by Milesians.   Now
the whole country that lies above the said seaboard
between the Borysthenes and the Ister consists,
first, of the Desert of the Getae;[6] then the country
of the Tyregetans;[7] and after it the country of the
Iazygian Sarmatians and that of the people called
the Basileians [8] and that of the Urgi,[9] who in general
are nomads, though a few are interested also in
farming; these people, it is said, dwell also along
the Ister, often on both sides.   In the interior
dwell, first, those Bastarnians whose country borders
on that of the Tyregetans and Germans—they also
being, one might say, of Germanic stock; and they
are divided up into several tribes, for a part of them
are called Atmoni and Sidoni, while those who took

[8] Called by Herodotus (4. 20, 22, 56, 57, 59) the "Basileian
('Royal') Scythians," but by Ptolemaeus (5. 9. 16) the
"Basileian Sarmatians."

[9] The "Urgi" are otherwise unknown.   In the margin of
Manuscript A, first hand, are these words: "Ungri" (cp.
'Hungarians') "now, though the same are also called Turci"
(cp. 'Turks').   But the editors in general regard "Urgi"
as corrupt, and conjecture either "Georgi" (literally,
"Farmers"; cp. 7. 4. 6 and Herodotus 4. 18) or "Agathyrsi"
(cp. Herodotus 4. 125).

Πεύκην κατασχόντες τὴν ἐν τῷ Ἴστρῳ νῆσον
Πευκῖνοι, Ῥωξολανοὶ δ᾽ ἀρκτικώτατοι τὰ μεταξὺ
τοῦ Τανάιδος καὶ τοῦ Βορυσθένους νεμόμενοι πεδία.
ἡ γὰρ προσάρκτιος πᾶσα ἀπὸ Γερμανίας μέχρι τῆς
Κασπίας πεδιάς ἐστιν, ἣν ἴσμεν· ὑπὲρ δὲ τῶν Ῥω-
ξολανῶν εἴ τινες οἰκοῦσιν, οὐκ ἴσμεν. οἱ δὲ Ῥωξολανοὶ καὶ πρὸς τοὺς Μιθριδάτου τοῦ Εὐπάτορος
στρατηγοὺς ἐπολέμουν, ἔχοντες ἡγεμόνα Τάσιον·
ἦκον δὲ Παλάκῳ συμμαχήσοντες τῷ Σκιλούρου,
καὶ ἐδόκουν μὲν εἶναι μάχιμοι· πρὸς μέντοι συντε-
ταγμένην φάλαγγα καὶ ὡπλισμένην καλῶς τὸ
βάρβαρον φῦλον ἀσθενὲς πᾶν ἐστι καὶ τὸ γυμνη-
τικόν. ἐκεῖνοι γοῦν περὶ πέντε μυριάδας πρὸς
ἑξακισχιλίους[1] τοὺς Διοφάντῳ, τῷ τοῦ Μιθριδάτου στρατηγῷ, συμπαραταξαμένους οὐκ ἀντέσχον, ἀλλ᾽ οἱ πλεῖστοι διεφθάρησαν. χρῶνται
δὲ ὠμοβοΐνοις κράνεσι καὶ θώραξι, γερροφόροι,
ἀμυντήρια δ᾽ ἔχοντες καὶ λόγχας καὶ τόξον καὶ
ξίφος· τοιοῦτοι δὲ καὶ τῶν ἄλλων οἱ πλείους.
C 307 τῶν δὲ Νομάδων αἱ σκηναὶ πιλωταὶ πεπήγασιν
ἐπὶ ταῖς ἁμάξαις, ἐν αἷς διαιτῶνται· περὶ δὲ τὰς
σκηνὰς τὰ βοσκήματα, ἀφ᾽ ὧν τρέφονται καὶ
γάλακτι καὶ τυρῷ καὶ κρέασιν· ἀκολουθοῦσι δὲ
ταῖς νομαῖς μεταλαμβάνοντες τόπους ἀεὶ τοὺς
ἔχοντας πόαν, χειμῶνος μὲν ἐν τοῖς ἕλεσι τοῖς
περὶ τὴν Μαιῶτιν, θέρους δὲ καὶ ἐν τοῖς πεδίοις.
18. Ἅπασα δ᾽ ἡ χώρα δυσχείμερός ἐστι μέχρι

----

[1] ἑξακισχιλίους, Tzschucke, for ἕξ; so the editors.

----

[1] The Dnieper.
[2] King of Pontus 120–63 B.C.

possession of Peuce, the island in the Ister, are called "Peucini," whereas the "Roxolani" (the most northerly of them all) roam the plains between the Tanaïs and the Borysthenes.[1] In fact, the whole country towards the north from Germany as far as the Caspian Sea is, so far as we know it, a plain, but whether any people dwell beyond the Roxolani we do not know. Now the Roxolani, under the leadership of Tasius, carried on war even with the generals of Mithridates Eupator;[2] they came for the purpose of assisting Palacus,[3] the son of Scilurus, as his allies, and they had the reputation of being warlike; yet all barbarian races and light-armed peoples are weak when matched against a well-ordered and well-armed phalanx. At any rate, those people, about fifty thousand strong, could not hold out against the six thousand men arrayed with Diophantus, the general of Mithridates, and most of them were destroyed. They use helmets and corselets made of raw ox-hides, carry wicker shields, and have for weapons spears, bow, and sword; and most of the other barbarians are armed in this way. As for the Nomads, their tents, made of felt, are fastened on the wagons in which they spend their lives; and round about the tents are the herds which afford the milk, cheese, and meat on which they live; and they follow the grazing herds, from time to time moving to other places that have grass, living only in the marsh-meadows about Lake Maeotis in winter, but also in the plains in summer.

18. The whole of the country has severe winters

[3] A prince in the Tauric Chersonese (now the Crimea); cp. 7. 4. 3.

τῶν ἐπὶ θαλάττῃ τόπων τῶν μεταξὺ Βορυσθένους
καὶ τοῦ στόματος τῆς Μαιώτιδος· αὐτῶν δὲ τῶν
ἐπὶ θαλάττῃ τὰ ἀρκτικώτατα τό τε στόμα τῆς
Μαιώτιδος καὶ ἔτι μᾶλλον τὸ τοῦ Βορυσθένους
καὶ [1] ὁ μυχὸς τοῦ Ταμυράκου κόλπου, καὶ [2]
Καρκινίτου,[3] καθ᾽ ὃν ὁ ἰσθμὸς τῆς μεγάλης
Χερρονήσου. δηλοῖ δὲ τὰ ψύχη, καίπερ ἐν
πεδίοις οἰκούντων· ὄνους τε γὰρ οὐ τρέφουσι
(δύσριγον γὰρ τὸ ζῷον), οἵ τε βόες οἱ μὲν ἄκερῳ
γεννῶνται, τῶν δ᾽ ἀπορρινῶσι τὰ κέρατα (καὶ
γὰρ τοῦτο δύσριγον τὸ μέρος), οἵ τε ἵπποι μικροί,
τὰ δὲ πρόβατα μεγάλα· ῥήττονται δὲ χαλκαῖ
ὑδρίαι, τὰ δ᾽ ἐνόντα συμπήττεται. τῶν δὲ πάγων
ἡ σφοδρότης μάλιστα ἐκ τῶν συμβαινόντων περὶ
τὸ στόμα τῆς Μαιώτιδος δῆλός ἐστιν. ἁμαξεύεται
γὰρ ὁ διάπλους ὁ εἰς Φαναγορίαν ἐκ τοῦ Παντικαπαίου, ὥστε καὶ πάγον [4] εἶναι καὶ ὁδόν· ὀρυκτοί
τέ εἰσιν ἰχθύες οἱ ἀποληφθέντες [5] ἐν τῷ κρυστάλλῳ
τῇ προσαγορευομένῃ γαγγάμῃ, καὶ μάλιστα οἱ

---

[1] καί, Tzschucke inserts ; so the later editors.
[2] τοῦ, before καί, Corais inserts, unnecessarily ; so the other
editors ; cp. Ταυρικὴν καὶ Σκυθικήν 7. 4. 1.
[3] Καρκινίτου, Xylander, for Καρπηνιήτου ; so the later
editors.
[4] πάγον, Jones, for πηλόν (mud), omitted by E, a space for
five letters being left. Others emend to πλοῦν (voyage). See
ἐπὶ τῷ πάγῳ (ice), 2. 1. 16. Capps conjectures πόρον, which is
most tempting.
[5] ἀποληφθέντες (E) ; ἀπολειφθέντες (ABCl).

---

[1] Now Karkinit Bay.
[2] The Tauric Chersonese, now the Crimea.
[3] See 2. 1. 16.

as far as the regions by the sea that are between
the Borysthenes and the mouth of Lake Maeotis;
but of the regions themselves that are by the sea
the most northerly are the mouth of the Maeotis
and, still more northerly, the mouth of the Borysthenes, and the recess of the Gulf of Tamyraces,[1]
or Carcinites, on which is the isthmus of the Great
Chersonesus.[2] The coldness of these regions, albeit
the people live in plains, is evident, for they do not
breed asses, an animal that is very sensitive to cold;
and as for their cattle, some are born without horns,
while the horns of others are filed off, for this part
of the animal is sensitive to cold; and the horses
are small, whereas the sheep are large; and bronze
water-jars burst[3] and their contents freeze solid.
But the severity of the frosts is most clearly
evidenced by what takes place in the region of the
mouth of Lake Maeotis: the waterway from Panticapaeum[4] across to Phanagoria[5] is traversed by
wagons, so that it is both ice and roadway. And
fish that become caught in the ice are obtained by
digging[6] with an implement called the " gangame," [7]
and particularly the antacaei,[8] which are about the

---

[4] Now Kertch.

[5] Near what is now Taman.

[6] Strabo seems to mean that the fish were imbedded in the
ice, and not that "the ice was first broken, and the fish
extracted from the water beneath with a net" (Tozer,
Selections from Strabo, p. 196).

[7] A pronged instrument like a trident. Tozer (*loc. cit.*)
takes "gangame" to mean here "a small round net;" but
see Stephanus, Thesaurus, and especially Hesychius (*s.v.*).

[8] A kind of sturgeon (see Herodotus 4. 53), being one of
the fish from the roe of which the Russian *caviar* is now
prepared.

225

ἀντακαῖοι, δελφῖσι πάρισοι τὸ μέγεθος. Νεοπτόλεμον[1] δέ φασι, τὸν τοῦ Μιθριδάτου στρατηγόν,
ἐν τῷ αὐτῷ πόρῳ θέρους μὲν ναυμαχίᾳ περιγε-
νέσθαι τῶν βαρβάρων, χειμῶνος δ᾽ ἱππομαχίᾳ·
φασὶ δὲ καὶ τὴν ἄμπελον ἐν τῷ Βοσπόρῳ κατο-
ρύττεσθαι χειμῶνος, ἐπαμώντων πολὺ τῆς γῆς.
λέγεται δὲ καὶ τὰ καύματα σφοδρὰ γίνεσθαι,
τάχα μὲν τῶν σωμάτων ἀηθιζομένων, τάχα δὲ
τῶν πεδίων ἀνηνεμούντων τότε, ἢ καὶ τοῦ πάχους
τοῦ ἀέρος ἐκθερμαινομένου πλέον, καθάπερ ἐν
τοῖς νέφεσιν οἱ παρήλιοι ποιοῦσιν. Ἀτέας δὲ
δοκεῖ τῶν πλείστων ἄρξαι τῶν ταύτῃ βαρβάρων
ὁ πρὸς Φίλιππον πολεμήσας τὸν Ἀμύντου.

19. Μετὰ δὲ τὴν πρὸ τοῦ Βορυσθένους νῆσον
ἑξῆς πρὸς ἀνίσχοντα ἥλιον ὁ πλοῦς ἐπὶ ἄκραν
τὴν τοῦ Ἀχιλλείου δρόμου, ψιλὸν μὲν χωρίον,
καλούμενον δ᾽[2] ἄλσος, ἱερὸν Ἀχιλλέως· εἶθ᾽ ὁ
Ἀχίλλειος Δρόμος, ἀλιτενὴς χερρόνησος· ἔστι
γὰρ ταινία τις ὅσον χιλίων σταδίων μῆκος ἐπὶ
τὴν ἔω, πλάτος δὲ τὸ μέγιστον δυεῖν σταδίων,

---

[1] Νεοπτόλεμον . . . ἱππομαχίᾳ, Meineke transposes back to
position after ὁδόν, unnecessarily (see footnote to translation).
[2] δ᾽, Corais inserts; so the later editors.

---

[1] This sentence is transposed by Meineke to a position
after the sentence that follows, but see footnote on "Carcinites," 7. 4. 1.
[2] Cp. 2. 1. 16.
[3] Aristotle (*Meteorologica* 3. 2. 6 and 3. 6. 5) refers to, and
explains, the phenomena of the "parhelia" ("mock-suns")
in the Bosporus region.
[4] According to Lucian (*Macrob.* 10) Anteas (*sic*) fell in the

size of dolphins.[1] It is said of Neoptolemus, the
general of Mithridates, that in the same strait he
overcame the barbarians in a naval engagement in
summer and in a cavalry engagement in winter.[2]
And it is further said that the vine in the Bosporus
region is buried during the winter, the people heap-
ing quantities of earth upon it. And it is said that
the heat too becomes severe, perhaps because the
bodies of the people are unaccustomed to it, or
perhaps because no winds blow on the plains at
that time, or else because the air, by reason of its
density, becomes superheated (like the effect of the
parhelia[3] in the clouds). It appears that Ateas,[4]
who waged war with Philip[5] the son of Amyntas,
ruled over most of the barbarians in this part of the
world.

19. After the island[6] that lies off the Borysthenes,
and next towards the rising sun, one sails to the
cape[7] of the Race Course of Achilles, which, though
a treeless place, is called *Alsos*[8] and is sacred to
Achilles. Then comes the Race Course of Achilles,
a peninsula[9] that lies flat on the sea; it is a ribbon-
like stretch of land, as much as one thousand stadia

war with Philip when about ninety years of age. The Roman
writers spell the name "Atheas."

[5] 359–336 B.C.; the father of Alexander the Great.

[6] See 7. 3. 17.

[7] Now Cape Tendra.

[8] *i.e.*, "a grove"; the word usually means a sacred
precinct planted with trees, but is often used of any sacred
precinct.

[9] The western part (now an island) of this peninsula is
called "Tendra," and the eastern, "Zharylgatch" (or
"Djarilgatch"). According to ancient legends Achilles
pursued Iphigeneia to this peninsula and there practised for
his races.

ἐλάχιστον τεττάρων πλέθρων, διέχουσα τῆς ἑκατέρωθεν τοῦ αὐχένος ἠπείρου σταδίους ἑξήκοντα,
C 308 ἀμμώδης, ὕδωρ ἔχουσα ὀρυκτόν· κατὰ μέσην δ'
ὁ τοῦ ἰσθμοῦ αὐχὴν ὅσον τετταράκοντα σταδίων·
τελευτᾷ δὲ πρὸς ἄκραν, ἣν Ταμυράκην καλοῦσιν,
ἔχουσαν ὕφορμον βλέπονταν πρὸς τὴν ἤπειρον·
μεθ' ἣν ὁ Καρκινίτης¹ κόλπος εὐμεγέθης, ἀνέχων
πρὸς τὰς ἄρκτους ὅσον ἐπὶ σταδίους χιλίους, οἱ
δὲ καὶ τριπλασίους φασὶ μέχρι τοῦ μυχοῦ· . . .²
καλοῦνται δὲ Τάφριοι.³ τὸν δὲ κόλπον καὶ
Ταμυράκην καλοῦσιν ὁμωνύμως τῇ ἄκρᾳ.

IV

1. Ἐνταῦθα δ' ἐστὶν ὁ ἰσθμὸς ὁ διείργων τὴν
Σαπρὰν λεγομένην λίμνην ἀπὸ τῆς θαλάττης,
σταδίων τεσσαράκοντα καὶ ποιῶν τὴν Ταυρικὴν
καὶ Σκυθικὴν λεγομένην χερρόνησον· οἱ δὲ τριακοσίων ἑξήκοντα τὸ πλάτος τοῦ ἰσθμοῦ φασιν.
ἡ δὲ Σαπρὰ λίμνη σταδίων μὲν καὶ τετρακισχιλίων
λέγεται, μέρος δ' ἐστὶ τῆς Μαιώτιδος τὸ πρὸς
δύσιν· συνεστόμωται γὰρ αὐτῇ στόματι μεγάλῳ.
ἑλώδης δ' ἐστὶ σφόδρα καὶ ῥαπτοῖς πλοίοις μόγις

¹ Καρκινίτης, the *Epit.*, for Καρπινηίτης ; so the editors.
² οἱ δ' ἐκεῖ, or something like it, seems to have fallen out of
the MSS. before καλοῦνται.
³ Τάφριοι (A *sec. m.*) for Τάφιοι ; so the editors.

¹ The plethron was one-sixth of a stadium, or 100 feet.
² We would call it "a sand-bank."
³ Now Cape Czile.　　　⁴ Isthmus of Perekop.
⁵ *i.e.* "Putrid"; called by Ptolemaeus (3. 5. 2) and other

228

in length, extending towards the east; its maximum breadth is only two stadia, and its minimum only four plethra,[1] and it is only sixty stadia distant from the mainland that lies on either side of the neck. It is sandy,[2] and water may be had by digging. The neck of the isthmus is near the centre of the peninsula and is about forty stadia wide. It terminates in a cape called Tamyrace,[3] which has a mooring-place that faces the mainland. And after this cape comes the Carcinites Gulf. It is a very large gulf, reaching up towards the north as far as one thousand stadia; some say, however, that the distance to its recess is three times as much. The people there are called Taphrians. The gulf is also called Tamyrace, the same name as that of the cape.

IV

1. Here is the isthmus [4] which separates what is called Lake Sapra [5] from the sea; it is forty stadia in width and forms what is called the Tauric, or Scythian, Chersonese. Some, however, say that the breadth of the isthmus is three hundred and sixty stadia. But though Lake Sapra is said to be as much as four thousand stadia,[6] it is only a part, the western part, of Lake Maeotis, for it is connected with the latter by a wide mouth. It is very marshy and is scarcely navigable for sewn boats,[7] for the

ancient writers "Byce"; now called by the Russians "Ghuiloje More."

[6] Strabo does not specify whether in breadth, length, or perimeter; he must mean perimeter, in which case the figure is, roughly speaking, correct.

[7] Boats made of hides sewn together.

πλόϊμος· οἱ γὰρ ἄνεμοι τὰ τενάγη ῥᾳδίως ἀνα-
καλύπτουσιν, εἶτα πάλιν πληροῦσιν, ὥστε τὰ
ἕλη τοῖς μείζοσι σκάφεσιν οὐ περάσιμά ἐστιν.
ἔχει δ' ὁ κόλπος νησίδια τρία καὶ προσβραχῆ
τινα καὶ χοιραδώδη ὀλίγα κατὰ τὸν παράπλουν.

2. Ἐκπλέοντι δ' ἐν ἀριστερᾷ πολίχνη καὶ ἄλλος[1]
λιμὴν Χερρονησιτῶν. ἔκκειται γὰρ ἐπὶ τὴν μεσημβρίαν ἄκρα μεγάλη κατὰ τὸν παράπλουν
ἐφεξῆς, μέρος οὖσα τῆς ὅλης Χερρονήσου, ἐφ'
ᾗ ἵδρυται πόλις Ἡρακλεωτῶν, ἄποικος τῶν ἐν
τῷ Πόντῳ, αὐτὸ τοῦτο καλουμένη Χερρόνησος,
διέχουσα τοῦ Τύρα παράπλουν[2] σταδίων τετρακισχιλίων τετρακοσίων· ἐν ᾗ τὸ τῆς Παρθένου

---

[1] ἄλλος, Corais (from conj. of Casaubon) emends to καλός.
Jones conjectures ἄλλος καλός.

[2] παράπλουν, all editors, for παράπλου (ABCE*l*).

---

[1] *i.e.* Carcinites. In numerous cases Strabo unexpectedly
reverts to a subject previously dismissed (cp. 7. 3. 18 and
footnote). The present instance, among others, clearly shows
that Groskurd, Forbiger, and Meineke are hardly justified in
transferring passages of the text to different positions.
However, they do not make a transfer here.

[2] Corais, from a conjecture of Casaubon, emends "another
harbour" to "Fair Harbour." But since Ptolemaeus (3. 5. 2)
refers to a Kalos Limen on the opposite coast, the present
translator conjectures that Strabo wrote "another Fair
Harbour." It is now known that there were two settlements of the Chersonesites north of the great bay on which
the city of Chersonesus was situated. and that their names
were "Cercinitis" and "Kalos Limen." See Latyschew,
and the inscription in *S. Ber. Akad. Berl.* 1892, 479 ; and
Pauly-Wissowa, *s.v.* "Bosporos," p. 772 and *s.v.* "Chersone-
sos," p. 2265.

[3] Also called the "Great Chersonesus" (the Crimea), as
distinguished from the "Little Chersonesus." Strabo means

winds readily uncover the shallow places and then cover them with water again, and therefore the marshes are impassable for the larger boats. The gulf[1] contains three small islands, and also some shoals and a few reefs along the coast.

2. As one sails out of the gulf, one comes, on the left, to a small city and another harbour[2] belonging to the Chersonesites. For next in order as one sails along the coast is a great cape which projects towards the south and is a part of the Chersonesus as a whole;[3] and on this cape is situated a city of the Heracleotae, a colony of the Heracleotae who live on the Pontus,[4] and this place itself[5] is called Chersonesus,[6] being distant as one sails along the coast[7] four thousand four hundred stadia from the Tyras. In this city is the temple of the Parthenos, a certain deity;[8] and the cape[9] which

that the cape in question and the Little Chersonesus are identical. The cape (or peninsula) was bounded on the north by the isthmus (later mentioned), and this isthmus was marked by a wall and trench (see 7. 4. 7) which connected Ctenus Harbour (now the Harbour of Sebastopol) with Symbolon Limen (now the Harbour of Balaklava).

[4] In the Paphlagonian city called Heracleia Pontica (now Erekli).   [5] The "city" just mentioned.

[6] "New Chersonesus," which is now in ruins near Sebastopol. "Old Chersonesus" (in ruins in Strabo's time) was near the isthmus of the little peninsula which terminates in Cape Fanary.

[7] That is, including the entire circuit around the coast of Karkinit Bay.

[8] "Parthenos" ("Virgin") usually means Athene; but in this case it means either the Tauric Artemis (see 5. 3. 12 and Diodorus Siculus, 4. 44), or (what is more likely) Iphigeneia (see Herodotus, 4. 103). In saying "deity," and not "goddess," Strabo seems purposely non-committal as between the two.   [9] Now Cape Fanary.

ἱερὸν, δαίμονός τινος, ἧς ἐπώνυμος καὶ ἡ ἄκρα ἡ
πρὸ τῆς πόλεώς ἐστιν ἐν σταδίοις ἑκατόν, καλουμένη Παρθένιον, ἔχον νεὼν τῆς δαίμονος καὶ
ξόανον. μεταξὺ δὲ τῆς πόλεως καὶ τῆς ἄκρας
λιμένες τρεῖς, εἶθ᾽ ἡ παλαιὰ Χερρόνησος κατε-
σκαμμένη καὶ μετ᾽ αὐτὴν λιμὴν στενόστομος, καθ᾽
ὃν μάλιστα οἱ Ταῦροι, Σκυθικὸν ἔθνος, τὰ λῃστήρια
συνίσταντο, τοῖς καταφεύγουσιν ἐπ᾽ αὐτὸν ἐπιχει-
ροῦντες· καλεῖται δὲ Συμβόλων Λιμήν. οὗτος δὲ
ποιεῖ πρὸς ἄλλον λιμένα Κτενοῦντα καλούμενον
τετταράκοντα σταδίων ἰσθμόν· οὗτος δ᾽ ἐστὶν
ὁ ἰσθμὸς ὁ κλείων τὴν μικρὰν Χερρόνησον, ἣν
ἔφαμεν τῆς μεγάλης Χερρονήσου μέρος, ἔχουσαν ἐν αὐτῇ[1] τὴν ὁμωνύμως λεγομένην πόλιν
Χερρόνησον.

3. Αὕτη δ᾽ ἦν πρότερον αὐτόνομος, πορθουμένη
δὲ ὑπὸ τῶν βαρβάρων ἠναγκάσθη προστάτην
C 309 ἑλέσθαι Μιθριδάτην τὸν Εὐπάτορα, στρατηγιῶντα
ἐπὶ τοὺς ὑπὲρ τοῦ ἰσθμοῦ μέχρι Βορυσθένους
βαρβάρους καὶ τοῦ Ἀδρίου·[2] ταῦτα δ᾽ ἦν ἐπὶ
Ῥωμαίους παρασκευή. ἐκεῖνος μὲν οὖν κατὰ
ταύτας τὰς ἐλπίδας ἄσμενος πέμψας εἰς τὴν
Χερρόνησον στρατιάν, ἅμα πρός τε τοὺς Σκύθας
ἐπολέμει Σκίλουρόν τε καὶ τοὺς Σκιλούρου παῖδας

---

[1] αὐτῇ, Meineke emends to αὑτῇ.
[2] καὶ τοῦ Ἀδρίου, Meineke relegates to foot of page.

---

[1] See 4. 1. 4. and footnote.
[2] "Signal Harbour"; now the Harbour of Balaklava.

is in front of the city, at a distance of one hundred stadia, is also named after this deity, for it is called the Parthenium, and it has a shrine and xoanon[1] of her. Between the city and the cape are three harbours. Then comes the Old Chersonesus, which has been razed to the ground; and after it comes a narrow-mouthed harbour, where, generally speaking, the Tauri, a Scythian tribe, used to assemble their bands of pirates in order to attack all who fled thither for refuge. It is called Symbolon Limen.[2] This harbour forms with another harbour called Ctenus Limen[3] an isthmus forty stadia in width; and this is the isthmus that encloses the Little Chersonesus, which, as I was saying, is a part of the Great Chersonesus and has on it the city of Chersonesus, which bears the same name as the peninsula.

3. This city[4] was at first self-governing, but when it was sacked by the barbarians it was forced to choose Mithridates Eupator as protector. He was then leading an army against the barbarians who lived beyond the isthmus[5] as far as the Borysthenes and the Adrias;[6] this, however, was preparatory to a campaign against the Romans. So, then, in accordance with these hopes of his he gladly sent an army to Chersonesus, and at the same time carried on war against the Scythians, not only against Scilurus, but also the sons of Scilurus—

[3] "Comb Harbour" (now the Harbour of Sebastopol); probably so called from the sharp indentations in the coast.

[4] Strabo is now thinking of the Old Chersonesus.

[5] Isthmus of Perekop.

[6] That is, the head of the Adriatic.

τοὺς περὶ Πάλακον, οὓς Ποσειδώνιος μὲν πεντή-
κοντά φησιν, Ἀπολλωνίδης δὲ ὀγδοήκοντα· ἅμα
δὲ τούτους τε ἐχειρώσατο βίᾳ καὶ Βοσπόρου
κατέστη κύριος παρ᾽ ἑκόντος λαβὼν Παρισάδου¹
τοῦ κατέχοντος. ἐξ ἐκείνου δὴ τοῦ χρόνου τοῖς
τοῦ Βοσπόρου δυνάσταις ἡ τῶν Χερρονησιτῶν
πόλις ὑπήκοος μέχρι νῦν ἐστι. τὸ δ᾽ ἴσον ὁ
Κτενοῦς διέχει τῆς τε τῶν Χερρονησιτῶν πόλεως
καὶ τοῦ Συμβόλων Λιμένος. μετὰ δὲ τὸν Συμβόλων Λιμένα μέχρι Θεοδοσίας πόλεως ἡ Ταυρικὴ
παραλία, χιλίων που σταδίων τὸ μῆκος, τραχεῖα
καὶ ὀρεινὴ καὶ καταιγίζουσα τοῖς Βορέαις ἵδρυται.
πρόκειται² δ᾽ αὐτῆς ἄκρα πολὺ πρὸς τὸ πέλαγος
καὶ τὴν μεσημβρίαν ἐκκειμένη κατὰ Παφλαγονίαν
καὶ Ἄμαστριν πόλιν, καλεῖται δὲ Κριοῦ Μέτωπον.
ἀντίκειται δ᾽ αὐτῇ τὸ τῶν Παφλαγόνων ἀκρωτήριον ἡ Κάραμβις τὸ διαιροῦν εἰς πελάγη δύο τὸν
Εὔξεινον πόντον τῷ ἑκατέρωθεν σφιγγομένῳ³
πορθμῷ. διέστηκε δ᾽ ἡ Κάραμβις τῆς μὲν τῶν
Χερρονησιτῶν πόλεως σταδίους δισχιλίους καὶ
πεντακοσίους, τοῦ δὲ Κριοῦ Μετώπου πολὺ ἐλάττους τὸν ἀριθμόν· συχνοὶ γοῦν τῶν διαπλευσάντων

¹ Πιρισίδου (ABC), Περισίδου (lno); Meineke reads Παιρι-
σάδου (the spelling on coins). But see C. Müller, Ind. Var.
Lect., p. 983; and footnote on Παρισάδην, 7. 4. 4.
² προσκεῖται (ABC).
³ σφιγγομένῳ (B, with correction, Cl).

¹ See 7. 3. 17.
² Little is known of this Apollonides. According to the
scholiast on Apollonius Rhodius (4. 983, 1175), he wrote a
geographical treatise entitled *Periplus of Europe*.
³ The Cimmerian Bosporus, the country about the strait of
Kertch. The capital was Panticapaeum (now Kertch).

Palacus [1] and the rest—who, according to Poseidonius were fifty in number, but according to
Apollonides [2] were eighty. At the same time, also,
he not only subdued all these by force, but also
established himself as lord of the Bosporus, [3] receiving the country as a voluntary gift from
Parisades [4] who held sway over it. So from that
time on down to the present the city of the
Chersonesites has been subject to the potentates of
the Bosporus. Again, Ctenus Limen is equidistant
from the city of the Chersonesites and Symbolon
Limen. And after Symbolon Limen, as far as the
city Theodosia, [5] lies the Tauric seaboard, which is
about one thousand stadia in length. It is rugged
and mountainous, and is subject to furious storms
from the north. And in front of it lies a promontory
which extends far out towards the high sea and the
south in the direction of Paphlagonia and the city
Amastris; [6] it is called Criumetopon. [7] And opposite
it lies that promontory of the Paphlagonians,
Carambis, [8] which, by means of the strait, which is
contracted on both sides, divides the Euxine Pontus
into two seas. [9] Now the distance from Carambis to
the city of the Chersonesites is two thousand five
hundred stadia, [10] but the number to Criumetopon is
much less; at any rate, many who have sailed across

[4] The correct spelling of the name seems to be "Paerisades" (so on coins), but several ancient writers spell it
Parisades.
[5] Now called Feodosia or Kaffa.
[6] Now Amasra.
[7] Literally, "Ram's-forehead"; now Cape Karadje.
[8] Now Cape Kerembe.
[9] Cp. 2. 5. 22, where the same thought is clearly expressed.
[10] But cp. 2. 5. 22.

τὸν πορθμὸν ἅμα φασὶν ἰδεῖν ἀμφοτέρας ἑκατέρωθεν τὰς ἄκρας. ἐν δὲ τῇ ὀρεινῇ τῶν Ταύρων καὶ τὸ ὄρος ἐστὶν ὁ Τραπεζοῦς, ὁμώνυμον τῇ πόλει τῇ περὶ τὴν Τιβαρανίαν καὶ τὴν Κολχίδα· καὶ ἄλλο δ' ἐστὶν ὄρος Κιμμέριον κατὰ τὴν αὐτὴν ὀρεινήν, δυναστευσάντων ποτὲ τῶν Κιμμερίων ἐν τῷ Βοσπόρῳ· καθ' ὃ καὶ Κιμμερικὸς Βόσπορος καλεῖται τοῦ πορθμοῦ πᾶν, ὃ ἐπέχει τὸ στόμα τῆς Μαιώτιδος.

4. Μετὰ δὲ τὴν ὀρεινὴν τὴν λεχθεῖσαν ἡ Θεοδοσία κεῖται πόλις, πεδίον εὔγαιον ἔχουσα καὶ λιμένα ναυσὶ καὶ ἑκατὸν ἐπιτήδειον· οὗτος δὲ ὅρος ἦν πρότερον τῆς τῶν Βοσπορηανῶν καὶ Ταύρων γῆς· καὶ ἡ ἑξῆς δ' ἐστὶν εὔγαιος χώρα μέχρι Παντικαπαίου, τῆς μητροπόλεως τῶν Βοσπορηανῶν, ἱδρυμένης ἐπὶ τῷ στόματι τῆς Μαιώτιδος. ἔστι δὲ τὸ μεταξὺ τῆς Θεοδοσίας καὶ τοῦ Παντικαπαίου στάδιοι περὶ πεντακόσιοι καὶ τριάκοντα, χώρα πᾶσα σιτοφόρος, κώμας ἔχουσα καὶ πόλιν εὐλίμενον τὸ Νύμφαιον καλούμενον. τὸ δὲ Παντικάπαιον λόφος ἐστὶ πάντῃ περιοικούμενος ἐν κύκλῳ σταδίων εἴκοσι· πρὸς ἔω δ' ἔχει λιμένα καὶ νεώρια ὅσον τριάκοντα νεῶν· ἔχει δὲ καὶ ἀκρόπολιν· κτίσμα δ' ἐστὶ Μιλησίων. ἐμοναρχεῖτο δὲ πολὺν χρόνον ὑπὸ δυναστῶν τῶν περὶ Λεύκωνα καὶ Σάτυρον[1] καὶ Παρισάδην[2] αὕτη

C 310

---

[1] Σάτυρον, Casaubon, for Σάγαυρον; so the later editors.
[2] Πιρισάδην (A); see Παρισάδου and footnote, 7. 4. 3.

---

[1] Cp. the footnote on seeing from Lilybaeum to the Carthaginian harbour, 6. 2. 1.

the strait say that they have seen both promontories, on either side, at the same time.[1] In the mountainous district of the Taurians is also the mountain Trapezus,[2] which has the same name as the city[3] in the neighbourhood of Tibarania and Colchis. And near the same mountainous district is also another mountain, Cimmerius,[4] so called because the Cimmerians once held sway in the Bosporus; and it is because of this fact that the whole of the strait[5] which extends to the mouth of Lake Maeotis is called the Cimmerian Bosporus.

4. After the aforesaid mountainous district is the city Theodosia. It is situated in a fertile plain and has a harbour that can accommodate as many as a hundred ships; this harbour in earlier times was a boundary between the countries of the Bosporians and the Taurians. And the country that comes next after that of Theodosia is also fertile, as far as Panticapaeum. Panticapaeum is the metropolis of the Bosporians and is situated at the mouth of Lake Maeotis. The distance between Theodosia and Panticapaeum is about five hundred and thirty stadia; the district is everywhere productive of grain, and it contains villages, as well as a city called Nymphaeum,[6] which possesses a good harbour. Panticapaeum is a hill inhabited on all sides in a circuit of twenty stadia. To the east it has a harbour, and docks for about thirty ships; and it also has an acropolis. It is a colony of the Milesians. For a long time it was ruled as a monarchy by the dynasty of Leuco, Satyrus, and Parisades, as were

---

[2] Now Tchadir-Dagh. [3] *i.e.* the Trebizond of to-day.
[4] Now Aghirmisch-Daghi. [5] The strait of Kertch.
[6] Now Kalati.

τε καὶ αἱ πλησιόχωροι κατοικίαι πᾶσαι αἱ περὶ τὸ στόμα τῆς Μαιώτιδος ἑκατέρωθεν μέχρι Παρισάδου τοῦ Μιθριδάτῃ παραδόντος τὴν ἀρχήν. ἐκαλοῦντο δὲ τύραννοι, καίπερ οἱ πλείους ἐπιεικεῖς γεγονότες, ἀρξάμενοι ἀπὸ Παρισάδου [1] καὶ Λεύκωνος. Παρισάδης δὲ καὶ θεὸς νενόμισται· τούτῳ δὲ ὁμώνυμος καὶ ὁ ὕστατος, ὃς [2] οὐχ οἷός τε ὢν ἀντέχειν πρὸς τοὺς βαρβάρους, φόρον πραττομένους μείζω τοῦ πρότερον, Μιθριδάτῃ τῷ Εὐπάτορι παρέδωκε τὴν ἀρχήν· ἐξ ἐκείνου δ᾽ ἡ βασιλεία γεγένηται Ῥωμαίοις ὑπήκοος. τὸ μὲν οὖν πλέον αὐτῆς μέρος ἐστὶν ἐπὶ τῆς Εὐρώπης, μέρος δέ τι καὶ ἐπὶ τῆς Ἀσίας.

5. Τὸ δὲ στόμα τῆς Μαιώτιδος καλεῖται μὲν Κιμμερικὸς Βόσπορος, ἄρχεται δὲ ἀπὸ μείζονος πλάτους, ἀπὸ ἑβδομήκοντά που σταδίων· καθ᾽ ὃ διαίρουσιν ἐκ τῶν περὶ Παντικάπαιον τόπων εἰς τὴν ἐγγυτάτω πόλιν τῆς Ἀσίας, τὴν Φαναγορίαν· τελευτᾷ δ᾽ εἰς πολὺ στενώτερον πορθμόν. διαιρεῖ δ᾽ ὁ στενωπὸς οὗτος τὴν Ἀσίαν ἀπὸ τῆς Εὐρώπης, καὶ ὁ Τάναϊς ποταμός, καταντικρὺ ῥέων ἀπὸ τῶν ἄρκτων εἴς τε τὴν λίμνην καὶ τὸ στόμα αὐτῆς· δύο δ᾽ ἔχει τὰς εἰς τὴν λίμνην ἐκβολὰς διεχούσας ἀλλήλων ὅσον σταδίους ἑξήκοντα. ἔστι δὲ καὶ πόλις ὁμώνυμος τῷ ποταμῷ, μέγιστον τῶν βαρβάρων ἐμπόριον μετὰ τὸ Παντικάπαιον. ἐν ἀριστερᾷ δ᾽ εἰσπλέοντι τὸν Κιμμερικὸν Βόσπορον

---

[1] Παρισέδου (AC).

[2] ὅς, Corais and Meineke insert, following Bno.

[1] His title seems to have been Paerisades V. On the titles and times of the monarchs in this dynasty, see Pauly-Wissowa, s.v. "Bosporus," p. 758.

also all the neighbouring settlements near the mouth of Lake Maeotis on both sides, until Parisades gave over the sovereignty to Mithridates. They were called tyrants, although most of them, beginning with Parisades and Leuco, proved to be equitable rulers. And Parisades was actually held in honour as god. The last[1] of these monarchs also bore the name Parisades, but he was unable to hold out against the barbarians, who kept exacting greater tribute than before, and he therefore gave over the sovereignty to Mithridates Eupator. But since the time of Mithridates the kingdom has been subject to the Romans. The greater part of it is situated in Europe, although a part of it is situated in Asia.[2]

5. The mouth of Lake Maeotis is called the Cimmerian Bosporus. It is rather wide at first—about seventy stadia—and it is here that people cross over from the regions of Panticapaeum to Phanagoria, the nearest city of Asia; but it ends in a much narrower channel. This strait separates Asia from Europe; and so does the Tanaïs[3] River, which is directly opposite and flows from the north into the lake and then into the mouth of it. The river has two outlets into the lake which are about sixty stadia distant from one another. There is also a city[4] which has the same name as the river, and next to Panticapaeum is the greatest emporium of the barbarians. On the left, as one sails into the

---

[2] According to Strabo, the boundary between Europe and Asia was formed by the Tanaïs (Don) River, Lake Maeotis (sea of Azof), and the Cimmerian Bosporus (strait of Kertch). See 2. 5. 26, 31 and 7. 4. 5.

[3] The Don.   [4] The site was near Nedrigofka.

πολίχνιόν ἐστι Μυρμήκιον ἐν εἴκοσι σταδίοις ἀπὸ
τοῦ Παντικαπαίου. τοῦ δὲ Μυρμηκίου διπλάσιον
διέχει κώμη Παρθένιον, καθ᾽ ἣν στενώτατος ὁ
εἴσπλους ἐστὶν ὅσον εἴκοσι σταδίων, ἔχων ἀντικει-
μένην ἐν τῇ Ἀσίᾳ κώμην, Ἀχίλλειον καλουμένην.
ἐντεῦθεν δ᾽ εὐθυπλοίᾳ μὲν ἐπὶ τὸν Τάναϊν καὶ
τὴν κατὰ τὰς ἐκβολὰς νῆσον στάδιοι δισχίλιοι
διακόσιοι, μικρὸν δ᾽ ὑπερβάλλει τοῦ ἀριθμοῦ
τούτου πλέοντι παρὰ τὴν Ἀσίαν· πλέον δ᾽ ἢ
τριπλάσιον ἐν ἀριστερᾷ πλέοντι μέχρι τοῦ
Τανάιδος, ἐν ᾧ παράπλῳ καὶ ὁ ἰσθμὸς ἵδρυται.
οὗτος μὲν οὖν ὁ παράπλους ἔρημος πᾶς ὁ παρὰ
τὴν Εὐρώπην, ὁ δ᾽ ἐν δεξιᾷ οὐκ ἔρημος· ὁ δὲ
σύμπας τῆς λίμνης κύκλος ἐννακισχιλίων ἱστορεῖ-
ται σταδίων. ἡ δὲ μεγάλη Χερρόνησος τῇ Πελοποννήσῳ προσέοικε καὶ τὸ σχῆμα καὶ τὸ
μέγεθος. ἔχουσι δ᾽ αὐτὴν οἱ τοῦ Βοσπόρου
δυνάσται κεκακωμένην πᾶσαν ὑπὸ τῶν συνεχῶν
πολέμων. πρότερον δ᾽ εἶχον ὀλίγην μὲν τὴν
πρὸς τῷ στόματι τῆς Μαιώτιδος καὶ τῷ Παντικα-
C 311 παίῳ μέχρι Θεοδοσίας τῶν Βοσπορίων τύραννοι,
τὴν δὲ πλείστην μέχρι τοῦ ἰσθμοῦ καὶ τοῦ κόλπου
τοῦ Καρκινίτου Ταῦροι, Σκυθικὸν ἔθνος· καὶ
ἐκαλεῖτο ἡ χώρα πᾶσα αὕτη, σχεδὸν δέ τι καὶ ἡ
ἔξω τοῦ ἰσθμοῦ μέχρι Βορυσθένους, μικρὰ Σκυθία·
διὰ δὲ τὸ πλῆθος τῶν ἐνθένδε περαιουμένων τόν
τε Τύραν καὶ τὸν Ἴστρον καὶ ἐποικούντων τὴν
γῆν καὶ ταύτης οὐκ ὀλίγη μικρὰ προσηγορεύθη
Σκυθία, τῶν Θρᾳκῶν τὰ μὲν τῇ βίᾳ συγχωρούν-

---

[1] On the site of, or near, Yenikale.
[2] Exact site unknown.   [3] Chosen by the Romans (7. 4. 7).

Cimmerian Bosporus, is a little city, Myrmecium,[1] at a distance of twenty stadia from Panticapaeum. And twice this distance from Myrmecium is the village of Parthenium;[2] here the strait is narrowest—about twenty stadia—and on the opposite side, in Asia, is situated a village called Achilleium. Thence, if one sails straight to the Tanaïs and the islands near its outlets, the distance is two thousand two hundred stadia, but if one sails along the coast of Asia, the distance slightly exceeds this; if, however, one sails on the left as far as the Tanaïs, following the coast where the isthmus is situated, the distance is more than three times as much. Now the whole of the seaboard along this coast, I mean on the European side, is desert, but the seaboard on the right is not desert; and, according to report, the total circuit of the lake is nine thousand stadia. The Great Chersonesus is similar to the Peloponnesus both in shape and in size. It is held by the potentates[3] of the Bosporus, though the whole of it has been devastated by continuous wars. But in earlier times only a small part of it—that which is close to the mouth of Lake Maeotis and to Panticapaeum and extends as far as Theodosia—was held by the tyrants of the Bosporians, whereas most of it, as far as the isthmus and the Gulf of Carcinites, was held by the Taurians, a Scythian tribe. And the whole of this country, together with about all the country outside the isthmus as far as the Borysthenes, was called Little Scythia. But on account of the large number of people who left Little Scythia and crossed both the Tyras and the Ister and took up their abode in the land beyond, no small portion of Thrace as well came to be called Little Scythia; the Thracians

STRABO

των, τὰ δὲ τῇ κακίᾳ τῆς χώρας· ἑλώδης γάρ
ἐστιν ἡ πολλὴ αὐτῆς.

6. Τῆς δὲ Χερρονήσου, πλὴν τῆς ὀρεινῆς τῆς
ἐπὶ τῇ θαλάττῃ μέχρι Θεοδοσίας, ἥ γε ἄλλη
πεδιὰς καὶ εὔγεώς ἐστι πᾶσα, σίτῳ δὲ καὶ
σφόδρα εὐτυχὴς τριακοντάχουν γοῦν[1] ἀποδίδωσι,
διὰ τοῦ τυχόντος ὀρύκτου[2] σχιζομένη. φόρον τε
ἐτέλουν ὀκτωκαίδεκα μυριάδας μεδίμνων Μιθριδάτῃ, τάλαντα δ' ἀργυρίου διακόσια σὺν τοῖς
Ἀσιανοῖς χωρίοις τοῖς περὶ τὴν Σινδικήν. κἂν
τοῖς πρόσθεν χρόνοις ἐντεῦθεν ἦν τὰ σιτοπομπεῖα
τοῖς Ἕλλησι, καθάπερ ἐκ τῆς λίμνης αἱ ταριχεῖαι.
Λεύκωνα δέ φασιν ἐκ τῆς Θεοδοσίας Ἀθηναίοις
πέμψαι μυριάδας μεδίμνων διακοσίας καὶ δέκα.
οἱ δ' αὐτοὶ οὗτοι καὶ Γεωργοὶ ἐκαλοῦντο ἰδίως διὰ
τὸ τοὺς ὑπερκειμένους Νομάδας εἶναι, τρεφομένους
κρέασιν ἄλλοις τε καὶ ἱππείοις, ἱππείῳ δὲ καὶ
τυρῷ καὶ γάλακτι καὶ ὀξυγάλακτι (τοῦτο δὲ καὶ
ὄψημά ἐστιν αὐτοῖς κατασκευασθέν πως)· διόπερ
ὁ ποιητὴς ἅπαντας εἴρηκε τοὺς ταύτῃ Γαλακτοφάγους. οἱ μὲν οὖν Νομάδες πολεμισταὶ μᾶλλόν

[1] τριακοντάχουν γοῦν, Kramer, for τριάκοντα γοῦν; but
Meineke reads τριακοντάχουν, emending ἀποδίδωσι to
ἀποδιδοῦσα.
[2] ὀρύκτου, Jones, for the common reading, ὀρυκτοῦ (cp.
ὀρύκτου, 15. 1. 18).

---

[1] Or perhaps, "plough-share."
[2] The Attic medimnus was about one bushel and a half.
[3] The Attic silver talent was about $1000.
[4] Leuco sent to Athens 400,000 medimni of wheat annually,

giving way to them partly as the result of force and partly because of the bad quality of the land, for the greater part of the country is marshy.

6. But the Chersonesus, except for the mountainous district that extends along the sea as far as Theodosia, is everywhere level and fertile, and in the production of grain it is extremely fortunate. At any rate, it yields thirty-fold if furrowed by any sort of a digging-instrument.[1] Further, the people of this region, together with those of the Asiatic districts round about Sindice, used to pay as tribute to Mithridates one hundred and eighty thousand medimni [2] and also two hundred talents of silver.[3] And in still earlier times the Greeks imported their supplies of grain from here, just as they imported their supplies of salt-fish from the lake. Leuco, it is said, once sent from Theodosia to Athens two million one hundred thousand medimni.[4] These same people used to be called Georgi,[5] in the literal sense of the term, because of the fact that the people who were situated beyond them were Nomads and lived not only on meats in general but also on the meat of horses, as also on cheese made from mare's milk, on mare's fresh milk, and on mare's sour milk, which last, when prepared in a particular way, is much relished by them. And this is why the poet calls all the people in that part of the world "Galactophagi." [6] Now although the Nomads

---

but in the year of the great famine (about 360 B.C.) he sent not only enough for Athens but a surplus which the Athenians sold at a profit of fifteen talents (Demosthenes, *Against Leptines*, 20. 32–33).

[5] *i.e.,* "Tillers of the soil."

[6] Cp. 7. 3. 3, 7, 9.

εἰσιν ἢ λῃστρικοί, πολεμοῦσι δὲ ὑπὲρ τῶν φόρων. ἐπιτρέψαντες γὰρ ἔχειν τὴν γῆν τοῖς ἐθέλουσι γεωργεῖν ἀντὶ ταύτης ἀγαπῶσι φόρους λαμβά-νοντες τοὺς συντεταγμένους μετρίους τινὰς οὐκ εἰς περιουσίαν, ἀλλ' εἰς τὰ ἐφήμερα καὶ τὰ ἀναγκαῖα τοῦ βίου· μὴ διδόντων δέ, αὐτοῖς πολε-μοῦσιν. οὕτω δὲ καὶ δικαίους ἅμα καὶ ἀβίους ὁ ποιητὴς εἴρηκε τοὺς αὐτοὺς τούτους ἄνδρας· ἐπεί, τῶν γε φόρων ἀπευτακτουμένων, οὐδ' ἂν καθίσταντο εἰς πόλεμον. οὐκ ἀπευτακτοῦσι δ' οἱ[1] δυνάμει πεποιθότες, ὥστε ἢ ἀμύνασθαι ῥᾳδίως ἐπιόντας ἢ κωλῦσαι τὴν ἔφοδον· καθάπερ Ἄσαν-δρον ποιῆσαί φησιν Ὑψικράτης, ἀποτειχίσαντα τὸν ἰσθμὸν τῆς Χερρονήσου τὸν πρὸς τῇ Μαιώτιδι, τριακοσίων ὄντα καὶ ἑξήκοντα σταδίων, ἐπιστή-σαντα πύργους καθ' ἕκαστον στάδιον δέκα.[2] οἱ δὲ Γεωργοὶ ταύτῃ μὲν ἡμερώτεροί τε ἅμα καὶ πολιτικώτεροι νομίζονται εἶναι, χρηματισταὶ δ' ὄντες καὶ θαλάττης ἁπτόμενοι λῃστηρίων οὐκ ἀπέχονται, οὐδὲ τῶν τοιούτων ἀδικιῶν καὶ πλεονεξιῶν.

C 312

7. Πρὸς δὲ τοῖς καταριθμηθεῖσι[3] τόποις[4] ἐν τῇ Χερρονήσῳ καὶ τὰ φρούρια ὑπῆρξεν, ἃ κατεσκεύ-

---

[1] δ' οὐ (ABC*l*); δ' οἱ (*no*), the editors.
[2] δέκα, Meineke emends to ἕνα (*one*); Forbiger and Tardieu following.
[3] τοῖς καταριθμηθεῖσι, Corais, for τὴν καταρίθμησιν; so the later editors.
[4] τόποις, the editors, for τύποις (A*l*), τύποι (BC), τῶν τόπων (*no*).

---

[1] Asander usurped the throne of the Bosporus in 47 (or 46) B.C., after he had overthrown and killed his chief, King Pharnaces, and had defeated and killed Mithridates of

244

are warriors rather than brigands, yet they go to war only for the sake of the tributes due them; for they turn over their land to any people who wish to till it, and are satisfied if they receive in return for the land the tribute they have assessed, which is a moderate one, assessed with a view, not to an abundance, but only to the daily necessities of life; but if the tenants do not pay, the Nomads go to war with them. And so it is that the poet calls these same men at the same time both "just" and "resourceless"; for if the tributes were paid regularly, they would never resort to war. But men who are confident that they are powerful enough either to ward off attacks easily or to prevent any invasion do not pay regularly; such was the case with Asander,[1] who, according to Hypsicrates,[2] walled off the isthmus of the Chersonesus which is near Lake Maeotis and is three hundred and sixty stadia in width, and set up ten towers for every stadium. But though the Georgi of this region are considered to be at the same time both more gentle and civilised, still, since they are money-getters and have to do with the sea, they do not hold aloof from acts of piracy, nor yet from any other such acts of injustice and greed.

7. In addition to the places in the Chersonesus which I have enumerated, there were also the three

Pergamon who sought the throne. His kingdom extended as far as the Don (see 11. 2. 11 and 13. 4. 3), and he built the fortifications above mentioned to prevent the invasions of the Scythians.

[2] Hypsicrates flourished in the time of Julius Caesar. He wrote a number of historical and geographical treatises, but the exact titles are unknown (see Pauly-Wissowa, s.v.).

ασε Σκίλουρος καὶ οἱ παῖδες, οἷσπερ καὶ ὁρμη-
τηρίοις ἐχρῶντο πρὸς τοὺς Μιθριδάτου στρατηγούς,
Παλάκιόν τε καὶ Χάβον καὶ Νεάπολις· ἦν δὲ καὶ
Εὐπατόριόν τι, κτίσαντος Διοφάντου[1] Μιθριδάτῃ[2]
στρατηγοῦντος.[3] ἔστι δ' ἄκρα διέχουσα τοῦ τῶν
Χερρονησιτῶν τείχους ὅσον πεντεκαίδεκα σταδίους, κόλπον ποιοῦσα εὐμεγέθη, νεύοντα πρὸς
τὴν πόλιν· τούτου δ' ὑπέρκειται λιμνοθάλαττα,
ἁλοπήγιον ἔχουσα· ἐνταῦθα δὲ καὶ ὁ Κτενοῦς ἦν.
ἵν' οὖν ἀντέχοιεν,[4] οἱ βασιλικοὶ πολιορκούμενοι
τῇ τε ἄκρᾳ τῇ λεχθείσῃ φρουρὰν ἐγκατέστησαν,
τειχίσαντες τὸν τόπον, καὶ τὸ στόμα τοῦ κόλπου
τὸ μέχρι τῆς πόλεως διέχωσαν, ὥστε πεζεύεσθαι
ῥᾳδίως καὶ τρόπον τινὰ μίαν εἶναι πόλιν ἐξ
ἀμφοῖν· ἐκ δὲ τούτου ῥᾷον ἀπεκρούοντο τοὺς
Σκύθας. ἐπεὶ δὲ καὶ τῷ διατειχίσματι τοῦ ἰσθμοῦ
τοῦ πρὸς τῷ Κτενοῦντι προσέβαλον καὶ τὴν
τάφρον ἐνέχουν καλάμῳ, τὸ μεθ' ἡμέραν γεφυ-
ρωθὲν μέρος νύκτωρ ἐνεπίμπρασαν οἱ βασιλικοὶ
καὶ ἀντεῖχον τέως, ἕως ἐπεκράτησαν. καὶ νῦν
ὑπὸ τοῖς τῶν Βοσπορανῶν βασιλεῦσιν, οὓς ἂν
Ῥωμαῖοι καταστήσωσιν, ἅπαντά ἐστιν.

[1] τοῦ, before Μιθριδάτου, Meineke inserts.
[2] Μιθριδάτῃ, Tzschucke, for Μιθριδάτου; so Corais, Müller-Dübner, and the versions of Guarinus and the Italian translator; see Stephanus, and Pausanias 9. 1. 2 (Ξέρξῃ στρατηγοῦντα). Meineke retains Μιθριδάτου.
[3] στρατηγοῦντος, Meineke emends to στρατηγοῦ, but στρατηγοῦ τινος (Kramer) would be better than that.
[4] ἀντέχοιεν, Corais, for ταῦτ' ἔχοιεν; so the later editors.

[1] The sites of these forts are unknown, but they must have been not far from the line of fortifications which ran along the eastern boundary of the Little Chersonesus (see 7. 4. 2).

forts which were built by Scilurus and his sons—
the forts which they used as bases of operations
against the generals of Mithridates—I mean Palacium,
Chabum, and Neapolis.[1] There was also a Fort
Eupatorium,[2] founded by Diophantus when he was
leading the army for Mithridates. There is a cape
about fifteen stadia distant from the wall of the
Chersonesites;[3] it forms a very large gulf which
inclines towards the city. And above this gulf is
situated a lagoon[4] which has salt-works. And here,
too, was the Ctenus Harbour. Now it was in order
that they might hold out that the besieged generals
of the king fortified the place, established a garrison
on the cape aforesaid, and filled up that part of the
mouth of the gulf which extends as far as the city,
so that there was now an easy journey on foot and,
in a way, one city instead of two. Consequently,
they could more easily beat off the Scythians. But
when the Scythians made their attack, near Ctenus,
on the fortified wall that extends across the isthmus,
and daily filled up the trench with straw, the generals
of the king set fire by night to the part thus bridged
by day, and held out until they finally prevailed over
them. And to-day everything is subject to whatever
kings of the Bosporians the Romans choose to set up.

[2] Fort Eupatorium is not to be identified with the city of
Eupatoria (mentioned by Ptolemaeus, 3. 6. 2), nor with the
modern Eupatoria (the Crimean Kozlof). It was situated on
what is now Cape Paul, where Fort Paul is, to the east of
Sebastopol (Becker, *Jahrb. für Philol.*, *Suppl. vol.*, 1856), or
else on the opposite cape between the Harbour of Sebastopol
and what is called Artillery Bay, where Fort Nicholas was
(C. Müller, note on Ptolemaeus, *l.c.*).

[3] *i.e.*, the wall of the city of New Chersonesus.

[4] Now Uschakowskaja Balka (Pauly-Wissowa, *s.v.* "Eupatoria ").

247

8. Ἴδιον δὲ τοῦ Σκυθικοῦ καὶ τοῦ Σαρματικοῦ παντὸς ἔθνους τὸ τοὺς ἵππους ἐκτέμνειν εὐπειθείας χάριν· μικροὶ μὲν γάρ εἰσιν, ὀξεῖς δὲ σφόδρα καὶ δυσπειθεῖς. θῆραι δ᾽ εἰσὶν ἐν μὲν τοῖς ἕλεσιν ἐλάφων καὶ συάγρων, ἐν δὲ τοῖς πεδίοις ὀνάγρων καὶ δορκάδων. ἴδιον δέ τι καὶ τὸ ἀετὸν μὴ γίνεσθαι ἐν τοῖς τόποις τούτοις. ἔστι δὲ τῶν τετραπόδων ὁ καλούμενος κόλος, μεταξὺ ἐλάφου καὶ κριοῦ τὸ μέγεθος, λευκός, ὀξύτερος τούτων τῷ δρόμῳ, πίνων τοῖς ῥώθωσιν εἰς τὴν κεφαλήν, εἶτ᾽ ἐντεῦθεν εἰς ἡμέρας ταμιεύων πλείους, ὥστ᾽ ἐν τῇ ἀνύδρῳ νέμεσθαι ῥᾳδίως. τοιαύτη μὲν ἡ ἐκτὸς Ἴστρου πᾶσα, ἡ μεταξὺ τοῦ Ῥήνου καὶ τοῦ Ταναΐδος ποταμοῦ, μέχρι τῆς Ποντικῆς θαλάττης καὶ τῆς Μαιώτιδος.

V.

1. Λοιπὴ δ᾽ ἐστὶ τῆς Εὐρώπης ἡ ἐντὸς Ἴστρου καὶ τῆς κύκλῳ θαλάττης, ἀρξαμένη ἀπὸ τοῦ μυχοῦ τοῦ Ἀδριατικοῦ, μέχρι τοῦ Ἱεροῦ στόματος τοῦ Ἴστρου, ἐν ᾗ ἐστιν ἥ τε Ἑλλὰς καὶ τὰ τῶν Μακεδόνων καὶ τῶν Ἠπειρωτῶν ἔθνη καὶ τὰ
C 313 ὑπὲρ τούτων πρὸς τὸν Ἴστρον[1] καθήκοντα καὶ πρὸς τὴν ἐφ᾽ ἑκάτερα θάλατταν, τήν τε Ἀδριατικὴν καὶ τὴν Ποντικήν, πρὸς μὲν τὴν Ἀδριατικὴν τὰ Ἰλλυρικά, πρὸς δὲ τὴν ἑτέραν μέχρι Προποντίδος καὶ Ἑλλησπόντου τὰ Θρᾴκια καὶ εἴ τινα τούτοις ἀναμέμικται Σκυθικὰ ἢ Κελτικά.

---

[1] Ἴστρον, Tyrwhitt, for ἰσθμόν; so the editors.

8. It is a peculiarity of the whole Scythian and Sarmatian race that they castrate their horses to make them easy to manage; for although the horses are small, they are exceedingly quick and hard to manage. As for game, there are deer and wild boars in the marshes, and wild asses and roe deer in the plains. Another peculiar thing is the fact that the eagle is not found in these regions. And among the quadrupeds there is what is called the "colos";[1] it is between the deer and ram in size, is white, is swifter than they, and drinks through its nostrils into its head, and then from this storage supplies itself for several days, so that it can easily live in the waterless country. Such, then, is the nature of the whole of the country which is outside the Ister between the Rhenus and the Tanaïs Rivers as far as the Pontic Sea and Lake Maeotis.

V

1. The remainder of Europe consists of the country which is between the Ister and the encircling sea, beginning at the recess of the Adriatic and extending as far as the Sacred Mouth[2] of the Ister. In this country are Greece and the tribes of the Macedonians and of the Epeirotes, and all those tribes above them whose countries reach to the Ister and to the seas on either side, both the Adriatic and the Pontic—to the Adriatic, the Illyrian tribes, and to the other sea as far as the Propontis and the Hellespont, the Thracian tribes and whatever Scythian or Celtic tribes are inter-

---

[1] "A large he-goat without horns" (Hesychius, s.v.).
[2] See 7. 3. 15.

δεῖ δ' ἀπὸ τοῦ Ἴστρου τὴν ἀρχὴν ποιήσασθαι, τὰ
ἐφεξῆς λέγοντας τοῖς περιοδευθεῖσι τόποις· ταῦτα
δ' ἐστὶ τὰ συνεχῆ τῇ Ἰταλίᾳ τε καὶ ταῖς Ἄλπεσι
καὶ Γερμανοῖς καὶ Δακοῖς καὶ Γέταις. δίχα δ' ἄν
τις καὶ ταῦτα διέλοι[1] τρόπον γάρ τινα τῷ Ἴστρῳ
παράλληλά ἐστι τά τε Ἰλλυρικὰ καὶ τὰ Παιονικὰ
καὶ τὰ Θρᾴκια ὄρη, μίαν πως γραμμὴν ἀποτε-
λοῦντα, διήκουσαν ἀπὸ τοῦ Ἀδρίου μέχρι πρὸς
τὸν Πόντον· ἧς προσάρκτια μέν ἐστι μέρη τὰ
μεταξὺ τοῦ Ἴστρου καὶ τῶν ὀρῶν, πρὸς νότον δ' ἥ
τε Ἑλλὰς καὶ ἡ συνεχὴς βάρβαρος μέχρι τῆς
ὀρεινῆς. πρὸς μὲν οὖν τῷ Πόντῳ τὸ Αἷμόν ἐστιν
ὄρος, μέγιστον τῶν ταύτῃ καὶ ὑψηλότατον, μέσην
πως διαιροῦν τὴν Θρᾴκην· ἀφ' οὗ φησι Πολύβιος
ἀμφοτέρας καθορᾶσθαι τὰς θαλάττας, οὐκ ἀληθῆ
λέγων· καὶ γὰρ τὸ διάστημα μέγα τὸ πρὸς τὸν
Ἀδρίαν καὶ τὰ ἐπισκοτοῦντα πολλά. πρὸς δὲ
τῷ Ἀδρίᾳ πᾶσα ἡ Ἀρδία σχεδόν τι, μέση δ' ἡ
Παιονία, καὶ αὐτὴ πᾶσα ὑψηλή. ἐφ' ἑκάτερα δ'
αὐτῆς, ἐπὶ μὲν τὰ Θρᾴκια ἡ Ῥοδόπη ὁμορεῖ,[2]
ὑψηλὸν[3] ὄρος μετὰ τὸν Αἷμον, ἐπὶ δὲ θάτερα πρὸς
ἄρκτον τὰ Ἰλλυρικά, ἥ τε τῶν Αὐταριατῶν[4] χώρα
καὶ ἡ Δαρδανική. λέγωμεν δὴ τὰ Ἰλλυρικὰ
πρῶτα, συνάπτοντα τῷ τε Ἴστρῳ καὶ ταῖς

---

[1] διέλοι, Corais, for διέλθοι; so the later editors.
[2] ὁμορεῖ, Meineke, for ὅμορον; so Müller-Dübner.
[3] ὑψηλόν, Meineke emends to ὑψηλότατον.
[4] Αὐταριατῶν, the editors, for Αὐγαριατῶν.

---

[1] See 7. 3. 2, 11.   [2] Cp. 7. 1. 1.   [3] Balkan.
[4] The southern part of Dalmatia, bounded by the River
Naro (now Narenta); but Strabo is thinking also of the

mingled[1] with them. But I must make my beginning at the Ister, speaking of the parts that come next in order after the regions which I have already encompassed in my description. These are the parts that border on Italy, on the Alps, and on the countries of the Germans, Dacians, and Getans. This country also[2] might be divided into two parts, for, in a way, the Illyrian, Paeonian, and Thracian mountains are parallel to the Ister, thus completing what is almost a straight line that reaches from the Adrias as far as the Pontus; and to the north of this line are the parts that are between the Ister and the mountains, whereas to the south are Greece and the barbarian country which borders thereon and extends as far as the mountainous country. Now the mountain called Haemus[3] is near the Pontus; it is the largest and highest of all mountains in that part of the world, and cleaves Thrace almost in the centre. Polybius says that both seas are visible from the mountain, but this is untrue, for the distance to the Adrias is great and the things that obscure the view are many. On the other hand, almost the whole of Ardia[4] is near the Adrias. But Paeonia is in the middle, and the whole of it too is high country. Paeonia is bounded on either side, first, towards the Thracian parts, by Rhodope,[5] a mountain next in height to the Haemus, and secondly, on the other side, towards the north, by the Illyrian parts, both the country of the Autariatae and that of the Dardanians.[6] So then, let me speak first of the Illyrian parts, which join the Ister and that part of

Adrian Mountain (now the Dinara; see 7. 5. 5), which runs through the centre of Dalmatia as far as the Naro.
[5] Now Despoto-Dagh.   [6] Cp. 7. 5. 6.

Ἄλπεσιν, αἳ¹ κεῖνται μεταξὺ τῆς Ἰταλίας καὶ τῆς Γερμανίας, ἀρξάμεναι² ἀπὸ τῆς λίμνης τῆς κατὰ τοὺς Οὐινδολικοὺς καὶ Ῥαιτοὺς καὶ Τοινίους.³

2. Μέρος μὲν δή τι τῆς χώρας ταύτης ἠρήμωσαν οἱ Δακοὶ καταπολεμήσαντες Βοΐους καὶ Ταυρίσκους, ἔθνη Κελτικὰ τὰ ὑπὸ Κριτασίρῳ,⁴ φάσκοντες εἶναι τὴν χώραν σφετέραν, καίπερ ποταμοῦ διείργοντος τοῦ Παρίσου, ῥέοντος ἀπὸ τῶν ὀρῶν ἐπὶ τὸν Ἴστρον κατὰ τοὺς Σκορδίσκους καλουμένους Γαλάτας· καὶ γὰρ οὗτοι τοῖς Ἰλλυρικοῖς ἔθνεσι καὶ τοῖς Θρακίοις ἀναμὶξ ᾤκησαν· ἀλλ' ἐκείνους μὲν οἱ Δακοὶ κατέλυσαν, τούτοις δὲ καὶ συμμάχοις ἐχρήσαντο πολλάκις. τὸ δὲ λοιπὸν ἔχουσι Παννόνιοι μέχρι Σεγεστικῆς καὶ Ἴστρου πρὸς ἄρκτον καὶ ἕω· πρὸς δὲ τἆλλα μέρη ἐπὶ πλέον διατείνουσιν. ἡ δὲ Σεγεστικὴ πόλις ἐστὶ Παννονίων ἐν συμβολῇ ποταμῶν πλειόνων, ἁπάντων πλωτῶν, εὐφυὲς ὁρμητήριον τῷ πρὸς Δακοὺς πολέμῳ· ὑποπέπτωκε γὰρ ταῖς Ἄλπεσιν, C 314 αἳ διατείνουσι μέχρι τῶν Ἰαπόδων, Κελτικοῦ τε ἅμα καὶ Ἰλλυρικοῦ ἔθνους· ἐντεῦθεν δὲ καὶ ποταμοὶ ῥέουσι πολὺν⁵ καταφέροντες εἰς αὐτὴν

---

¹ αἵ, Corais, for ἅ ; so the later editors.
² ἀρξάμεναι, Corais, for ἀρξάμενα ; so the later editors.
³ Τοινίους, Corais emends to Ἐλουητίους, and so Meineke; C. Müller to Τωυγένους. See note to translation.
⁴ Ἐκρετοσείρῳ (ABC𝑙), Κρετοσίρῳ (C), but see 7. 3. 11.
⁵ πολύν, Corais and Meineke emend to πολλοί.

---

¹ Lake Constance (the Bodensee), see 7. 1. 5.
² Meineke emends "Toenii" (otherwise unknown) to

the Alps which lies between Italy and Germany and begins at the lake [1] which is near the country of the Vindelici, Rhaeti, and Toenii.[2]

2. A part of this country was laid waste by the Dacians when they subdued the Boii and Taurisci, Celtic tribes under the rule of Critasirus.[3] They alleged that the country was theirs, although it was separated from theirs by the River Parisus,[4] which flows from the mountains to the Ister near the country of the Scordisci who are called Galatae,[5] for these too [6] lived intermingled with the Illyrian and the Thracian tribes. But though the Dacians destroyed the Boii and Taurisci, they often used the Scordisci as allies. The remainder of the country in question is held by the Pannonii as far as Segestica [7] and the Ister, on the north and east, although their territory extends still farther in the other directions. The city Segestica, belonging to the Pannonians, is at the confluence of several rivers,[8] all of them navigable, and is naturally fitted to be a base of operations for making war against the Dacians; for it lies beneath that part of the Alps which extends as far as the country of the Iapodes, a tribe which is at the same time both Celtic and Illyrian. And thence, too, flow rivers which bring down into Segestica much merchandise

---

"Helvetii," the word one would expect here (cp. 7. 1. 5); but (on textual grounds) "Toygeni" (cp. 7. 2. 2) is almost certainly the correct reading.

[3] Cp. 7. 3. 11.

[4] The "Parisus" (otherwise unknown) should probably be emended to "Pathissus" (now the Lower Theiss), the river mentioned by Pliny (4. 25) in connection with the Daci.

[5] *i.e.* Gauls. [6] Cp. 7. 5. 1 and footnote.

[7] Now Sissek. [8] Cp. 4. 6. 10.

τόν τε ἄλλον καὶ τὸν ἐκ τῆς Ἰταλίας φόρτον. εἰς γὰρ Ναύπορτον¹ ἐξ Ἀκυληίας ὑπερθεῖσι² τὴν Ὄκραν εἰσὶ στάδιοι τριακόσιοι πεντήκοντα, εἰς ἣν αἱ ἁρμάμαξαι κατάγονται, τῶν Ταυρίσκων οὖσαν κατοικίαν· ἔνιοι δὲ πεντακοσίους φασίν. ἡ δ' Ὄκρα ταπεινότατον μέρος τῶν Ἄλπεών ἐστι τῶν διατεινουσῶν ἀπὸ τῆς Ῥαιτικῆς μέχρι Ἰαπό- δων· ἐντεῦθεν δ' ἐξαίρεται τὰ ὄρη πάλιν ἐν τοῖς Ἰάποσι καὶ καλεῖται Ἄλβια. ὁμοίως δὲ καὶ ἐκ Τεργέστε, κώμης Καρνικῆς, ὑπέρθεσίς ἐστι διὰ τῆς Ὄκρας εἰς ἕλος Λούγεον καλούμενον. πλη- σίον δὲ τοῦ Ναυπόρτου³ ποταμός ἐστι Κορκόρας, ὁ δεχόμενος τὰ φορτία· οὗτος μὲν οὖν εἰς τὸν Σάον⁴ ἐμβάλλει, ἐκεῖνος δ' εἰς τὸν Δράβον· ὁ δὲ εἰς τὸν Νόαρον κατὰ τὴν Σεγεστικήν. ἐντεῦθεν δ' ἤδη ὁ Νόαρος πλήθει προσλαβὼν τὸν διὰ τῶν Ἰαπόδων ῥέοντα ἐκ τοῦ Ἀλβίου ὄρους Κόλαπιν, συμβάλλει τῷ Δανουΐῳ κατὰ τοὺς Σκορδίσκους. ὁ δὲ πλοῦς τὰ πολλὰ τοῖς ποταμοῖς ἐπὶ τὰς ἄρκτους ἐστίν· ὁδὸς δ'⁵ ἀπὸ Τεργέστε ἐπὶ τὸ Δανούιον σταδίων ὅσον χιλίων καὶ διακοσίων. ἐγγὺς δὲ τῆς Σεγεστικῆς ἐστι καὶ ἡ Σισκία φρούριον καὶ Σίρμιον, ἐν ὁδῷ κείμεναι τῇ εἰς Ἰταλίαν.

¹ Ναύπορτον, Casaubon, for Ναύποντον; so the later editors.
² ὑπερθεῖσι, Meineke emends to ὑπερτιθεῖσι.
³ Ναυπόρτου, Casaubon, for Ναυπόντου.
⁴ Σάον, Tzschucke, for Σαὖον; so Corais and the MSS. on 4. 6. 10. Meineke reads Σάβον (E).
⁵ δ', Corais inserts; so the later editors.

¹ The Julian Alps.	² Now Ober-Laibach.
³ Cp. 4. 6. 1.	⁴ Now Trieste.
⁵ Now Lake Zirknitz.	⁶ Now the Gurk.

both from other countries and from Italy. For if
one passes over Mount Ocra[1] from Aquileia to
Nauportus,[2] a settlement of the Taurisci, whither
the wagons are brought, the distance is three
hundred and fifty stadia, though some say five
hundred. Now the Ocra is the lowest part of that
portion of the Alps which extends from the country
of the Rhaeti to that of the Iapodes. Then the
mountains rise again, in the country of the Iapodes,
and are called "Albian."[3] In like manner, also,
there is a pass which leads over Ocra from Tergeste,[4]
a Carnic village, to a marsh called Lugeum.[5] Near
Nauportus there is a river, the Corcoras,[6] which
receives the cargoes. Now this river empties into
the Saüs, and the Saüs into the Dravus, and the
Dravus into the Noarus[7] near Segestica. Immediately below Nauportus the Noarus is further
increased in volume by the Colapis,[8] which flows
from the Albian Mountain through the country of
the Iapodes and meets the Danuvius near the
country of the Scordisci. The voyage on these
rivers is, for the most part, towards the north.
The road from Tergeste to the Danuvius is about
one thousand two hundred stadia. Near Segestica,
and on the road to Italy, are situated both Siscia,[9] a
fort, and Sirmium.[10]

---

[7] Something is wrong here. In 4. 6. 10 Strabo rightly
makes the Saüs (Save) flow past Segestica (Sissek) and empty
into the Danube, not the Drave. The Drave, too, empties
into the Danube, not into some Noarus River. Moreover,
the Noarus is otherwise unknown, except that it is again
mentioned in 7. 5. 12 as "flowing past Segestica."

[8] Now the Kulpa.

[9] The usual name for Segestica itself was Siscia.

[10] Now Mitrovitza.

3. Ἔθνη δ' ἐστὶ τῶν Παννονίων Βρεῦκοι καὶ Ἀνδιζήτιοι καὶ Διτίωνες καὶ Πειροῦσται καὶ Μαζαῖοι καὶ Δαισιτιᾶται, ὧν Βάτων ἡγεμών, καὶ ἄλλα ἀσημότερα μικρά, ἃ¹ διατείνει μέχρι Δαλματίας, σχεδὸν δέ τι καὶ Ἀρδιαίων,² ἰόντι πρὸς νότον. ἅπασα δ'³ ἡ ἀπὸ τοῦ μυχοῦ τοῦ Ἀδρίου παρήκουσα ὀρεινὴ μέχρι τοῦ Ῥιζονικοῦ κόλπου καὶ τῆς Ἀρδιαίων⁴ γῆς Ἰλλυρική ἐστι,⁵ μεταξὺ πίπτουσα τῆς τε θαλάττης καὶ τῶν Παννονίων ἐθνῶν. σχεδὸν δέ τι καὶ ἐντεῦθεν τὴν ἀρχὴν ποιητέον τῆς συνεχοῦς περιοδείας ἀναλαβοῦσι μικρὰ τῶν λεχθέντων πρότερον. ἔφαμεν δ' ἐν τῇ περιοδείᾳ τῆς Ἰταλίας Ἴστρους εἶναι πρώτους τῆς Ἰλλυρικῆς παραλίας, συνεχεῖς τῇ Ἰταλίᾳ καὶ τοῖς Κάρνοις, καὶ διότι μέχρι Πόλας, Ἰστρικῆς πόλεως, προήγαγον οἱ νῦν ἡγεμόνες τοὺς τῆς Ἰταλίας ὅρους. οὗτοι μὲν οὖν περὶ ὀκτακοσίους σταδίους εἰσὶν ἀπὸ τοῦ μυχοῦ, τοσοῦτοι δ' εἰσὶ καὶ ἀπὸ τῆς ἄκρας τῆς πρὸ τῶν Πολῶν ἐπὶ Ἀγκῶνα ἐν δεξιᾷ ἔχοντι τὴν Ἑνετικήν. ὁ δὲ πᾶς Ἰστρικὸς παράπλους χίλια τριακόσια.

¹ ἅ, Corais inserts; so the later editors.
² Σαρδιαίων (ABC*l*); Ἀρδειέων (E).
³ δ' Corais inserts; so the later editors.
⁴ Σαρδιαίων (ABC*l*); Ἀρδειέων (E).
⁵ After γῆς Jones inserts Ἰλλυρική ἐστι; Groskurd inserts ἡ Ἰλλυρικὴ παραλία ἐστί; Meineke merely indicates a lacuna.

---

¹ It is doubtful whether "is" or "was" (so others translate) should be supplied from the context here. Certainly "is" is more natural. This passage is important as having a bearing on the time of the composition and retouching of Strabo's work. See the *Introduction*, pp. xxiv ff.

3. The tribes of the Pannonii are: the Breuci, the Andizetii, the Ditiones, the Peirustae, the Mazaei, and the Daesitiatae, whose leader is[1] Bato,[2] and also other small tribes of less significance which extend as far as Dalmatia and, as one goes south, almost as far as the land of the Ardiaei. The whole of the mountainous country that stretches alongside Pannonia from the recess of the Adriatic as far as the Rhizonic Gulf[3] and the land of the Ardiaei is Illyrian, falling as it does between the sea and the Pannonian tribes. But this[4] is about where I should begin my continuous geographical circuit—though first I shall repeat a little of what I have said before.[5] I was saying in my geographical circuit of Italy that the Istrians were the first people on the Illyrian seaboard; their country being a continuation of Italy and the country of the Carni; and it is for this reason that the present Roman rulers have advanced the boundary of Italy as far as Pola, an Istrian city. Now this boundary is about eight hundred stadia from the recess, and the distance from the promontory[6] in front of Pola to Ancona, if one keeps the Henetic[7] country on the right, is the same. And the entire distance along the coast of Istria is one thousand three hundred stadia.

[2] Bato the Daesitiatian and Bato the Breucian made common cause against the Romans in 6 A.D. (Cassius Dio 55. 29). The former put the latter to death in 8 A.D. (*op. cit.* 55. 34), but shortly afterwards surrendered to the Romans (Velleius Paterculus, 2. 114).

[3] Now the Gulf of Cattaro.

[4] The Rhizonic Gulf. [5] 5. 1. 1, 5. 1. 9 and 6. 3. 10.

[6] Polaticum Promontorium; now Punta di Promontore.

[7] See 5. 1. 4.

4. Ἑξῆς δ' ἐστὶν ὁ Ἰαποδικὸς παράπλους χιλίων σταδίων· ἵδρυνται γὰρ οἱ Ἰάποδες ἐπὶ τῷ Ἀλβίῳ ὄρει τελευταίῳ τῶν Ἄλπεων ὄντι, ὑψηλῷ σφόδρα, τῇ μὲν ἐπὶ τοὺς Παννονίους καὶ τὸν Ἴστρον καθήκοντες, τῇ δ' ἐπὶ τὸν Ἀδρίαν, ἀρειμάνιοι μέν, ἐκπεπονημένοι[1] δὲ ὑπὸ τοῦ Σεβαστοῦ τελέως· πόλεις δ' αὐτῶν Μέτουλον,

C 315 Ἀρουπῖνοι,[2] Μονήτιον, Οὐένδων· λυπρὰ δὲ τὰ χωρία, καὶ ζειᾷ καὶ κέγχρῳ τὰ πολλὰ τρεφομένων· ὁ δ' ὁπλισμὸς Κελτικός· κατάστικτοι δ' ὁμοίως[3] τοῖς ἄλλοις Ἰλλυριοῖς καὶ Θρᾳξί. μετὰ δὲ τὸν τῶν Ἰαπόδων ὁ Λιβυρνικὸς παράπλους ἐστί, μείζων τοῦ προτέρου σταδίοις πεντακοσίοις,[4] ἐν δὲ τῷ παράπλῳ ποταμὸς φορτίοις ἀνάπλουν ἔχων μέχρι Δαλματέων, καὶ Σκάρδων, Λιβυρνὴ πόλις.

5. Παρ' ὅλην δ' ἣν εἶπον παραλίαν νῆσοι μὲν αἱ Ἀψυρτίδες, περὶ ἃς ἡ Μήδεια λέγεται δισφθεῖραι τὸν ἀδελφὸν Ἄψυρτον διώκοντα αὐτήν. ἔπειτα ἡ Κυρικτικὴ κατὰ τοὺς Ἰάποδας· εἶθ' αἱ Λιβυρνίδες περὶ τετταράκοντα τὸν ἀριθμόν· εἶτ' ἄλλαι νῆσοι, γνωριμώταται δ' Ἴσσα, Τραγούριον,

---

[1] ἐκπεποιημένοι (ACl).

[2] Ἀρουπῖνοι, Kramer, for Ἀρουπῖνος (ACl); so Müller-Dübner and Meineke; cp. Ἀρουπῖνοι, 4. 6. 10.

[3] καί (after ὁμοίως), the *Epit.* omits; so Corais, Meineke, and others.

[4] πεντακοσίοις, Xylander inserts, from the *Epit.*; so the later editors.

---

[1] Cp. 4. 6. 10.

[2] Probably what is now the village of Metule, east of Lake Zirknitz.

[3] Probably what is now Auersberg.   [4] Now Möttnig.

4. Next in order comes the voyage of one thousand stadia along the coast of the country of the Iapodes; for the Iapodes are situated on the Albian Mountain, which is the last mountain of the Alps, is very lofty, and reaches down to the country of the Pannonians on one side and to the Adrias on the other. They are indeed a war-mad people, but they have been utterly worn out by Augustus. Their cities[1] are Metulum,[2] Arupini,[3] Monetium,[4] and Vendo.[5] Their lands are poor, the people living for the most part on spelt and millet. Their armour is Celtic, and they are tattooed like the rest of the Illyrians and the Thracians. After the voyage along the coast of the country of the Iapodes comes that along the coast of the country of the Liburni, the latter being five hundred stadia longer than the former; on this voyage is a river,[6] which is navigable inland for merchant-vessels as far as the country of the Dalmatians, and also a Liburnian city, Scardo.[7]

5. There are islands along the whole of the aforesaid seaboard: first, the Apsyrtides,[8] where Medeia is said to have killed her brother Apsyrtus who was pursuing her; and then, opposite the country of the Iapodes, Cyrictica,[9] then the Liburnides,[10] about forty in number; then other islands, of which the best known are Issa,[11] Tragurium[12]

---

[5] But the proper spelling is " Avendo," which place was near what are now Crkvinje Kampolje, south-east of Zeng (see Tomaschek, Pauly-Wissowa, *s.v.* "Avendo").

[6] The Titius, now Kerka.   [7] Now Scardona.

[8] Now Ossero and Cherso.   [9] Now Veglia.

[10] Now Arbo, Pago, Isola Longa, and the rest.

[11] Now Lissa.   [12] Now Trau.

Ἰσσέων κτίσμα, Φάρος, ἡ πρότερον Πάρος, Παρίων κτίσμα, ἐξ ἧς Δημήτριος ὁ Φάριος, καὶ [1] ἡ τῶν Δαλματέων παραλία καὶ τὸ ἐπίνειον αὐτῶν Σάλων. ἔστι δὲ τῶν πολὺν χρόνον πολεμησάντων πρὸς Ῥωμαίους τὸ ἔθνος τοῦτο· κατοικίας δ᾽ ἔσχεν ἀξιολόγους εἰς πεντήκοντα, ὧν τινας καὶ πόλεις, Σάλωνά τε καὶ Πριάμωνα [2] καὶ Νινίαν καὶ Σινώτιον, τό τε νέον καὶ τὸ παλαιόν, ἃς ἐνέπρησεν ὁ Σεβαστός. ἔστι δὲ καὶ Ἀνδήτριον [3] ἐρυμνὸν χωρίον, Δάλμιον [4] δὲ μεγάλη πόλις, ἧς ἐπώνυμον τὸ ἔθνος, μικρὰν δ᾽ ἐποίησε Νασικᾶς καὶ τὸ πεδίον μηλόβοτον διὰ τὴν πλεονεξίαν τῶν ἀνθρώπων. ἴδιον δὲ τῶν Δαλματέων τὸ διὰ ὀκταετηρίδος χώρας ἀναδασμὸν ποιεῖσθαι· τὸ δὲ μὴ χρῆσθαι νομίσμασι πρὸς μὲν τοὺς ἐν τῇ παραλίᾳ ταύτῃ ἴδιον, πρὸς ἄλλους [5] δὲ τῶν βαρβάρων πολλοὺς κοινόν. Ἄδριον [6] δὲ ὄρος ἐστί, μέσην [7] τέμνον τὴν Δαλματικήν, τὴν μὲν ἐπιθαλάττιον, τὴν δ᾽ ἐπὶ θάτερα. εἶθ᾽ ὁ Νάρων ποταμὸς καὶ οἱ περὶ αὐτὸν Δαόριζοι καὶ Ἀρδιαῖοι καὶ Πληραῖοι, ὧν τοῖς μὲν πλησιάζει νῆσος ἡ Μέλαινα Κόρκυρα καλουμένη καὶ πόλις, Κνιδίων

---

[1] καί, Jones restores ; Meineke emends to εἶτα.

[2] Πριάμωνα, Meineke emends to Πρόμωνα, perhaps rightly.

[3] Ἀνδήτριον, Cellarius and Tzschucke, for Ἀνδρήτριον (ABl), Ἀδρήτριον (C) ; so the later editors.

[4] Δάλμιον, Xylander, for Δαίμμιον ; so the later editors.

[5] ἄλλους, Casaubon, for ἀλλήλους ; so the later editors.

[6] Xylander conj. Ἄρδιον for Ἄδριον (Ἀνδριον, E) ; perhaps rightly.

[7] μέσην, Corais, for μέσον ; so Meineke.

---

[1] In 384 B.C. (Diodorus Siculus, 15. 13).

[2] Demetrius of Pharos, on making common cause with the

(founded by the people of Issa), and Pharos (formerly Paros, founded by the Parians [1]), the native land of Demetrius [2] the Pharian. Then comes the seaboard of the Dalmatians, and also their sea-port, Salo. [3] This tribe is one of those which carried on war against the Romans for a long time ; it had as many as fifty noteworthy settlements ; and some of these were cities—Salo, Priamo, Ninia, and Sinotium (both the Old and the New), all of which were set on fire by Augustus. And there is Andretium, a fortified place ; and also Dalmium [4] (whence the name of the tribe), which was once a large city, but because of the greed of the people Nasica [5] reduced it to a small city and made the plain a mere sheep-pasture. The Dalmatians have the peculiar custom of making a redistribution of land every seven years ; and that they make no use of coined money is peculiar to them as compared with the other peoples in that part of the world, although as compared with many other barbarian peoples it is common. And there is Mount Adrium, [6] which cuts the Dalmatian country through the middle into two parts, one facing the sea and the other in the opposite direction. Then come the River Naro and the people who live about it—the Daorizi, the Ardiaei, and the Pleraei. An island called the Black Corcyra [7] and also a city [8] founded by the

Romans in 229 B.C., was made ruler of most of Illyria instead of Queen Teuta (Polybius, 2–10 ff.).

[3] Now Salona, between Klissa and Spalato.

[4] Also spelled Delminium ; apparently what is now Duvno (see Pauly-Wissowa, s.v. "Delminium ").

[5] P. Cornelius Scipio Nasica Corculum, in 155 B.C.

[6] The Dinara.   [7] Now Curzola.   [8] Of the same name.

κτίσμα, τοῖς δὲ Ἀρδιαίοις ἡ Φάρος, Πάρος
λεγομένη πρότερον· Παρίων γάρ ἐστι κτίσμα.

6. Οὐαρδαίους δ' οἱ ὕστερον ἐκάλεσαν τοὺς
Ἀρδιαίους· ἀπέωσαν δ' αὐτοὺς εἰς τὴν μεσόγαιαν
ἀπὸ τῆς θαλάττης Ῥωμαῖοι, λυμαινομένους αὐτὴν
διὰ τῶν λῃστηρίων, καὶ ἠνάγκασαν γεωργεῖν.
τραχεῖα δὲ χώρα καὶ λυπρὰ καὶ οὐ γεωργῶν,
ἀνθρώπων, ὥστ' ἐξέφθαρται τελέως,[1] μικροῦ δὲ
καὶ ἐκλέλοιπε. τοῦτο δὲ καὶ τοῖς ἄλλοις ἔθνεσι
τοῖς ταύτῃ συνέβη· οἱ γὰρ πλεῖστον δυνάμενοι
πρότερον τελέως ἐταπεινώθησαν καὶ ἐξέλιπον,
Γαλατῶν μὲν Βόιοι καὶ Σκορδίσται, Ἰλλυριῶν δὲ
Αὐταριάται καὶ Ἀρδιαῖοι καὶ Δαρδάνιοι, Θρᾳκῶν
C 316 δὲ Τριβαλλοί, ὑπ' ἀλλήλων μὲν ἐξ ἀρχῆς, ὕστερον
δ' ὑπὸ Μακεδόνων καὶ Ῥωμαίων ἐκπολεμούμενοι.

7. Μετὰ δ' οὖν τὴν τῶν Ἀρδιαίων καὶ Πλη-
ραίων παραλίαν ὁ Ῥιζονικός[2] κόλπος ἐστὶ καὶ
Ῥίζων πόλις καὶ ἄλλα πολίχνια καὶ Δρίλων
ποταμός, ἀνάπλουν ἔχων πρὸς ἔω μέχρι τῆς
Δαρδανικῆς, ἣ[3] συνάπτει τοῖς Μακεδονικοῖς
ἔθνεσι καὶ τοῖς Παιονικοῖς πρὸς μεσημβρίαν,
καθάπερ καὶ οἱ Αὐταριάται καὶ Δασαρήτιοι,
ἄλλοι κατ' ἄλλα μέρη συνεχεῖς ἀλλήλοις ὄντες
καὶ τοῖς Αὐταριάταις. τῶν δὲ Δαρδανιατῶν εἰσι

---

[1] After τελέως Groskurd inserts τὸ ἔθνος, perhaps rightly;
so Meineke.
[2] Ῥιζονικός, Meineke for ῥιζαί.
[3] ἥ, Pletho inserts; so the later editors.

---

[1] Now Risano.   [2] Now the Drin.
[3] The exact meaning and connection of "different . . .
Autariatae" is doubtful. Corais and others emend Auta-

Cnidians are close to the Pleraei, while Pharos (formerly called Paros, for it was founded by Parians) is close to the Ardiaei.

6. The Ardiaei were called by the men of later times "Vardiaei." Because they pestered the sea through their piratical bands, the Romans pushed them back from it into the interior and forced them to till the soil. But the country is rough and poor and not suited to a farming population, and therefore the tribe has been utterly ruined and in fact has almost been obliterated. And this is what befell the rest of the peoples in that part of the world; for those who were most powerful in earlier times were utterly humbled or were obliterated, as, for example, among the Galatae the Boii and the Scordistae, and among the Illyrians the Autariatae, Ardiaei, and Dardanii, and among the Thracians the Triballi; that is, they were reduced in warfare by one another at first and then later by the Macedonians and the Romans.

7. Be this as it may, after the seaboard of the Ardiaei and the Pleraei come the Rhizonic Gulf, and the city Rhizo,[1] and other small towns, and also the River Drilo,[2] which is navigable inland towards the east as far as the Dardanian country. This country borders on the Macedonian and the Paeonian tribes on the south, as do also the Autariatae and the Dassaretii—different peoples on different sides being contiguous to one another and to the Autariatae.[3] To the Dardaniatae belong also the

riatae to Dardaniatae; others would omit "and to the Autariatae"; and still others would make the clause read "and different tribes which on different sides are contiguous to one another and to the Autariatae." The last seems most probable.

καὶ οἱ Γαλάβριοι, παρ' οἷς πόλις ἀρχαία, καὶ οἱ
Θουνᾶται, οἳ¹ Μέδοις,² ἔθνει Θρᾳκίῳ, πρὸς ἔω
συνάπτουσιν. ἄγριοι δ' ὄντες οἱ Δαρδάνιοι
τελέως, ὥσθ' ὑπὸ ταῖς κοπρίαις ὀρύξαντες σπή-
λαια ἐνταῦθα διαίτας ποιεῖσθαι, μουσικῆς δ' ὅμως
ἐπεμελήθησαν, μουσικοῖς³ ἀεὶ χρώμενοι καὶ
αὐλοῖς καὶ τοῖς ἐντατοῖς ὀργάνοις. οὗτοι μὲν
οὖν ἐν τῇ μεσογαίᾳ· μνησθησόμεθα δ' αὐτῶν καὶ
ὕστερον.

8. Μετὰ δὲ τὸν Ῥιζονικὸν κόλπον Λίσσος ἐστὶ
πόλις καὶ Ἀκρόλισσος καὶ Ἐπίδαμνος, Κερκυραίων κτίσμα, ἡ νῦν Δυρράχιον ὁμωνύμως τῇ
χερρονήσῳ λεγομένη, ἐφ' ἧς ἵδρυται. εἶθ' ὁ
Ἄψος ποταμὸς καὶ ὁ Ἄωος, ἐφ' ᾧ Ἀπολλωνία
πόλις εὐνομωτάτη, κτίσμα Κορινθίων καὶ Κερκυραίων, τοῦ ποταμοῦ μὲν ἀπέχουσα σταδίους δέκα,
τῆς θαλάττης δὲ ἑξήκοντα. τὸν δ' Ἄωον Αἴαντα
καλεῖ Ἑκαταῖος καί φησιν ἀπὸ τοῦ αὐτοῦ τόπου,
τοῦ περὶ Λάκμον, μᾶλλον δὲ τοῦ αὐτοῦ μυχοῦ,
τόν τε Ἴναχον ῥεῖν εἰς Ἄργος πρὸς νότον καὶ τὸν
Αἴαντα πρὸς ἑσπέραν καὶ πρὸς τὸν Ἀδρίαν. ἐν
δὲ τῇ χώρᾳ τῶν Ἀπολλωνιατῶν καλεῖταί τι
Νυμφαῖον, πέτρα δ' ἐστὶ πῦρ ἀναδιδοῦσα· ὑπ'

¹ οἵ, Meineke inserts.
² Μέδοις (the reading of all MSS.), Jones restores, for
Μαίδοις. Cp. Μέδων, 7. 5. 12 and *Frag.* 36.
³ μουσικοῖς, Meineke deletes, perhaps rightly.

¹ These Galabrii, who are otherwise unknown, are thought
by Patsch (Pauly-Wissowa, *s. v.*) and others to be the
ancestors of the Italian Calabri.
² The name of this city, now unknown, seems to have
fallen out of the text.

Galabrii,[1] among whom is an ancient city,[2] and the Thunatae, whose country joins that of the Medi,[3] a Thracian tribe on the east. The Dardanians are so utterly wild that they dig caves beneath their dung-hills and live there, but still they care for music, always making use of musical instruments, both flutes and stringed instruments. However, these people live in the interior, and I shall mention them again later.

8. After the Rhizonic Gulf comes the city of Lissus,[4] and Acrolissus,[5] and Epidamnus,[6] founded by the Corcyraeans, which is now called Dyrrachium, like the peninsula on which it is situated. Then comes the Apsus[7] River; and then the Aoüs,[8] on which is situated Apollonia,[9] an exceedingly well-governed city, founded by the Corinthians and the Corcyraeans, and ten stadia distant from the river and sixty from the sea. The Aoüs is called "Aeas"[10] by Hecataeus, who says that both the Inachus and the Aeas flow from the same place, the region of Lacmus,[11] or rather from the same subterranean recess, the former towards the south into Argos and the latter towards the west and towards the Adrias. In the country of the Apolloniates is a place called Nymphaeum; it is a rock that gives

---

[3] "Maedi" is the usual spelling in other authors. But cp. "Medobithyni," 7. 3. 2 and "Medi," 7. 5. 12 and *Frag.* 36.

[4] Now Alessio. [5] A fortress near Lissus.
[6] Now Durazzo. [7] Now the Semeni.
[8] Now the Viosa. [9] Now Pollina.
[10] Cp. 6. 2. 4, and Pliny, 3. 26.
[11] More often spelled Lacmon; one of the heights of Pindus.

STRABO

αὐτῇ δὲ κρῆναι ῥέουσι χλιαροῦ καὶ ἀσφάλτου,
καιομένης, ὡς εἰκός, τῆς βώλου τῆς ἀσφαλτίτιδος·
μέταλλον δ' αὐτῆς ἐστι πλησίον ἐπὶ λόφου· τὸ
δὲ τμηθὲν ἐκπληροῦται πάλιν τῷ χρόνῳ, τῆς
ἐγχωννυμένης εἰς τὰ ὀρύγματα γῆς μεταβαλλού-
σης εἰς ἄσφαλτον, ὥς φησι Ποσειδώνιος. λέγει δ'
ἐκεῖνος καὶ τὴν ἀμπελῖτιν γῆν ἀσφαλτώδη τὴν ἐν
Σελευκείᾳ τῇ Πιερίᾳ μεταλλευομένην ἄκος τῆς
φθειριώσης ἀμπέλου· χρισθεῖσαν γὰρ μετ' ἐλαίου
φθείρειν τὸ θηρίον, πρὶν ἐπὶ τοὺς βλαστοὺς τῆς
ῥίζης ἀναβῆναι· τοιαύτην δ' εὑρεθῆναι καὶ ἐν
Ῥόδῳ, πρυτανεύοντος αὐτοῦ, πλείονος δ' ἐλαίου
δεῖσθαι. μετὰ δ' Ἀπολλωνίαν Βυλλιακὴ καὶ
Ὠρικὸν καὶ τὸ ἐπίνειον αὐτοῦ ὁ Πάνορμος καὶ τὰ
Κεραύνια ὄρη, ἡ ἀρχὴ τοῦ στόματος τοῦ Ἰονίου
κόλπου καὶ τοῦ Ἀδρίου.

9. Τὸ μὲν οὖν στόμα κοινὸν ἀμφοῖν ἐστι, δια-
φέρει δὲ ὁ Ἰόνιος, διότι τοῦ πρώτου μέρους τῆς
C 317 θαλάττης ταύτης ὄνομα τοῦτ' ἐστίν, ὁ δ' Ἀδρίας
τῆς ἐντὸς μέχρι τοῦ μυχοῦ, νυνὶ δὲ καὶ τῆς
συμπάσης. φησὶ δὲ ὁ Θεόπομπος τῶν ὀνομάτων
τὸ μὲν ἥκειν ἀπὸ ἀνδρὸς ἡγησαμένου τῶν τόπων,
ἐξ Ἴσσης[1] τὸ γένος, τὸν Ἀδρίαν δὲ ποταμοῦ

---

[1] Ἴσης (ACl).

---

[1] Now Kabousi, at the foot of the Djebel-Arsonz (Mt.
Pieria), on the boundary of Cilicia and Syria.

[2] In private communications to Professor C. R. Crosby of
Cornell University, Dr. Paul Marchal and Professor F. Sil-
vestri of Portici identify the insect in question as the *Pseudo-
coccus Vitis* (also called *Dactylopius Vitis*, Nedzelsky). This
insect, in conjunction with the fungus Bornetina Corium,
still infests the vine in the region mentioned by Poseidonius

forth fire; and beneath it flow springs of warm water and asphalt—probably because the clods of asphalt in the earth are burned by the fire. And near by, on a hill, is a mine of asphalt; and the part that is trenched is filled up again in the course of time, since, as Poseidonius says, the earth that is poured into the trenches changes to asphalt. He also speaks of the asphaltic vine-earth which is mined at the Pierian Seleuceia[1] as a cure for the infested vine; for, he says, if it is smeared on together with olive oil, it kills the insects[2] before they can mount the sprouts of the roots;[3] and, he adds, earth of this sort was also discovered in Rhodes when he was in office there as Prytanis,[4] but it required more olive oil. After Apollonia comes Bylliaca,[5] and Oricum[6] and its seaport Panormus, and the Ceraunian Mountains, where the mouth of the Ionian Gulf[7] and the Adrias begins.

9. Now the mouth is common to both, but the Ionian is different in that it is the name of the first part of this sea, whereas Adrias is the name of the inside part of the sea as far as the recess; at the present time, however, Adrias is also the name of the sea as a whole. According to Theopompus, the first name came from a man,[8] a native of Issa,[9] who once ruled over the region, whereas the Adrias

[3] For a discussion of this passage, see Mangin and Viala, *Revue de Viticulture*, 1903, Vol. XX, pp. 583-584.

[4] President, or chief presiding-officer.

[5] The territory (not the city of Byllis) between Apollonia and Oricum.

[6] Now Erico.   [7] See 6. 1. 7 and the footnote.

[8] Ionius, an Illyrian according to the Scholiasts (quoting Theopompus) on Apollonius (*Argonautica*, 4. 308) and Pindar (*Pythian Odes*, 3. 120).   [9] The isle of Issa (7. 5. 5).

ἐπώνυμον γεγονέναι. στάδιοι δ' ἀπὸ τῶν Λιβυρ-
νῶν ἐπὶ τὰ Κεραύνια μικρῷ πλείους ἢ δισχίλιοι.
Θεόπομπος δὲ τὸν πάντα ἀπὸ τοῦ μυχοῦ πλοῦν
ἡμερῶν ἓξ εἴρηκε, πεζῇ δὲ τὸ μῆκος τῆς Ἰλλυρίδος
καὶ τριάκοντα· πλεονάζειν δέ μοι δοκεῖ. καὶ
ἄλλα δ' οὐ πιστὰ λέγει, τό τε συντετρῆσθαι τὰ
πελάγη¹ ἀπὸ τοῦ εὑρίσκεσθαι κέραμόν τε Χῖον
καὶ Θάσιον ἐν τῷ Νάρωνι, καὶ τὸ ἄμφω κατο-
πτεύεσθαι τὰ πελάγη ἀπό τινος ὄρους, καὶ τῶν
νήσων τῶν Λιβυρνίδων τινὰ² τιθεὶς³ ὥστε
κύκλον ἔχειν σταδίων καὶ πεντακοσίων, καὶ τὸ
τὸν Ἴστρον ἑνὶ τῶν στομάτων εἰς τὸν Ἀδρίαν
ἐμβάλλειν. τοιαῦτα δὲ καὶ τοῦ Ἐρατοσθένους
ἔνια παρακούσματά ἐστι λαοδογματικά,⁴ καθάπερ
Πολύβιός φησι καὶ περὶ αὐτοῦ καὶ τῶν ἄλλων
λέγων συγγραφέων.

10. Τὸν μὲν οὖν παράπλουν ἅπαντα τὸν Ἰλλυ-
ρικὸν σφόδρα εὐλίμενον εἶναι συμβαίνει καὶ ἐξ
αὐτῆς τῆς συνεχοῦς ᾐόνος καὶ ἐκ τῶν πλησίον

---

¹ Meineke thinks that τεκμαιρόμενος or something of the
kind has fallen out after πελάγη.
² τινά, Jones inserts.
³ τιθεὶς, Meineke suspects ; Corais emends to τὴν θέσιν.
⁴ λαοδογματικά, Tyrwhitt, for λαοδογματικῶς; so the editors.
Cp. 2. 4. 2 and 10. 3. 5.

---

¹ Called by Ptolemaeus (3. 1. 21) "Atrianus," emptying
into the lagoons of the Padus (now Po) near the city of
Adria (cp. 5. 1. 8), or Atria (now Atri). This river, now the
Tartara, is by other writers called the Tartarus.
² Strabo's estimate for the length of the Illyrian *seaboard*,
all told (cp. 7. 5. 3–4), amounts to 5,800 stadia. In objecting
to Theopompus' length of the Illyrian *country on foot*, he

was named after a river.[1] The distance from the country of the Liburnians to the Ceraunian Mountains is slightly more than two thousand stadia. Theopompus states that the whole voyage from the recess takes six days, and that on foot the length of the Illyrian country is as much as thirty days, though in my opinion he makes the distance too great.[2] And he also says other things that are incredible : first, that the seas[3] are connected by a subterranean passage, from the fact that both Chian and Thasian pottery are found in the Naro River ; secondly, that both seas are visible from a certain mountain ;[4] and thirdly, when he puts down a certain one of the Liburnides islands as large enough to have a circuit of five hundred stadia ;[5] and fourthly, that the Ister empties by one of its mouths into the Adrias. In Eratosthenes, also, are some false hearsay statements of this kind—"popular notions,"[6] as Polybius calls them when speaking of him and the other historians.

10. Now the whole Illyrian seaboard is exceedingly well supplied with harbours, not only on the continuous coast itself but also in the neighbouring islands, although the reverse is the case with that

obviously wishes, among other things, to make a liberal deduction for the *seaboard* of the Istrian peninsula. Cp. 6. 3. 10.

[3] The Adriatic and the Aegaean.

[4] The Haemus (cp. 7. 5. 1).

[5] The coastline of Arbo is not much short of 500 stadia. The present translator inserts "a certain one"; others emend so as to make Theopompus refer to the circuit of *all* the Liburnides, or insert "the least" ($\tau\grave{\eta}\nu$ $\grave{\epsilon}\lambda\alpha\chi\acute{\iota}\sigma\tau\eta\nu$), or leave the text in doubt.

[6] See 2. 4. 2 and 10. 3. 5.

νήσων, ὑπεναντίως τῷ Ἰταλικῷ τῷ ἀντικειμένῳ,
ἀλιμένῳ ὄντι· ἀλεεινοὶ δὲ καὶ χρηστόκαρποι
ὁμοίως· ἐλαιόφυτοι γὰρ καὶ εὐάμπελοι, πλὴν
εἴ πού τι σπάνιον ἐκτετράχυνται τελέως. τοιαύτη
δ᾽ οὖσα ὠλιγωρεῖτο πρότερον ἡ Ἰλλυρικὴ παραλία, τάχα μὲν καὶ κατ᾽ ἄγνοιαν τῆς ἀρετῆς, τὸ
μέντοι πλέον διὰ τὴν ἀγριότητα τῶν ἀνθρώπων
καὶ τὸ λῃστρικὸν ἔθος.[1] ἡ δ᾽ ὑπερκειμένη ταύτης
πᾶσα ὀρεινὴ καὶ ψυχρὰ καὶ νιφόβολός ἐστιν, ἡ δὲ
προσάρκτιος καὶ μᾶλλον, ὥστε καὶ τῶν ἀμπέλων
σπάνιν εἶναι καὶ ἐν ταῖς ὑψώσεσι καὶ ἐν τοῖς
ἐπιπεδωτέροις. ὀροπέδια δ᾽ ἐστὶ ταῦτα, ἃ κατέ-
χουσιν οἱ Παννόνιοι, πρὸς νότον μὲν μέχρι
Δαλματέων καὶ Ἀρδιαίων διατείνοντα, πρὸς
ἄρκτον δὲ ἐπὶ τὸν Ἴστρον τελευτῶντα, πρὸς ἕω
δὲ Σκορδίσκοις συνάπτοντα, τῇ δὲ[2] παρὰ τὰ ὄρη
τῶν Μακεδόνων καὶ Θρακῶν.

11. Αὐταριάται μὲν οὖν τὸ μέγιστον καὶ ἄρισ-
τον τῶν Ἰλλυριῶν ἔθνος ὑπῆρξεν, ὃ πρότερον μὲν
πρὸς Ἀρδιαίους συνεχῶς ἐπολέμει περὶ ἁλῶν
ἐν μεθορίοις πηγνυμένων ἐξ ὕδατος ῥέοντος ὑπὸ
ἄγκει[3] τινὶ τοῦ ἔαρος· ἀρυσαμένοις γὰρ καὶ
ἀποθεῖσιν ἡμέρας πέντε ἐξεπήγνυντο οἱ ἅλες.
συνέκειτο δὲ παρὰ μέρος χρῆσθαι τῷ ἁλοπηγίῳ,
C 318 παραβαίνοντες δὲ τὰ συγκείμενα ἐπολέμουν·
καταστρεψάμενοι δέ ποτε οἱ Αὐταριάται Τρι-
βαλλοὺς ἀπὸ Ἀγριάνων μέχρι τοῦ Ἴστρου καθή-

---

[1] ἔθος, Tyrwhitt, for ἔθνος ; so the editors.
[2] Before τῇ δέ, Meineke indicates a lacuna. But see C.
Müller, Ind. Var. Lect., p. 985.
[3] ἄγκει, the Epit. and the editors, for ἄγγει.

part of the Italian seaboard which lies opposite, since it is harbourless. But both seaboards in like manner are sunny and good for fruits, for the olive and the vine flourish there, except, perhaps, in places here or there that are utterly rugged. But although the Illyrian seaboard is such, people in earlier times made but small account of it—perhaps in part owing to their ignorance of its fertility, though mostly because of the wildness of the inhabitants and their piratical habits. But the whole of the country situated above this is mountainous, cold, and subject to snows, especially the northerly part, so that there is a scarcity of the vine, not only on the heights but also on the levels. These latter are the mountain-plains occupied by the Pannonians; on the south they extend as far as the country of the Dalmatians and the Ardiaei, on the north they end at the Ister, while on the east they border on the country of the Scordisci, that is, on the country that extends along the mountains of the Macedonians and the Thracians.

11. Now the Autariatae were once the largest and best tribe of the Illyrians. In earlier times they were continually at war with the Ardiaei over the salt-works on the common frontiers. The salt was made to crystallise out of water which in the spring-time flowed at the foot of a certain mountain-glen; for if they drew off the water and stowed it away for five days the salt would become thoroughly crystallised. They would agree to use the salt-works alternately, but would break the agreements and go to war. At one time when the Autariatae had subdued the Triballi, whose territory extended from that of the Agrianes as far as the Ister, a

κοντας ἡμερῶν πεντεκαίδεκα ὁδὸν ἐπῆρξαν καὶ
τῶν ἄλλων Θρᾳκῶν τε καὶ Ἰλλυριῶν· κατελύθησαν δ' ὑπὸ Σκορδίσκων πρότερον, ὕστερον δ'
ὑπὸ Ῥωμαίων, οἳ[1] καὶ τοὺς Σκορδίσκους αὐτοὺς
κατεπολέμησαν πολὺν χρόνον ἰσχύσαντας.

12. Ὤκησαν δ' οὗτοι παρὰ τὸν Ἴστρον, διῃρημένοι δίχα, οἱ μὲν μεγάλοι Σκορδίσκοι καλούμενοι,
οἱ δὲ μικροί, οἱ μὲν μεταξὺ δυεῖν ποταμῶν[2]
ἐμβαλλόντων εἰς τὸν Ἴστρον, τοῦ τε Νοάρου τοῦ
παρὰ τὴν Σεγεστικὴν ῥέοντος καὶ τοῦ Μάργου[3]
(τινὲς δὲ Βάργον φασίν)· οἱ δὲ μικροὶ τούτου
πέραν, συνάπτοντες Τριβαλλοῖς καὶ Μυσοῖς.
εἶχον δὲ καὶ τῶν νήσων τινὰς οἱ Σκορδίσκοι· ἐπὶ
τοσοῦτον δ' ηὐξήθησαν, ὥστε καὶ μέχρι τῶν
Ἰλλυρικῶν καὶ τῶν Παιονικῶν καὶ Θρᾳκίων
προῆλθον ὀρῶν· κατέσχον οὖν καὶ τὰς νήσους
τὰς ἐν τῷ Ἴστρῳ τὰς πλείους, ἦσαν δὲ καὶ
πόλεις αὐτοῖς Ἑόρτα καὶ Καπέδουνον. μετὰ
δὲ τὴν τῶν Σκορδίσκων χώραν παρὰ μὲν
τὸν Ἴστρον ἡ τῶν Τριβαλλῶν καὶ Μυσῶν
ἐστιν, ὧν ἐμνήσθημεν πρότερον, καὶ τὰ ἕλη
τὰ τῆς μικρᾶς καλουμένης Σκυθίας τῆς ἐντὸς
Ἴστρου· καὶ τούτων ἐμνήσθημεν. ὑπεροικοῦσι
δ' οὗτοί τε καὶ Κρόβυζοι καὶ οἱ Τρωγλοδύται
λεγόμενοι τῶν περὶ Κάλλατιν καὶ Τομέα καὶ

---

[1] οἳ, the editors insert.
[2] οἰκεῖν (οἰκοῦντες, Bno), after ποταμῶν, the editors either
bracket or delete.
[3] Μάργου, Pletho, for Μάρτου; so the editors.

---

[1] See 7. 5. 2.   [2] Now the Morava.
[3] i.e. east of the Margus.

journey of fifteen days, they held sway also over the
rest of the Thracians and the Illyrians; but they
were overpowered, at first by the Scordisci, and later
on by the Romans, who also subdued the Scordisci
themselves, after these had been in power for a long
time.

12. The Scordisci lived along the Ister and were
divided into two tribes called the Great Scordisci
and the Little Scordisci. The former lived between
two rivers that empty into the Ister—the Noarus,[1]
which flows past Segestica, and the Margus [2] (by
some called the Bargus), whereas the Little Scordisci
lived on the far side of this river,[3] and their territory
bordered on that of the Triballi and the Mysi. The
Scordisci also held some of the islands; and they
increased to such an extent that they advanced as
far as the Illyrian, Paeonian, and Thracian mountains; accordingly, they also took possession of most
of the islands in the Ister. And they also had two
cities—Heorta and Capedunum.[4] After the country
of the Scordisci, along the Ister, comes that of the
Triballi and the Mysi (whom I have mentioned
before),[5] and also the marshes of that part of what
is called Little Scythia which is this side the Ister
(these too I have mentioned).[6] These people, as
also the Crobyzi and what are called the Troglodytae,
live above [7] the region round about Callatis,[8] Tomis,[9]

---

[4] The sites of these places are unknown. Groskurd and
Forbiger identify them with what are now Heortberg (Hart-
berg) and Kappenberg (Kapfenstein).

[5] 7. 3 7, 8, 10, 13.   [6] 7. 4. 5,

[7] *i.e.* "in the interior and back of."

[8] Now Mangalia, on the Black Sea.

[9] Now Kostanza.

Ἴστρον τόπων. εἶθ' οἱ περὶ τὸ Αἷμον καὶ οἱ ὑπ'
αὐτῷ[1] οἰκοῦντες μέχρι τοῦ Πόντου Κόραλλοι
καὶ Βέσσοι καὶ Μέδων[2] τινὲς καὶ Δανθηλητῶν.
πάντα μὲν οὖν ταῦτα λῃστρικώτατα ἔθνη· Βέσσοι
δὲ οὕπερ[3] τὸ πλέον τοῦ ὄρους νέμονται τοῦ Αἵμου,
καὶ ὑπὸ τῶν λῃστῶν λῃσταὶ προσαγορεύονται,
καλυβῖταί τινες καὶ λυπρόβιοι, συνάπτοντες τῇ
τε Ῥοδόπῃ καὶ τοῖς Παίοσι καὶ τῶν Ἰλλυριῶν
τοῖς τε Αὐταριάταις καὶ τοῖς Δαρδανίοις. μεταξὺ
δὲ τούτων τε καὶ τῶν Ἀρδιαίων οἱ Δασσαρήτιοί
εἰσι καὶ Ὑβριᾶνες[4] καὶ ἄλλα ἄσημα ἔθνη, ἃ
ἐπόρθουν οἱ Σκορδίσκοι, μέχρι ἠρήμωσαν τὴν
χώραν, καὶ δρυμῶν ἀβάτων ἐφ' ἡμέρας πλείους
ἐποίησαν μεστήν.

VI

1. Λοιπὴ δ' ἐστὶ τῆς μεταξὺ Ἴστρου καὶ τῶν
ὀρῶν τῶν ἐφ' ἑκάτερα τῆς Παιονίας ἡ Ποντικὴ
παραλία, ἡ ἀπὸ τοῦ Ἱεροῦ στόματος τοῦ Ἴστρου
μέχρι τῆς περὶ τὸν Αἷμον ὀρεινῆς, καὶ μέχρι τοῦ
στόματος τοῦ κατὰ Βυζάντιον. καθάπερ δὲ τὴν
Ἰλλυρικὴν παραλίαν ἐπιόντες μέχρι τῶν Κεραυ-

---

[1] ὑπ' αὐτῷ (αὐτοῦ A) ; Meineke emends to ὑπὲρ αὐτοῦ.
[2] Μέδων, Jones restores, for Μαίδων ; see note on Μεδοβιθυνοί, 7. 3. 2 ; also see Μέδων, 7. 5. 7, and *Frag.* 36.
[3] οὕπερ, Meineke, for ὑπέρ.
[4] Ὑβριᾶνες, Meineke emends to Ἀγριᾶνες ; C. Müller
proposes Βρυγιᾶνες.

---

[1] Now Karanasib.   [2] Cp. 7. 5. 7 and the footnote.

and Ister.[1] Then come the peoples who live in the neighbourhood of the Haemus Mountain and those who live at its base and extend as far as the Pontus —I mean the Coralli, the Bessi, and some of the Medi[2] and Dantheletae. Now these tribes are very brigandish themselves, but the Bessi, who inhabit the greater part of the Haemus Mountain, are called brigands even by the brigands. The Bessi live in huts and lead a wretched life; and their country borders on Mount Rhodope, on the country of the Paeonians, and on that of two Illyrian peoples—the Autariatae, and the Dardanians. Between these[3] and the Ardiaei are the Dassaretii, the Hybrianes,[4] and other insignificant tribes, which the Scordisci kept on ravaging until they had depopulated the country and made it full of trackless forests for a distance of several days' journey.

VI

1. The remainder of the country between the Ister and the mountains on either side of Paeonia consists of that part of the Pontic seaboard which extends from the Sacred Mouth of the Ister as far as the mountainous country in the neighbourhood of the Haemus and as far as the mouth at Byzantium. And just as, in traversing the Illyrian seaboard, I

[3] The word "these" would naturally refer to the Autariatae and the Dardanians, but it might refer to the Bessi (see next footnote).

[4] The "Hybrianes" are otherwise unknown. Casaubon and Meineke emend to "Agrianes" (cp. 7. 5. 11 and *Fragments* 36, 37 and 41). If this doubtful emendation be accepted, then "these" (see preceding footnote) must refer to the Bessi.

νίων ὀρῶν προὔβημεν ἔξω τῆς Ἰλλυρικῆς πιπ-
τόντων ὀρεινῆς, ἐχόντων δέ τι οἰκεῖον πέρας, τὰ
μεσόγαια δ' ἔθνη τούτοις ἀφωρίσμεθα, νομίζοντες
σημειωδεστέρας ἔσεσθαι τὰς τοιαύτας παρα-
γραφὰς [1] καὶ πρὸς τὰ νῦν καὶ πρὸς τὰ ὕστερον.
οὕτω κἀνταῦθα ἡ παραλία, κἂν ὑπερπίπτῃ τὴν
ὀρεινὴν γραμμήν, ὅμως εἰς οἰκεῖόν τι πέρας τελευ-
C 319 τήσει τὸ τοῦ Πόντου στόμα καὶ πρὸς τὰ νῦν καὶ
πρὸς τὰ ἐφεξῆς. ἔστιν οὖν ἀπὸ τοῦ Ἱεροῦ στόματος τοῦ Ἴστρου ἐν δεξιᾷ ἔχοντι τὴν συνεχῆ
παραλίαν Ἴστρος πολίχνιον ἐν πεντακοσίοις
σταδίοις, Μιλησίων κτίσμα· εἶτα Τόμις, ἕτερον
πολίχνιον ἐν διακοσίοις πεντήκοντα σταδίοις·
εἶτα πόλις Κάλλατις ἐν διακοσίοις ὀγδοήκοντα,
Ἡρακλεωτῶν ἄποικος· εἶτ' Ἀπολλωνία ἐν χιλίοις
τριακοσίοις σταδίοις, ἄποικος Μιλησίων, τὸ πλέον
τοῦ κτίσματος ἱδρυμένον ἔχουσα ἐν νησίῳ τινί,
ὅπου [2] ἱερὸν τοῦ Ἀπόλλωνος, ἐξ οὗ Μάρκος
Λεύκολλος τὸν κολοσσὸν ἦρε καὶ ἀνέθηκεν ἐν
τῷ Καπετωλίῳ τὸν τοῦ Ἀπόλλωνος, Καλάμιδος
ἔργον. ἐν τῷ μεταξὺ δὲ διαστήματι τῷ ἀπὸ
Καλλάτιδος εἰς Ἀπολλωνίαν Βιζώνη τέ ἐστιν,
ἧς κατεπόθη πολὺ μέρος ὑπὸ σεισμῶν, καὶ

---

[1] παραγραφάς, "marks" (the reading of all MSS.), Jones
restores. Corais and the later editors emend to περιγραφάς,
"outlines," wrongly. See 17. 1. 48 and Sophocles' *Lexicon*.
[2] ὅπου appears only in Bno; so read the editors in general.

---

[1] Others wrongly emend "marks" to "outlines." See
critical note to Greek text, and especially cp. 17. 1. 48
where the "marks" on the wall of the well indicate the
risings of the Nile.

proceeded as far as the Ceraunian Mountains, because, although they fall outside the mountainous country of Illyria, they afford an appropriate limit, and just as I determined the positions of the tribes of the interior by these mountains, because I thought that marks[1] of this kind would be more significant as regards both the description at hand and what was to follow, so also in this case the seaboard, even though it falls beyond the mountain-line, will nevertheless end at an appropriate limit—the mouth of the Pontus—as regards both the description at hand and that which comes next in order. So, then, if one begins at the Sacred Mouth of the Ister and keeps the continuous seaboard on the right, one comes, at a distance of five hundred stadia, to a small town, Ister, founded by the Milesians; then, at a distance of two hundred and fifty stadia, to a second small town, Tomis; then, at two hundred and eighty stadia, to a city Callatis,[2] a colony of the Heracleotae;[3] then, at one thousand three hundred stadia, to Apollonia,[4] a colony of the Milesians. The greater part of Apollonia was founded on a certain isle, where there is a temple of Apollo, from which Marcus Lucullus carried off the colossal statue of Apollo, a work of Calamis,[5] which he set up in the Capitolium. In the interval between Callatis and Apollonia come also Bizone,[6] of which a considerable part was engulfed by earthquakes,[7] Cruni,[8]

---

[2] On these three places, see 7. 5. 12.
[3] Cp. 7. 4. 2.   [4] Now Sizeboli.
[5] Flourished at Athens about 450 B.C. This colossal statue was thirty cubits high and cost 500 talents (Pliny 34. 18).
[6] Now Kavarna.   [7] Cp. 1. 3. 10.
[8] Now Baltchik.

Κρουνοὶ[1] καὶ Ὀδησσός, Μιλησίων ἄποικος, καὶ
Ναύλοχος, Μεσημβριανῶν πολίχνιον. εἶτα τὸ
Αἷμον ὄρος μέχρι τῆς δεῦρο θαλάττης διῆκον·
εἶτα Μεσημβρία Μεγαρέων ἄποικος, πρότερον
δὲ Μενεβρία (οἶον Μένα πόλις, τοῦ κτίσαντος
Μένα καλουμένου, τῆς δὲ πόλεως βρίας καλουμένης Θρᾳκιστί· ὡς καὶ ἡ τοῦ Σήλυος πόλις
Σηλυβρία προσηγόρευται, ἥ τε Αἶνος Πολτυοβρία
ποτὲ ὠνομάζετο)· εἶτ᾽ Ἀγχιάλη πολίχνιον Ἀπολλωνιατῶν, καὶ αὐτὴ ἡ Ἀπολλωνία. ἐν δὲ ταύτῃ
τῇ παραλίᾳ ἐστὶ ἡ Τίριζις[2] ἄκρα, χωρίον ἐρυμνόν,
ᾧ ποτε καὶ Λυσίμαχος ἐχρήσατο γαζοφυλακίῳ.
πάλιν δ᾽ ἀπὸ τῆς Ἀπολλωνίας ἐπὶ Κυανέας
στάδιοί εἰσι περὶ χιλίους καὶ πεντακοσίους, ἐν δὲ
τῷ μεταξὺ ἥ τε Θυνιάς, τῶν Ἀπολλωνιατῶν
χώρα, (Ἀγχιάλη καὶ αὐτὴ Ἀπολλωνιατῶν),[3]
καὶ Φινόπολις[4] καὶ Ἀνδριάκη, συνάπτουσαι τῷ
Σαλμυδησσῷ. ἔστι δ᾽ οὗτος ἔρημος αἰγιαλὸς
καὶ λιθώδης, ἀλίμενος, ἀναπεπταμένος πολὺς
πρὸς τοὺς βορέας, σταδίων ὅσον ἑπτακοσίων
μέχρι Κυανέων τὸ μῆκος, πρὸς ὃν οἱ ἐκπίπτοντες
ὑπὸ τῶν Ἀστῶν διαρπάζονται τῶν ὑπερκειμένων,
Θρᾳκίου ἔθνους. αἱ δὲ Κυάνεαι πρὸς τῷ στόματι

---

[1] Κρουνοί, Xylander, for Κρούλιοι; so the later editors.
[2] ἡ Τίριζις, Kramer for κητίριζις; so later editors.
[3] Meineke relegates the words in parenthesis to the foot of
the page, as being a gloss. Corais conj. καὶ ἀκτὴ ἄλλη; no
have καί before Ἀγχιάλη.
[4] Φινόπολις, Xylander, for Φθινόπολις; so the later editors.

---

[1] Now Varna.
[2] In Pliny (4. 18), "Tetranaulochus"; site unknown.

Odessus,[1] a colony of the Milesians, and Naulochus,[2] a small town of the Mesembriani. Then comes the Haemus Mountain, which reaches the sea here;[3] then Mesembria, a colony of the Megarians, formerly called "Menebria" (that is, "city of Menas," because the name of its founder was Menas, while "bria" is the word for "city" in the Thracian language. In this way, also, the city of Selys is called Selybria;[4] and Aenus[5] was once called Poltyobria[6]). Then come Anchiale,[7] a small town belonging to the Apolloniatae, and Apollonia itself. On this coast-line is Cape Tirizis,[8] a stronghold, which Lysimachus[9] once used as a treasury. Again, from Apollonia to the Cyaneae the distance is about one thousand five hundred stadia; and in the interval are Thynias,[10] a territory belonging to the Apolloniatae (Anchiale, which also belongs to the Apolloniatae[11]), and also Phinopolis and Andriaca,[12] which border on Salmydessus.[13] Salmydessus is a desert and stony beach, harbourless and wide open to the north winds, and in length extends as far as the Cyaneae, a distance of about seven hundred stadia; and all who are cast ashore on this beach are plundered by the Astae, a Thracian tribe who are situated above it. The

---

[3] In Cape Emineh-bouroun ("End of Haemus").
[4] Or Selymbria; now Selivri.
[5] Now Aenos.
[6] Or Poltymbria; city of Poltys.
[7] Now Ankhialo.
[8] Cape Kaliakra. ⁹ See 7. 3. 8, 14.
[10] Now Cape Iniada.
[11] The parenthesised words seem to be merely a gloss (see critical note).
[12] The sites of these two places are unknown.
[13] Including the city of Salmydessus (now Midia).

τοῦ Πόντου εἰσὶ δύο νησίδια, τὸ μὲν τῇ Εὐρώπῃ
προσεχές, τὸ δὲ τῇ Ἀσίᾳ, πορθμῷ διειργόμενα
ὅσον εἴκοσι σταδίων, τοσοῦτον δὲ διέχει καὶ τοῦ
ἱεροῦ τοῦ Βυζαντίων, καὶ τοῦ ἱεροῦ τοῦ Χαλκη-
δονίων· ὅπερ ἐστὶ τοῦ στόματος τοῦ Εὐξείνου
τὸ στενώτατον. προϊόντι γὰρ δέκα σταδίους
ἄκρα ἐστὶ πεντασταδίον ποιοῦσα τὸν πορθμόν,
εἶτα διίσταται ἐπὶ πλέον καὶ ποιεῖν ἄρχεται τὴν
Προποντίδα.

2. Ἀπὸ μὲν οὖν τῆς ἄκρας τῆς τὸ πεντασταδίον
ποιούσης ἐπὶ τὸν ὑπὸ τῇ Συκῇ καλούμενον λιμένα
στάδιοι πέντε καὶ τριάκοντα, ἐντεῦθεν δ' ἐπὶ τὸ
C 320 Κέρας τὸ Βυζαντίων πέντε. ἔστι δὲ τὸ Κέρας,
προσεχὲς τῷ Βυζαντίων τείχει, κόλπος ἀνέχων
ὡς πρὸς δύσιν ἐπὶ σταδίους ἐξήκοντα, ἐοικὼς
ἐλάφου κέρατι· εἰς γὰρ πλείστους σχίζεται
κόλπους, ὡς ἂν κλάδους τινάς, εἰς οὓς ἐμπίπτουσα
ἡ πηλαμὺς ἁλίσκεται ῥᾳδίως διά τε τὸ πλῆθος
αὐτῆς καὶ τὴν βίαν τοῦ συνελαύνοντος ῥοῦ καὶ
τὴν στενότητα τῶν κόλπων, ὥστε καὶ χερσὶν
ἁλίσκεσθαι διὰ τὴν στενοχωρίαν.[1] γεννᾶται μὲν
οὖν τὸ ζῷον ἐν τοῖς ἕλεσι τῆς Μαιώτιδος, ἰσχῦσαν
δὲ μικρὸν ἐκπίπτει διὰ τοῦ στόματος ἀγεληδὸν

[1] διὰ τὴν στενοχωρίαν, Meineke relegates to foot of page.

---

[1] Cp. 1. 2. 10 and 3. 2. 12. The islet, or rock, on the
Asiatic side was visible in the sixteenth century, but "is
now submerged,"—"on the bight of Kabakos" (Tozer,
op. cit., p. 198). Tozer (loc. cit.) rightly believes that the
ancients often restricted the Cyanean Rocks to those on the
European side—what are now the Oräkje Tashy (see Pliny
4. 27).

[2] These temples were called the Sarapieium and the temple

Cyaneae[1] are two islets near the mouth of the Pontus, one close to Europe and the other to Asia; they are separated by a channel of about twenty stadia and are twenty stadia distant both from the temple of the Byzantines and from the temple of the Chalcedonians.[2] And this is the narrowest part of the mouth of the Euxine, for when one proceeds only ten stadia farther one comes to a headland which makes the strait only five stadia[3] in width, and then the strait opens to a greater width and begins to form the Propontis.

2. Now the distance from the headland that makes the strait only five stadia wide to the harbour which is called "Under the Fig-tree"[4] is thirty-five stadia; and thence to the Horn of the Byzantines,[5] five stadia. The Horn, which is close to the wall of the Byzantines, is a gulf that extends approximately towards the west for a distance of sixty stadia; it resembles a stag's horn,[6] for it is split into numerous gulfs—branches, as it were. The *pelamydes*[7] rush into these gulfs and are easily caught—because of their numbers, the force of the current that drives them together, and the narrowness of the gulfs; in fact, because of the narrowness of the area, they are even caught by hand. Now these fish are hatched in the marshes of Lake Maeotis, and when they have gained a little strength they rush out through

of Zeno Urius; and they were on the present sites of the two Turkish forts which command the entrance to the Bosporus (Tozer).

[3] But cp. "four stadia" in 2. 5. 23.
[4] Now Galata.   [5] The Golden Horn.
[6] So the harbour of Brindisi (6. 3. 6).
[7] A kind of tunny-fish.

καὶ φέρεται παρὰ τὴν Ἀσιανὴν ἠιόνα μέχρι
Τραπεζοῦντος καὶ Φαρνακίας· ἐνταῦθα δὲ πρότερον
συνίστασθαι συμβαίνει τὴν θήραν, οὐ πολλὴ δ'
ἐστίν· οὐ γάρ πω τὸ προσῆκον ἔχει μέγεθος· εἰς
δὲ Σινώπην προϊοῦσα[1] ὡραιοτέρα πρός τε τὴν
θήραν καὶ τὴν ταριχείαν ἐστίν· ἐπειδὰν δὲ ἤδη
συνάψῃ τοῖς Κυανέαις καὶ παραλλάξῃ ταύτας,
ἐκ τῆς Χαλκηδονιακῆς ἀκτῆς λευκή τις πέτρα
προπίπτουσα φοβεῖ τὸ ζῷον, ὥστ' εὐθὺς εἰς τὴν
περαίαν τρέπεσθαι· παραλαβὼν δ' ὁ ἐνταῦθα
ῥοῦς, ἅμα καὶ τῶν τόπων εὐφυῶν ὄντων πρὸς τὸ
τὸν ἐκεῖ ῥοῦν τῆς θαλάττης ἐπὶ τὸ Βυζάντιον καὶ
τὸ πρὸς αὐτῷ Κέρας τετράφθαι, φυσικῶς συνε-
λαύνεται δεῦρο καὶ παρέχει τοῖς Βυζαντίοις καὶ
τῷ δήμῳ τῶν Ῥωμαίων πρόσοδον ἀξιόλογον.
Χαλκηδόνιοι δ' ἐπὶ τῆς περαίας ἱδρυμένοι πλησίον
οὐ μετέχουσι τῆς εὐπορίας ταύτης διὰ τὸ μὴ
προσπελάζειν τοῖς λιμέσιν αὐτῶν τὴν πηλαμύδα·
ἦ δὴ καὶ τὸν Ἀπόλλω φασὶ τοῖς κτίσασι τὸ
Βυζάντιον ὕστερον μετὰ τὴν ὑπὸ Μεγαρέων
Χαλκηδόνος κτίσιν χρηστηριαζομένοις προστάξαι
ποιήσασθαι τὴν ἵδρυσιν ἀπεναντίον τῶν τυφλῶν,
τυφλοὺς καλέσαντα τοὺς Χαλκηδονίους, ὅτι πρότερον[2] πλεύσαντες τοὺς τόπους, ἀφέντες τὴν
πέραν κατασχεῖν τοσοῦτον πλοῦτον[3] ἔχουσαν,
εἵλοντο τὴν λυπροτέραν.

[1] προσιοῦσα (ABCl).
[2] πρότερον, Meineke emends to πρότεροι.
[3] πλοῦτον, Casaubon, for πλούτου (no), πλοῦν (ABCl); so
the later editors.

---

[1] Pharnacia (cp. 12. 3. 19).

the mouth of the lake in schools and move along the Asian shore as far as Trapezus and Pharnacia. It is here[1] that the catching of the fish first takes place, though the catch is not considerable, for the fish have not yet grown to their normal size. But when they reach Sinope, they are mature enough for catching and salting. Yet when once they touch the Cyaneae and pass by these, the creatures take such fright at a certain white rock which projects from the Chalcedonian shore that they forthwith turn to the opposite shore. There they are caught by the current, and since at the same time the region is so formed by nature as to turn the current of the sea there to Byzantium and the Horn at Byzantium, they naturally are driven together thither and thus afford the Byzantines and the Roman people considerable revenue. But the Chalcedonians, though situated near by, on the opposite shore, have no share in this abundance, because the *pelamydes* do not approach their harbours; hence the saying that Apollo, when the men who founded Byzantium at a time subsequent to the founding of Chalcedon[2] by the Megarians consulted the oracle, ordered them to "make their settlement opposite the blind," thus calling the Chalcedonians "blind" because, although they sailed the regions in question at an earlier time, they failed to take possession of the country on the far side, with all its wealth, and chose the poorer country.

[2] Byzantium appears to have been founded about 659 B.C. (see Pauly-Wissowa, *s.v.*). According to Herodotus (4. 144), Chalcedon (now Kadi Koi) was founded seventeen years earlier. Both were Megarian colonies.

Μέχρι μὲν δὴ Βυζαντίου προήλθομεν, ἐπειδὴ
πόλις ἐπιφανὴς πλησιάζουσα μάλιστα τῷ στόματι
εἰς γνωριμώτερον πέρας ἀπὸ τοῦ Ἴστρου τὸν
παράπλουν τελευτῶντα ἀπέφαινεν. ὑπέρκειται
δὲ τοῦ Βυζαντίου τὸ τῶν Ἀστῶν ἔθνος, ἐν ᾧ πόλις
Καλύβη, Φιλίππου τοῦ Ἀμύντου τοὺς πονηρο-
τάτους ἐνταῦθα ἱδρύσαντος.

VII

1. Τὰ μὲν οὖν ἀφοριζόμενα ἔθνη τῷ τε Ἴστρῳ καὶ
τοῖς ὄρεσι τοῖς[1] Ἰλλυρικοῖς καὶ Θρᾳκίοις ταῦτ᾽
ἐστίν, ὧν ἄξιον μνησθῆναι, κατέχοντα τὴν Ἀδριατικὴν παραλίαν πᾶσαν, ἀπὸ τοῦ μυχοῦ ἀρξάμενα,[2]
καὶ τὴν τὰ[3] Ἀριστερὰ τοῦ Πόντου λεγομένην
ἀπὸ Ἴστρου ποταμοῦ μέχρι Βυζαντίου. λοιπὰ
δέ ἐστι τὰ νότια μέρη τῆς λεχθείσης ὀρεινῆς καὶ
C 321 ἑξῆς τὰ ὑποπίπτοντα χωρία, ἐν οἷς ἐστιν ἥ τε
Ἑλλὰς καὶ ἡ προσεχὴς βάρβαρος μέχρι τῶν ὁρῶν.
Ἑκαταῖος μὲν οὖν ὁ Μιλήσιος περὶ τῆς Πελοποννήσου φησίν, διότι πρὸ τῶν Ἑλλήνων ᾤκησαν
αὐτὴν βάρβαροι. σχεδὸν δέ τι καὶ ἡ σύμπασα

---

[1] τοῖς, Meineke deletes, transferring ὄρεσι to a position
after Ἰλλυρικοῖς.
[2] ἀρξάμενα (no, C?), for ἀρξαμένων; so most editors.
[3] κατά, before τά, Meineke deletes (see 12. 3. 2).

---

[1] i.e., " Hut," called by Ptolemaeus (3. 11) and others
"Cabyle"; to be identified, apparently, with the modern
Tauschan-tépé, on the Toundja River.
[2] Suidas (s. v. Δούλων πόλις) quotes Theopompus as saying
that Philip founded in Thrace a small city called Poneropolis

I have now carried my description as far as Byzantium, because a famous city, lying as it does very near to the mouth, marked a better-known limit to the coasting-voyage from the Ister. And above Byzantium is situated the tribe of the Astae, in whose territory is a city Calybe,[1] where Philip the son of Amyntas settled the most villainous people of his kingdom.[2]

VII

1. These alone, then, of all the tribes that are marked off by the Ister and by the Illyrian and Thracian mountains, deserve to be mentioned, occupying as they do the whole of the Adriatic seaboard beginning at the recess, and also the sea-board that is called "the left parts of the Pontus," and extends from the Ister River as far as Byzantium. But there remain to be described the southerly parts of the aforesaid[3] mountainous country and next thereafter the districts that are situated below them, among which are both Greece and the adjacent barbarian country as far as the mountains. Now Hecataeus of Miletus says of the Peloponnesus that before the time of the Greeks it was inhabited by barbarians. Yet one might say that in the ancient

("City of Villains"), settling the same with about two thousand men—the false-accusers, false-witnesses, lawyers, and all other bad men : but Poneropolis is not to be identified with Cabyle if the positions assigned to the two places by Ptolemaeus (3. 11) are correct. However, Ptolemaeus does not mention Poneropolis. but Philippopolis, which latter, according to Pliny (4. 18), was the later name of Poneropolis.

[3] See 7. 5. 1.

Ἑλλὰς κατοικία βαρβάρων ὑπῆρξε τὸ παλαιόν,
ἀπ' αὐτῶν λογιζομένοις τῶν μνημονευομένων·
Πέλοπος μὲν ἐκ τῆς Φρυγίας ἐπαγαγομένου[1]
λαοὺς[2] εἰς τὴν ἀπ' αὐτοῦ κληθεῖσαν Πελοπόννησον, Δαναοῦ δὲ ἐξ Αἰγύπτου, Δρυόπων τε
καὶ Καυκώνων καὶ Πελασγῶν καὶ Λελέγων καὶ
ἄλλων τοιούτων κατανειμαμένων τὰ ἐντὸς Ἰσθμοῦ
καὶ τὰ ἐκτὸς δέ· τὴν μὲν γὰρ Ἀττικὴν οἱ μετὰ
Εὐμόλπου Θρᾷκες ἔσχον, τῆς δὲ Φωκίδος τὴν
Δαυλίδα Τηρεύς, τὴν δὲ Καδμείαν οἱ μετὰ
Κάδμου Φοίνικες, αὐτὴν δὲ τὴν Βοιωτίαν Ἄονες
καὶ Τέμμικες καὶ Ὕαντες· ὡς[3] δὲ Πίνδαρός
φησιν,

> ἦν ὅτε σύας[4] Βοιώτιον ἔθνος ἔνεπον.

καὶ ἀπὸ τῶν ὀνομάτων δὲ ἐνίων τὸ βάρβαρον
ἐμφαίνεται, Κέκροψ καὶ Κόδρος καὶ Ἄϊκλος καὶ
Κόθος καὶ Δρύμας καὶ Κρίνακος. οἱ δὲ Θρᾷκες
καὶ Ἰλλυριοὶ καὶ Ἠπειρῶται καὶ μέχρι νῦν ἐν
πλευραῖς εἰσιν· ἔτι μέντοι μᾶλλον πρότερον ἢ
νῦν, ὅπου γε καὶ τῆς ἐν τῷ παρόντι Ἑλλάδος
ἀναντιλέκτως οὔσης τὴν πολλὴν οἱ βάρβαροι
ἔχουσι, Μακεδονίαν μὲν Θρᾷκες καί τινα μέρη
τῆς Θετταλίας, Ἀκαρνανίας δὲ καὶ Αἰτωλίας τὰ

---

[1] ἐπαγαγομένου, Corais, for ἐπαγομένου; so Meineke.
[2] λαούς, Tzschucke, for ἀλέους; so most editors; but
Meineke, λαόν. See λαούς, 7. 7. 2.
[3] ὡς . . . ἔνεπον, Meineke relegates to foot of page.
[4] σοίας (ABC), ὕας (lno), σύας (Epit.).

---

[1] See 8. 3. 31, 4. 4, 5. 5 and 12. 8. 2.

times the whole of Greece was a settlement of
barbarians, if one reasons from the traditions themselves: Pelops[1] brought over peoples[2] from Phrygia
to the Peloponnesus that received its name from
him; and Danaüs[3] from Egypt; whereas the
Dryopes, the Caucones, the Pelasgi, the Leleges,
and other such peoples, apportioned among themselves the parts that are inside the isthmus—and
also the parts outside, for Attica was once held by
the Thracians who came with Eumolpus,[4] Daulis in
Phocis by Tereus,[5] Cadmeia[6] by the Phoenicians
who came with Cadmus, and Boeotia itself by the
Aones and Temmices and Hyantes. According to
Pindar,[7] there was a time when the Boeotian tribe
was called "Syes."[8] Moreover, the barbarian origin
of some is indicated by their names—Cecrops, Codrus,
Aïclus, Cothus, Drymas, and Crinacus. And even to
the present day the Thracians, Illyrians, and
Epeirotes live on the flanks of the Greeks (though
this was still more the case formerly than now);
indeed most of the country that at the present time
is indisputably Greece is held by the barbarians—
Macedonia and certain parts of Thessaly by the
Thracians, and the parts above Acarnania and

[2] See the quotation from Hesiod (§ 2 following) and footnote on "peoples."
[3] See 8. 6. 9, 10.
[4] Son of Poseidon, king of the Thracians, and reputed
founder of the Eleusinian Mysteries.
[5] See 9. 3. 13.
[6] Thebes and surrounding territory (9. 2. 3, 32).
[7] A dithyrambic fragment (Bergk, *Frags.* Dith. 83); cp.
Pindar, *Olymp.* 6. 152.
[8] Strabo identifies "Hyantes" with "Syes"="Hyes,"
i.e. "swine."

ἄνω Θεσπρωτοὶ καὶ Κασσωπαῖοι[1] καὶ Ἀμφίλοχοι
καὶ Μολοττοὶ καὶ Ἀθαμᾶνες, Ἠπειρωτικὰ ἔθνη.

2. Περὶ μὲν οὖν Πελασγῶν εἴρηται, τοὺς δὲ
Λέλεγάς τινες μὲν τοὺς αὐτοὺς Καρσὶν εἰκάζουσιν,
οἱ δὲ συνοίκους μόνον καὶ συστρατιώτας· διόπερ
ἐν τῇ Μιλησίᾳ Λελέγων κατοικίας λέγεσθαί τινας,
πολλαχοῦ δὲ τῆς Καρίας τάφους Λελέγων καὶ
ἐρύματα ἔρημα, Λελέγια καλούμενα. ἥ τε Ἰωνία
νῦν λεγομένη πᾶσα ὑπὸ Καρῶν ᾠκεῖτο καὶ
Λελέγων· ἐκβαλόντες δὲ τούτους οἱ Ἴωνες αὐτοὶ
τὴν χώραν κατέσχον, ἔτι δὲ πρότερον οἱ τὴν
Τροίαν ἑλόντες ἐξήλασαν τοὺς Λέλεγας ἐκ τῶν
περὶ τὴν Ἴδην τόπων τῶν κατὰ Πήδασον καὶ
τὸν Σατνιόεντα ποταμόν. ὅτι μὲν οὖν βάρβαροι
ἦσαν οὗτοι, καὶ αὐτὸ τὸ κοινωνῆσαι τοῖς Καρσὶ
νομίζοιτ’ ἂν σημεῖον· ὅτι δὲ πλάνητες καὶ μετ’
ἐκείνων καὶ χωρὶς καὶ ἐκ παλαιοῦ, καὶ αἱ
Ἀριστοτέλους πολιτεῖαι δηλοῦσιν. ἐν μὲν γὰρ
τῇ Ἀκαρνάνων φησὶ τὸ μὲν ἔχειν αὐτῆς Κουρῆτας,
τὸ δὲ προσεσπέριον Λέλεγας, εἶτα Τηλεβόας· ἐν
C 322 δὲ τῇ Αἰτωλῶν τοὺς νῦν Λοκροὺς Λέλεγας καλεῖ,
κατασχεῖν δὲ καὶ τὴν Βοιωτίαν αὐτούς φησιν·
ὁμοίως δὲ καὶ ἐν τῇ Ὀπουντίων καὶ Μεγαρέων·
ἐν δὲ τῇ Λευκαδίων καὶ αὐτόχθονά τινα Λέλεγα
ὀνομάζει, τούτου δὲ θυγατριδοῦν Τηλεβόαν, τοῦ
δὲ παῖδας δύο καὶ εἴκοσι Τηλεβόας, ὧν τινας

---

[1] Κασσωπαῖοι, Xylander, for Ἀσσωπαῖαι ; so the later
editors.

---

[1] 5. 2. 4.
[2] Only fragments of this work are now extant (see Didot
Edition, Vol. IV, pp. 219–296).

Aetolia by the Thesproti, the Cassopaei, the Amphilochi, the Molossi, and the Athamanes—Epeirotic tribes.

2. As for the Pelasgi, I have already discussed them.[1] As for the Leleges, some conjecture that they are the same as the Carians, and others that they were only fellow-inhabitants and fellow-soldiers of these; and this, they say, is why, in the territory of Miletus, certain settlements are called settlements of the Leleges, and why, in many places in Caria, tombs of the Leleges and deserted forts, known as "Lelegian forts," are so called. However, the whole of what is now called Ionia used to be inhabited by Carians and Leleges; but the Ionians themselves expelled them and took possession of the country, although in still earlier times the captors of Troy had driven the Leleges from the region about Ida that is near Pedasus and the Satnioïs River. So then, the very fact that the Leleges made common cause with the Carians might be considered a sign that they were barbarians. And Aristotle, in his *Polities*,[2] also clearly indicates that they led a wandering life, not only with the Carians, but also apart from them, and from earliest times; for instance, in the *Polity of the Acarnanians* he says that the Curetes held a part of the country, whereas the Leleges, and then the Teleboae, held the westerly part; and in the *Polity of the Aetolians* (and likewise in that of the Opuntii and the Megarians) he calls the Locri of to-day Leleges and says that they took possession of Boeotia too; again, in the *Polity of the Leucadians* he names a certain indigenous Lelex, and also Teleboas, the son of a daughter of Lelex, and twenty-two sons of Teleboas, some of

289

οἰκῆσαι τὴν Λευκάδα. μάλιστα δ᾽ ἄν τις Ἡσιόδῳ πιστεύσειεν οὕτως περὶ αὐτῶν εἰπόντι·

ἤτοι γὰρ Λοκρὸς Λελέγων ἡγήσατο λαῶν,
τοὺς ῥά ποτε Κρονίδης Ζεύς, ἄφθιτα μήδεα
εἰδώς,
λεκτοὺς ἐκ γαίης λαοὺς[1] πόρε Δευκαλίωνι·

τῇ γὰρ ἐτυμολογίᾳ τὸ συλλέκτους γεγονέναι τινὰς ἐκ παλαιοῦ καὶ μιγάδας αἰνίττεσθαί μοι δοκεῖ, καὶ διὰ τοῦτο[2] ἐκλελοιπέναι τὸ γένος· ἅπερ ἄν τις καὶ περὶ Καυκώνων λέγοι, νῦν οὐδαμοῦ ὄντων, πρότερον δ᾽ ἐν πλείοσι τόποις κατῳκισμένων.

3. Πρότερον μὲν οὖν, καίπερ μικρῶν καὶ πολλῶν καὶ ἀδόξων ὄντων τῶν ἐθνῶν, ὅμως διὰ τὴν εὐανδρίαν καὶ τὸ βασιλεύεσθαι κατὰ σφᾶς οὐ πάνυ ἦν χαλεπὸν διαλαβεῖν τοὺς ὅρους αὐτῶν, νυνὶ δ᾽ ἐρήμου τῆς πλείστης χώρας γεγενημένης καὶ τῶν κατοικιῶν, καὶ μάλιστα τῶν πόλεων, ἠφανισμένων, οὐδ᾽ εἰ δύναιτό τις ἀκριβοῦν ταῦτα, οὐδὲν ἂν ποιοίη χρήσιμον διὰ τὴν ἀδοξίαν καὶ τὸν ἀφανισμὸν αὐτῶν, ὃς ἐκ πολλοῦ χρόνου λαβὼν τὴν ἀρχὴν οὐδὲ νῦν πω πέπαυται κατὰ πολλὰ μέρη διὰ τὰς ἀποστάσεις· ἀλλ᾽ ἐνστρατοπεδεύουσιν αὐτοῖς Ῥωμαῖοι τοῖς οἴκοις, κατασταθέντες

---

[1] λαούς, Tzschucke, for ἀλέους (cp. λαούς, 7. 7. 1); so Groskurd, Forbiger, Meineke, and *Etym. Magn.* But Corais, ἀλέας.

[2] τοῦτο, Pletho, for τό; so the later editors.

---

[1] Now Santa Maura (cp. 10. 2. 2).

[2] In the Greek word for " peoples" (λαούς) Hesiod alludes to the Greek word for "stones" (λᾶας). Pindar (*Olymp.* 9. 46 ff.) clearly derives the former word from the latter:

whom, he says, dwelt in Leucas.[1]   But in particular
one might believe Hesiod when he says concerning
them :   " For verily Locrus was chieftain of the
peoples of the Leleges, whom once Zeus the son
of Cronus, who knoweth devices imperishable, gave
to Deucalion—peoples [2] picked out of earth " ; [3] for
by his etymology [4] he seems to me to hint that from
earliest times they were a collection of mixed
peoples and that this was why the tribe disappeared.
And the same might be said of the Caucones, since
now they are nowhere to be found, although in earlier
times they were settled in several places.

3. Now although in earlier times the tribes in
question were small, numerous, and obscure, still,
because of the density of their population and
because they lived each under its own king, it
was not at all difficult to determine their boundaries ; but now that most of the country has
become depopulated and the settlements, particularly the cities, have disappeared from sight, it
would do no good, even if one could determine
their boundaries with strict accuracy, to do so,
because of their obscurity and their disappearance.
This process of disappearing began a long time ago,
and has not yet entirely ceased in many regions
because the people keep revolting ; indeed, the
Romans, after being set up as masters by the inhabi-

" Pyrrha and Deucalion, without bed of marriage, founded
a Stone Race, who were called Laoi."   One might now infer
that the resemblance of the two words gave rise to the myth
of the stones.

[3] A fragment otherwise unknown (Paulson, *Frag.* 141. 3).

[4] That is, of " Leleges."   In the Greek the root *leg* appears
in (1) " Leleges," (2) " picked," and (3) " collection."

STRABO

ὑπ' αὐτῶν δυνάσται. τῶν δ' οὖν[1] Ἠπειρωτῶν
ἑβδομήκοντα πόλεις Πολύβιός φησιν ἀνατρέψαι
Παῦλον μετὰ τὴν Μακεδόνων καὶ Περσέως κατάλυσιν (Μολοττῶν δ' ὑπάρξαι τὰς πλείστας), πέντε
δὲ καὶ δέκα μυριάδας ἀνθρώπων ἐξανδραποδί-
σασθαι. ὅμως δ' οὖν ἐγχειρήσομεν, ἐφ' ὅσον τῇ
γραφῇ τε προσήκει καὶ ἡμῖν ἐφικτόν, ἐπελθεῖν τὰ
καθ' ἕκαστα, ἀρξάμενοι ἀπὸ τῆς κατὰ τὸν Ἰόνιον
κόλπον παραλίας· αὕτη δ' ἐστίν, εἰς ἣν ὁ ἔκπλους
ὁ ἐκ τοῦ Ἀδρίου τελευτᾷ.

4. Ταύτης δὴ τὰ πρῶτα μέρη τὰ περὶ Ἐπίδαμνον καὶ Ἀπολλωνίαν ἐστίν. ἐκ δὲ τῆς
Ἀπολλωνίας εἰς Μακεδονίαν ἡ Ἐγνατία ἐστὶν
ὁδὸς πρὸς ἔω, βεβηματισμένη κατὰ μίλιον καὶ
κατεστηλωμένη μέχρι Κυψέλων καὶ Ἕβρου
ποταμοῦ· μιλίων δ' ἐστὶ πεντακοσίων τριάκοντα
πέντε· λογιζομένῳ δέ, ὡς μὲν οἱ πολλοί, τὸ μίλιον
ὀκτωστάδιον τετρακισχίλιοι ἂν εἶεν στάδιοι καὶ
ἐπ' αὐτοῖς διακόσιοι ὀγδοήκοντα, ὡς δὲ Πολύβιος,
προστιθεὶς τῷ ὀκτασταδίῳ δίπλεθρον, ὅ ἐστι
τρίτον σταδίου, προσθετέον ἄλλους σταδίους
ἑκατὸν ἑβδομήκοντα ὀκτώ, τὸ τρίτον τοῦ τῶν
μιλίων ἀριθμοῦ. συμβαίνει δ' ἀπὸ ἴσου διαστήματος συμπίπτειν εἰς τὴν αὐτὴν ὁδὸν τούς τ' ἐκ
τῆς Ἀπολλωνίας ὁρμηθέντας καὶ τοὺς ἐξ Ἐπι-
δάμνου. ἡ μὲν οὖν πᾶσα Ἐγνατία καλεῖται,
ἡ δὲ πρώτη ἐπὶ Κανδαουίας λέγεται, ὄρους
Ἰλλυρικοῦ, διὰ Λυχνιδοῦ[2] πόλεως καὶ Πυλῶνος,

C 323

[1] δ' οὖν, Meineke emends to γοῦν.
[2] Λυχνιδοῦ, Tzschucke, for Λυχνιδίου; so the later editors.

[1] Now standing empty.   [2] Book XXX, Frag. 16.
[3] Aemilius Paulus Macedonicus (consul 182 and 168 B.C.)
in 168 B.C.

tants, encamp in their very houses.[1] Be this as it
may, Polybius [2] says that Paulus,[3] after his subjection
of Perseus and the Macedonians, destroyed seventy
cities of the Epeirotes (most of which, he adds,
belonged to the Molossi),[4] and reduced to slavery
one hundred and fifty thousand people. Nevertheless, I shall attempt, in so far as it is appropriate to
my description and as my knowledge reaches, to
traverse the several different parts, beginning at the
seaboard of the Ionian Gulf—that is, where the
voyage out of the Adrias ends.

4. Of this seaboard, then, the first parts are those
about Epidamnus and Apollonia. From Apollonia
to Macedonia one travels the Egnatian Road, towards
the east; it has been measured by Roman miles and
marked by pillars as far as Cypsela [5] and the Hebrus [6]
River—a distance of five hundred and thirty-five
miles. Now if one reckons as most people do, eight
stadia to the mile, there would be four thousand
two hundred and eighty stadia, whereas if one
reckons as Polybius does, who adds two plethra,
which is a third of a stadium, to the eight stadia,
one must add one hundred and seventy-eight stadia
—the third of the number of miles. And it so
happens that travellers setting out from Apollonia
and Epidamnus meet at an equal distance from the
two places on the same road.[7] Now although the
road as a whole is called the Egnatian Road, the
first part of it is called the Road to Candavia (an
Illyrian mountain) and passes through Lychnidus,[8]
a city, and Pylon, a place on the road which marks

[4] See 7. 7. 8.   [5] Now Ipsala.   [6] Now the Maritza.
[7] Or, as we should say, the junction of the roads is equidistant from the two places.
[8] Now Ochrida.

τόπου ὁρίζοντος ἐν τῇ ὁδῷ τήν τε Ἰλλυρίδα καὶ
τὴν Μακεδονίαν· ἐκεῖθεν δ᾽ ἐστὶ παρὰ Βαρνοῦντα
διὰ Ἡρακλείας καὶ Λυγκηστῶν καὶ Ἐορδῶν εἰς
Ἔδεσσαν καὶ Πέλλαν μέχρι Θεσσαλονικείας·
μίλια δ᾽ ἐστί, φησὶ Πολύβιος, ταῦτα διακόσια
ἑξήκοντα ἑπτά. ταύτην δὴ τὴν ὁδὸν ἐκ τῶν περὶ
τὴν Ἐπίδαμνον καὶ τὴν Ἀπολλωνίαν τόπων ἰοῦσιν
ἐν δεξιᾷ μέν ἐστι τὰ Ἠπειρωτικὰ ἔθνη, κλυζόμενα
τῷ Σικελικῷ πελάγει, μέχρι τοῦ Ἀμβρακικοῦ
κόλπου, ἐν ἀριστερᾷ δὲ τὰ ὄρη τὰ τῶν Ἰλλυριῶν,
ἃ προδιήλθομεν, καὶ τὰ ἔθνη τὰ παροικοῦντα
μέχρι Μακεδονίας καὶ Παιόνων. εἶτ᾽ ἀπὸ μὲν
Ἀμβρακικοῦ κόλπου τὰ νεύοντα ἐφεξῆς πρὸς ἔω,
τὰ ἀντιπαρήκοντα τῇ Πελοποννήσῳ, τῆς Ἑλλάδος
ἐστίν· εἶτ᾽ ἐκπίπτει εἰς τὸ Αἰγαῖον πέλαγος,[1] ἀπο-
λιπόντα ἐν δεξιᾷ τὴν Πελοπόννησον ὅλην. ἀπὸ
δὲ τῆς ἀρχῆς τῶν Μακεδονικῶν ὀρῶν[2] καὶ τῶν
Παιονικῶν μέχρι Στρυμόνος ποταμοῦ Μακεδόνες
τε οἰκοῦσι καὶ Παίονες καί τινες τῶν ὀρεινῶν
Θρᾳκῶν· τὰ δὲ πέραν Στρυμόνος ἤδη μέχρι τοῦ
Ποντικοῦ στόματος καὶ τοῦ Αἵμου πάντα Θρᾳκῶν
ἐστι πλὴν τῆς παραλίας. αὕτη δ᾽ ὑφ᾽ Ἑλλήνων
οἰκεῖται, τῶν μὲν ἐπὶ τῇ Προποντίδι ἱδρυμένων,
τῶν δὲ ἐφ᾽ Ἑλλησπόντῳ καὶ τῷ Μέλανι κόλπῳ,
τῶν δ᾽ ἐπὶ τῷ Αἰγαίῳ. τὸ δ᾽ Αἰγαῖον πέλαγος

---

[1] εἰς τὸ Αἰγαῖον πέλαγος, Pletho, for τοῦ Αἰγαίου πελάγους;
so the later editors.
[2] ὀρῶν, Kramer, for ἐθνῶν; so the later editors.

---

[1] Now the Neretschka Planina Mountain.
[2] Heracleia Lyncestis ; now Monastir.
[3] Now Vodena.

the boundary between the Illyrian country and
Macedonia. From Pylon the road runs to Barnus [1]
through Heracleia [2] and the country of the Lyncestae
and that of the Eordi into Edessa [3] and Pella [4] and
as far as Thessaloniceia; [5] and the length of this
road in miles, according to Polybius, is two hundred
and sixty-seven. So then, in travelling this road
from the region of Epidamnus and Apollonia, one
has on the right the Epeirotic tribes whose coasts
are washed by the Sicilian Sea and extend as far as
the Ambracian Gulf,[6] and, on the left, the mountains
of Illyria, which I have already described in detail,
and those tribes which live along them and extend
as far as Macedonia and the country of the Paeonians.
Then, beginning at the Ambracian Gulf, all the
districts which, one after another, incline towards
the east and stretch parallel to the Peloponnesus
belong to Greece; they then leave the whole of the
Peloponnesus on the right and project into the
Aegaean Sea. But the districts which extend from
the beginning of the Macedonian and the Paeonian
mountains as far as the Strymon [7] River are inhabited
by the Macedonians, the Paeonians, and by some of
the Thracian mountaineers; whereas the districts
beyond the Strymon, extending as far as the mouth
of the Pontus and the Haemus, all belong to the
Thracians, except the seaboard. This seaboard is
inhabited by Greeks, some being situated on the
Propontis,[8] others on the Hellespont and the Gulf
of Melas,[9] and others on the Aegaean. The Aegaean

---

[4] The capital of Macedonia; now in ruins and called Hagii
Apostoli.   [5] Now Thessaloniki or Saloniki.
[6] The Gulf of Arta.   [7] Now the Struma.
[8] Now the Sea of Marmara.   [9] Now the Gulf of Saros.

δύο κλύζει πλευρὰς τῆς Ἑλλάδος, τὴν μὲν πρὸς
ἕω βλέπουσαν, τείνουσαν δὲ ἀπὸ Σουνίου πρὸς
τὴν ἄρκτον μέχρι τοῦ Θερμαίου κόλπου καὶ
Θεσσαλονικείας, Μακεδονικῆς πόλεως, ἣ νῦν
μάλιστα τῶν ἄλλων εὐανδρεῖ, τὴν δὲ πρὸς νότον
τὴν Μακεδονικὴν ἀπὸ Θεσσαλονικείας μέχρι
Στρυμόνος· τινὲς δὲ καὶ τὴν ἀπὸ Στρυμόνος
μέχρι Νέστου τῇ Μακεδονίᾳ προσνέμουσιν, ἐπειδὴ
Φίλιππος ἐσπούδασε διαφερόντως περὶ ταῦτα τὰ
χωρία, ὥστ᾽ ἐξιδιώσασθαι, καὶ συνεστήσατο προσ-
όδους μεγίστας ἐκ τῶν μετάλλων καὶ τῆς ἄλλης
εὐφυΐας τῶν τόπων. ἀπὸ δὲ Σουνίου μέχρι Πελοποννήσου τὸ Μυρτῷόν ἐστι καὶ Κρητικὸν πέλαγος
καὶ Λιβυκὸν σὺν τοῖς κόλποις μέχρι τοῦ Σικελικοῦ·
τοῦτο δὲ καὶ τὸν Ἀμβρακικὸν καὶ Κορινθιακὸν
καὶ Κρισαῖον ἐκπληροῖ κόλπον.

5. Τῶν μὲν οὖν Ἠπειρωτῶν ἔθνη φησὶν εἶναι
Θεόπομπος τετταρεσκαίδεκα, τούτων δ᾽ ἐνδοξό-
τατα Χάονες καὶ Μολοττοὶ διὰ τὸ ἄρξαι ποτὲ
πάσης τῆς Ἠπειρώτιδος, πρότερον μὲν Χάονας,
C 324 ὕστερον δὲ Μολοττούς, οἳ καὶ διὰ τὴν συγγένειαν
τῶν βασιλέων ἐπὶ πλέον ηὐξήθησαν, τῶν γὰρ
Αἰακιδῶν ἦσαν, καὶ διὰ τὸ παρὰ τούτοις εἶναι τὸ
ἐν Δωδώνῃ μαντεῖον, παλαιόν τε καὶ ὀνομαστὸν
ὄν. Χάονες μὲν οὖν καὶ Θεσπρωτοὶ καὶ μετὰ
τούτους ἐφεξῆς Κασσωπαῖοι (καὶ οὗτοι δ᾽ εἰσὶ
Θεσπρωτοί) τὴν ἀπὸ τῶν Κεραυνίων ὀρῶν μέχρι

---

[1] Now Cape Colonna.   [2] Now the Gulf of Saloniki.
[3] Now the Mesta.   [4] See footnote on 6. 1. 7
[5] Aeacus was son of Zeus and Aegina, was king of the Isle
of Aegina, was noted for his justice and piety, and was finally
made one of the three judges in Hades.

Sea washes Greece on two sides : first, the side that faces towards the east and stretches from Sunium,[1] towards the north as far as the Thermaean Gulf[2] and Thessaloniceia, a Macedonian city, which at the present time is more populous than any of the rest ; and secondly, the side that faces towards the south, I mean the Macedonian country, extending from Thessaloniceia as far as the Strymon. Some, however, also assign to Macedonia the country that extends from the Strymon as far as the Nestus River,[3] since Philip was so specially interested in these districts that he appropriated them to himself, and since he organized very large revenues from the mines and the other natural resources of the country. But from Sunium to the Peloponnesus lie the Myrtoan, the Cretan, and the Libyan Seas, together with their gulfs, as far as the Sicilian Sea ; and this last fills out the Ambracian, the Corinthian, and the Crisaean[4] Gulfs.

5. Now as for the Epeirotes, there are fourteen tribes of them, according to Theopompus, but of these the Chaones and the Molossi are the most famous, because of the fact that they once ruled over the whole of the Epeirote country—the Chaones earlier and later the Molossi ; and the Molossi grew to still greater power, partly because of the kinship of their kings, who belonged to the family of the Aeacidae,[5] and partly because of the fact that the oracle at Dodona[6] was in their country, an oracle both ancient and renowned. Now the Chaones and the Thesproti and, next in order after these, the Cassopaei (these, too, are Thesproti) inhabit the

---

[6] Dodona was situated to the south of Lake Pambotis (now Janina), near what is now Dramisi.

τοῦ Ἀμβρακικοῦ κόλπου παραλίαν νέμονται,
χώραν εὐδαίμονα ἔχοντες· ὁ δὲ πλοῦς ἀπὸ τῶν
Χαόνων ἀρξαμένῳ πρὸς ἀνίσχοντα ἥλιον καὶ
πρὸς τὸν Ἀμβρακικὸν κόλπον καὶ τὸν Κορινθια-
κόν, ἐν δεξιᾷ ἔχοντι τὸ Αὐσόνιον πέλαγος, ἐν
ἀριστερᾷ δὲ τὴν Ἤπειρον, εἰσὶ χίλιοι καὶ τριακόσιοι στάδιοι ἀπὸ τῶν Κεραυνίων ἐπὶ τὸ στόμα
τοῦ Ἀμβρακικοῦ κόλπου. ἐν τούτῳ δ' ἐστὶ τῷ
διαστήματι Πάνορμός¹ τε λιμὴν μέγας, ἐν μέσοις
τοῖς Κεραυνίοις ὄρεσι, καὶ μετὰ ταῦτα Ὄγχησμος,²
λιμὴν ἄλλος, καθ' ὃν τὰ δυσμικὰ ἄκρα τῆς
Κορκυραίας ἀντίκειται, καὶ πάλιν ἄλλος, Κασ-
σιόπη,⁵ ἀφ' οὗ ἐπὶ Βρεντέσιον χίλιοι ἑπτακόσιοι
στάδιοι· οἱ δ' ἴσοι καὶ ἐπὶ Τάραντα ἀπὸ ἄλλου
ἀκρωτηρίου νοτιωτέρου τῆς Κασσιόπης, ὃ καλοῦσι
Φαλακρόν. μετὰ δὲ Ὄγχησμον Ποσείδιον καὶ
Βουθρωτὸν ἐπὶ τῷ στόματι τοῦ Πηλώδους καλουμένου λιμένος, ἱδρυμένον ἐν τόπῳ χερρονησίζοντι,
ἐποίκους ἔχον Ῥωμαίους, καὶ τὰ Σύβοτα. εἰσὶ
δὲ νησῖδες τὰ Σύβοτα, τῆς μὲν Ἠπείρου μικρὸν
ἀπέχουσαι, κατὰ δὲ τὸ ἑῷον ἄκρον τῆς Κορκυραίας τὴν Λευκίμμαν κείμεναι. καὶ ἄλλαι δ' ἐν τῷ
παράπλῳ νησῖδες εἰσὶν οὐκ ἄξιαι μνήμης. ἔπειτα
ἄκρα Χειμέριον καὶ Γλυκὺς Λιμήν, εἰς ὃν ἐμβάλλει

---

¹ See 2. 5. 20, 2. 5. 29, 5. 3. 6.   ² Now Panormo.
³ Now Santi Quaranta.   ⁴ Now Kerkyra or Corfu.
⁵ "Cassope" is probably the correct spelling ; now Cassopo,
the name of a harbour and cape of Corfu.

seaboard which extends from the Ceraunian Mountains as far as the Ambracian Gulf, and they have a
fertile country. The voyage, if one begins at the
country of the Chaones and sails towards the rising
sun and towards the Ambracian and Corinthian
Gulfs, keeping the Ausonian Sea [1] on the right and
Epeirus on the left, is one thousand three hundred
stadia, that is, from the Ceraunian Mountains to the
mouth of the Ambracian Gulf. In this interval is
Panormus,[2] a large harbour at the centre of the
Ceraunian Mountains, and after these mountains one
comes to Onchesmus,[3] another harbour, opposite
which lie the western extremities of Corcyraea,[4] and
then still another harbour, Cassiope,[5] from which
the distance to Brentesium is one thousand seven
hundred stadia. And the distance to Taras from
another cape, which is farther south than Cassiope
and is called Phalacrum,[6] is the same. After Onchesmus comes Poseidium,[7] and also Buthrotum [8]
(which is at the mouth of what is called Pelodes
Harbour, is situated on a place that forms a
peninsula, and has alien settlers consisting of
Romans), and the Sybota.[9] The Sybota are small
islands situated only a short distance from the
mainland and opposite Leucimma, the eastern headland of Corcyraea. And there are still other small
islands as one sails along this coast, but they are not
worth mentioning. Then comes Cape Cheimerium,
and also Glycys Limen,[10] into which the River

[6] Now Cape Drasti, at the southern extremity of Corfu.
[7] In Thesprotia (see Ptolemaeus, 3. 13. 3); now Cape
Scala.
[8] Now Butrinto.   [9] Now called the Syvota.
[10] "Sweet Harbour"; now Port Splantza (Phanari).

STRABO

ὁ Ἀχέρων ποταμός, ῥέων ἐκ τῆς Ἀχερουσίας
λίμνης καὶ δεχόμενος πλείους ποταμούς, ὥστε καὶ
γλυκαίνειν τὸν κόλπον· ῥεῖ δὲ καὶ ὁ Θύαμις
πλησίον. ὑπέρκειται δὲ τούτου μὲν τοῦ κόλπου
Κίχυρος, ἡ πρότερον Ἔφυρα, πόλις Θεσπρωτῶν·
τοῦ δὲ κατὰ Βουθρωτὸν ἡ Φοινίκη. ἐγγὺς δὲ τῆς
Κιχύρου πολίχνιον Βουχέτιον¹ Κασσωπαίων,
μικρὸν ὑπὲρ τῆς θαλάττης ὄν, καὶ Ἐλάτρια καὶ
Πανδοσία καὶ Βατίαι ἐν μεσογαίᾳ· καθήκει δ᾽
αὐτῶν ἡ χώρα μέχρι τοῦ κόλπου. μετὰ δὲ Γλυ-
κὺν Λιμένα ἐφεξῆς εἰσι δύο ἄλλοι λιμένες, ὁ μὲν
ἐγγυτέρω καὶ ἐλάττων Κόμαρος, ἰσθμὸν ποιῶν
ἑξήκοντα σταδίων πρὸς τὸν Ἀμβρακικὸν κόλπον
καὶ τὸ τοῦ Σεβαστοῦ Καίσαρος κτίσμα, τὴν
Νικόπολιν· ὁ δὲ ἀπωτέρω καὶ μείζων καὶ ἀμείνων
πλησίον τοῦ στόματος τοῦ κόλπου, διέχων τῆς
Νικοπόλεως ὅσον δώδεκα σταδίους.

6. Ἐφεξῆς δὲ τὸ στόμα τοῦ Ἀμβρακικοῦ
C 325 κόλπου· τούτου δὲ τοῦ κόλπου τὸ μὲν στόμα
μικρῷ τοῦ τετρασταδίου μεῖζον, ὁ δὲ κύκλος καὶ
τριακοσίων σταδίων, εὐλίμενος δὲ πᾶς. οἰκοῦσι
δὲ τὰ μὲν ἐν δεξιᾷ εἰσπλέουσι τῶν Ἑλλήνων
Ἀκαρνᾶνες, καὶ ἱερὸν τοῦ Ἀκτίου Ἀπόλλωνος
ἐνταῦθά ἐστι πλησίον τοῦ στόματος, λόφος τις,
ἐφ᾽ ᾧ ὁ νεώς, καὶ ὑπ᾽ αὐτῷ πεδίον ἄλσος ἔχον καὶ
νεώρια, ἐν οἷς ἀνέθηκε Καῖσαρ τὴν δεκαναΐαν

¹ Βουχέτιον, Groskurd, for Βουχαίτιον; so the later
editors.

¹ Now the Phanariotikos.   ² Now Lago di Fusaro.
³ Now the Kalamas.

300

Acheron[1] empties. The Acheron flows from the Acherusian Lake[2] and receives several rivers as tributaries, so that it sweetens the waters of the gulf. And also the Thyamis[3] flows near by. Cichyrus,[4] the Ephyra of former times, a city of the Thesprotians, lies above this gulf, whereas Phoenice[5] lies above that gulf which is at Buthrotum. Near Cichyrus is Buchetium, a small town of the Cassopaeans, which is only a short distance above the sea; also Elatria, Pandosia, and Batiae, which are in the interior, though their territory reaches down as far as the gulf. Next in order after Glycys Limen come two other harbours—Comarus,[6] the nearer and smaller of the two, which forms an isthmus of sixty stadia[7] with the Ambracian Gulf, and Nicopolis, a city founded by Augustus Caesar, and the other, the more distant and larger and better of the two, which is near the mouth of the gulf and is about twelve stadia distant from Nicopolis.[8]

6. Next comes the mouth of the Ambracian Gulf. Although the mouth of this gulf is but slightly more than four stadia wide, the circumference is as much as three hundred stadia; and it has good harbours everywhere. That part of the country which is on the right as one sails in is inhabited by the Greek Acarnanians. Here too, near the mouth, is the sacred precinct of the Actian Apollo—a hill on which the temple stands; and at the foot of the hill is a plain which contains a sacred grove and a naval station, the naval station where Caesar

---

[4] The exact side of Cichyrus is uncertain (see Pauly-Wissowa, *s.v.* " Ephyre ").
[5] Now Phiniki.   [6] Now Gomaro.
[7] In width.   [8] Now in ruins near Prevesa.

ἀκροθίνιον, ἀπὸ μονοκρότου μέχρι δεκήρους· ὑπὸ
πυρὸς δ' ἠφανίσθαι καὶ οἱ νεώσοικοι λέγονται καὶ
τὰ πλοῖα· ἐν ἀριστερᾷ δὲ ἡ Νικόπολις καὶ τῶν
Ἠπειρωτῶν οἱ Κασσωπαῖοι μέχρι τοῦ μυχοῦ τοῦ
κατὰ Ἀμβρακίαν· ὑπέρκειται δὲ αὕτη τοῦ μυχοῦ
μικρόν, Γόργου τοῦ Κυψέλου κτίσμα· παραρρεῖ
δ' αὐτὴν ὁ Ἄρατθος [1] ποταμός, ἀνάπλουν ἔχων ἐκ
θαλάττης εἰς αὐτὴν ὀλίγων σταδίων, ἀρχόμενος
ἐκ Τύμφης [2] ὄρους καὶ τῆς Παρωραίας. ηὐτύχει
μὲν οὖν καὶ πρότερον ἡ πόλις αὕτη διαφερόντως
(τὴν γοῦν ἐπωνυμίαν ἐντεῦθεν ἔσχηκεν ὁ κόλπος),
μάλιστα δ' ἐκόσμησεν αὐτὴν Πύρρος, βασιλείῳ
χρησάμενος τῷ τόπῳ· Μακεδόνες δ' ὕστερον καὶ
Ῥωμαῖοι καὶ ταύτην καὶ τὰς ἄλλας κατεπόνησαν
τοῖς συνεχέσι πολέμοις διὰ τὴν ἀπείθειαν, ὥστε
τὸ τελευταῖον ὁ Σεβαστὸς ὁρῶν ἐκλελειμμένας
τελέως τὰς πόλεις εἰς μίαν συνῴκισε τὴν ὑπ'
αὐτοῦ κληθεῖσαν Νικόπολιν ἐν τῷ κόλπῳ τούτῳ,
ἐκάλεσε δ' ἐπώνυμον τῆς νίκης, ἐν ᾗ κατε-
ναυμάχησεν Ἀντώνιον πρὸ τοῦ στόματος τοῦ
κόλπου καὶ τὴν Αἰγυπτίων βασίλισσαν Κλεο-
πάτραν, παροῦσαν ἐν τῷ ἀγῶνι καὶ αὐτήν. ἡ
μὲν οὖν Νικόπολις εὐανδρεῖ καὶ λαμβάνει καθ'
ἡμέραν ἐπίδοσιν, χώραν τε ἔχουσα πολλὴν καὶ
τὸν ἐκ τῶν λαφύρων κόσμον, τό τε κατασκευασθὲν
τέμενος ἐν τῷ προαστείῳ τὸ μὲν εἰς τὸν ἀγῶνα τὸν

---

[1] Ἄραχθος (C), the spelling in other writers; perhaps
rightly.
[2] Τύμφης, Corais, for Ξτύμφης; so the later editors.

---

[1] In the Battle of Actium, 31 B.C.
[2] Now Arta.

dedicated as first fruits of his victory [1] the squadron of ten ships—from vessel with single bank of oars to vessel with ten ; however, not only the boats, it is said, but also the boat-houses have been wiped out by fire. On the left of the mouth are Nicopolis and the country of the Epeirote Cassopaeans, which extends as far as the recess of the gulf near Ambracia.[2] Ambracia lies only a short distance above the recess ; it was founded by Gorgus, the son of Cypselus. The River Aratthus [3] flows past Ambracia; it is navigable inland for only a few stadia, from the sea to Ambracia, although it rises in Mount Tymphe and the Paroraea. Now this city enjoyed an exceptional prosperity in earlier times (at any rate the gulf was named after it), and it was adorned most of all by Pyrrhus, who made the place his royal residence. In later times, however, the Macedonians and the Romans, by their continuous wars, so completely reduced both this and the other Epeirote cities because of their disobedience that finally Augustus, seeing that the cities had utterly failed, settled what inhabitants were left in one city together—the city on this gulf which was called by him Nicopolis ; [4] and he so named it after the victory which he won in the naval battle before the mouth of the gulf over Antonius and Cleopatra the queen of the Egyptians, who was also present at the fight. Nicopolis is populous, and its numbers are increasing daily, since it has not only a considerable territory and the adornment taken from the spoils of the battle, but also, in its suburbs, the thoroughly equipped sacred precinct—one part of it being in

[3] Otherwise called Arachthus ; now the Arta.
[4] "Victory-city."

STRABO

πεντετηρικὸν ἐν ἄλσει ἔχοντι γυμνάσιόν τε καὶ
στάδιον, τὸ δ' ἐν τῷ ὑπερκειμένῳ τοῦ ἄλσους ἱερῷ
λόφῳ τοῦ Ἀπόλλωνος· ἀποδέδεικται δ' ὁ ἀγὼν
Ὀλύμπιος, τὰ Ἄκτια, ἱερὸς τοῦ Ἀκτίου Ἀπόλλωνος, τὴν δ' ἐπιμέλειαν ἔχουσιν αὐτοῦ Λακεδαιμόνιοι. αἱ δ' ἄλλαι κατοικίαι περιπόλιοι τῆς
Νικοπόλεώς εἰσιν. ἤγετο δὲ καὶ πρότερον τὰ
Ἄκτια τῷ θεῷ, στεφανίτης ἀγών, ὑπὸ τῶν περι-
οίκων· νυνὶ δ' ἐντιμότερον ἐποίησεν ὁ Καῖσαρ.

7. Μετὰ δὲ τὴν Ἀμβρακίαν τὸ Ἄργος ἐστὶ τὸ
Ἀμφιλοχικόν, κτίσμα Ἀλκμαίωνος καὶ τῶν παίδων. Ἔφορος μὲν οὖν φησι τὸν Ἀλκμαίωνα
μετὰ τὴν Ἐπιγόνων ἐπὶ τὰς Θήβας στρατείαν,
παρακληθέντα ὑπὸ Διομήδους, συνελθεῖν εἰς
Αἰτωλίαν αὐτῷ καὶ συγκατακτήσασθαι ταύτην
τε καὶ τὴν Ἀκαρνανίαν· καλοῦντος δ' αὐτοὺς ἐπὶ
C 326 τὸν Τρωικὸν πόλεμον Ἀγαμέμνονος, τὸν μὲν
Διομήδη πορευθῆναι, τὸν δ' Ἀλκμαίωνα, μείναντα
ἐν τῇ Ἀκαρνανίᾳ, τὸ Ἄργος κτίσαι, καλέσαι δ'
Ἀμφιλοχικὸν ἐπώνυμον τοῦ ἀδελφοῦ, Ἴναχον δὲ
τὸν διὰ τῆς χώρας ῥέοντα ποταμὸν εἰς τὸν κόλπον
ἀπὸ τοῦ κατὰ τὴν Ἀργείαν προσαγορεῦσαι.
Θουκυδίδης δέ φησιν αὐτὸν Ἀμφίλοχον μετὰ τὴν
ἐκ Τροίας ἐπάνοδον, δυσαρεστοῦντα τοῖς ἐν Ἄργει,
παρελθεῖν εἰς τὴν Ἀκαρνανίαν, διαδεξάμενον δὲ
τὴν τἀδελφοῦ δυναστείαν κτίσαι τὴν πόλιν
ἐπώνυμον ἑαυτοῦ.

---

[1] The *Ludi Quinquennales*, celebrated every four years
(see Dio Cassius 51. 1).

[2] So in the course of time games at numerous places
(including Athens, Ephesus, Naples, Smyrna, Tarsus) came
to be called "Olympian" in imitation of those at Olympia.

a sacred grove that contains a gymnasium and a stadium for the celebration of the quinquennial games,[1] the other part being on the hill that is sacred to Apollo and lies above the grove. These games—the Actia, sacred to Actian Apollo—have been designated as Olympian,[2] and they are superintended by the Lacedaemonians. The other settlements are dependencies of Nicopolis. In earlier times also the Actian Games were wont to be celebrated in honour of the god by the inhabitants of the surrounding country—games in which the prize was a wreath—but at the present time they have been set in greater honour by Caesar.

7. After Ambracia comes Argos Amphilochicum, founded by Alcmaeon and his children. According to Ephorus, at any rate, Alcmaeon, after the expedition of the Epigoni against Thebes, on being invited by Diomedes, went with him into Aetolia and helped him acquire both this country and Acarnania; and when Agamemnon summoned them to the Trojan war, Diomedes went, but Alcmaeon stayed in Acarnania, founded Argos, and named it Amphilochicum after his brother; and he named the river which flows through the country into the Ambracian Gulf "Inachus," after the river in the Argeian country. But according to Thucydides,[3] Amphilochus himself, after his return from Troy, being displeased with the state of affairs at Argos, passed on into Acarnania, and on succeeding to his brother's dominion founded the city that is named after him.

The actual term used, for those at Tarsus at least, was Ἰσολύμπια, "equal to the Olympian" (C. I. 4472).
  [3] 2. 68.

8. Ἠπειρῶται δ' εἰσὶ καὶ Ἀμφίλοχοι καὶ οἱ ὑπερκείμενοι καὶ συνάπτοντες τοῖς Ἰλλυρικοῖς ὄρεσι, τραχεῖαν οἰκοῦντες χώραν, Μολοττοί τε καὶ Ἀθαμᾶνες καὶ Αἴθικες καὶ Τυμφαῖοι καὶ Ὀρέσται Παρωραῖοί τε καὶ Ἀτιντᾶνες, οἱ μὲν πλησιάζοντες τοῖς Μακεδόσι μᾶλλον, οἱ δὲ τῷ Ἰονίῳ κόλπῳ. λέγεται δὲ τὴν Ὀρεστιάδα κατα-σχεῖν ποτε Ὀρέστης, φεύγων τὸν τῆς μητρὸς φόνον, καὶ καταλιπεῖν ἐπώνυμον ἑαυτοῦ τὴν χώραν, κτίσαι δὲ καὶ πόλιν, καλεῖσθαι δ' αὐτὴν Ἄργος Ὀρεστικόν. ἀναμέμικται δὲ τούτοις τὰ Ἰλλυρικὰ ἔθνη τὰ πρὸς τῷ νοτίῳ μέρει τῆς ὀρεινῆς καὶ τὰ ὑπὲρ τοῦ Ἰονίου κόλπου· τῆς γὰρ Ἐπι-δάμνου καὶ τῆς Ἀπολλωνίας μέχρι τῶν Κεραυνίων ὑπεροικοῦσι Βυλλίονές τε καὶ Ταυλάντιοι καὶ Παρθῖνοι καὶ Βρῦγοι· πλησίον δέ που καὶ τὰ ἀργυρεῖα τὰ ἐν Δαμαστίῳ, περὶ ἃ Δυέσται[1] συνεστήσαντο τὴν δυναστείαν καὶ Ἐγχελείοις οὓς[2] καὶ Σεσαρηθίους καλοῦσι· πρὸς δὲ τούτοις Λυγ-κησταί τε καὶ ἡ Δευρίοπος καὶ ἡ τριπολῖτις[3] Πελαγονία καὶ Ἐορδοὶ καὶ Ἐλίμεια καὶ Ἐράτυρα. ταῦτα δὲ πρότερον μὲν κατεδυναστεύετο ἕκαστα, ὧν ἐν τοῖς Ἐγχελείοις[4] οἱ Κάδμου καὶ Ἁρμονίας ἐπίγονοι ἦρχον, καὶ τὰ μυθευόμενα περὶ αὐτῶν

---

[1] περὶ ἃ Δυέσται, Meineke, for περεσάδυές τε ; Casaubon had already conjectured περὶ ἅ.

[2] Ἐγχελείοις οὓς καί, Meineke, for Ἐγχελέους καί.

[3] τριπολῖτις, Meineke wrongly emends to τριπόλις (cp. τριπολῖτις and Τριπολίτιδος, 7. 7. 9).

[4] Ἐγχελείοις, Meineke, for Ἐγχελίοις (C), Ἐγχελέοις (k).

---

[1] The site of Damastium is unknown. Imhoof-Blumer (*Ztschr. f. Numism.* 1874, Vol. I. pp. 99 ff.) think that it

8. The Amphilochians are Epeirotes; and so are the peoples who are situated above them and border on the Illyrian mountains, inhabiting a rugged country—I mean the Molossi, the Athamanes, the Aethices, the Tymphaei, the Orestae, and also the Paroraei and the Atintanes, some of them being nearer to the Macedonians and others to the Ionian Gulf. It is said that Orestes once took possession of Orestias—when in exile on account of the murder of his mother—and left the country bearing his name; and that he also founded a city and called it Argos Oresticum. But the Illyrian tribes which are near the southern part of the mountainous country and those which are above the Ionian Gulf are intermingled with these peoples; for above Epidamnus and Apollonia as far as the Ceraunian Mountains dwell the Bylliones, the Taulantii, the Parthini, and the Brygi. Somewhere near by are also the silver mines of Damastium,[1] around which the Dyestae and the Encheleii (also called Sesarethii) together established their dominion ; and near these people are also the Lyncestae, the territory Deuriopus, Pelagonian Tripolitis, the Eordi, Elimeia, and Eratyra. In earlier times these peoples were ruled separately, each by its own dynasty. For instance, it was the descendants of Cadmus and Harmonia who ruled over the Encheleii ; and the scenes of the stories told about them are still pointed out there. These

---

[1] might be identified with what is now Tepeleni, on the Viosa River. But so far as is now known, there is no silver ore in Epeirus or Southern Illyria. Philippson (Pauly-Wissowa, s.v. "Damastion") suggests that Argyrium (now Argyrocastro, on the Viosa) might be connected with the presence of silver.

ἐκεῖ δείκνυται. οὗτοι μὲν οὖν οὐχ ὑπὸ ἰθαγενῶν
ἤρχοντο· οἱ δὲ Λυγκησταὶ ὑπ' Ἀρραβαίῳ ἐγένοντο, τοῦ Βακχιαδῶν γένους ὄντι· τούτου δ' ἦν
θυγατριδῆ ἡ Φιλίππου μήτηρ τοῦ Ἀμύντου
Εὐρυδίκη, Σίρρα[1] δὲ θυγάτηρ· καὶ τῶν Ἠπειρωτῶν δὲ Μολοττοὶ ὑπὸ Πύρρῳ τῷ Νεοπτολέμου[2]
τοῦ Ἀχιλλέως καὶ τοῖς ἀπογόνοις αὐτοῦ, Θετταλοῖς οὖσι, γεγονότες· οἱ λοιποὶ δὲ ὑπὸ ἰθαγενῶν
ἤρχοντο· εἶτ' ἐπικρατούντων ἀεί τινων κατέ-
στρεψεν ἅπαντα εἰς τὴν Μακεδόνων ἀρχήν, πλὴν
ὀλίγων τῶν ὑπὲρ τοῦ Ἰονίου κόλπου. καὶ δὴ καὶ
τὰ περὶ Λύγκον[3] καὶ Πελαγονίαν καὶ Ὀρεστιάδα
καὶ Ἐλίμειαν τὴν ἄνω Μακεδονίαν ἐκάλουν, οἱ
δ' ὕστερον καὶ ἐλευθέραν· ἔνιοι δὲ καὶ σύμπασαν
τὴν μέχρι Κορκύρας Μακεδονίαν προσαγορεύουσιν,
C 327 αἰτιολογοῦντες ἅμα, ὅτι καὶ κουρᾷ καὶ διαλέκτῳ καὶ
χλαμύδι καὶ ἄλλοις τοιούτοις χρῶνται παραπλη-
σίως· ἔνιοι δὲ καὶ δίγλωττοί εἰσι. καταλυθείσης δὲ
τῆς Μακεδόνων ἀρχῆς, ὑπὸ Ῥωμαίοις ἔπεσε. διὰ
δὲ τούτων ἐστὶ τῶν ἐθνῶν ἡ Ἐγνατία ὁδὸς ἐξ Ἐπι-
δάμνου καὶ Ἀπολλωνίας· περὶ δὲ τὴν ἐπὶ Κανδαουίας ὁδὸν αἵ τε λίμναι εἰσὶν αἱ περὶ Λυχνιδόν,
ταριχείας ἰχθύων αὐτάρκεις ἔχουσαι, καὶ ποταμοὶ
οἵ τε εἰς τὸν Ἰόνιον κόλπον ἐκπίπτοντες καὶ οἱ
ἐπὶ τὰ νότια μέρη, ὅ τ' Ἴναχος καὶ ὁ Ἄρατθος[4]

---

[1] Σίρρα, Meineke, for Ἴρρα.
[2] Νεοπτολέμου, Spengel and Kramer, for Νεοπτολέμῳ; so
the later editors.
[3] Λύγκον, Meineke, for Λυγκηστόν.
[4] Ἄρατθος, Kramer, for ρατῶος; so the later editors.

---

[1] That is, to those of the Macedonians.
[2] See 7. 7. 4. [3] Now Ochrida.

people, I say, were not ruled by men of native stock ;
and the Lyncestae became subject to Arrabaeus,
who was of the stock of the Bacchiads (Eurydice,
the mother of Philip, Amyntas' son, was Arrabaeus'
daughter's daughter and Sirra was his daughter);
and again, of the Epeirotes, the Molossi became
subject to Pyrrhus, the son of Neoptolemus the son
of Achilles, and to his descendants, who were
Thessalians. But the rest were ruled by men of
native stock. Then, because one tribe or another
was always getting the mastery over others, they all
ended in the Macedonian empire, except a few who
dwelt above the Ionian Gulf. And in fact the
regions about Lyncus, Pelagonia, Orestias, and
Elimeia, used to be called Upper Macedonia, though
later on they were by some also called Free
Macedonia. But some go so far as to call the
whole of the country Macedonia, as far as Corcyra,
at the same time stating as their reason that in
tonsure, language, short cloak, and other things
of the kind, the usages of the inhabitants are
similar,[1] although, they add, some speak both
languages. But when the empire of the Macedonians was broken up, they fell under the power
of the Romans. And it is through the country of
these tribes that the Egnatian Road [2] runs, which
begins at Epidamnus and Apollonia. Near the Road
to Candavia [2] are not only the lakes which are in
the neighbourhood of Lychnidus,[3] on the shores of
which are salt-fish establishments that are independent of other waters, but also a number of
rivers, some emptying into the Ionian Gulf and
others flowing in a southerly direction—I mean the
Inachus, the Aratthus, the Acheloüs and the

STRABO

καὶ ὁ Ἀχελῷος καὶ ὁ Εὔηνος ὁ Λυκόρμας πρότερον
καλούμενος, ὁ μὲν εἰς τὸν κόλπον τὸν Ἀμβρακικὸν
ἐμβάλλων, ὁ δὲ εἰς τὸν Ἀχελῷον, αὐτὸς δὲ ὁ
Ἀχελῷος εἰς τὴν θάλατταν καὶ ὁ Εὔηνος, ὁ μὲν
τὴν Ἀκαρνανίαν διεξιών, ὁ δὲ τὴν Αἰτωλίαν· ὁ δὲ
Ἐρίγων πολλὰ δεξάμενος ῥεύματα ἐκ τῶν Ἰλλυρικῶν ὀρῶν καὶ Λυγκηστῶν καὶ Βρύγων καὶ Δευριόπων καὶ Πελαγόνων[1] εἰς τὸν Ἀξιὸν ἐκδίδωσι.

9. Πρότερον μὲν οὖν καὶ πόλεις ἦσαν ἐν τοῖς
ἔθνεσι τούτοις· τριπολῖτις[2] γοῦν ἡ Πελαγονία
ἐλέγετο, ἧς καὶ Ἄζωρος ἦν, καὶ ἐπὶ τῷ Ἐρίγωνι
πᾶσαι αἱ τῶν Δευριόπων πόλεις ᾤκηντο, ὧν τὸ
Βρυάνιον καὶ Ἀλαλκομεναὶ καὶ Στύβαρα· Κύδραι
δὲ Βρύγων,[3] Αἰγίνιον δὲ Τυμφαίων, ὅμορον Αἰθικίᾳ
καὶ Τρίκκῃ· πλησίον δ' ἤδη τῆς τε Μακεδονίας
καὶ τῆς Θετταλίας περὶ τὸ Ποῖον ὄρος καὶ τὴν
Πίνδον Αἰθικές τε καὶ τοῦ Πηνειοῦ πηγαί, ὧν
ἀμφισβητοῦσι Τυμφαῖοί τε καὶ οἱ ὑπὸ τῇ Πίνδῳ
Θετταλοί, καὶ πόλις Ὀξύνεια παρὰ τὸν Ἴωνα
ποταμόν, ἀπέχουσα Ἀζώρου τῆς Τριπολίτιδος
σταδίους ἑκατὸν εἴκοσι· πλησίον δὲ καὶ Ἀλαλκομεναὶ καὶ Αἰγίνιον καὶ Εὔρωπος καὶ αἱ τοῦ Ἴωνος
εἰς τὸν Πηνειὸν συμβολαί. τότε μὲν οὖν, ὡς
εἶπον, καίπερ οὖσα τραχεῖα καὶ ὀρῶν πλήρης,
Τομάρου[4] καὶ Πολυάνου καὶ ἄλλων πλειόνων,
ὅμως εὐάνδρει ἥ τε Ἤπειρος πᾶσα καὶ ἡ Ἰλλυρίς·
νῦν δὲ τὰ πολλὰ μὲν ἐρημία κατέχει, τὰ δ'

[1] Πελαγόνων, Corais, for πλειόνων; so the later editors.
[2] τριπολῖτις, Meineke emends to τρίπολις (see note on
τριπολῖτις, 7. 7. 8).
[3] Βρύγων, Tzschucke, for Βυρσῶν; so the later editors.
[4] Τομάρου, Corais, for Ταμάρου; so the later editors.

Evenus (formerly called the Lycormas); the Aratthus emptying into the Ambracian Gulf, the Inachus
into the Acheloüs, the Acheloüs itself and the
Evenus into the sea—the Acheloüs after traversing
Acarnania and the Evenus after traversing Aetolia.
But the Erigon, after receiving many streams from
the Illyrian mountains and from the countries of
the Lyncestae, Brygi, Deuriopes, and Pelagonians,
empties into the Axius.

9. In earlier times there were also cities among
these tribes; at any rate, Pelagonia used to be called
Tripolitis,[1] one of which was Azorus; and all the
cities of the Deuriopes on the Erigon River were
populous, among which were Bryanium, Alalcomenae,
and Stubara. And Cydrae belonged to the Brygi,
while Aeginium, on the border of Aethicia and
Tricca,[2] belonged to the Tymphaei. When one is
already near to Macedonia and to Thessaly, and in
the neighbourhood of the Poeus and the Pindus
Mountains, one comes to the country of the Aethices
and to the sources of the Peneius River, the possession of which is disputed by the Tymphaei and those
Thessalians who live at the foot of the Pindus, and
to the city Oxineia, situated on the Ion River one
hundred and twenty stadia from Azorus in Tripolitis.
Near by are Alalcomenae, Aeginium, Europus, and
the confluence of the Ion River with the Peneius.
Now although in those earlier times, as I have said,
all Epeirus and the Illyrian country were rugged
and full of mountains, such as Tomarus and Polyanus
and several others, still they were populous; but at
the present time desolation prevails in most parts,

---

[1] "Country of three cities."   [2] Now Trikala.

STRABO

οἰκούμενα κωμηδὸν καὶ ἐν ἐρειπίοις λείπεται. ἐκλέλοιπε δέ πως καὶ τὸ μαντεῖον τὸ ἐν Δωδώνῃ, καθάπερ τἆλλα.

10. Ἔστι δ᾽, ὥς φησιν Ἔφορος, Πελασγῶν ἵδρυμα· οἱ δὲ Πελασγοὶ τῶν περὶ τὴν Ἑλλάδα δυναστευσάντων ἀρχαιότατοι λέγονται· καὶ ὁ ποιητής φησιν οὕτω·

Ζεῦ ἄνα Δωδωναῖε, Πελασγικέ·

ὁ δ᾽ Ἡσίοδος·

Δωδώνην φηγόν τε, Πελασγῶν ἕδρανον, ἦεν.

περὶ μὲν οὖν τῶν Πελασγῶν ἐν τοῖς Τυρρηνικοῖς C 328 εἴρηται, περὶ δὲ Δωδώνης τοὺς μὲν περιοικοῦντας τὸ ἱερὸν διότι βάρβαροι διασαφεῖ καὶ ὁ Ὅμηρος ἐκ τῆς διαίτης, ἀνιπτόποδας, χαμαιεύνας λέγων· πότερον δὲ χρὴ λέγειν Ἑλλούς, ὡς Πίνδαρος, ἢ Σελλούς, ὡς ὑπονοοῦσι παρ᾽ Ὁμήρῳ κεῖσθαι, ἡ γραφὴ ἀμφίβολος οὖσα οὐκ ἐᾷ διισχυρίζεσθαι. Φιλόχορος δέ φησι καὶ τὸν περὶ Δωδώνην τόπον, ὥσπερ τὴν Εὔβοιαν, Ἑλλοπίαν κληθῆναι· καὶ γὰρ Ἡσίοδον οὕτω λέγειν·

ἔστι τις Ἑλλοπίη, πολυλήιος ἠδ᾽ εὐλείμων· ἐνθάδε Δωδώνη τις ἐπ᾽ ἐσχατιῇ πεπόλισται.

οἴονται δέ, φησὶν ὁ Ἀπολλόδωρος, ἀπὸ τῶν ἑλῶν τῶν περὶ τὸ ἱερὸν οὕτω καλεῖσθαι, τὸν μέντοι

---

[1] See articles s.v. "Dodona" in Pauly-Wissowa and Encyclopedia Britannica.
[2] Iliad 16. 233. [3] Frag. 212 (Rzach). [4] 5. 2. 4.

while the parts that are still inhabited survive only
in villages and in ruins. And even the oracle at
Dodona,[1] like the rest, is virtually extinct.

10. This oracle, according to Ephorus, was founded
by the Pelasgi. And the Pelasgi are called the
earliest of all peoples who have held dominion in
Greece. And the poet speaks in this way: "O Lord
Zeus, Dodonaean, Pelasgian";[2] and Hesiod: "He
came to Dodona and the oak-tree, seat of the
Pelasgi."[3] The Pelasgi I have already discussed in
my description of Tyrrhenia;[4] and as for the people
who lived in the neighbourhood of the temple of
Dodona, Homer too makes it perfectly clear from
their mode of life, when he calls them "men with
feet unwashen, men who sleep upon the ground,"[5]
that they were barbarians; but whether one should
call them "Helli," as Pindar does, or "Selli," as is
conjectured to be the true reading in Homer, is a
question to which the text, since it is doubtful, does
not permit a positive answer. Philochorus says that
the region round about Dodona, like Euboea, was
called Hellopia, and that in fact Hesiod speaks of
it in this way: "There is a land called Hellopia,
with many a corn-field and with goodly meadows;
on the edge of this land a city called Dodona hath
been built."[6] It is thought, Apollodorus says, that
the land was so called from the marshes[7] around
the temple; as for the poet, however, Apollodorus
takes it for granted that he did not call the people

---

[5] *Iliad* 16. 235.

[6] *Frag.* 134 (Rzach); see the Schol. on Sophocles *Trachiniae*
1137.

[7] The Greek for marshes is "Helê."

STRABO

ποιητὴν οὐχ[1] οὕτω λέγειν Ἑλλούς, ἀλλὰ Σελλούς[2] ὑπολαμβάνει τοὺς περὶ τὸ ἱερόν, προσθείς, ὅτι καὶ Σελλήεντά τινα ὀνομάζει ποταμόν. ὀνομάζει μὲν οὖν, ὅταν φῇ·

τηλόθεν ἐξ Ἐφύρης ποταμοῦ ἄπο Σελλήεντος.

οὐ μέντοι, ὁ Σκήψιός φησι, τῆς[3] ἐν Θεσπρωτοῖς Ἐφύρας, ἀλλὰ τῆς ἐν τοῖς Ἠλείοις· ἐκεῖ γὰρ εἶναι τὸν Σελλήεντα, ἐν δὲ Θεσπρωτοῖς οὐδένα, οὐδ᾽ ἐν Μολοττοῖς. τὰ δὲ μυθευόμενα περὶ τῆς δρυὸς καὶ τῶν πελειῶν, καὶ εἴ τινα ἄλλα τοιαῦτα, καθάπερ καὶ περὶ Δελφῶν, τὰ μὲν ποιητικωτέρας ἐστὶ διατριβῆς, τὰ δ᾽ οἰκεῖα τῆς νῦν περιοδείας.

11. Ἡ Δωδώνη τοίνυν τὸ μὲν παλαιὸν ὑπὸ Θεσπρωτοῖς ἦν καὶ τὸ ὄρος ὁ Τόμαρος ἢ Τμάρος (ἀμφοτέρως γὰρ λέγεται), ὑφ᾽ ᾧ κεῖται τὸ ἱερόν, καὶ οἱ τραγικοὶ δὲ[4] καὶ Πίνδαρος Θεσπρωτίδα εἰρήκασι τὴν Δωδώνην· ὕστερον δὲ ὑπὸ Μολοττοῖς ἐγένετο·[5] ἀπὸ δὲ τοῦ Τομάρου τοὺς ὑπὸ τοῦ ποιητοῦ λεγομένους ὑποφήτας τοῦ Διός, οὓς καὶ ἀνιπτόποδας, χαμαιεύνας καλεῖ, τομούρους φασὶ λεχθῆναι· καὶ ἐν μὲν τῇ Ὀδυσσείᾳ οὕτω γράφουσί τινες ἅ φησιν Ἀμφίνομος,[6] συμβουλεύων τοῖς

---

[1] οὐχ, Kramer inserts; so the later editors.
[2] Ἑλλούς, ἀλλὰ Σελλούς, Tzschucke, for ἑλλοὺς ἑλλὰς ἑλλούς; so the later editors.
[3] οὐ μέντοι, ὁ Σκήψιός φησι, τῆς, Meineke inserts, deleting the δέ of the MSS. before Θεσπρωτοῖς. Tzschucke and Groskurd had proposed similar words. See 8. 3. 6.

314

who lived about the temple "Helli," but "Selli,"
since (Apollodorus adds) the poet also named a
certain river Selleeïs. He names it, indeed, when he
says, "From afar, out of Ephyra, from the River
Selleeïs" ; [1] however, as Demetrius of Scepsis says,
the poet is not referring to the Ephyra among the
Thesprotians, but to that among the Eleians, for the
Selleeïs is among the Eleians, he adds, and there is
no Selleeïs among the Thesprotians, nor yet among
the Molossi. And as for the myths that are told
about the oak-tree and the doves, and any other
myths of the kind, although they, like those told
about Delphi, are in part more appropriate to poetry,
yet they also in part properly belong to the present
geographical description.

11. In ancient times, then, Dodona was under
the rule of the Thesprotians; and so was Mount
Tomarus, [2] or Tmarus (for it is called both ways), at
the base of which the temple is situated. And both
the tragic poets and Pindar have called Dodona
"Thesprotian Dodona." But later on it came under
the rule of the Molossi. And it is after the Tomarus,
people say, that those whom the poet calls interpreters of Zeus—whom he also calls "men with feet
unwashen, men who sleep upon the ground" [3]—were
called "tomouroi" ; and in the *Odyssey* some so write
the words of Amphinomus, when he counsels the

---

[1] *Iliad* 2. 659 ; 15. 531.   [2] Now Mt. Olytsika.
[3] *Iliad* 16. 235.

---

[4] δέ, Corais, for τε ; so the later editors.
[5] ἐγένετο, Corais, for ἐλέγετο ; so the later editors.
[6] Ἀμφίνομος (*Epit.*), for Ἀμφίλοχος ; so Xylander and later
editors.

μνηστῆρσι μὴ πρότερον ἐπιτίθεσθαι τῷ Τηλε-
μάχῳ, πρὶν ἂν τὸν Δία ἔρωνται·

εἰ μὲν κ᾽ αἰνήσωσι Διὸς μεγάλοιο τομοῦροι,
αὐτός τε κτανέω, τούς τ᾽ ἄλλους πάντας
ἀνώξω·
εἰ δέ κ᾽ ἀποτρεπέῃσι θεός, παύεσθαι ἄνωγα.

βέλτιον γὰρ εἶναι τομούρους ἢ θέμιστας γράφειν·
οὐδαμοῦ γοῦν τὰ μαντεῖα θέμιστας λέγεσθαι παρὰ
τῷ ποιητῇ, ἀλλὰ τὰς βουλὰς καὶ τὰ πολιτεύ-
ματα καὶ νομοθετήματα· τομούρους δ᾽ εἰρῆσθαι ἐπι-
C 329 τετμημένους τομαρούρους,[1] οἷον τομαροφύλακας.
οἱ μὲν οὖν νεώτεροι λέγουσιν τομούρους, παρ᾽[2]
Ὁμήρῳ δ᾽ ἁπλούστερον δεῖ δέχεσθαι θέμιστας,
καταχρηστικῶς καὶ βουλάς, τὰ προστάγματα
καὶ τὰ βουλήματα τὰ μαντικά, καθάπερ καὶ τὰ
νόμιμα· τοιοῦτον γὰρ καὶ τὸ

ἐκ δρυὸς ὑψικόμοιο Διὸς βουλὴν ἐπακοῦσαι.

12. Κατ᾽ ἀρχὰς μὲν οὖν ἄνδρες ἦσαν οἱ προφη-
τεύοντες· καὶ τοῦτ᾽ ἴσως καὶ ὁ ποιητὴς ἐμφαίνει·
ὑποφήτας γὰρ καλεῖ, ἐν οἷς τάττοιντο κἂν οἱ
προφῆται· ὕστερον δ᾽ ἀπεδείχθησαν τρεῖς γραῖαι,
ἐπειδὴ καὶ σύνναος τῷ Διὶ προσαπεδείχθη καὶ
ἡ Διώνη. Σουίδας μέντοι Θετταλοῖς μυθώδεις
λόγους προσχαριζόμενος, ἐκεῖθέν τέ φησιν εἶναι
τὸ ἱερὸν μετενηνεγμένον ἐκ τῆς περὶ Σκοτοῦσσαν

---

[1] τομαρούρους, Corais, for τμάρους, which Meineke deletes.
[2] παρ᾽, Tzschucke inserts ; so the later editors.

---

[1] *Odyssey* 16. 403–5.
[2] "Guardians of Mt. Tomarus."

wooers not to attack Telemachus until they inquire
of Zeus: "If the tomouroi of great Zeus approve, I
myself shall slay, and I shall bid all the rest to aid,
whereas if god averts it, I bid you stop." [1]   For it
is better, they argue, to write "tomouroi" than
"themistes"; at any rate, nowhere in the poet are
the oracles called "themistes," but it is the decrees,
statutes, and laws that are so called; and the people
have been called "tomouroi" because "tomouroi"
is a contraction of "tomarouroi," the equivalent of
"tomarophylakes." [2]   Now although the more recent
critics say "tomouroi," yet in Homer one should
interpret "themistes" (and also "boulai") in a
simpler way, though in a way that is a misuse of
the term, as meaning those orders and decrees that
are oracular, just as one also interprets "themistes"
as meaning those that are made by law.   For example,
such is the case in the following: "to give ear to
the decree [3] of Zeus from the oak-tree of lofty
foliage." [4]

12. At the outset, it is true, those who uttered
the prophecies were men (this too perhaps the poet
indicates, for he calls them "hypophetae," [5] and the
prophets might be ranked among these), but later
on three old women were designated as prophets,
after Dione also had been designated as temple-
associate of Zeus.   Suidas, [6] however, in his desire to
gratify the Thessalians with mythical stories, says
that the temple was transferred from Thessaly, from
the part of Pelasgia which is about Scotussa (and

---

[3] "Boulê."   [4] *Odyssey* 14. 328.
[5] "interpreters."
[6] Little is known of this Suidas except that he wrote a
History of Thessaly and a *History of Euboea.*

Πελασγίας ἔστι δ' ἡ Σκοτοῦσσα τῆς Πελασγιώτιδος Θετταλίας συνακολουθῆσαί τε γυναῖκας
τὰς πλείστας, ὧν ἀπογόνους εἶναι τὰς νῦν προφή-
τιδας· ἀπὸ δὲ τούτου καὶ Πελασγικὸν Δία κε-
κλῆσθαι· Κινέας δ' ἔτι μυθωδέστερον. . . .

Scotussa does belong to the territory called Thessalia Pelasgiotis), and also that most of the women whose descendants are the prophetesses of to-day went along at the same time; and it is from this fact that Zeus was also called "Pelasgian." But Cineas tells a story that is still more mythical. . . .

ΑΠΟΣΠΑΣΜΑΤΙΑ ΕΚ ΤΟΥ Ζ΄

1. Κινέας δέ φησι πόλιν ἐν Θετταλίᾳ εἶναι
καὶ φηγὸν καὶ τὸ τοῦ Διὸς μαντεῖον εἰς Ἤπειρον μετενεχθῆναι. (Stephanus Byzantinus s.v.
Δωδώνη.)

1a. Ἦν δὲ πρότερον περὶ Σκοτοῦσσαν πόλιν
τῆς Πελασγιώτιδος τὸ χρηστήριον· ἐμπρησθέντος
δ᾽ ὑπό τινων τοῦ δένδρου, μετηνέχθη κατὰ χρη-

---

¹ Corais and Groskurd offer only 27 *Fragments*; Kramer
has 57, his numbers running from 1 to 58 inclusive, except
that number 42 is missing ; Müller-Dübner have the same 57,
though they correct the numbering from 42 to 57 ; Meineke,
like Kramer, has no number 42, but changes Kramer's 1 to
1a and inserts seven new fragments, 1, 11a, 16a, 16b, 23a,
58a, and 58b (the last two being 59 and 60 in the present
edition). The present editor adds 28 more. Of these, five
(1b, 16c, 27a, 55a, 61) are quotations from Strabo himself ;
nine (11b, 20a, 21a, 21b, 45a, 47a, 51a, 55b, 58) are from
Stephanus Byzantinus ; twelve (1c, 12a, 15a, 16d, 16e, 25a,
44a, 47b, 50a, 62, 63, 64) are from the notes of Eustathius on
the *Iliad* and *Odyssey ;* and two (65, 66) from his notes on the
geographical poem of Dionysius Periegetes. All these fragments from Eustathius, except no. 62, are citations from
"the Geographer," not from "Strabo," and so is 23a, which
Meineke inserted ; but with the help of the editor, John Paul
Pritchard, Fellow in Greek and Latin at Cornell University,
starting with the able articles of Kunze on this subject
(*Rheinisches Museum*, 1902, LVII, pp. 43 ff. and 1903, LVIII,
pp. 126 ff.), has established beyond all doubt that "the
Geographer" is "Strabo," and in due time the complete
proof will be published. To him the editor is also indebted

FRAGMENTS OF BOOK VII[1]

THE rest of Book VII, containing the description of Macedonia and Thrace, has been lost, but the following fragments, gathered chiefly from the Vatican and Palatine Epitomes and from Eustathius, seem to preserve most of the original matter.[2]

1. Cineas says that there was a city in Thessaly,[3] and that an oak-tree and the oracle of Zeus were transferred from there to Epeirus.

1a. In earlier times the oracle was in the neighbourhood of Scotussa, a city of Pelasgiotis; but when the tree was set on fire by certain people the oracle was transferred in accordance with an oracle which

for fragment no. 66 (hitherto unnoticed, we believe), and for the elimination of certain doubtful passages suggested by Kunze. Meineke's numbers, where different from those of the present edition, are given in parentheses.

[2] Manuscript A has already lost a whole quaternion (about 13 Casaubon pages = about 26 Greek pages in the present edition) in each of two places, namely, from ἡ Λιβύη (2. 5. 26) to περὶ αὐτῆς (3. 1. 6) and from καθ' αὑτούς (5. 3. 2) to ρεντῖνος ἐνάμιλλος (5. 4. 3). In the present case A leaves off at μετὰ δέ (7. 7. 5) and resumes at the beginning of Book VIII. Assuming the loss of a third quaternion from A, and taking into account that portion of it which is preserved in other manuscripts, Ὀγχησμον (7. 7. 5) to μυθωδέστερον (7. 7. 12), only about one-sixth of Book VII is missing; and if this be true, the fragments herein given, although they contain some repetitions, account for most of the original matter of the missing one-sixth.

[3] i. e. a city called Dodona.

STRABO

σμὸν τοῦ Ἀπόλλωνος ἐν Δωδώνῃ. ἐχρησμῴδει
δ᾽ οὐ διὰ λόγων, ἀλλὰ διά τινων συμβόλων,
ὥσπερ τὸ ἐν Λιβύῃ Ἀμμωνιακόν. ἴσως δέ τινα
πτῆσιν αἱ τρεῖς περιστεραὶ ἐπέτοντο ἐξαίρετον,
ἐξ ὧν αἱ ἱέρειαι παρατηρούμεναι προεθέσπιζον.
φασὶ δὲ καὶ κατὰ τὴν τῶν Μολοττῶν καὶ
Θεσπρωτῶν γλῶτταν τὰς γραίας πελίας καλεῖσθαι
καὶ τοὺς γέροντας πελίους. καὶ ἴσως οὐκ ὄρνεα
ἦσαν αἱ θρυλούμεναι πελειάδες, ἀλλὰ γυναῖκες
γραῖαι τρεῖς περὶ τὸ ἱερὸν σχολάζουσαι. (Epitome edita.)

1b. Τῆς δὲ Σκοτούσσης ἐμνήσθημεν καὶ ἐν τοῖς
περὶ Δωδώνης λόγοις καὶ τοῦ μαντείου τοῦ ἐν
Θετταλίᾳ, διότι περὶ τοῦτον ὑπῆρξε τὸν τόπον.
(Strabo 9. 5. 20.)

1c. Ἱερὰ δὲ κατὰ τὸν Γεωγράφον δρῦς τιμᾶται
ἐν Δωδώνῃ, ἀρχαιότατον ὑπολειφθεῖσα φυτὸν καὶ
πρῶτον τροφὴν ἀνθρώποις παρασχόν. ὁ δ᾽ αὐτὸς
καὶ εἰς τὰς ἐκεῖ λεγομένας μαντικὰς πελείας φησὶν
ὅτι αἱ πέλειαι εἰς οἰωνοσκοπίαν ὑπονοοῦνται, καθὰ
καὶ κορακομάντεις ἦσάν τινες. (Eustathius on
Od. 14. 327.)

2. Ὅτι κατὰ Θεσπρωτοὺς καὶ Μολοττοὺς τὰς
γραίας πελίας[1] καὶ τοὺς γέροντας πελίους,
καθάπερ καὶ παρὰ Μακεδόσι· πελιγόνας γοῦν
καλοῦσιν ἐκεῖνοι τοὺς ἐν τιμαῖς, καθὰ παρὰ
Λάκωσι καὶ Μασσαλιώταις τοὺς γέροντας. ὅθεν
καὶ τὰς ἐν τῇ Δωδωναίᾳ δρυῒ μεμυθεῦσθαι πελείας
φασίν. (Epitome Vaticana.)

[1] πελίας, Kramer and later editors, for πελείας (MSS.);
cp. Eustathius (on Od. 14. 327) and Hesychius (s.vv. πέλειαι
and πελείους).

322

Apollo gave out at Dodona. However, he gave out
the oracle, not through words, but through certain
symbols, as was the case at the oracle of Zeus
Ammon in Libya. Perhaps there was something
exceptional about the flight of the three pigeons
from which the priestesses were wont to make
observations and to prophesy. It is further said
that in the language of the Molossians and the
Thesprotians old women are called "peliai"[1] and
old men "pelioi."[1] And perhaps the much talked
of Peleiades were not birds, but three old women
who busied themselves about the temple.

1b. I mentioned Scotussa also in my discussion of
Dodona and of the oracle in Thessaly, because the
oracle was originally in the latter region.

1c. According to the Geographer, a sacred oak-
tree is revered in Dodona, because it was thought to
be the earliest plant created and the first to supply
men with food. And the same writer also says in
reference to the oracular doves there, as they are
called, that the doves are observed for the purposes
of augury, just as there were some seers who divined
from ravens.

2. Among the Thesprotians and the Molossians old
women are called "peliai" and old men "pelioi," as
is also the case among the Macedonians; at any rate,
those people call their dignitaries "peligones"
(compare the "gerontes"[2] among the Laconians
and the Massaliotes).[3] And this, it is said, is the
origin of the myth about the pigeons in the
Dodonaean oak-tree.

---

[1] "Pigeons."

[2] The senators at Sparta were called "gerontes," literally
"old men," "senators."   [3] Cp. 4. 1. 5.

3. Ὅτι ἡ παροιμία, Τὸ ἐν Δωδώνῃ χαλκεῖον, ἐντεῦθεν ὠνομάσθη· χαλκεῖον ἦν ἐν τῷ ἱερῷ, ἔχον ὑπερκείμενον ἀνδριάντα, κρατοῦντα μάστιγα χαλκῆν, ἀνάθημα Κορκυραίων· ἡ δὲ μάστιξ ἦν τριπλῆ, ἀλυσιδωτή, ἀπηρτημένους ἔχουσα ἐξ αὐτῆς ἀστραγάλους, οἳ πλήττοντες τὸ χαλκεῖον συνεχῶς, ὁπότε αἰωροῖντο ὑπὸ τῶν ἀνέμων, μακροὺς ἤχους ἀπειργάζοντο, ἕως ὁ μετρῶν τὸν χρόνον ἀπὸ τῆς ἀρχῆς τοῦ ἤχου μέχρι τέλους καὶ ἐπὶ τετρακόσια προέλθοι· ὅθεν καὶ ἡ παροιμία ἐλέχθη, Ἡ Κερκυραίων μάστιξ. (Epit. ed.)

4. Ἡ δὲ Παιονία τούτοις μέν ἐστι πρὸς ἕω τοῖς ἔθνεσι, πρὸς δύσιν δὲ τοῖς Θρᾳκίοις ὄρεσι, πρὸς ἄρκτον δ' ὑπέρκειται τοῖς Μακεδόσι, διὰ Γορτυνίου πόλεως καὶ Στόβων ἔχουσα τὰς εἰσβολὰς ἐπὶ τὰ πρὸς [1] . . . (δι' ὧν ὁ Ἀξιὸς ῥέων δυσείσβολον ποιεῖ τὴν Μακεδονίαν ἐκ τῆς Παιονίας, ὡς ὁ Πηνειὸς διὰ τῶν Τεμπῶν φερόμενος ἀπὸ τῆς Ἑλλάδος αὐτὴν ἐρυμνοῖ), πρὸς νότον δὲ [2] τοῖς Αὐταριάταις καὶ Δαρδανίοις καὶ Ἀρδιαίοις ὁμορεῖ· ἐκτέταται δὲ καὶ μέχρι Στρυμόνος ἡ Παιονία. (Epit. Vat.)

5. Ὅτι ὁ Ἁλιάκμων εἰς τὸν Θερμαῖον κόλπον ῥεῖ. (Epit. Vat.)

6. Ἡ δ' Ὀρεστὶς πολλή, καὶ ὄρος ἔχει μέγα

---

[1] Between πρὸς and δι' ὧν the MSS. leave a space for about ten letters. Kramer conjectures τὴν Πέλλαν and Tafel νότον στενά (see footnote to translation).
[2] δέ, after νότον, Kramer inserts; so the later editors.

---

[1] The phrase was used in reference to incessant talkers (Stephanus Byzantinus, s.v. Δωδώνη).

3. The proverbial phrase, "the copper vessel in Dodona,"[1] originated thus: In the temple was a copper vessel with a statue of a man situated above it and holding a copper scourge, dedicated by the Corcyraeans; the scourge was three-fold and wrought in chain fashion, with bones strung from it; and these bones, striking the copper vessel continuously when they were swung by the winds, would produce tones so long that anyone who measured the time from the beginning of the tone to the end could count to four hundred. Whence, also, the origin of the proverbial term, "the scourge of the Corcyraeans."

4. Paeonia is on the east of these tribes and on the west of the Thracian mountains, but it is situated on the north of the Macedonians; and, by the road that runs through the city Gortynium[2] and Stobi,[3] it affords a passage to . . .[4] (through which the Axius[5] flows, and thus makes difficult the passage from Paeonia to Macedonia—just as the Peneius flows through Tempe and thus fortifies Macedonia on the side of Greece). And on the south Paeonia borders on the countries of the Autariatae, the Dardanii, and the Ardiaei; and it extends as far as the Strymon.

5. The Haliacmon[6] flows into the Thermaean Gulf.

6. Orestis is of considerable extent, and has a

[2] Gortynium (or Gortynia) was situated in Macedonia, to the south of the narrow pass now called "Demir Kapu," or (in Bulgarian) "Prusak."
[3] Now Sirkovo, to the north of the Demir Kapu Pass.
[4] The words to be supplied here are almost certainly "the narrow pass on the south."
[5] The Vardar.   [6] The Vistritza.

μέχρι τοῦ Κόρακος τῆς Αἰτωλίας καθῆκον καὶ
τοῦ Παρνασσοῦ, περιοικοῦσι δ' αὐτοί τε 'Ορέσται
καὶ Τυμφαῖοι καὶ οἱ ἐκτὸς 'Ισθμοῦ ''Ελληνες οἱ
περὶ Παρνασσὸν καὶ τὴν Οἴτην καὶ Πίνδον. ἐνὶ
μὲν δὴ κοινῷ ὀνόματι καλεῖται Βόιον τὸ ὄρος,
κατὰ μέρη δὲ πολυώνυμόν ἐστιν. φασὶ δ' ἀπὸ
τῶν ὑψηλοτάτων σκοπιῶν ἀφορᾶσθαι τό τε Αἰγαῖον πέλαγος καὶ τὸ 'Αμβρακικὸν καὶ τὸ 'Ιόνιον,
πρὸς ὑπερβολήν, οἶμαι, λέγοντες. καὶ τὸ Πτε-
λεὸν ἱκανῶς ἐστιν ἐν ὕψει τὸ περικείμενον τῷ
'Αμβρακικῷ κόλπῳ, τῇ μὲν ἐκτεινόμενον μέχρι
τῆς Κερκυραίας, τῇ δ' ἐπὶ τὴν κατὰ Λευκάδα
θάλασσαν. (Epit. Vat.)

7. ''Οτι ἐπὶ γέλωτι ἐν παροιμίας μέρει γελᾶται
Κέρκυρα ταπεινωθεῖσα τοῖς πολλοῖς πολέμοις.
(Epit. Vat.)

8. ''Οτι ἡ Κόρκυρα τὸ παλαιὸν εὐτυχὴς ἦν καὶ
δύναμιν ναυτικὴν πλείστην εἶχεν, ἀλλ' ὑπὸ πολέμων τινῶν καὶ τυράννων ἐφθάρη· καὶ ὕστερον
ὑπὸ 'Ρωμαίων ἐλευθερωθεῖσα οὐκ ἐπηνέθη, ἀλλ'
ἐπὶ λοιδορίᾳ παροιμίαν ἔλαβεν·

ἐλευθέρα Κόρκυρα, χέζ' ὅπου θέλεις. (Epit.
ed.)

9. Λοιπὴ δ' ἐστὶ τῆς Εὐρώπης ἥ τε Μακεδονία
καὶ τῆς Θράκης τὰ συνεχῆ ταύτῃ μέχρι Βυζαντίου
καὶ ἡ 'Ελλὰς καὶ αἱ προσεχεῖς νῆσοι. ἔστι μὲν
οὖν 'Ελλὰς καὶ ἡ Μακεδονία· νυνὶ μέντοι τῇ
φύσει τῶν τόπων ἀκολουθοῦντες καὶ τῷ σχήματι
χωρὶς ἔγνωμεν αὐτὴν ἀπὸ τῆς ἄλλης 'Ελλάδος
τάξαι καὶ συνάψαι πρὸς τὴν ὅμορον αὐτῇ Θράκην
μέχρι τοῦ στόματος τοῦ Εὐξείνου καὶ τῆς Προ-

large mountain which reaches as far as Mount Corax[1] in Aetolia and Mount Parnassus. About this mountain dwell the Orestae themselves, the Tymphaei, and the Greeks outside the isthmus that are in the neighbourhood of Parnassus, Oeta, and Pindus. As a whole the mountain is called by a general name, Boëum, but taken part by part it has many names. People say that from the highest peaks one can see both the Aegaean Sea and the Ambracian and Ionian Gulfs, but they exaggerate, I think. Mount Pteleum, also, is fairly high ; it is situated around the Ambracian Gulf, extending on one side as far as the Corcyraean country and on the other to the sea at Leucas.

7. Corcyra is proverbially derided as a joke because it was humbled by its many wars.

8. Corcyra in early times enjoyed a happy lot and had a very large naval force, but was ruined by certain wars and tyrants. And later on, although it was set free by the Romans, it got no commendation, but instead, as an object of reproach, got a proverb : " Corcyra is free, dung where thou wilt."

9. There remain of Europe, first, Macedonia and the parts of Thrace that are contiguous to it and extend as far as Byzantium; secondly, Greece ; and thirdly, the islands that are close by. Macedonia, of course, is a part of Greece, yet now, since I am following the nature and shape of the places geographically, I have decided to classify it apart from the rest of Greece and to join it with that part of Thrace which borders on it and extends as far as the mouth of the Euxine and the Propontis. Then,

[1] Vardusia.

ποντίδος. εἶτα μετ᾽ ὀλίγα μέμνηται Κυψέλων καὶ τοῦ Ἕβρου[1] ποταμοῦ. καταγράφει δὲ καί τι σχῆμα παραλληλόγραμμον, ἐν ᾧ ἡ σύμπασα Μακεδονία ἐστίν. (*Epit. Vat.*)

10. Ὅτι ἡ Μακεδονία περιορίζεται ἐκ μὲν δυσμῶν τῇ παραλίᾳ τοῦ Ἀδρίου, ἐξ ἀνατολῶν δὲ τῇ παραλλήλῳ ταύτης μεσημβρινῇ γραμμῇ τῇ διὰ τῶν ἐκβολῶν Ἕβρου ποταμοῦ καὶ Κυψέλων πόλεως, ἐκ βορρᾶ δὲ τῇ νοουμένῃ εὐθείᾳ γραμμῇ τῇ διὰ Βερτίσκου ὄρους καὶ Σκάρδου καὶ Ὀρβήλου καὶ Ῥοδόπης καὶ Αἵμου· τὰ γὰρ ὄρη ταῦτα, ἀρχόμενα ἀπὸ τοῦ Ἀδρίου, διῆκει κατὰ εὐθεῖαν γραμμὴν ἕως τοῦ Εὐξείνου, ποιοῦντα χερρόνησον μεγάλην πρὸς νότον, τήν τε Θρᾴκην ὁμοῦ καὶ Μακεδονίαν καὶ Ἤπειρον καὶ Ἀχαΐαν· ἐκ νότου δὲ τῇ Ἐγνατίᾳ ὁδῷ ἀπὸ Δυρραχίου πόλεως πρὸς ἀνατολὰς ἰούσῃ[2] ἕως Θεσσαλονικείας· καὶ ἔστι τὸ σχῆμα τοῦτο τῆς Μακεδονίας παραλληλόγραμμον[3] ἔγγιστα. (*Epit. ed.*)

11. Ὅτι Ἡμαθία ἐκαλεῖτο πρότερον ἡ νῦν Μακεδονία. ἔλαβε δὲ τοὔνομα τοῦτο ἀπ᾽ ἀρχαίου τινὸς τῶν ἡγεμόνων Μακεδόνος. ἦν δὲ καὶ πόλις Ἡμαθία πρὸς θαλάσσῃ. κατεῖχον δὲ τὴν χώραν ταύτην Ἠπειρωτῶν τινες καὶ Ἰλλυριῶν, τὸ δὲ πλεῖστον Βοττιαῖοι καὶ Θρᾷκες· οἱ μὲν ἐκ Κρήτης, ὥς φασι, τὸ γένος ὄντες, ἡγεμόνα ἔχοντες Βόττωνα.[4]

---

[1] Ἕβρου (*mqo*), for Εὕρου ; so the editors.

[2] ἰούσῃ, Meineke, following Corais, emends to ἰοῦσι.

[3] παραλληλόγραμμον, Meineke, following Corais, emends to παραλληλογράμμου.

[4] Βόττωνα, Kramer and later editors, for Βούτωνα; cp. *Etym. Magn.*, p. 206, 6.

a little further on, Strabo mentions Cypsela and the
Hebrus River, and also describes a sort of parallelogram in which the whole of Macedonia lies.

10. Macedonia is bounded, first, on the west, by
the coastline of the Adrias; secondly, on the east,
by the meridian line which is parallel to this coast-
line and runs through the outlets of the Hebrus
River and through the city Cypsela; thirdly, on the
north, by the imaginary straight line which runs
through the Bertiscus Mountain,[1] the Scardus,[2] the
Orbelus,[3] the Rhodope,[4] and the Haemus;[5] for these
mountains, beginning at the Adrias, extend on a
straight line as far as the Euxine, thus forming
towards the south a great peninsula which comprises
Thrace together with Macedonia, Epeirus, and
Achaea; and fourthly, on the south, by the Egnatian
Road,[6] which runs from the city Dyrrhachium towards
the east as far as Thessaloniceia. And thus [7] the
shape of Macedonia is very nearly that of a parallelogram.

11. What is now called Macedonia was in earlier
times called Emathia. And it took its present
name from Macedon, one of its early chieftains.
And there was also a city Emathia close to the sea.
Now a part of this country was taken and held by
certain of the Epeirotes and the Illyrians, but most
of it by the Bottiaei and the Thracians. The
Bottiaei came from Crete originally, so it is said,[8]
along with Botton as chieftain. As for the Thracians,

---

[1] It is uncertain what mountain Strabo refers to (see Pauly-
Wissowa, *s.v.* "Bertiskos").
[2] Now the Char-dagh.   [3] Now the Perim-dagh.
[4] Now the Despoto-dagh.
[5] Now the Balkan Mountains.   [6] See 7. 7. 4.
[7] Cp. 7. 7. 8.   [8] Cp. 6. 3. 2.

Θρακῶν δὲ Πίερες μὲν ἐνέμοντο τὴν Πιερίαν καὶ τὰ περὶ τὸν Ὄλυμπον, Παίονες δὲ τὰ[1] περὶ τὸν Ἀξιὸν ποταμὸν καὶ τὴν καλουμένην διὰ τοῦτο Ἀμφαξῖτιν, Ἠδωνοὶ δὲ καὶ Βισάλται τὴν λοιπὴν μέχρι Στρυμόνος· ὧν οἱ μὲν αὐτὸ τοῦτο προσηγορεύοντο Βισάλται, Ἠδωνῶν δ' οἱ μὲν Μυγδόνες, οἱ δὲ Ἠδῶνες, οἱ δὲ Σιθῶνες. τούτων δὲ πάντων οἱ Ἀργεάδαι καλούμενοι κατέστησαν κύριοι καὶ Χαλκιδεῖς οἱ ἐν Εὐβοίᾳ. ἐπῆλθον δὲ καὶ Χαλκιδεῖς οἱ ἐν Εὐβοίᾳ ἐπὶ τὴν τῶν Σιθώνων καὶ συνῴκισαν πόλεις ἐν αὐτῇ περὶ τριάκοντα, ἐξ ὧν ὕστερον ἐκβαλλόμενοι συνῆλθον εἰς μίαν οἱ πλείους αὐτῶν, εἰς τὴν Ὄλυνθον· ὠνομάζοντο δ' οἱ ἐπὶ Θράκης Χαλκιδεῖς. (*Epit. Vat.*)

11*a*. Τὸ δὲ ἐθνικὸν τοῦ Βόττεια διὰ τοῦ ι, ὡς Στράβων ἐν ζ'. καλεῖται δὲ ἀπὸ Βόττωνος Κρητὸς ἡ πόλις. (*Etymologicum Magnum*, p. 206, 6.)

11*b*. Ἀμφάξιον· δύο μέρη λόγου. πόλις.[2] τὸ ἐξ αὐτοῦ Ἀμφαξίτης. Στράβων ἑβδόμῃ. (Stephanus Byzantinus under Ἀμφάξιον.)

12. Ὅτι Πηνειὸς μὲν ὁρίζει τὴν κάτω καὶ πρὸς θαλάττῃ Μακεδονίαν ἀπὸ Θετταλίας καὶ Μαγνησίας, Ἁλιάκμων δὲ τὴν ἄνω, καὶ ἔτι τοὺς

---

[1] τά, before περί, Kramer inserts; so Meineke.
[2] πόλις (cod. Vossianus), Jones, for ποταμός (cp. Pauly-Wissowa, *s.v.* "Amphaxitis").

---

[1] The name appears to have been derived from the Macedonian Argos, *i.e.* Argos Oresticum (7. 7. 8).
[2] *i.e.* the name of the tribe which corresponds to the name of the city.

the Pieres inhabited Pieria and the region about
Olympus; the Paeones, the region on both sides of
the Axius River, which on that account is called Amphaxitis; the Edoni and Bisaltae, the rest of the
country as far as the Strymon. Of these two peoples
the latter are called Bisaltae alone, whereas a part of
the Edoni are called Mygdones, a part Edones, and a
part Sithones. But of all these tribes the Argeadae,[1]
as they are called, established themselves as masters,
and also the Chalcidians of Euboea; for the Chalcidians of Euboea also came over to the country of
the Sithones and jointly peopled about thirty cities
in it, although later on the majority of them were
ejected and came together into one city, Olynthus;
and they were named the Thracian Chalcidians.

11a. The ethnic[2] of Botteia[3] is spelled with the
i,[4] according to Strabo in his Seventh Book. And
the city is called[5] after Botton the Cretan.[6]

11b. Amphaxion. Two parts of speech.[7] A city.
The ethnic of Amphaxion is Amphaxites.

12. The Peneius forms the boundary between
Lower Macedonia, or that part of Macedonia which
is close to the sea, and Thessaly and Magnesia; the
Haliacmon forms the boundary of Upper Macedonia;
and the Haliacmon also, together with the Erigon

---

[3] "A city in Macedonia" (*Etymologicum Magnum, s.v.*)

[4] *i. e.* not with the *e*, as is Βοττεάτης the ethnic of Βόττεα
(see *Etym. Magn., l.c.*), but with the *i*, as is Βοττιαῖοι.

[5] *sc.* Botteia.

[6] The *country* was called "Bottiaea" (6. 3. 6), "Bottia,"
and "Bottiaeis," and the *inhabitants* "Bottiaei" (6. 3. 2).
See Pauly-Wissowa, *s. vv.* Βόττια and Βοττική; and Meritt,
Am. Jour. Arch., 1923, pp. 336 ff.

[7] *i. e.* the preposition "amphi" ("on both sides of") and
the noun "Axius" (the "Axius" River).

Ἠπειρώτας καὶ τοὺς Παίονας καὶ αὐτὸς καὶ ὁ
Ἐρίγων καὶ ὁ Ἀξιὸς καὶ ἕτεροι. (*Epit. Vat.*)

12α. Εἰ γὰρ κατὰ τὸν Γεωγράφον ἀπὸ Πηλίου
καὶ Πηνειοῦ τῶν Θετταλικῶν πρὸς μεσόγαιαν
παράκεινται Μακεδόνες μέχρι Παιονίας καὶ τῶν
Ἠπειρωτικῶν ἐθνῶν, ἐκ δὲ Παιόνων συμμαχίαν
ἐν Τροίᾳ εἶχον οἱ Ἕλληνες, δυσχερὲς νοῆσαι τοῖς
Τρωσὶν ἐλθεῖν συμμαχίαν ἐκ τῶν ῥηθέντων
πορρωτέρω Παιόνων. (Eustathius on *Iliad* 2.
848.)

13. Ὅτι ἐστὶ τῆς παραλίας τῆς Μακεδονικῆς
ἀπὸ τοῦ μυχοῦ τοῦ Θερμαίου κόλπου καὶ Θεσσαλονικείας ἡ μὲν τεταμένη πρὸς νότον μέχρι
Σουνίου, ἡ δὲ πρὸς ἕω μέχρι τῆς Θρακίας χερρονήσου, γωνίαν τινὰ ποιοῦσα κατὰ τὸν μυχόν.
εἰς ἑκάτερον δὲ καθηκούσης τῆς Μακεδονίας, ἀπὸ
τῆς προτέρας λεχθείσης ἀρκτέον. τὰ μὲν δὴ
πρῶτα μέρη τὰ περὶ Σούνιον ὑπερκειμένην ἔχει
τὴν Ἀττικὴν σὺν τῇ Μεγαρικῇ μέχρι τοῦ Κρι-
σαίου κόλπου· μετὰ δὲ ταύτην ἡ Βοιωτικὴ ἐστι
παραλία ἡ πρὸς Εὔβοιαν· ὑπέρκειται δ᾽ αὐτῆς ἡ
λοιπὴ Βοιωτία ἐπὶ δύσιν παράλληλος τῇ Ἀττικῇ.
λέγει δὲ καὶ τὴν Ἐγνατίαν ὁδὸν τελευτᾶν εἰς
Θεσσαλονίκειαν ἀπὸ τοῦ Ἰονίου κόλπου. (*Epit.
Vat.*)

14. Τῶν ταινιῶν, φησίν, ἀφοριοῦμεν πρώτους
τοὺς περὶ Πηνειὸν οἰκοῦντας καὶ τὸν Ἁλιάκμονα
πρὸς θαλάττῃ. ῥεῖ δ᾽ ὁ Πηνειὸς ἐκ τοῦ Πίνδου
ὄρους διὰ μέσης τῆς Θετταλίας πρὸς ἕω· διελθὼν
δὲ τὰς τῶν Λαπιθῶν πόλεις καὶ Περραιβῶν τινας

---

[1] *sc.* Strabo.   [2] Cp. 7. 3. 19.

and the Axius and another set of rivers, form the boundary of the Epeirotes and the Paeonians.

12*a.* For if, according to the Geographer, Macedonia stretches from the Thessalian Pelion and Peneius towards the interior as far as Paeonia and the Epeirote tribes, and if the Greeks had at Troy an allied force from Paeonia, it is difficult to conceive that an allied force came to the Trojans from the aforesaid more distant part of Paeonia.

13. Of the Macedonian coastline, beginning at the recess of the Thermaean Gulf and at Thessaloniceia, there are two parts—one extending towards the south as far as Sunium and the other towards the east as far as the Thracian Chersonese, thus forming at the recess a sort of angle. Since Macedonia extends in both directions, I must begin with the part first mentioned. The first portion, then, of this part—I mean the region of Sunium—has above it Attica together with the Megarian country as far as the Crisaean Gulf; after this is that Boeotian coastline which faces Euboea, and above this coastline lies the rest of Boeotia, extending in the direction of the west, parallel to Attica. And he[1] says that the Egnatian Road, also, beginning at the Ionian Gulf, ends at Thessaloniceia.

14. As for the ribbon-like[2] stretches of land, he[3] says, I shall first mark off the boundary of the peoples who live in the one which is beside the sea near the Peneius and the Haliacmon. Now the Peneius flows from the Pindus Mountain through the middle of Thessaly towards the east; and after it passes through the cities of the Lapithae and some cities of the Perrhaebians, it reaches Tempe,

[3] *sc.* Strabo.

333

STRABO

συνάπτει τοῖς Τέμπεσι· παραλαβὼν πλείους ποτα
μούς, ὧν καὶ ὁ Εὔρωπος, ὃν Τιταρήσιον εἶπεν ὁ
ποιητής, τὰς πηγὰς ἔχοντα ἀπὸ τοῦ Τιταρίου ὄρους
συμφυοῦς τῷ Ὀλύμπῳ, ὃ κἀντεῦθεν ἄρχεται διο
ρίζειν τὴν Μακεδονίαν ἀπὸ τῆς Θετταλίας. ἔστι
γὰρ τὰ Τέμπη στενὸς αὐλὼν μεταξὺ Ὀλύμπου
καὶ Ὄσσης. φέρεται δ᾽ ὁ Πηνειὸς ἀπὸ τῶν στε
νῶν τούτων ἐπὶ σταδίους τετταράκοντα, ἐν ἀρισ
τερᾷ μὲν ἔχων τὸν Ὄλυμπον, Μακεδονικὸν ὄρος
μετεωρότατον, ἐν δὲ δεξιᾷ τὴν Ὄσσαν,[1] πλησίον[2]
τῶν ἐκβολῶν τοῦ ποταμοῦ. ἐπὶ μὲν δὴ ταῖς
ἐκβολαῖς τοῦ Πηνειοῦ ἐν δεξιᾷ Γυρτὼν ἵδρυται,
Περραιβικὴ πόλις καὶ Μαγνῆτις, ἐν ᾗ Πειρίθους
τε καὶ Ἰξίων ἐβασίλευσαν·[3] ἀπέχει δ᾽ ὅσον
σταδίους ἑκατὸν τῆς Γυρτῶνος πόλις Κραννών,
καί φασιν, ὅταν εἴπῃ ὁ ποιητὴς "τὼ μὲν ἄρ᾽ ἐκ
Θράκης" καὶ τὰ ἑξῆς, Ἐφύρους μὲν λέγεσθαι
τοὺς Κραννωνίους, Φλεγύας δὲ τοὺς Γυρτωνίους.
ἐπὶ δὲ θάτερα ἡ Πιερία. (*Epit. Vat.*)

15. Ὅτι ὁ Πηνειὸς ποταμός, ῥέων διὰ τῶν
Τεμπῶν, καὶ ἀρχόμενος ἀπὸ τοῦ Πίνδου ὄρους,
καὶ διὰ μέσης Θεσσαλίας καὶ τῶν Λαπιθῶν καὶ
Περραιβῶν, δεχόμενός τε τὸν Εὔρωπον ποταμόν,
ὃν Ὅμηρος Τιταρήσιον ὠνόμασε, διορίζει Μακε
δονίαν μὲν πρὸς βορρᾶν, Θεσσαλίαν δὲ πρὸς νότον.
αἱ δὲ τοῦ Εὐρώπου ποταμοῦ πηγαὶ ἐκ τοῦ Τιτα
ρίου ὄρους ἄρχονται, ὅ ἐστι συνεχὲς τῷ Ὀλύμπῳ.
καὶ ἔστιν ὁ μὲν Ὄλυμπος τῆς Μακεδονίας, ἡ δὲ
Ὄσσα τῆς Θεσσαλίας καὶ τὸ Πήλιον. (*Epit. ed.*)

[1] ἐν δὲ δεξιᾷ τὴν Ὄσσαν, Kramer conjectures, from
Eustathius (note on *Iliad* 2. 750); Meineke inserts.
[2] πλησίον, Jones inserts; ἐγγύς, Kramer and Meineke.

after having received the waters of several rivers,
among which is the Europus, which the poet called
Titaresius,[1] since it has its sources in the Titarius
Mountain ; the Titarius Mountain joins Olympus,
and thence Olympus begins to mark the boundary
between Macedonia and Thessaly ; for Tempe is a
narrow glen between Olympus and Ossa, and from
these narrows the Peneius flows for a distance of
forty stadia with Olympus, the loftiest mountain in
Macedonia, on the left, and with Ossa, near the
outlets of the river, on the right. So then, Gyrton,
the Perrhaebian and Magnetan city in which
Peirithoüs and Ixion reigned, is situated near the
outlets of the Peneius on the right ; and the city of
Crannon lies at a distance of as much as one hundred
stadia from Gyrton ; and writers say that when the
poet says, " Verily these twain from Thrace "[2] and
what follows, he means by "Ephyri" the Crannonians
and by " Phlegyae " the Gyrtonians. But Pieria is
on the other side of the Peneius.

15. The Peneius River rises in the Pindus Mountain and flows through Tempe and through the
middle of Thessaly and of the countries of the
Lapithae and the Perrhaebians, and also receives
the waters of the Europus River, which Homer
called Titaresius ; it marks the boundary between
Macedonia[3] on the north and Thessaly on the south.
But the source-waters of the Europus rise in the
Titarius Mountain, which is continuous with Olympus.
And Olympus belongs to Macedonia, whereas Ossa
and Pelion belong to Thessaly.

[1] *Iliad* 2. 751.   [2] *Iliad* 13. 301.
[3] Including Lower Macedonia (cp. *Frag.* 12).

---

[3] ἐβασίλευσαν, Eustathius (note on *Iliad* 2. 752), for
ἐβασίλευσεν ; so Meineke.

15a. Ἄρχεται δὲ κατὰ τὸν Γεωγράφον ἐκ Πίνδου ὄρους ὁ Πηνειός, περὶ ὃ οἱ Περραιβοί. . . . περὶ δὲ Πηνειοῦ καὶ ταῦτα ἐν τοῖς τοῦ Στράβωνος φέρεται· Πηνειὸς ἄρχεται ἐκ Πίνδου· ἐν ἀριστερᾷ δ᾽ ἀφεὶς Τρίκκην φέρεται περὶ Ἄτρακα καὶ Λάρισσαν καὶ τοὺς ἐν Θετταλίᾳ δεξάμενος ποταμοὺς πρόεισι διὰ τῶν Τεμπῶν. καὶ ὅτι διὰ μέσης ῥέει Θετταλίας πολλοὺς δεχόμενος ποταμούς, καὶ ὅτι Πηνειὸς φέρεται ἐν ἀριστερᾷ μὲν ἔχων Ὄλυμπον, ἐν δεξιᾷ δὲ Ὄσσαν. ἐπὶ δὲ ταῖς ἐκβολαῖς τοῦ Πηνειοῦ ἐν δεξιᾷ Μαγνῆτις πόλις ἡ Γυρτών, ἐν ᾗ Πειρίθους καὶ Ἰξίων ἐβασίλευσαν· ἀπέχει δ᾽ αὐτῆς οὐ πολὺ πόλις Κραννών, ἧς οἱ πολῖται Ἔφυροι ἑτερωνύμως, ὡς καὶ οἱ τῆς Γυρτῶνος Φλεγύαι. (Eustathius on *Iliad* 2. 750.)

16. Ὅτι ὑπὸ ταῖς ὑπωρείαις τοῦ Ὀλύμπου παρὰ τὸν Πηνειὸν ποταμὸν Γυρτών ἐστι, πόλις Περραιβικὴ καὶ Μαγνῆτις, ἐν ᾗ Πειρίθους τε καὶ Ἰξίων ἦρξαν. ἀπέχει δὲ ἑκατὸν τῆς Γυρτῶνος[1] Κραννών, καί φασιν, ὅταν εἴπῃ ὁ ποιητὴς " τὼ μὲν ἄρ᾽ ἐκ Θρῄκης," Ἐφύρους μὲν λέγεσθαι τοὺς Κραννωνίους, Φλεγύας δὲ τοὺς Γυρτωνίους. (*Epit. ed.*)

16a. Ἀπέχει δὲ σταδίους ἑκατὸν Γυρτῶνος Κραννὼν πόλις, ὥς φησι Στράβων. (Stephanus under Κραννών.)

16b. Ὁμόλιον πόλις Μακεδονίας καὶ Μαγνησίας. Στράβων ἑβδόμη. (Stephanus under Ὁμόλιον.)

16c. Εἴρηται ἐν τοῖς Μακεδονικοῖς ὅτι ἐστὶ (*scil.* τὸ Ὁμόλιον) πρὸς τῇ Ὄσσῃ κατὰ τὴν

15a. The Peneius rises, according to the Geographer, in that part of the Pindus Mountain about which the Perrhaebians live. . . . And Strabo also makes the following statements concerning the Peneius : The Peneius rises in the Pindus ; and leaving Tricca on the left it flows around Atrax and Larissa, and after receiving the rivers in Thessaly passes on through Tempe. And he says that the Peneius flows through the centre of Thessaly, receiving many rivers, and that in its course it keeps Olympus on the left and Ossa on the right. And at its outlets, on the right, is a Magnetan city, Gyrton, in which Peirithoüs and Ixion reigned ; and not far from Gyrton is a city Crannon, whose citizens were called by a different name, "Ephyri," just as the citizens of Gyrton were called " Phlegyae."

16. Below the foot-hills of Olympus, along the Peneius River, lies Gyrton, the Perrhaebian and Magnetan city, in which Peirithoüs and Ixion ruled ; and Crannon is at a distance of one hundred stadia from Gyrton, and writers say that when the poet says, " Verily these twain from Thrace," he means by " Ephyri " the Crannonians and by " Phlegyae " the Gyrtonians.[1]

16a. The city of Crannon is at a distance of one hundred stadia from Gyrton, according to Strabo.

16b. Homolium, a city of Macedonia and Magnesia. Strabo in his Seventh Book.

16c. I have said in my description of Macedonia that Homolium is close to Ossa and is where the

---

[1] Cp. *Frag.* 14.

---

[1] δὲ ἑκατὸν τῆς Γυρτῶνος (as in Stephanus, *s.v.* Κραννών), for δ᾽ ἡ Γυρτὼν τῆς Τύρρηνος ; so other editors, including Meineke.

337

ἀρχὴν τῆς τοῦ Πηνειοῦ διὰ τῶν Τεμπῶν διεκβολῆς. (Strabo, 9. 5. 22.)

16d. Διάφοροι δὲ Ἔφυραι, εἴπερ ὁ Γεωγράφος καὶ εἰς ἐννέα ταύτας μετρεῖ. (Eustathius on *Iliad* 2. 659.)

16e. Γυρτῶνα δὲ πόλιν λέγει (*sc.* ὁ Γεωγράφος) Μαγνῆτιν πρὸς ταῖς τοῦ Πηνειοῦ ἐκβολαῖς. (Eustathius on *Iliad* 13. 301; see also Strabo 9. 5. 19.)

17. Ὅτι τὸ Δῖον ἡ πόλις οὐκ ἐν τῷ αἰγιαλῷ τοῦ Θερμαίου κόλπου ἐστὶν ἐν ταῖς ὑπωρείαις τοῦ Ὀλύμπου, ἀλλ᾽ ὅσον ἑπτὰ ἀπέχει σταδίους· ἔχει δ᾽ ἡ πόλις τὸ Δῖον κώμην πλησίον Πίμπλειαν, ἔνθα Ὀρφεὺς διέτριβεν. (*Epit. ed.*)

18. Ὅτι ὑπὸ τῷ Ὀλύμπῳ πόλις Δῖον. ἔχει δὲ κώμην πλησίον Πίμπλειαν· ἐνταῦθα τὸν Ὀρφέα διατρῖψαί φασι[1] τὸν Κίκονα, ἄνδρα γόητα ἀπὸ μουσικῆς ἅμα καὶ μαντικῆς καὶ τῶν περὶ τὰς τελετὰς ὀργιασμῶν ἀγυρτεύοντα τὸ πρῶτον, εἶτ᾽ ἤδη καὶ μείζονων[2] ἀξιοῦντα ἑαυτὸν καὶ ὄχλον καὶ δύναμιν κατασκευαζόμενον· τοὺς μὲν οὖν ἑκουσίως ἀποδέχεσθαι, τινὰς δ᾽ ὑπιδομένους ἐπιβουλὴν καὶ βίαν ἐπισυστάντας διαφθεῖραι αὐτόν. ἐνταῦθα πλησίον καὶ τὰ Λείβηθρα. (*Epit. Vat.*)

19. Ὅτι τὸ παλαίον οἱ μάντεις καὶ μουσικὴν εἰργάζοντο. (*Epit. ed.*)

20. Μετὰ δὲ τὸ Δῖον αἱ τοῦ Ἁλιάκμονος ἐκβολαί· εἶτα Πύδνα, Μεθώνη, Ἄλωρος καὶ ὁ Ἐρίγων ποταμὸς καὶ Λουδίας, ὁ μὲν ἐκ Τρικλάρων ῥέων

[1] φασί, Meineke emends to φησί.

Peneius, flowing through Tempe, begins to discharge its waters.[1]

16*d*. There were several different Ephyras, if indeed the Geographer counts as many as nine.[2]

16*e*. He (the Geographer) speaks of a city Gyrton, a Magnetan city near the outlets of the Peneius.

17. The city Dium, in the foot-hills of Olympus, is not on the shore of the Thermaean Gulf, but is at a distance of as much as seven stadia from it. And the city Dium has a village near by, Pimpleia, where Orpheus lived.

18. At the base of Olympus is a city Dium. And it has a village near by, Pimpleia. Here lived Orpheus, the Ciconian, it is said—a wizard who at first collected money from his music, together with his soothsaying and his celebration of the orgies connected with the mystic initiatory rites, but soon afterwards thought himself worthy of still greater things and procured for himself a throng of followers and power. Some, of course, received him willingly, but others, since they suspected a plot and violence, combined against him and killed him. And near here, also, is Leibethra.

19. In the early times the soothsayers also practised music.

20. After Dium come the outlets of the Haliacmon; then Pydna, Methone, Alorus, and the Erigon and Ludias Rivers. The Erigon flows from the country

---

[1] See 9. 5. 22, from which this *Fragment* is taken.
[2] Our text of Strabo mentions only seven. Benseler's Lexicon names nine and Pauly-Wissowa eight.

---

[2] μειζόνων, Eustathius (note on *Iliad* 2. 596), for μείζονα; so other editors, including Meineke.

STRABO

δι' Ὀρεστῶν καὶ τῆς Πελλαίας,[1] ἐν ἀριστερᾷ
ἀφιεὶς τὴν πόλιν καὶ συμβάλλων τῷ Ἀξιῷ· ὁ δὲ
Λουδίας εἰς Πέλλαν ἀνάπλουν ἔχων σταδίων
ἑκατὸν καὶ εἴκοσι· μέση δ' οὖσα ἡ Μεθώνη τῆς
μὲν Πύδνης ὅσον τετταράκοντα σταδίων ἀπέχει,
τῆς Ἀλώρου δὲ ἑβδομήκοντα. ἔστι δ' ἡ Ἄλωρος
τὸ μυχαίτατον τοῦ Θερμαίου κόλπου. λέγεται δὲ
Θεσσαλονίκεια διὰ[2] τὴν ἐπιφάνειαν. τὴν μὲν
οὖν Ἄλωρον Βοτταϊκὴν νομίζουσι, τὴν δὲ Πύδναν
Πιερικήν. Πέλλα ἐστὶ μὲν τῆς κάτω Μακεδονίας,
ἣν Βοττιαῖοι κατεῖχον· ἐνταῦθ' ἦν πάλαι τὸ τῆς
Μακεδονίας χρηματιστήριον· ηὔξησε τὴν πόλιν
ἐκ μικρᾶς Φίλιππος, τραφεὶς ἐν αὐτῇ. ἔχει δ'
ἄκραν ἐν λίμνῃ τῇ καλουμένῃ Λουδίᾳ· ἐκ ταύτης
ὁ Λουδίας ἐκδίδωσι ποταμός, αὐτὴν δὲ πληροῖ
τοῦ Ἀξιοῦ τι ἀπόσπασμα. ὁ δὲ Ἀξιὸς ἐκδίδωσι
μεταξὺ Χαλάστρας καὶ Θέρμης· ἐπίκειται δὲ τῷ
ποταμῷ τούτῳ χωρίον ἐρυμνόν, ὃ νῦν μὲν καλεῖται
Ἀβυδῶν, Ὅμηρος δ' Ἀμυδῶνα καλεῖ, καί φησι
τοὺς Παίονας ἐντεῦθεν εἰς Τροίαν ἐπικούρους
ἐλθεῖν·

τηλόθεν ἐξ Ἀμυδῶνος ἀπ' Ἀξιοῦ εὐρυρέοντος.

κατεσκάφη δ' ὑπὸ τῶν Ἀργεαδῶν.   (*Epit. Vat.*)

---

[1] Πελλαίας, Meineke emends to Πελαγονίας, following Tafel
and Kramer.   See footnote to translation.
[2] The letters δι in διά have fallen out of the MSS.

---

[1] Otherwise unknown.
[2] Tafel, Kramer, Meineke, and Forbiger think that Strabo
wrote "Pelagonia" instead of "Pellaea" (or "the Pellaean
country") and that "the city" which the Erigon leaves
"on the left" is Heracleia Lyncestis (now Bitolia), for
"Pellaea" seems to be used by no other writer and the
Erigon leaves "the city" Pella "on the right," not "on

of the Triclari [1] through that of the Orestae and through Pellaea, leaves the city on the left,[2] and meets the Axius; the Ludias is navigable inland to Pella, a distance of one hundred and twenty stadia. Methone, which lies between the two cities, is about forty stadia from Pydna and seventy from Alorus. Alorus is in the inmost recess of the Thermaean Gulf, and it is called Thessaloniceia because of its fame.[3] Now Alorus is regarded as a Bottiaean city, whereas Pydna is regarded as a Pierian.[4] Pella belongs to Lower Macedonia, which the Bottiaei used to occupy; in early times the treasury of Macedonia was here. Philip enlarged it from a small city, because he was reared in it. It has a headland in what is called Lake Ludias; and it is from this lake that the Ludias River issues, and the lake itself is supplied by an offshoot of the Axius. The Axius empties between Chalastra and Therma; and on this river lies a fortified place which now is called Abydon, though Homer [5] calls it Amydon, and says that the Paeonians went to the aid of Troy from there, "from afar, out of Amydon, from wide-flowing Axius." The place was destroyed by the Argeadae.

the left." But both this fragment and *Frag.* 22 contain other errors which seem to defy emendation (cp. C. Müller, *Index Variae Lectionis*); for example, both make the Haliacmon empty between Dium and Pydna (and so does Ptolemaeus, 3. 12). But lack of space requires that this whole matter be reserved for special discussion.

[3] The text as it stands seems impossible, for Thessaloniceia, not Alorus, was in the innermost part of the gulf—unless, indeed, we assume that Strabo wrongly identified Alorus with Thessaloniceia. In any case, we should probably interpret "it" as referring to "the Thermaean Gulf" and "its" as meaning "Thessaloniceia's."

[4] Cp. *Frag.* 22.   [5] *Iliad* 2. 849.

20a. Ἀβυδων, Ἀβυδῶνος· χωρίον Μακεδονίας, ὡς Στράβων. (Stephanus Byzantinus, s.v. Ἀβυδών.)

21. Ὅτι ὁ Ἀξιὸς θολερὸς ῥεῖ· ὁ δ᾽ Ὅμηρος Ἀξιοῦ κάλλιστον ὕδωρ φησίν, ἴσως διὰ τὴν πηγὴν τὴν καλουμένην Αἶαν, ἢ καθαρώτατον ἐκδιδοῦσα ὕδωρ εἰς τοῦτον ἐλέγχει φαύλην ὑπάρχουσαν τὴν νῦν φερομένην γραφὴν παρὰ τῷ ποιητῇ. μετὰ δὲ Ἀξιὸν Ἐχέδωρος ἐν σταδίοις εἴκοσιν· εἶτα Θεσσαλονίκεια Κασσάνδρου[1] κτίσμα ἐν ἄλλοις τετταράκοντα καὶ ἡ Ἐγνατία ὁδός. ἐπωνόμασε δὲ τὴν πόλιν ἀπὸ τῆς ἑαυτοῦ γυναικὸς Θεσσαλονίκης, Φιλίππου δὲ τοῦ Ἀμύντου θυγατρός, καθελὼν τὰ ἐν τῇ Κρουσίδι πολίσματα καὶ τὰ ἐν τῷ Θερμαίῳ κόλπῳ περὶ ἓξ καὶ εἴκοσι καὶ συνοικίσας εἰς ἕν· ἡ δὲ μητρόπολις τῆς νῦν Μακεδονίας ἐστί. τῶν δὲ συνοικισθεισῶν ἦν Ἀπολλωνία καὶ Χαλάστρα καὶ Θέρμα καὶ Γαρησκὸς καὶ Αἰνέα[2] καὶ Κισσός, ὧν τὴν Κισσὸν ὑπονοήσειεν ἄν τις τῷ Κισσῇ προσήκειν, οὗ μέμνηται ὁ ποιητής· Κισσῆς τόν γ᾽ ἔθρεψε, τὸν Ἰφιδάμαντα λέγων. (Epit. Vat.)

21a. Κρουσίς· μοῖρα τῆς Μυγδονίας. Στράβων ἑβδόμη. (Stephanus Byzantinus, s.v. Κρουσίς.)

21b. Χαλάστρα· πόλις Θρᾴκης περὶ Θερμαῖον κόλπον . . . Στράβων δ᾽ ἐν ἑβδόμῃ Μακεδονίας αὐτὴν καλεῖ. (Stephanus Byzantinus, s.v. Χαλάστρα.)

22. Ὅτι μετὰ τὸ Δῖον πόλιν ὁ Ἁλιάκμων

---

[1] Κασσάνδρου, Jones, for Κασάνδρου (cp. Frag. 25 and footnote).

FRAGMENTS OF BOOK VII

20*a*. Abydon, Abydonis; a place in Macedonia, according to Strabo.

21. The Axius is a muddy stream; but Homer[1] calls it "water most fair," perhaps on account of the spring called Aea, which, since it empties purest water into the Axius, proves that the present current reading[2] of the passage in the poet is faulty. After the Axius, at a distance of twenty stadia, is the Echedorus;[3] then, forty stadia farther on, Thessaloniceia, founded by Cassander, and also the Egnatian Road. Cassander named the city after his wife Thessalonice, daughter of Philip son of Amyntas, after he had rased to the ground the towns in Crusis and those on the Thermaean Gulf, about twenty-six in number, and had settled all the inhabitants together in one city; and this city is the metropolis of what is now Macedonia. Among those included in the settlement were Apollonia, Chalastra, Therma, Garescus, Aenea, and Cissus; and of these one might suspect that Cissus belonged to Cisses,[4] whom the poet mentions in speaking of Iphidamas, "whom Cisses reared."[5]

21*a*. Crusis; a portion of Mygdonia. Strabo in his Seventh Book.

21*b*. Chalastra: a city of Thrace near the Thermaean Gulf—though Strabo, in his Seventh Book, calls it a city of Macedonia.

22. After the city Dium comes the Haliacmon

---

[1] *Iliad* 21. 158.　　[2] See *Frag.* 23.　　[3] Now the Gallico.
[4] Also spelled "Cisseus" (wrongly, it seems), as in *Frag.* 24 *q.v.*
[5] *Iliad* 11. 223.

---

[2] Αἰνέα, Meineke emends to Αἴνεια; cp. Αἰνέαν, *Frag.* 24.

ποταμός ἐστιν, ἐκβάλλων εἰς τὸν Θερμαῖον κόλπον· καὶ τὸ ἀπὸ τούτου ἡ πρὸς βορρᾶν τοῦ κόλπου παραλία Πιερία καλεῖται ἕως τοῦ Ἀξιοῦ ποταμοῦ, ἐν ᾗ καὶ πόλις Πύδνα, ἡ νῦν Κίτρον καλεῖται· εἶτα Μεθώνη καὶ Ἄλωρος πόλεις· εἶτα Ἐρίγων καὶ Λουδίας ποταμοί· ἀπὸ δὲ Λουδίου εἰς Πέλλαν πόλιν ἀνάπλους στάδια ἑκατὸν εἴκο-σιν. ἀπέχει δ' ἡ Μεθώνη τῆς μὲν Πύδνης στάδια τετταράκοντα, τῆς Ἀλώρου δὲ ἑβδομήκοντα στά-δια. ἡ μὲν οὖν Πύδνα Πιερική ἐστι πόλις· ἡ δὲ Ἄλωρος Βοττιαϊκή. ἐν μὲν οὖν τῷ πρὸ τῆς Πύδνης πεδίῳ Ῥωμαῖοι Περσέα καταπολεμήσαντες καθεῖ-λον τὴν τῶν Μακεδόνων βασιλείαν, ἐν δὲ τῷ πρὸ τῆς Μεθώνης πεδίῳ γενέσθαι συνέβη Φιλίππῳ τῷ Ἀμύντου τὴν ἐκκοπὴν τοῦ δεξιοῦ ὀφθαλμοῦ καταπελτικῷ βέλει κατὰ τὴν πολιορκίαν τῆς πόλεως. (Epit. ed.)

23. Ὅτι τὴν Πέλλαν, οὖσαν μικρὰν πρότερον, Φίλιππος εἰς μῆκος ηὔξησε, τραφεὶς ἐν αὐτῇ· ἔχει δὲ λίμνην πρὸ αὐτῆς, ἐξ ἧς ὁ Λουδίας ποταμὸς ῥεῖ· τὴν δὲ λίμνην πληροῖ τοῦ Ἀξιοῦ τι ποταμοῦ ἀπόσπασμα. εἶτα ὁ Ἀξιός, διαιρῶν τήν τε Βοττιαίαν καὶ τὴν Ἀμφαξῖτιν γῆν, καὶ παραλαβὼν τὸν Ἐρίγωνα ποταμὸν ἐξίησι μεταξὺ Χαλάστρας καὶ Θέρμης· ἐπίκειται δὲ τῷ Ἀξιῷ ποταμῷ χωρίον, ὅπερ Ὅμηρος Ἀμυδῶνα καλεῖ, καί φησι τοὺς Παίονας ἐντεῦθεν εἰς Τροίαν ἐπικού-ρους ἐλθεῖν·

τηλόθεν ἐξ Ἀμυδῶνος ἀπ' Ἀξιοῦ εὐρυρέοντος.

ἀλλ' ἐπεὶ ὁ μὲν Ἀξιὸς θολερός ἐστι, κρήνη δέ τις ἐξ Ἀμυδῶνος ἀνίσχουσα καὶ ἐπιμιγνυμένη

River, which empties into the Thermaean Gulf. And the part after this, the seaboard of the gulf towards the north as far as the Axius River, is called Pieria, in which is the city Pydna, now called Citrum. Then come the cities Methone and Alorus. Then the Rivers Erigon and Ludias; and from[1] Ludias to the city of Pella the river is navigable, a distance of one hundred and twenty stadia. Methone is forty stadia distant from Pydna and seventy stadia from Alorus. Now Pydna is a Pierian city, whereas Alorus is Bottiaean.[2] Now it was in the plain before Pydna that the Romans defeated Perseus in war and destroyed the kingdom of the Macedonians, and it was in the plain before Methone that Philip the son of Amyntas, during the siege of the city, had the misfortune to have his right eye knocked out by a bolt from a catapult.

23. As for Pella, though it was formerly small, Philip greatly enlarged it, because he was reared in it. It has a lake before it; and it is from this lake that the Ludias River flows, and the lake is supplied by an offshoot of the Axius. Then the Axius, dividing both Bottiaea and the land called Amphaxitis, and receiving the Erigon River, discharges its waters between Chalastra and Therma. And on the Axius River lies the place which Homer[3] calls Amydon, saying that the Paeonians went to the aid of Troy from there, "from afar, out of Amydon, from wide-flowing Axius."[4] But since the Axius is muddy and since a certain spring rises in Amydon and mingles "water most fair" with it,

---

[1] *sc.* "the mouth of the" (cp. *Frag.* 20).
[2] Cp. *Frag.* 20.　　[3] *Iliad* 2. 849.　　[4] Cp. *Frag.* 20.

αὐτῷ καλλίστου ὕδατος, διὰ τοῦτο τὸν ἐξῆς στίχον,

Ἀξιοῦ, οὗ κάλλιστον ὕδωρ ἐπικίδναται Αἶαν,

μεταγράφουσιν οὕτως·

Ἀξιοῦ, ᾧ κάλλιστον ὕδωρ ἐπικίδναται Αἴης·

οὐ γὰρ τὸ τοῦ Ἀξιοῦ ὕδωρ κάλλιστον τῆς γῆς τῇ ὄψει ἐπικίδναται, ἀλλὰ τὸ τῆς πηγῆς τῷ Ἀξίῳ.[1] (Epit. ed.)

23a. Ἐν δὲ τῷ " ἐπικίδναται αἴη " ἢ " αἶαν " (διττῶς γὰρ ἡ γραφή) " αἶαν " τινὲς οὐ τὴν γῆν ἐνόησαν, ἀλλά τινα πηγήν, ὡς δῆλον ἐξ ὧν ὁ γεωγράφος φησί, λέγων ὅτι ἡ παρ' Ὁμήρῳ Ἀμυδὼν Ἀβυδὼν ὕστερον ἐκλήθη, κατεσκάφη δέ. πηγὴ δὲ πλησίον Ἀμυδῶνος Αἶα καλουμένη καθαρώτατον ὕδωρ ἐκδιδοῦσα εἰς τὸν Ἄξιον, ὃς ἐκ πολλῶν πληρούμενος ποταμῶν θολερὸς ῥέει. φαύλη οὖν, φησίν, ἡ φερομένη γραφὴ "'Ἀξίου κάλλιστον ὕδωρ ἐπικίδναται Αἴη," ὡς δηλαδὴ οὐ τοῦ Ἀξίου ἐπικιδνάντος τὸ ὕδωρ τῇ πηγῇ, ἀλλ' ἀνάπαλιν· εἶτα ὑποδυσκόλως αἰτιώμενος ὁ γεωγράφος καὶ τὸ νοῆσαι τὴν αἶαν ἐπὶ τῆς γῆς ἔοικε παντελῶς ἐθέλειν ἐκβαλεῖν τοῦ Ὁμηρικοῦ ἔπους τὴν τοιαύτην λέξιν. (Eustathius on Iliad 2. 850.)

24. Ὅτι μετὰ τὸν Ἀξιὸν ποταμὸν ἡ Θεσσαλονίκη ἐστὶ πόλις, ἢ πρότερον Θέρμη ἐκαλεῖτο· κτίσμα δ' ἐστὶ Κασσάνδρου, ὃς ἐπὶ τῷ ὀνόματι τῆς ἑαυτοῦ γυναικός, παιδὸς δὲ Φιλίππου τοῦ

[1] τῆς γῆς τῇ ὄψει ἐπικίδναται, ἀλλὰ τὸ τῆς πηγῆς τῷ Ἀξίῳ, Corais, for τῆς γῆς τῇ ὄψει κίδναται, ἀλλὰ τῆς γῆς τῷ Ἀξίῳ. Meineke, following Politus (note on Eustathius in Eust., Vol. II, p. 779), reads τῇ πηγῇ ἐπικίδναται, ἀλλὰ τὸ τῆς πηγῆς

therefore the next line, "Axius, whose water most fair is spread o'er Aea," [1] is changed to read thus, "Axius, o'er which is spread Aea's water most fair"; for it is not the "water most fair" of the Axius that is spread over the face of the earth, but that of the spring o'er the Axius.

23a. In the phrase 'spread o'er Aiai,' or 'Aian,' [2] (for it is written in two ways), some are of the opinion that 'Aea' means, not the earth, but a certain spring, as is clear from what the Geographer says, namely: the Amydon in Homer was later called Abydon, but it was destroyed; and there is a spring near Amydon called Aea, which empties purest water into the Axius; and this river, since it is filled from many rivers, flows muddy. Therefore, he says, the current reading, 'Axius's water most fair spreads o'er Aea,' is faulty, because it is clearly not the water of the Axius that spread o'er the spring, but the reverse. Then the Geographer goes on somewhat gruffly to find fault with the opinion that Aea refers to the earth, and appears disposed to eject such diction from the Homeric poem altogether.

24. After the Axius River comes Thessalonica, a city which in earlier times was called Therma. It was founded by Cassander, who named it after his wife, the daughter of Philip the son of Amyntas.

---

[1] The usual meaning of "aea" in Homer is "earth."

[2] The Greek dative and accusative forms, respectively, of *Aia* (*Aea*).

τῷ 'Αξίῳ, perhaps rightly. But cp. the phrase ἡ ὄψις τῆς γῆς in O.T., Septuagint Version, *passim*, *e.g. Exod.* 2. 5. and *Num.* 22. 5.

Ἀμύντου, ὠνόμασε· μετῴκισε δὲ τὰ πέριξ πολίχνια εἰς αὐτήν, οἷον Χαλάστραν, Αἰνέαν,[1]
Κισσὸν καί τινα καὶ ἄλλα. ἐκ δὲ τοῦ Κισσοῦ
τούτου ὑπονοήσειεν ἄν τις γενέσθαι καὶ τὸν παρ'
Ὁμήρῳ Ἰφιδάμαντα,[2] οὗ ὁ πάππος Κισσεὺς
ἔθρεψεν αὐτόν, φησίν, ἐν Θρῄκῃ, ἣ νῦν Μακεδονία
καλεῖται. (Epit. ed.)

25. Ὅτι αὐτοῦ που καὶ τὸ Βέρμιον ὄρος, ὃ
πρότερον κατεῖχον Βρίγες, Θρᾳκῶν ἔθνος, ὧν
τινες διαβάντες εἰς τὴν Ἀσίαν Φρύγες μετωνο-
μάσθησαν. μετὰ δὲ Θεσσαλονίκειάν ἐστι τὰ
λοιπὰ τοῦ Θερμαίου κόλπου μέχρι τοῦ Καναστραίου.[3] τοῦτο δ' ἐστὶν ἄκρα χερρονησίζουσα,
ἀνταίρουσα τῇ Μαγνήτιδι· ὄνομα δὲ τῇ χερρονήσῳ Παλλήνη· πεντεστάδιον δ' ἔχει τὸν ἰσθμὸν
διορωρυγμένον· κεῖται δ' ἐπ' αὐτῷ πόλις ἡ
πρότερον μὲν Ποτίδαια, Κορινθίων κτίσμα, ὕστερον δὲ Κασσάνδρεια[4] ἀπὸ τοῦ αὐτοῦ βασιλέως
Κασσάνδρου,[4] ἀναλαβόντος αὐτὴν ἀνατετραμ-
μένην· ὁ περίπλους ταύτης τῆς χερρονήσου
πεντακοσίων καὶ ἑβδομήκοντα. ἔτι δὲ πρότερον
τοὺς Γίγαντας ἐνταῦθα γενέσθαι φασὶ καὶ τὴν
χώραν ὀνομάζεσθαι Φλέγραν οἱ μὲν μυθολογοῦν-
τες, οἱ δὲ πιθανώτερον ἔθνος τι βάρβαρον καὶ
ἀσεβὲς ἀποφαίνοντες τὸ κατέχον τὸν τόπον, κατα-

---

[1] Αἰνέαν, Meineke emends to Αἴνειαν ; cp. Αἰνέα, Frag. 22.
[2] Ἰφιδάμαντα, Kramer, for Ἀμφιδάμαντα ; so the later editors.
[3] Καναστραίου, Kramer, for Καλασυραίου ; so the later editors.

And he transferred to it the towns in the surrounding country, as, for instance, Chalastra, Aenea, Cissus, and also some others. And one might suspect that it was from this Cissus that Homer's Iphidamas came, whose grandfather Cisseus "reared him," Homer says, in Thrace, which now is called Macedonia.

25. Mt. Bermium,[1] also, is somewhere in this region; in earlier times it was occupied by Briges, a tribe of Thracians; some of these crossed over into Asia and their name was changed to Phryges. After Thessaloniceia come the remaining parts of the Thermaean Gulf as far as Canastraeum;[2] this is a headland which forms a peninsula and rises opposite to Magnetis. The name of the peninsula is Pallene; and it has an isthmus five stadia in width, through which a canal is cut. On the isthmus is situated a city founded by the Corinthians, which in earlier times was called Potidaea, although later on it was called Cassandreia, after the same King Cassander,[3] who restored it after it had been destroyed. The distance by sea around this peninsula is five hundred and seventy stadia. And further, writers say that in earlier times the giants lived here and that the country was named Phlegra;[4] the stories of some are mythical, but the account of others is more plausible, for they tell of a certain barbarous and impious tribe which occupied the

---

[1] Now Doxa. [2] Cape Paliuri.
[3] Cp. *Frag.* 21. [4] Cp. 5. 4. 4, 6.

---

[4] Κασσάνδρεια and Κασσάνδρου, Jones, for Κασάνδρεια and Κασάνδρου; cp. spelling in *Frags.* 24, 27, and in Ptolemaeus (3. 10).

STRABO

λυθὲν δ᾽ ὑπὸ Ἡρακλέους, ἡνίκα τὴν Τροίαν ἑλὼν ἀνέπλει εἰς τὴν οἰκείαν. κἀνταῦθα δὲ τῆς λύμης αἱ Τρωάδες αἴτιαι λέγονται, ἐμπρήσασαι τὰς ναῦς, ἵνα μὴ ταῖς γυναιξὶ τῶν ἑλόντων αὐτὰς δουλεύοιεν. (*Epit. Vat.*)

25a. Ὅτι δὲ Βρίγες καὶ οἱ Φρύγες ἐλέγοντο, δηλοῖ ὁ γεωγράφος. (Eustathius on *Od.* 1. 101.)

26. Ὅτι ἡ Βέροια πόλις ἐν ταῖς ὑπωρείαις κεῖται τοῦ Βερμίου ὄρους. (*Epit. ed.*)

27. Ὅτι ἡ Παλλήνη χερρόνησος, ἧς ἐν τῷ ἰσθμῷ κεῖται ἡ πρὶν μὲν Ποτίδαια, νῦν δὲ Κασσάνδρεια, Φλέγρα τὸ πρὶν ἐκαλεῖτο· ᾤκουν δ᾽ αὐτὴν οἱ μυθευόμενοι Γίγαντες, ἔθνος ἀσεβὲς καὶ ἄνομον, οὓς Ἡρακλῆς διέφθειρεν· ἔχει δὲ πόλεις τέσσαρας, Ἄφυτιν, Μένδην, Σκιώνην, Σάνην. (*Epit. ed.*)

27a. Ὁ δὲ Σκήψιος (scil. Δημήτριος) οὔτε τὴν τούτου (scil. Ἐφόρου) δόξαν ἔοικεν ἀποδεξάμενος οὔτε τῶν περὶ τὴν Παλλήνην τοὺς Ἀλιζώνους ὑπολαβόντων, ὧν ἐμνήσθημεν ἐν τοῖς Μακεδονικοῖς. (Strabo 12. 3. 22.)

28. Ὅτι διεῖχε Ποτιδαίας Ὄλυνθος ἑβδομήκοντα σταδίους. (*Epit. Vat.*)

29. Ὅτι τῆς Ὀλύνθου ἐπίνειόν ἐστι Μηκύπερνα ἐν τῷ Τορωναίῳ κόλπῳ. (*Epit. ed.*)

30. Ὅτι πλησίον Ὀλύνθου χωρίον ἐστὶ κοῖλον, καλούμενον Κανθαρώλεθρον, ἐκ τοῦ συμβεβηκότος· τὸ γὰρ ζῷον ὁ κάνθαρος πέριξ τῆς [1] χώρας γινόμενος, ἡνίκα ψαύσῃ τοῦ χωρίου ἐκείνου, διαφθείρεται. (*Epit. ed.*)

31. Μετὰ δὲ Κασσάνδρειαν [2] ἐφεξῆς ἡ λοιπὴ

---

[1] πέριξ τῆς ; Meineke reads τῆς πέριξ.

place but was broken up by Heracles when, after capturing Troy, he sailed back to his home-land. And here, too, the Trojan women were guilty of their crime, it is said, when they set the ships on fire in order that they might not be slaves to the wives of their captors.[1]

25a. The Geographer points out that the Phrygians too were called Brigians.

26. The city Beroea lies in the foot-hills of Mt. Bermium.

27. The peninsula Pallene, on whose isthmus is situated the city formerly called Potidaea and now Cassandreia, was called Phlegra in still earlier times. It used to be inhabited by the giants of whom the myths are told, an impious and lawless tribe, whom Heracles destroyed. It has four cities, Aphytis, Mende, Scione, Sane.

27a. The Scepsian[2] apparently accepts the opinion neither of this man[3] nor of those who suppose them[4] to be the Halizoni near Pallene, whom I have mentioned in my description of Macedonia.

28. Olynthus was seventy stadia distant from Potidaea.

29. The naval station of Olynthus is Macyperna, on the Toronaean Gulf.

30. Near Olynthus is a hollow place which is called Cantharolethron[5] from what happens there; for when the insect called the Cantharos, which is found all over the country, touches that place, it dies.

31. After Cassandreia, in order, comes the re-

---

[1] Cp. 6. 1. 12.   [2] Demetrius.   [3] Ephorus.
     [4] The Amazons.   [5] "Beetle-death."

---

[2] Κασσάνδρειαν, Jones, for Κασάνδρειαν; cp. spelling in *Frags.* 24, 27, and in Ptolemaeus (3. 10).

τοῦ Τορωνικοῦ κόλπου παραλία μέχρι Δέρρεως·
ἄκρα δ᾽ ἐστὶν ἀνταίρουσα τῷ Καναστραίῳ καὶ
ποιοῦσα τὸν κόλπον. ἀπαντικρὺ δὲ τῆς Δέρρεως
πρὸς ἔω τὰ ἄκρα τοῦ Ἄθω, μεταξὺ δὲ ὁ Σιγγιτι-
κὸς[1] κόλπος ἀπὸ τῆς ἐν αὐτῷ πόλεως ἀρχαίας
κατεσκαμμένης Σίγγου τοὔνομα. Μεθ᾽ ἣν Ἄκανθος
ἐπὶ τῷ ἰσθμῷ τοῦ Ἄθω κειμένη πόλις, Ἀνδρίων
κτίσμα, ἀφ᾽ ἧς συχνοὶ καὶ τὸν κόλπον Ἀκάνθιον
καλοῦσι. (Epit. Vat.)

32. Ὅτι ἀντικρὺ Καναστρου, ἄκρου τῆς Παλ-
λήνης, ἡ Δέρρις ἐστὶν ἄκρα, πλησίον Κωφοῦ
Λιμένος, καὶ ὁ Τορωναῖος κόλπος ὑπὸ τούτων
ἀφορίζεται. καὶ πρὸς ἀνατολὰς αὖθις κεῖται τὸ
ἄκρον τοῦ Ἄθωνος, ὃ ἀφορίζει τὸν Σιγγιτικὸν
κόλπον, ὡς εἶναι ἐφεξῆς κόλπους τοῦ Αἰγαίου
πελάγους πρὸς βορρᾶν, ἀλλήλων ἀπέχοντας
οὕτως· Μαλιακόν, Παγασιτικόν, Θερμαῖον, Το-
ρωναῖον, Σιγγιτικόν, Στρυμονικόν. τὰ δὲ ἄκρα
Ποσείδιον μὲν τὸ μεταξὺ Μαλιακοῦ καὶ Παγα-
σιτικοῦ, τὸ δὲ ἐφεξῆς πρὸς βορρᾶν Σηπιάς, εἶτα
τὸ ἐν Παλλήνῃ Κάναστρον, εἶτα Δέρρις, εἶτα
Νυμφαῖον ἐν τῷ Ἄθωνι πρὸς τῷ Σιγγιτικῷ, τὸ
δὲ πρὸς τῷ Στρυμονικῷ Ἀκράθως ἄκρον, ὧν
μεταξὺ ὁ Ἄθων, οὗ πρὸς ἀνατολὰς ἡ Λῆμνος·
πρὸς δὲ βορρᾶν ἀφορίζει τὸν Στρυμονικὸν κόλπον
ἡ Νεάπολις. (Epit. ed.)

33. Ὅτι Ἄκανθος πόλις ἐν τῷ Σιγγιτικῷ

_____

[1] Σιγγιτικός, Jones, for Σιγγικός, as in Frags. 32, 33, and in
Ptolemaeus (3. 9).

_____

[1] Cape Nymphaeum (now Hagios Georgios) is meant.

mainder of the seaboard of the Toronic Gulf,
extending as far as Derrhis. Derrhis is a headland
that rises opposite to Canastraeum and forms the
gulf; and directly opposite Derrhis, towards the east,
are the capes[1] of Athos; and between[2] is the Singitic
Gulf, which is named after Singus, the ancient city
that was on it, now in ruins. After this city comes
Acanthus, a city situated on the isthmus of Athos;
it was founded by the Andrii, and from it many call
the gulf the Acanthian Gulf.

32. Opposite Canastrum,[3] a cape of Pallene, is
Derrhis, a headland near Cophus Harbour; and
these two mark off the limits of the Toronaean
Gulf. And towards the east, again, lies the cape
of Athos, which marks off the limit of the Singitic
Gulf. And so the gulfs of the Aegaean Sea lie in
order, though at some distance from one another,
towards the north, as follows: the Maliac, the
Pagasitic, the Thermaean, the Toronaean, the Singitic, the Strymonic. The capes are, first, Poseidium,
the one between the Maliac and the Pegasitic;
secondly, the next one towards the north, Sepias;
then the one on Pallene, Canastrum; then Derrhis;
then come Nymphaeum, on Athos on the Singitic
Gulf, and Acrathos, the cape that is on the Strymonic
Gulf (Mt. Athos is between these two capes, and
Lemnos is to the east of Mt. Athos); on the north,
however, the limit of the Strymonic Gulf is marked
by Neapolis.[4]

33. Acanthus, a city on the Singitic Gulf, is on

---

[2] Derrhis and Nymphaeum (cp. *Frag.* 32).

[3] The same as "Canastraeum" (*Frags.* 25 and 31).

[4] Now Kavala.

κόλπῳ ἐστὶ παράλιος πλησίον τῆς τοῦ Ξέρξου διώρυχος· ἔχει δ' ὁ Ἄθων πέντε πόλεις, Δῖον, Κλεωνάς, Θύσσον,[1] Ὀλόφυξιν, Ἀκροθώους·[2] αὕτη δὲ πρὸς τῇ κορυφῇ τοῦ Ἄθωνος κεῖται. ἔστι δ' ὁ Ἄθων ὄρος μαστοειδές, ὀξύτατον, ὑψηλότατον· οὗ οἱ τὴν κορυφὴν οἰκοῦντες ὁρῶσι τὸν ἥλιον ἀνατέλλοντα πρὸ ὡρῶν τριῶν τῆς ἐν τῇ παραλίᾳ ἀνατολῆς. καὶ ἔστιν ἀπὸ πόλεως τῆς Ἀκάνθου ὁ περίπλους τῆς χερρονήσου ἕως Σταγείρου, πόλεως τοῦ Ἀριστοτέλους, στάδια τετρακόσια, ἐν ᾗ λιμὴν ὄνομα Κάπρος καὶ νησίον ὁμώνυμον τῷ λιμένι· εἶτα αἱ τοῦ Στρυμόνος ἐκβολαί· εἶτα Φάγρης, Γαληψός, Ἀπολλωνία, πᾶσαι πόλεις· εἶτα τὸ Νέστου[3] στόμα τοῦ διορίζοντος Μακεδονίαν καὶ Θρᾴκην, ὡς Φίλιππος καὶ Ἀλέξανδρος, ὁ τούτου παῖς, διώριζον ἐν τοῖς κατ' αὐτοὺς χρόνοις. εἰσὶ δὲ περὶ τὸν Στρυμονικὸν κόλπον πόλεις καὶ ἕτεραι, οἷον Μύρκινος, Ἄργιλος, Δραβῆσκος, Δάτον, ὅπερ καὶ ἀρίστην ἔχει χώραν καὶ εὔκαρπον καὶ ναυπήγια καὶ χρυσοῦ μέταλλα· ἀφ' οὗ καὶ παροιμία Δάτον ἀγαθῶν, ὡς καὶ Ἀγαθῶν ἀγαθῖδας. (Epit. ed.)

34. Ὅτι πλεῖστα μέταλλά ἐστι χρυσοῦ ἐν ταῖς Κρηνίσιν, ὅπου νῦν οἱ Φίλιπποι πόλις ἵδρυται, πλησίον τοῦ Παγγαίου ὄρους· καὶ αὐτὸ δὲ τὸ Παγγαῖον ὄρος χρυσεῖα καὶ ἀργυρεῖα ἔχει μέταλλα καὶ ἡ πέραν καὶ ἡ ἐντὸς τοῦ Στρυμόνος ποταμοῦ μέχρι Παιονίας· φασὶ δὲ καὶ τοὺς τὴν Παιονίαν γῆν ἀροῦντας εὑρίσκειν χρυσοῦ τινα μόρια. (Epit. ed.)

---

[1] Θύσσον, the editors, for Θύσσαν.
[2] Ἀκροθώους, the editors, for Ἀκρεσθώους.

the coast near the canal of Xerxes. Athos has five cities, Dium, Cleonae, Thyssus, Olophyxis, Acrothoï; and Acrothoï is near the crest of Athos. Mt. Athos is breast-shaped, has a very sharp crest, and is very high, since those who live on the crest see the sun rise three hours before it rises on the seaboard. And the distance by sea around the peninsula from the city Acanthus as far as Stageirus,[1] the city of Aristotle, is four hundred stadia. On this coast is a harbour, Caprus by name, and also an isle with the same name as the harbour. Then come the outlets of the Strymon; then Phagres, Galepsus, Apollonia, all cities; then the mouth of the Nestus,[2] which is the boundary between Macedonia and Thrace as fixed by Philip and his son Alexander in their times. There is also another set of cities about the Strymonic Gulf, as, for instance, Myrcinus, Argilus, Drabescus, and Datum.[3] The last named has not only excellent and fruitful soil but also dock-yards and gold mines; and hence the proverb, "a Datum of good things," like that other proverb, "spools of good things."

34. There are very many gold mines in Crenides, where the city Philippi[4] now is situated, near Mt. Pangaeum.[5] And Mt. Pangaeum as well has gold and silver mines, as also the country across, and the country this side, the Strymon River as far as Paeonia. And it is further said that the people who plough the Paeonian land find nuggets of gold.

---

[1] Now in ruins near Nizvoro.   [2] Now Mesta.
[3] See footnote on "Datum," *Frag.* 36.
[4] Now Filibedjik (see footnote on "Datum," *Frag.* 36).
[5] Now Pirnari.

---

[3] Νέστου, the editors, for Νέσσου.

STRABO

35. Ἔστι δ' ὁ Ἄθως ὄρος ὑψηλὸν καὶ μαστοειδές, ὥστε τοὺς ἐν ταῖς κορυφαῖς ἤδη ἀνίσχοντος
ἡλίου κάμνειν ἀροῦντας, ἡνίκα ἀλεκτοροφωνίας
ἀρχὴ παρὰ τοῖς τὴν ἀκτὴν οἰκοῦσίν ἐστιν. ἐν δὲ
τῇ ἀκτῇ ταύτῃ Θάμυρις ὁ Θρᾷξ ἐβασίλευσε, τῶν
αὐτῶν ἐπιτηδευμάτων γεγονώς, ὧν καὶ Ὀρφεύς.
ἐνταῦθα δὲ καὶ διῶρυξ δείκνυται ἡ περὶ τὴν
Ἄκανθον, καθ' ἣν Ξέρξης τὸν Ἄθω διορύξαι
λέγεται καὶ διαγαγεῖν ἐκ τοῦ Στρυμονικοῦ κόλπου
διὰ τοῦ ἰσθμοῦ, δεξάμενος τὴν θάλασσαν εἰς τὴν
διώρυγα. Δημήτριος δ' ὁ Σκήψιος οὐκ οἴεται
πλευσθῆναι τὴν διώρυγα ταύτην· μέχρι μὲν γὰρ
δέκα σταδίων εὔγεων καὶ ὀρυκτὴν εἶναι, διορω-
ρύχθαι δ' ἐπὶ πλάτος πλεθριαῖον, εἶθ' ὑψηλὸν
εἶναι πλαταμῶνα σταδιαῖον σχεδόν τι τὸ μῆκος,
ὅσον οὐκ ἐνὸν ἐκλατομηθῆναι δι' ὅλου μέχρι
θαλάσσης· εἰ δὲ καὶ μέχρι δεῦρο, οὔ γε καὶ κατὰ
βυθοῦ, ὥστε πόρον γενέσθαι πλωτόν· ὅπου
Ἀλέξαρχον τὸν Ἀντιπάτρου πόλιν ὑποδείμασθαι
τὴν Οὐρανόπολιν τριάκοντα σταδίων τὸν κύκλον
ἔχουσαν. ᾤκησαν δὲ τὴν χερρόνησον ταύτην τῶν
ἐκ Λήμνου Πελασγῶν τινες, εἰς πέντε διῃρημένοι
πολίσματα, Κλεωνάς, Ὀλόφυξιν, Ἀκροθώους,
Δῖον, Θύσσον. μετὰ δὲ Ἄθω ὁ Στρυμονικὸς
κόλπος μέχρι Νέστου,[1] τοῦ ποταμοῦ τοῦ ἀφορί-
ζοντος τὴν κατὰ Φίλιππον καὶ Ἀλέξανδρον
Μακεδονίαν· εἰς μέντοι τἀκριβὲς ἄκρα τίς ἐστι
ἡ ποιοῦσα τὸν κόλπον πρὸς τὸν Ἄθω, πόλιν

---

[1] Νέστου, the editors, for Νέσου.

[1] The third watch of the night.

356

FRAGMENTS OF BOOK VII

35. Mt. Athos is high and breast-shaped; so high that on its crests the sun is up and the people are weary of ploughing by the time cock-crow[1] begins among the people who live on the shore. It was on this shore that Thamyris the Thracian reigned, who was a man of the same pursuits as Orpheus.[2] Here, too, is to be seen a canal, in the neighbourhood of Acanthus, where Xerxes dug a canal across Athos, it is said, and, by admitting the sea into the canal, brought his fleet across from the Strymonic Gulf through the isthmus. Demetrius of Scepsis, however, does not believe that this canal was navigable, for, he says, although as far as ten stadia the ground is deep-soiled and can be dug, and in fact a canal one plethrum in width has been dug, yet after that it is a flat rock, almost a stadium in length, which is too high and broad to admit of being quarried out through the whole of the distance as far as the sea; but even if it were dug thus far, certainly it could not be dug deep enough to make a navigable passage; this, he adds, is where Alexarchus, the son of Antipater,[3] laid the foundation of Uranopolis, with its circuit of thirty stadia. Some of the Pelasgi from Lemnos took up their abode on this peninsula, and they were divided into five cities, Cleonae, Olophyxis, Acrothoï, Dium, Thyssus. After Athos comes the Strymonic Gulf extending as far as the Nestus, the river which marks off the boundary of Macedonia as fixed by Philip and Alexander; to be accurate, however, there is a cape which with Athos forms the Strymonic Gulf, I mean the cape which

[2] See *Frag.* 18.
[3] One of the foremost Macedonian generals (b. 497–d. 319 B.C.); also the father of Cassander.

ἐσχηκυῖα τὴν Ἀπολλωνίαν. ἐν δὲ τῷ κόλπῳ
πρώτη μετὰ τὸν Ἀκανθίων λιμένα Στάγειρα,
ἔρημος, καὶ αὐτὴ τῶν Χαλκιδικῶν, Ἀριστοτέλους
πατρίς, καὶ λιμὴν αὐτῆς Κάπρος καὶ νησίον
ὁμώνυμον τούτῳ· εἶθ᾽ ὁ Στρυμὼν καὶ ὁ ἀνάπλους
εἰς Ἀμφίπολιν εἴκοσι σταδίων· ἔστι δ᾽ Ἀθηναίων
κτίσμα ἐν τῷ τόπῳ ἱδρυμένον τούτῳ, ὃς καλεῖται
Ἐννέα Ὁδοί· εἶτα Γαληψὸς καὶ Ἀπολλωνία,
κατεσκαμμέναι ὑπὸ Φιλίππου. (*Epit. Vat.*)

36. Ἀπὸ Πηνειοῦ φησιν εἰς Πύδναν σταδίους
ἑκατὸν[1] εἴκοσι. παρὰ δὲ τὴν παραλίαν τοῦ
Στρυμόνος καὶ Δατηνῶν πόλις Νεάπολις καὶ αὐτὸ
τὸ Δάτον, εὔκαρπα πεδία καὶ λίμνην[2] καὶ ποταμοὺς καὶ ναυπήγια καὶ χρυσεῖα λυσιτελῆ ἔχον,
ἀφ᾽ οὗ καὶ παροιμιάζονται Δάτον ἀγαθῶν, ὡς καὶ
Ἀγαθῶν ἀγαθίδας. ἔστι δ᾽ ἡ χώρα ἡ πρὸς τὸ
Στρυμόνος πέραν, ἡ μὲν ἐπὶ τῇ θαλάττῃ καὶ τοῖς
περὶ Δάτον τόποις Ὀδομάντεις καὶ Ἠδωνοὶ καὶ
Βισάλται, οἵ τε αὐτόχθονες καὶ οἱ ἐκ Μακεδονίας

---

[1] ἑκατόν (ρ') probably should be emended to τριακοσίους (τ'),
as Kramer suggests.
[2] λίμνην, Tafel would emend to λιμένα; so C. Müller.

---

[1] The same Apollonia mentioned in *Frag.* 33. It was
rased to the ground by Philip. It must have been somewhere between Neapolis and the mouth of the Nestus. Cp.
Frag. 32, where Neapolis is spoken of as marking the northern
limit of the gulf.
[2] Now Kapronisi.   [3] "Nine Roads."
[4] Appian (*Bellum Civile* 4. 105) and also Harpocration say
that Datum was the earlier name of Philippi and that
Crenides was the name of the same place in still earlier
times. Leake (*Northern Greece*, Vol. III, pp. 223–4), Kiepert
(*Alte Geographie* 315), Forbiger (Strabo Vol. II, p. 140, footnote, 175), Besnier (*Lexique Géog. Ancienne s.v.* "Neapolis"),

has had on it a city called Apollonia.[1] The first city on this gulf after the harbour of the Acanthians is Stageira, the native city of Aristotle, now deserted; this too belongs to the Chalcidians and so do its harbour, Caprus, and an isle[2] bearing the same name as the harbour. Then come the Strymon and the inland voyage of twenty stadia to Amphipolis. Amphipolis was founded by the Athenians and is situated in that place which is called Ennea Hodoi.[3] Then come Galepsus and Apollonia, which were rased to the ground by Philip.

36. From the Peneius, he says, to Pydna is one hundred and twenty stadia. Along the seaboard of the Strymon and the Dateni are, not only the city Neapolis, but also Datum[4] itself, with its fruitful plains, lake, rivers, dock-yards, and profitable gold mines; and hence the proverb, "a Datum of good things," like that other proverb, "spools of good things." Now the country that is on the far side of the Strymon, I mean that which is near the sea and those places that are in the neighbourhood of Datum, is the country of the Odomantes and the Edoni and the Bisaltae, both those who are indigenous and those who crossed over from Macedonia, amongst whom

Lolling (*Hellenische Landeskunde*, 220, 230) identify Datum with Neapolis. But Heuzey (quoted by Philippson, Pauly-Wissowa *s.v.* "Datum") tries to reconcile these disagreements and the above statement of Strabo by assuming that originally Datum was that territory east of Mt. Pangarum which comprised the Plain of Philippi, the basin of the Angites River (including Drabescus now Drama), and the adjacent coast; and that later Neapolis (now Kavala) was founded on the coast and Datum was founded on the site of Crenides, and still later the city of Datum was named Philippi.

διαβάντες, ἐν οἷς Ῥῆσος ἐβασίλευσεν. ὑπὲρ δὲ τῆς Ἀμφιπόλεως Βισάλται καὶ μέχρι πόλεως Ἡρακλείας, ἔχοντες αὐλῶνα εὔκαρπον, ὃν διαιρεῖ[1] ὁ Στρυμών, ὡρμημένος ἐκ τῶν περὶ Ῥοδόπην Ἀγριάνων, οἷς παράκειται τῆς Μακεδονίας ἡ Παρορβηλία,[2] ἐν μεσογαίᾳ ἔχουσα κατὰ τὸν αὐλῶνα τὸν ἀπὸ Εἰδομένης Καλλίπολιν, Ὀρθό-πολιν, Φιλιππούπολιν, Γαρησκόν.

Ἐν δὲ τοῖς Βισάλταις ἀνὰ ποταμὸν ἰόντι τὸν Στρυμόνα καὶ ἡ Βέργη ἵδρυται, κώμη ἀπέχουσα Ἀμφιπόλεως περὶ διακοσίους σταδίους. ἐπὶ δὲ ἄρκτους ἰόντι ἀπὸ Ἡρακλείας καὶ τὰ στενά, δι' ὧν ὁ Στρυμὼν φέρεται, δεξιὸν ἔχοντι τὸν ποταμόν, ἐκ μὲν τῶν εὐωνύμων ἐστὶν ἡ Παιονία καὶ τὰ περὶ τὸν Δόβηρον καὶ τὴν Ῥοδόπην καὶ τὸν Αἷμον ὄρος, ἐν δεξιᾷ δὲ τὰ περὶ τὸν Αἷμον.[3] ἐντὸς δὲ τοῦ Στρυμόνος πρὸς αὐτῷ μὲν τῷ ποταμῷ ἡ Σκοτοῦσσά ἐστι· πρὸς δὲ τῇ λίμνῃ τῇ Βόλβῃ Ἀρέθουσα. καὶ δὴ καὶ μάλιστα λέγονται Μυγ-δόνες οἱ περὶ τὴν λίμνην. οὐ μόνον δ' ὁ Ἀξιὸς ἐκ Παιόνων ἔχει τὴν ῥύσιν, ἀλλὰ καὶ ὁ Στρυμών· ἐξ Ἀγριάνων γὰρ διὰ Μέδων[4] καὶ Σιντῶν εἰς τὰ

---

[1] διαιρεῖ, Jones restores, for διαρρεῖ (the conjecture of Kramer).

[2] Παρορβηλία, Kramer, for Γαρορβηδία; so the later editors.

[3] καὶ τὴν Ῥοδόπην καὶ τὸν Αἷμον ὄρος, ἐν δεξιᾷ δὲ περὶ τὸν Αἷμον (MSS.), C. Müller would emend to read as follows: ἐν δεξιᾷ δὲ τὰ περὶ τὴν Ῥοδόπην καὶ τὸν Αἷμον, or else simply delete καὶ τὴν Ῥοδόπην καὶ τὸν Αἷμον ὄρος. See note to translation.

[4] Μέδων, Jones restores, for Μαίδων; cp. Μέδων, 7. 5. 7 and 7. 5. 12.

Rhesus reigned. Above Amphipolis, however, and as far as the city Heracleia,[1] is the country of the Bisaltae, with its fruitful valley; this valley is divided into two parts by the Strymon, which has its source in the country of the Agrianes who live round about Rhodope; and alongside this country lies Parorbelia, a district of Macedonia, which has in its interior, along the valley that begins at Eidomene, the cities Callipolis, Orthopolis, Philippopolis, Garescus.

If one goes up the Strymon, one comes to Berge;[2] it, too, is situated in the country of the Bisaltae, and is a village about two hundred stadia distant from Amphipolis. And if one goes from Heracleia towards the north and the narrows through which the Strymon flows, keeping the river on the right, one has Paeonia and the region round about Doberus,[3] Rhodope, and the Haemus Mountain on the left, whereas on the right one has the region round about the Haemus.[4] This side the Strymon are Scotussa, near the river itself, and Arethusa, near Lake Bolbe.[5] Furthermore, the name Mygdones is applied especially to the people round about the lake. Not only the Axius flows out of the country of the Paeonians, but also the Strymon, for it flows out of the country of the Agrianes through that of the Medi and Sinti

---

[1] Heracleia Sintica (now Zervokhori.).

[2] Now Tachyno (Leake, *Northern Greece*, Vol. III, p. 229).

[3] The site of the city Doberus is uncertain (see Pauly-Wissowa, *s.v.*), though it appears to have been somewhere near Tauriana (now Doiran).

[4] The text, which even Meineke retains, is translated as it stands, but Strabo probably wrote as follows: "one has Paeonia and the region round about Doberus on the left, whereas on the right one has the parts round about Rhodope and the Haemus Mountain."

[5] Now Beschikgoel.

μεταξὺ Βισαλτῶν καὶ Ὀδομάντων ἐκπίπτει. (*Epit. Vat.*)

37. Ὅτι ὁ Στρυμὼν ποταμὸς ἄρχεται ἐκ τῶν περὶ τὴν Ῥοδόπην Ἀγριάνων. (*Epit. ed.*)

38. Τοὺς δὲ Παίονας οἱ μὲν ἀποίκους Φρυγῶν, οἱ δ᾽ ἀρχηγέτας ἀποφαίνουσι, καὶ τὴν Παιονίαν μέχρι Πελαγονίας καὶ Πιερίας ἐκτετάσθαι φασί· καλεῖσθαι δὲ πρότερον Ὀρεστίαν[1] τὴν Πελαγονίαν, τὸν δὲ Ἀστεροπαῖον, ἕνα τῶν ἐκ Παιονίας στρατευσάντων ἐπ᾽ Ἴλιον ἡγεμόνων, οὐκ ἀπεικότως υἱὸν λέγεσθαι Πηλεγόνος, καὶ αὐτοὺς τοὺς Παίονας καλεῖσθαι Πελαγόνας. (*Epit. Vat.*)

39. Ὅτι ὁ παρ᾽ Ὁμήρῳ Ἀστεροπαῖος, υἱὸς Πηλεγόνος, ἐκ Παιονίας ὢν τῆς ἐν Μακεδονίᾳ ἱστορεῖται· διὸ καὶ Πηλεγόνος υἱός· οἱ γὰρ Παίονες Πελαγόνες ἐκαλοῦντο. (*Epit. ed.*)

40. Ἐπεὶ δὲ ὁ παιανισμὸς τῶν Θρᾳκῶν τιτανισμὸς ὑπὸ τῶν Ἑλλήνων λέγεται κατὰ μίμησιν τῆς ἐν παιᾶσι φωνῆς, καὶ οἱ Τιτᾶνες ἐκλήθησαν Πελαγόνες. (*Epit. ed.*)

41. Ὅτι καὶ πάλαι καὶ νῦν οἱ Παίονες φαίνονται πολλὴν τῆς νῦν Μακεδονίας κατεσχηκότες, ὡς καὶ Πέρινθον πολιορκῆσαι καὶ Κρηστωνίαν καὶ Μυγδονίδα πᾶσαν καὶ τὴν Ἀγριάνων μέχρι Παγγαίου ὑπ᾽ αὐτοῖς γενέσθαι. τῆς δ᾽ ἐν τῷ Στρυμονικῷ κόλπῳ παραλίας τῆς ἀπὸ Γαληψοῦ μέχρι Νέστου ὑπέρκεινται οἱ Φίλιπποι[2] καὶ τὰ περὶ Φιλίππους. οἱ δὲ Φίλιπποι Κρηνίδες ἐκαλοῦντο πρότερον, κατοικία μικρά· ηὐξήθη δὲ μετὰ τὴν περὶ Βροῦτον καὶ Κάσσιον ἧτταν. (*Epit. Vat.*)

---

[1] Ὀρεστίαν, Kramer, for Ὀργεστίαν; so the later editors.
[2] Φίλιπποι, Kramer inserts; so the later editors.

and empties into the parts that are between the Bisaltae and the Odomantes.

37. The Strymon River rises in the country of the Agrianes who live round about Rhodope.

38. Some represent the Paeonians as colonists from the Phrygians, while others represent them as independent founders. And it is said that Paeonia has extended as far as Pelagonia and Pieria; that Pelagonia was called Orestia in earlier times; that Asteropaeus, one of the leaders who made the expedition from Paeonia to Troy, was not without good reason called "son of Pelegon," and that the Paeonians themselves were called Pelagonians.

39. The Homeric "Asteropaeus son of Pelegon"[1] was, as history tells us, from Paeonia in Macedonia; wherefore "son of Pelegon," for the Paeonians were called Pelagonians.

40. Since the "paeanismos"[2] of the Thracians is called "titanismos" by the Greeks, in imitation of the cry[3] uttered in paeans, the Titans too were called Pelagonians.

41. It is clear that in early times, as now, the Paeonians occupied much of what is now Macedonia, so that they could not only lay siege to Perinthus but also bring under their power all Crestonia and Mygdonis and the country of the Agrianes as far as Pangaeum.[4] Philippi and the region about Philippi lie above that part of the seaboard of the Strymonic Gulf which extends from Galepsus as far as Nestus. In earlier times Philippi was called Crenides, and was only a small settlement, but it was enlarged after the defeat of Brutus and Cassius.[5]

---

[1] *Iliad* 21. 141. [2] *i. e.* "the chanting of the paean."
[3] The cry to Titan. [4] See *Frag.* 34.
[5] In 42 B.C., after which it was made a Roman colony.

42 (43). Ὅτι οἱ νῦν Φίλιπποι πόλις Κρηνίδες ἐκαλοῦντο τὸ παλαιόν. (*Epit. ed.*)

43 (44). Πρόκεινται δὲ τῆς παραλίας ταύτης δύο νῆσοι, Λῆμνος καὶ Θάσος. μετὰ δὲ τὸν εἰς Θάσον πορθμὸν [1] Ἄβδηρα καὶ τὰ περὶ Ἀβδήρου μυθευόμενα. ᾤκησαν δ᾽ αὐτὴν Βίστονες Θρᾷκες, ὧν Διομήδης ἦρχεν· οὐ μένει δ᾽ ὁ Νέστος ἐπὶ ταὐτοῦ ῥείθρου διὰ παντός, ἀλλὰ κατακλύζει τὴν χώραν πολλάκις. εἶτα Δίκαια, πόλις ἐν κόλπῳ [2] κειμένη καὶ λιμήν· ὑπέρκειται δὲ τούτων ἡ Βιστονὶς λίμνη κύκλον ἔχουσα ὅσον διακοσίων σταδίων. φασὶ δὲ τοῦ πεδίου κοίλου παντάπασιν ὄντος καὶ ταπεινοτέρου τῆς θαλάττης, ἱπποκρατούμενον τὸν Ἡρακλέα, ἡνίκα ἦλθεν ἐπὶ τὰς τοῦ Διομήδους ἵππους, διορύξαι τὴν ἠιόνα καὶ τὴν θάλατταν ἐπαφέντα τῷ πεδίῳ κρατῆσαι τῶν ἐναντίων. δείκνυται δὲ καὶ τὸ βασίλειον Διομήδους ἀπὸ τοῦ συμβεβηκότος καλούμενον Καρτερὰ [3] Κώμη διὰ τὴν ἐρυμνότητα. μετὰ δὲ τὴν ἀνὰ μέσον λίμνην Ξάνθεια, Μαρώνεια καὶ Ἴσμαρος, αἱ τῶν Κικόνων πόλεις· καλεῖται δὲ νῦν Ἴσμαρα πλησίον τῆς Μαρωνείας· πλησίον δὲ καὶ ἡ Ἰσμαρὶς ἐξίησι λίμνη· καλεῖται δὲ τὸ

---

[1] Θάσον πορθμόν, Kramer inserts ; so the later editors.
[2] κόλπῳ, Schneidewin, for Ἰωλκῷ ; so Meineke.
[3] Καρτερά, Kramer, for . . . τερά, space for three letters being left in the *Epitome* ; so the later editors.

FRAGMENTS OF BOOK VII

42 (43). What is now the city Philippi was called Crenides in early times.

43 (44). Off this seaboard lie two islands, Lemnos and Thasos. And after the strait of Thasos one comes to Abdera[1] and the scene of the myths connected with Abderus. It was inhabited by the Bistonian Thracians over whom Diomedes ruled. The Nestus River does not always remain in the same bed, but oftentimes floods the country. Then come Dicaea,[2] a city situated on a gulf, and a harbour. Above these lies the Bistonis,[3] a lake which has a circuit of about two hundred stadia. It is said that, because this plain was altogether a hollow and lower than the sea, Heracles, since he was inferior in horse when he came to get the mares of Diomedes, dug a canal through the shore and let in the water of the sea upon the plain and thus mastered his adversaries. One is shown also the royal residence[4] of Diomedes, which, because of its naturally strong position and from what is actually the case, is called Cartera Come.[5] After the lake, which is midway between, come Xantheia,[6] Maroneia,[7] and Ismarus,[8] the cities of the Cicones. Ismarus, however, is now called Ismara; it is near Maroneia. And near here, also, Lake Ismaris sends forth its stream; this stream

[1] Now Balastra.
[2] Now, perhaps, Kurnu.
[3] Now Bourougoel.
[4] That is, the town of the royal palace, as "Camici" (6. 2. 6) was the "royal residence" of Cocalus.
[5] "Strong Village."
[6] Xantheia was situated on the mountain now called Xanthi.
[7] Now Maronia.   [8] Now Ismahan.

STRABO

ῥεῖθρον Ὀδύσσειον·[1] αὐτοῦ δὲ καὶ αἱ Θασίων λεγόμεναι κεφαλαί. Σαπαῖοι δ᾽ εἰσὶν οἱ ὑπερκείμενοι. (Epit. Vat.)

44 (45). Ὅτι τὰ Τόπειρά ἐστι πρὸς Ἀβδήροις καὶ Μαρωνεία. (Epit. Vat.)

44a. Ἡ ῥηθεῖσα Ἴσμαρος ἡ καὶ Ἴσμαρα ὕστερον, Κικόνων, φασί, πόλις, ἐγγὺς Μαρωνείας, ἔνθα καὶ λίμνη, ἧς τὸ ῥεῖθρον Ὀδύσσειον καλεῖται. ἐκεῖ δὲ καὶ Μάρωνος ἡρῷον, ὡς ὁ Γεωγράφος ἱστορεῖ. (Eustathius on Od. 9. 30.)

45 (46). Ὅτι Σιντοί, ἔθνος Θρακικόν, κατῴκει τὴν Λῆμνον νῆσον· ὅθεν Ὅμηρος Σίντιας αὐτοὺς καλεῖ, λέγων·

ἔνθα με Σίντιες ἄνδρες.

45a. Λῆμνος· ᾠκίσθη δὲ πρῶτον ὑπὸ Θρακῶν, οἳ Σίντιες ἐκαλοῦντο, ὡς Στράβων. (Stephanus Byzantinus, s.v. Λῆμνος.)

46 (47). Ὅτι μετὰ τὸν Νέστον ποταμὸν πρὸς ἀνατολὰς Ἄβδηρα πόλις, ἐπώνυμος Ἀβδήρου, ὃν οἱ τοῦ Διομήδους ἵπποι ἔφαγον· εἶτα Δίκαια πόλις πλησίον, ἧς ὑπέρκειται λίμνη μεγάλη, ἡ Βιστονίς· εἶτα πόλις Μαρώνεια. (Epit. ed.)

47 (48). Ἔστι δ᾽ ἡ Θράκη σύμπασα ἐκ δυεῖν καὶ εἴκοσιν ἐθνῶν συνεστῶσα· δύναται δὲ στέλλειν, καίπερ οὖσα περισσῶς ἐκπεπονημένη, μυρίους καὶ πεντακισχιλίους ἱππέας, πεζῶν δὲ καὶ εἴκοσι μυριάδας. μετὰ δὲ τὴν Μαρώνειαν Ὀρθαγορία πόλις καὶ τὰ περὶ Σέρριον,

---

[1] Ὀδύσσειον, Jones, for ἤδυ ... γειον (γιον scrip. supra), following Kunze's suggestion (Rheinisches Museum, 1903, Vol. LVIII, p. 126), based on Eustathius (note on the Odyssey

is called Odysseium. And here, too, are what are called the Thasiôn Cephalae.[1] But the people situated in the interior are Sapaei.

44 (45). Topeira is near Abdera and Maroneia.

44a. The aforesaid Ismarus, in later times called Ismara, is, they say, a city of the Cicones; it is near Maroneia, where is also a lake, the stream of which is called Odysseium; here too is a hero-temple of Maron, as the Geographer records.

45 (46). The Sinti, a Thracian tribe, inhabit the island Lemnos; and from this fact Homer calls them Sinties, when he says, "where me the Sinties . . ."[2]

45a. Lemnos: first settled by the Thracians who were called Sinties, according to Strabo.

46 (47). After the Nestus River, towards the east, is the city Abdera, named after Abderus, whom the horses of Diomedes devoured; then, near by, the city Dicaea, above which lies a great lake, Bistonis; then the city Maroneia.

47 (48). Thrace as a whole consists of twenty-two tribes. But although it has been devastated to an exceptional degree, it can send into the field fifteen thousand cavalry and also two hundred thousand infantry. After Maroneia one comes to the city Orthagoria and to the region about Serrhium[3] (a

---

[1] Literally, "Heads of the Thasii"; referring, apparently, to certain headlands occupied by Thasians.
[2] *Iliad* 1. 594; cp. Thucydides 2. 98.
[3] Cape Makri.

---

9. 30), who says of the lake in question: Ἰσμάρα . . . . ἐγγὺς Μαρονείας. ἔνθα καὶ λίμνη ἧς τὸ ῥεῖθρον Ὀδύσσειον καλεῖται . . . . . ὡς ὁ Γεωγράφος ἱστορεῖ. In the *Epitome* space is left for three (or four) letters between ἡδυ and γειον.

STRABO

παράπλους τραχύς, καὶ τὸ τῶν Σαμοθράκων
πολίχνιον Τέμπυρα καὶ ἄλλο Καράκωμα[1] οὗ
πρόκειται ἡ Σαμοθράκη νῆσος καὶ Ἴμβρος οὐ
πολὺ ἄποθεν ταύτης· πλέον δ᾽ ἢ διπλάσιον ἡ
Θάσος. ἀπὸ δὲ Καρακώματος[2] Δορίσκος, ὅπου
ἐμέτρησε Ξέρξης τῆς στρατιᾶς τὸ πλῆθος. Εἶθ᾽
Ἕβρος, ἀνάπλουν ἔχων εἰς Κύψελα ἑκατὸν[3]
εἴκοσι· τῆς Μακεδονίας φησὶ τοῦτο ὅριον, ἣν
ἀφείλοντο Περσέα Ῥωμαῖοι καὶ μετὰ ταῦτα τὸν
Ψευδοφίλιππον. Παῦλος μὲν οὖν ὁ τὸν Περσέα
ἑλὼν συνάψας τῇ Μακεδονίᾳ καὶ τὰ Ἠπειρωτικὰ
ἔθνη εἰς τέτταρα μέρη διέταξε τὴν χώραν, καὶ τὸ
μὲν προσένειμεν Ἀμφιπόλει, τὸ δὲ Θεσσαλονικείᾳ,
τὸ δὲ Πέλλῃ, τὸ δὲ Πελαγόσι. Παροικοῦσι δὲ
τὸν Ἕβρον Κορπῖλοι καὶ Βρέναι ἔτι ἀνωτέρω, εἶτ᾽
ἔσχατοι Βέσσοι· μέχρι γὰρ δεῦρο ὁ ἀνάπλους.
ἄπαντα δὲ τὰ ἔθνη ληστρικὰ ταῦτα, μάλιστα
δ᾽ οἱ Βέσσοι, οὓς λέγει γειτονεύειν Ὀδρύσαις
καὶ Σαπαίοις. Ἀστῶν[4] δὲ βασίλειον ἦν Βιζύη.[5]
Ὀδρύσας δὲ καλοῦσιν ἔνιοι πάντας τοὺς ἀπὸ
Ἕβρου καὶ Κυψέλων μέχρι Ὀδησσοῦ τῆς παραλίας ὑπεροικοῦντας, ὧν ἐβασίλευσεν Ἀμάδοκος

---

[1] Καράκωμα, Kramer and the later editors emend to
χαράκωμα, perhaps rightly; but both Καράκωμα and χαράκωμα
are otherwise unknown.
[2] Καρακώματος, Kramer and the later editors emend to
χαρακώματος.
[3] For ἑκατόν (ρ'), C. Müller suggests διακοσίους (σ').
[4] Ἀστῶν, Kramer, for Γετῶν; so the later editors.
[5] Βιζύη, the editors, for Βιζύης.

---

[1] Caracoma (or Characoma, meaning a fortress?) is otherwise
unknown.
[2] Now Tusla.   [7] Now Ipsala.   [4] sc. Strabo.

rough coasting-voyage) and to Tempyra, the little
town of the Samothracians, and to Caracoma,[1] another
little town, off which lies the island Samothrace, and
to Imbros, which is not very far from Samothrace;
Thasos, however, is more than twice as far from
Samothrace as Imbros is. From Caracoma one comes
to Doriscus,[2] where Xerxes enumerated his army;
then to the Hebrus, which is navigable inland to
Cypsela,[3] a distance of one hundred and twenty
stadia. This, he [4] says, was the boundary of the
Macedonia which the Romans first took away from
Perseus and afterwards from the Pseudo-Philip.[5]
Now Paulus,[6] who captured Perseus, annexed the
Epeirotic tribes to Macedonia, divided the country
into four parts for purposes of administration, and
apportioned one part to Amphipolis, another to
Thessaloniceia, another to Pella, and another to the
Pelagonians. Along the Hebrus live the Corpili,
and, still farther up the river, the Brenae, and then,
farthermost of all, the Bessi, for the river is navigable
thus far. All these tribes are given to brigandage,
but most of all the Bessi, who, he [7] says, are neighbours to the Odrysae and the Sapaei. Bizye [8] was
the royal residence of the Astae. The term
"Odrysae" is applied by some to all the peoples
living above the seaboard from the Hebrus and
Cypsela as far as Odessus [9]—the peoples over whom

[5] The younger brother of Perseus, whom Perseus regarded
as his heir.
[6] Aemilius Paulus Macedonicus, in his second consulship,
168 B.C., defeated Perseus near Pydna.
[7] sc Strabo.
[8] Bizye (now Viza) was the home of King Tereus (in the
story of Philomela and Procne) and was the residence of
the last Thracian dynasty, which was of the stock of the
Odrysae.   [9] Now Varna.

καὶ Κερσοβλέπτης καὶ Βηρισάδης [1] καὶ Σεύθης [2] καὶ Κότυς. (Epit. Vat.)

47a. Ὀδρύσαι· ἔθνος Θρᾴκης. Στράβων ἑβδόμῃ. (Stephanus Byzantinus, s.v. Ὀδρύσαι.)

47b. Ὁ δὲ Γεωγράφος καὶ τὸ πολὺ τῆς Θρᾳκικῆς περιοχῆς δηλῶν λέγει ὡς ἡ Θράκη σύμπασα ἐκ δύο καὶ εἴκοσι ἐθνῶν συνέστηκεν. (Eustathius on Iliad 2. 844.)

48 (49). Ὅτι ὁ νῦν ποταμὸς Ῥηγινία ἐν Θρᾴκῃ καλούμενος Ἐρίγων [3] ἦν καλούμενος. (Epit. ed.)

49 (50). Ὅτι τὴν Σαμοθρᾴκην Ἰασίων καὶ Δάρδανος ἀδελφοὶ ᾤκουν· κεραυνωθέντος δὲ Ἰασίωνος διὰ τὴν εἰς Δήμητρα ἁμαρτίαν, ὁ Δάρδανος ἀπάρας ἐκ Σαμοθρᾴκης, ἐλθὼν ᾤκησεν ἐν τῇ ὑπωρείᾳ τῆς Ἴδης, τὴν πόλιν Δαρδανίαν καλέσας, καὶ ἐδίδαξε τοὺς Τρῶας τὰ ἐν Σαμοθρᾴκῃ μυστήρια· ἐκαλεῖτο δὲ ἡ Σαμοθρᾴκη Σάμος πρίν. (Epit. ed.)

50 (51). Ὅτι τοὺς ἐν τῇ Σαμοθρᾴκῃ τιμωμένους θεοὺς εἰρήκασι πολλοὶ τοὺς αὐτοὺς τοῖς Καβείροις, οὐδ᾽ αὐτοὺς ἔχοντες λέγειν τοὺς Καβείρους, οἵ τινές εἰσι, καθάπερ τοὺς Κύρβαντας καὶ Κορύβαντας, ὡς δ᾽ αὕτως Κουρῆτας καὶ Ἰδαίους Δακτύλους. (Epit. Vat.)

50a. Ἡ Θρᾳκικὴ αὕτη κατὰ τὸν Γεωγράφον Σάμος καλεῖται διὰ τὸ ὕψος. σάμοι γάρ, φησί, τὰ ὕψη . . . λέγει δὲ ὁ Γεωγράφος ὅτι Σάμιοι ἐκ Μυκάλης πάλαι ᾤκισαν ἐν αὐτῇ, ἐρημωθείσῃ κατὰ ἀφορίαν καρπῶν, ὥστε καὶ οὕτω κληθῆναι Σάμον. . . . ἱστορεῖ δὲ ὁ Γεωγράφος καὶ Μελίτην πρότερον τὴν Σαμοθρᾴκην καλεῖσθαι καὶ πλου-

---

[1] Βηρισάδης, the editors, for Βηρισιάδης.

370

Amadocus, Cersobleptes, Berisades, Seuthes, and Cotys reigned as kings.

47a. Odrysae: a tribe of Thrace; Strabo in his Seventh Book.

47b. The Geographer, in pointing out the great extent of Thrace, says also that Thrace as a whole consists of twenty-two tribes.

48 (49). The river in Thrace that is now called Rheginia used to be called Erigon.

49 (50). Iasion and Dardanus, two brothers, used to live in Samothrace. But when Iasion was struck by a thunderbolt because of his sin against Demeter, Dardanus sailed away from Samothrace, went and took up his abode at the foot of Mount Ida, calling the city Dardania, and taught the Trojans the Samothracian Mysteries. In earlier times, however, Samothrace was called Samos.

50 (51). Many writers have identified the gods that are worshipped in Samothrace with the Cabeiri, though they cannot say who the Cabeiri themselves are, just as the Cyrbantes and Corybantes, and likewise the Curetes and the Idaean Dactyli, are identified with them.

50a. This Thracian island, according to the Geographer, is called Samos because of its height; for "samoi," he says, means "heights." . . . And the Geographer says that in olden times Samians from Mycale settled in the island, which had been deserted because of a dearth of crops, and that in this way it was called Samos. . . . And the Geographer records also that in earlier times Samothrace was called Melite, as also that it was rich; for

---

² Σεύθης, the editors, for Θησεύς.

³ Ἐρίγων may be an error for Ἐργῖνος.

σίαν δὲ εἶναι. Κίλικες γάρ, φησί, πειραταὶ προσπεσόντες λάθρα τὸ ἐν Σαμοθράκῃ ἐσύλησαν ἱερὸν καὶ ἀπήνεγκαν τάλαντα πλείω χιλίων. (Eustathius on *Iliad* 13. 12.)

51 (52). Πρὸς δὲ τῇ ἐκβολῇ τοῦ Ἕβρου, δι-στόμου ὄντος, πόλις Αἶνος ἐν τῷ Μέλανι κόλπῳ κεῖται, κτίσμα Μιτυληναίων καὶ Κυμαίων, ἔτι δὲ πρότερον Ἀλωπεκοννησίων· εἶτ᾽ ἄκρα Σαρπηδών· εἶθ᾽ ἡ Χερρόνησος ἡ Θρᾳκία καλουμένη, ποιοῦσα τήν τε Προποντίδα καὶ τὸν Μέλανα κόλπον καὶ τὸν Ἑλλήσποντον· ἄκρα γὰρ ἔκκειται πρὸς εὐρόνοτον, συνάπτουσα τὴν Εὐρώπην πρὸς τὴν Ἀσίαν ἑπτασταδίῳ πορθμῷ τῷ κατὰ Ἄβυδον καὶ Σηστόν, ἐν ἀριστερᾷ μὲν τὴν Προποντίδα ἔχουσα, ἐν δεξιᾷ δὲ τὸν Μέλανα κόλπον, καλού-μενον οὕτως ἀπὸ τοῦ Μέλανος ἐκδιδόντος εἰς αὐτόν, καθάπερ Ἡρόδοτος καὶ Εὔδοξος· εἴρηκε δέ, φησίν, ὁ Ἡρόδοτος μὴ ἀνταρκέσαι τὸ ῥεῖθρον τῇ Ξέρξου στρατιᾷ τοῦτο· ἰσθμῷ δὲ κλείεται τετταράκοντα σταδίων ἡ λεχθεῖσα ἄκρα. ἐν μέσῳ μὲν οὖν τοῦ ἰσθμοῦ Λυσιμάχεια πόλις ἵδρυται ἐπώνυμος τοῦ κτίσαντος βασιλέως· ἑκα-τέρωθεν δ᾽ ἐπὶ μὲν τῷ Μέλανι κόλπῳ Καρδία κεῖται, μεγίστη τῶν ἐν τῇ Χερρονήσῳ πόλεων, Μιλησίων καὶ Κλαζομενίων κτίσμα, ὕστερον δὲ καὶ Ἀθηναίων, ἐν δὲ τῇ Προποντίδι Πακτύη. μετὰ δὲ Καρδίαν Δράβος καὶ Λίμναι· εἶτ᾽ Ἀλωπεκόννησος, εἰς ἣν τελευτᾷ μάλιστα ὁ Μέλας κόλπος· εἶτ᾽ ἄκρα μεγάλη Μαζουσία· εἶτ᾽ ἐν

---

[1] Now Enos.
[2] Gulf of Saros.

Cilician pirates, he says, secretly broke into the temple in Samothrace, robbed it, and carried off more than a thousand talents.

51 (52). Near the outlet of the Hebrus, which has two mouths, lies the city Aenus,[1] on the Melas Gulf;[2] it was founded by Mitylenaeans and Cumaeans, though in still earlier times by Alopeconnesians. Then comes Cape Sarpedon; then what is called the Thracian Chersonesus, which forms the Propontis and the Melas Gulf and the Hellespont; for it is a cape which projects towards the south-east, thus connecting Europe with Asia by the strait, seven stadia wide, which is between Abydus and Sestus, and thus having on the left the Propontis and on the right the Melas Gulf—so called, just as Herodotus[3] and Eudoxus say, from the Melas River[4] which empties into it. But Herodotus,[5] he[6] says, states that this stream was not sufficient to supply the army of Xerxes. The aforesaid cape is closed in by an isthmus forty stadia wide. Now in the middle of the isthmus is situated the city Lysimacheia, named after the king who founded it; and on either side of it lies a city—on the Melas Gulf, Cardia, the largest of the cities on the Chersonesus, founded by Milesians and Clazomenians but later refounded by Athenians, and on the Propontis, Pactye. And after Cardia come Drabus and Limnae; then Alopeconnesus, in which the Melas Gulf comes approximately to an end; then the large headland, Mazusia;

[3] 7. 58.   [4] Now called by the Turks "Kavatch Su."
[5] 7. 58.   [6] *sc.* Strabo.

STRABO

κόλπῳ Ἐλεοῦς,[1] ὅπου τὸ Πρωτεσιλάειον, καθ᾽
ὃ τὸ Σίγειον ἀπὸ τεττεράκοντα σταδίων ἐστίν,
ἄκρα τῆς Τρῳάδος· καὶ σχεδὸν τοῦτ᾽ ἔστι τὸ
νοτιώτατον ἄκρον τῆς Χερρονήσου, σταδίους
μικρῷ πλείους τῶν τετρακοσίων ἀπὸ Καρδίας·
καὶ οἱ λοιποὶ δ᾽ ἐπὶ θάτερον μέρος τοῦ ἰσθμοῦ
μικρῷ τοῦ διαστήματος τούτου πλείους περι-
πλέοντι. (*Epit. Vat.*)

51a. Αἶνος· πόλις Θρᾴκης, Ἄψυνθος καλουμένη. Στράβων ζ'· ἐν δὲ τῇ ἐκβολῇ τοῦ Ἕβρου
διστόμου ὄντος πόλις Αἶνος, καὶ κτίσμα Κυμαίων,
κληθῆναι δὲ αὐτὴν ὅτι πλησίον τῆς Ὄσσης ἦν
Αἶνιος[2] ποταμὸς καὶ κώμη ὁμώνυμος. (Stephanus
Byzantinus, *s.v.* Αἶνος.)

52 (53). Ὅτι ἡ ἐν Θρᾴκῃ Χερρόνησος τρεῖς
ποιεῖ θαλάσσας· Προποντίδα ἐκ βορρᾶ, Ἑλλήσποντον ἐξ ἀνατολῶν καὶ τὸν Μέλανα κόλπον
ἐκ νότου, ὅπου καὶ ὁ Μέλας ποταμὸς ἐκβάλλει,[3]
ὁμώνυμος τῷ κόλπῳ. (*Epit. ed.*)

53 (54). Ὅτι ἐν τῷ ἰσθμῷ τῆς Χερρονήσου
τρεῖς πόλεις κεῖνται· πρὸς μὲν τῷ Μέλανι κόλπῳ
Καρδία, πρὸς δὲ τῇ Προποντίδι Πακτύη, πρὸς
δὲ τῇ μεσογαίᾳ Λυσιμαχεία· μῆκος τοῦ ἰσθμοῦ
στάδια τεσσαράκοντα. (*Epit. ed.*)

54 (55). Ὅτι ἡ πόλις ὁ Ἐλεοῦς[4] ἀρσενικῶς
λέγεται· τάχα δὲ καὶ ὁ Τραπεζοῦς. (*Epit. ed.*)

55 (56). Ἔστι δ᾽ ἐν τῷ περίπλῳ τούτῳ τῷ

---

[1] Ἐλεοῦς, Meineke emends to Ἐλαιοῦς, but the name was
spelled both ways after 400 B.C. (Pauly-Wissowa, *s.v.*
"Flaeus").

[2] Αἶνιος, Jones, for Αἶμος. (Cp. Stephanus Byzantinus,
s.v. Αἰνία, and Pauly-Wissowa (*s.vv.* "Ainios" and "Ainos").

374

then, on a gulf, Eleus,[1] where is the temple of
Protesilaus, opposite which, forty stadia distant, is
Sigeium,[2] a headland of the Troad; and this is about
the most southerly extremity of the Chersonesus,
being slightly more than four hundred stadia from
Cardia; and if one sails around the rest of the circuit,
towards the other side of the isthmus, the distance is
slightly more than this.

51a. Aenus; a city of Thrace, called Apsinthus.
Strabo in his Seventh Book. The city Aenus is in
the outlet of the Hebrus, which has two mouths,
and was founded by Cumaeans; and it was so called
because there was an Aenius River and also a village
of the same name near Ossa.

52 (53). The Thracian Chersonesus forms three
seas: the Propontis in the north, the Hellespont
in the east, and the Melas Gulf in the south, into
which empties the Melas River, which bears the
same name as the gulf.

53 (54). On the isthmus of the Chersonesus are
situated three cities: near the Melas Gulf, Cardia,
and near the Propontis, Pactye, and near the middle,
Lysimacheia. The length [3] of the isthmus is forty
stadia.

54 (55). The name of the city Eleus is masculine;
and perhaps also that of the city Trapezus.

55 (56). On this voyage along the coast of the

---

[1] The better spelling of the name is " Elaeus."
[2] Now Yeni-scheher.
[3] " Length " here means " breadth " (see *Frag.* 51).

---

[3] ἐκβάλλει, Meineke, for βάλλει.
[4] Ἐλεοῦς, Meineke emends to Ἐλαιοῦς.

μετὰ Ἐλεοῦντα¹ ἡ εἰσβολὴ πρῶτον ἡ εἰς τὴν
Προποντίδα διὰ τῶν στενῶν, ἥν φασιν ἀρχὴν
εἶναι τοῦ Ἑλλησπόντου· ἐνταῦθα δ' ἐστὶ τὸ
Κυνὸς Σῆμα ἄκρα, οἱ δ' Ἑκάβης φασί· καὶ γὰρ
δείκνυται κάμψαντι τὴν ἄκραν τάφος αὐτῆς. Εἶτα
Μάδυτος καὶ Σηστιὰς ἄκρα, καθ' ἣν τὸ Ξέρξου
ζεῦγμα, καὶ μετὰ ταῦτα Σηστός. ἀπὸ δὲ Ἐλεοῦντος
ἐπὶ τὸ ζεῦγμα ἑκατὸν ἑβδομήκοντα· μετὰ δὲ
Σηστὸν ἐπὶ Αἰγὸς ποταμοὺς² ὀγδοήκοντα, πολίχνην κατεσκαμμένην, ὅπου φασὶ τὸν λίθον
πεσεῖν κατὰ τὰ Περσικά· εἶτα Καλλίπολις, ἀφ'
ἧς εἰς Λάμψακον δίαρμα εἰς τὴν Ἀσίαν τεττα-
ράκοντα· εἶτα πολίχνιον κατεσκαμμένον Κριθωτή·
εἶτα Πακτύη· εἶτα τὸ Μακρὸν Τεῖχος καὶ Λευκὴ
ἀκτὴ καὶ τὸ Ἱερὸν Ὄρος καὶ Πέρινθος, Σαμίων
κτίσμα· εἶτα Σηλυβρία. ὑπέρκειται δ' αὐτῶν
Σίλτα, καὶ τὸ Ἱερὸν Ὄρος τιμᾶται ὑπὸ τῶν
ἐγχωρίων καὶ ἔστιν οἷον ἀκρόπολις τῆς χώρας.
ἄσφαλτον δ' ἐξίησιν εἰς τὴν θάλασσαν, καθ' ὃν
τόπον ἡ Προκόννησος ἐγγυτάτω τῆς γῆς ἐστι ἀπὸ
ἑκατὸν εἴκοσι σταδίων, τὸ μέταλλον ἔχουσα τῆς
λευκῆς μαρμάρου πολύ τε καὶ σπουδαῖον. μετὰ δὲ

¹ Ἐλεοῦντα, Meineke emends to Ἐλαιοῦντα.
² διακόσιοι (σ'), after ποταμούς, Jones deletes.

---

¹ *i.e.* "Bitch's Monument"; according to one story
Hecabe (Hecuba) was metamorphosed into a bitch.
² The text reads "two hundred and eighty," but this is
clearly an error of the copyist.

FRAGMENTS OF BOOK VII

Chersonesus after leaving Eleus, one comes first to the entrance which leads through the narrows into the Propontis; and this entrance is called the beginning of the Hellespont. And here is the cape called the Cynos-Sema;[1] though some call it Hecabe's Sema, and in fact her tomb is pointed out after one has doubled the cape. Then one comes to Madytus, and to Cape Sestias, where the pontoon-bridge of Xerxes was built; and, after these, to Sestus. The distance from Eleus to the place of the pontoon-bridge is one hundred and seventy stadia. After Sestus one comes to Aegospotami, eighty[2] stadia, a town which has been rased to the ground, where it is said, the stone[3] fell at the time of the Persian war. Then comes Callipolis,[4] from which the distance across to Lampsacus in Asia is forty stadia; then Crithote, a little town which has been rased to the ground; then Pactye; then Macron Teichos,"[5] Leuce Acte,[6] Hieron Oros,[7] and Perinthus, founded by the Samians: then Selybria.[8] Above these places lies Silta;[9] and the Hieron Oros is revered by all the natives and is a sort of acropolis of the country. The Hieron Oros discharges asphalt into the sea, near the place where the Proconnesus,[10] only one hundred and twenty stadia distant, is nearest to the land; and the quarry of white marble in the Proconnesus is both large and excellent. After Selybria come the

---

[3] On this meteor, see Aristotle, *Meteorologica*, 1. 7, and Pliny, *Nat. Hist.* 2. 58 (59).
[4] Now Gallipoli.   [5] "Long Wall."
[6] "White Strand."   [7] "Sacred Mountain."
[8] Also spelled "Selymbria."
[9] What is now Schandu, apparently.
[10] Now the Isle of Marmara.

Σηλυβρίαν Ἀθύρας ἐστὶ ποταμὸς καὶ Βαθυνίας·[1]
εἶτα Βυζάντιον καὶ τὰ ἐφεξῆς μέχρι Κυανέων
Πετρῶν. (*Epit. Vat.*)

55a. Περὶ δὲ Σηστοῦ καὶ τῆς ὅλης Χερρονήσου
προείπομεν ἐν τοῖς περὶ τῆς Θρᾴκης τόποις.
(Strabo 13. 1. 22.)

55b. Σηστὸς μέν, Λεσβίων ἄποικος, καθὰ καὶ
ἡ Μάδυτος, ὡς ὁ Γεωγράφος φησί, Χερρονησία
πόλις, Ἀβύδου διέχουσα σταδίους λ΄, ἐκ λιμένος
εἰς λιμένα. (Stephanus Byzantinus, *s.v.* Σηστός.)

56 (57). Ὅτι ἐκ Περίνθου εἰς Βυζάντιόν εἰσιν
ἑξακόσιοι τριάκοντα· ἀπὸ δὲ Ἕβρου καὶ Κυψέλων
εἰς Βυζάντιον μέχρι Κυανέων τρισχίλιοι ἑκατόν,
ὥς φησιν Ἀρτεμίδωρος· τὸ δὲ σύμπαν μῆκος
ἀπὸ Ἰονίου κόλπου τοῦ κατὰ Ἀπολλωνίαν μέχρι
Βυζαντίου ἑπτακισχίλιοι τριακόσιοι εἴκοσι, προσ-
τίθησι δ᾽ ὁ Πολύβιος καὶ ἄλλους ἑκατὸν ὀγδοήκοντα, τὸ τρίτον τοῦ σταδίου προσλαμβάνων
ἐπὶ τοῖς ὀκτὼ τοῦ μιλίου σταδίοις. Δημήτριος
δ᾽ ὁ Σκήψιος ἐν τοῖς περὶ τοῦ Τρωικοῦ διακόσμου
τὸ μὲν ἐκ Περίνθου μέχρι Βυζαντίου φησὶν ἑξακοσίους σταδίους, τὸ δ᾽ ἴσον μέχρι Παρίου. τὴν
δὲ Προποντίδα μήκει μὲν χιλίων καὶ τετρακοσίων
ἀποφαίνει σταδίων, εἰς εὖρος δὲ πεντακοσίων.
τοῦ δὲ Ἑλλησπόντου τὸ στενώτατον ἑπταστάδιόν
φησι, μῆκος δὲ τετρακοσίων. (*Epit. Vat.*)

57 (58). Ὅτι Ἑλλήσποντος οὐχ ὁμολογεῖται

---

[1] Βαθυνίας, Meineke (following conj. of Kramer), for
. . . ουνιας.

[1] This work consisted of thirty books, and was written
as an interpretation of Homer's catalogue (62 lines) of the

Rivers Athyras and Bathynias; and then, Byzantium and the places which come in order thereafter as far as the Cyanean Rocks.

55a. As for Sestus and the whole of the Chersonesus, I have already discussed them in my description of the regions of Thrace.

55b. Sestus, a colony of the Lesbians, as is also Madytus, as the Geographer says, is a Chersonesian city thirty stadia distant from Abydus, from harbour to harbour.

56 (57). The distance from Perinthus to Byzantium is six hundred and thirty stadia; but from the Hebrus and Cypsela to Byzantium, as far as the Cyanean Rocks, three thousand one hundred, as Artemidorus says; and the entire distance from the Ionian Gulf at Apollonia as far as Byzantium is seven thousand three hundred and twenty stadia, though Polybius adds one hundred and eighty more, since he adds a third of a stadium to the eight stadia in the mile. Demetrius of Scepsis, however, in his work *On the Marshalling of the Trojan Forces* [1] calls the distance from Perinthus to Byzantium six hundred stadia and the distance to Parium equal thereto; and he represents the Propontis as one thousand four hundred stadia in length and five hundred in breadth; while as for the Hellespont, he calls its narrowest breadth seven stadia and its length four hundred.

57 (58). There is no general agreement in the

Trojan forces (*Iliad* 2. 816–877), as Strabo says elsewhere (13. 1. 45).

παρὰ πᾶσιν ὁ αὐτός, ἀλλὰ δόξαι περὶ αὐτοῦ λέγονται πλείους. οἱ μὲν γὰρ ὅλην τὴν Προποντίδα καλοῦσιν Ἑλλήσποντον, οἱ δὲ μέρος τῆς Προποντίδος τὸ ἐντὸς Περίνθου. οἱ δὲ προσλαμβάνουσι καὶ τῆς ἔξω θαλάσσης τῆς πρὸς τὸ Αἰγαῖον πέλαγος καὶ τὸν Μέλανα κόλπον ἀνεῳγμένης, καὶ οὗτοι ἄλλος ἄλλα ἀποτεμνόμενος· οἱ μὲν τὸ ἀπὸ Σιγείου ἐπὶ Λάμψακον καὶ Κύζικον ἢ Πάριον ἢ Πρίαπον, ὁ δὲ προσλαμβάνων καὶ τὸ ἀπὸ Σιγρίου τῆς Λεσβίας. οὐκ ὀκνοῦσι δέ τινες καὶ τὸ μέχρι τοῦ Μυρτῴου πελάγους ἄπαν καλεῖν Ἑλλήσποντον, εἴπερ, ὥς φησιν ἐν τοῖς ὕμνοις Πίνδαρος, οἱ μεθ' Ἡρακλέους ἐκ Τροίας πλέοντες διὰ παρθένιον Ἕλλας πορθμόν, ἐπεὶ τῷ Μυρτῴῳ συνῆψαν, εἰς Κῶν ἐπαλινδρόμησαν Ζεφύρου ἀντιπνεύσαντος. Οὕτω δὲ καὶ τὸ Αἰγαῖον πέλαγος μέχρι τοῦ Θερμαίου κόλπου καὶ τῆς κατὰ Θετταλίαν καὶ Μακεδονίαν θαλάσσης ἄπαν ἀξιοῦσι Ἑλλήσποντον προσαγορεύειν δεῖν, μάρτυρα καὶ Ὅμηρον καλοῦντες. φησὶ γάρ·

ὄψεαι, ἢν ἐθέλησθα καὶ αἴ κέν τοι τὰ μεμήλῃ,
ἠρι μάλ' Ἑλλήσποντον ἐπ' ἰχθυόεντα πλεούσας
νῆας ἐμάς.

ἐλέγχεται δὲ τὸ τοιοῦτον ἐκ τῶν ἐπῶν ἐκείνων·

ἥρως¹ Ἰμβρασίδης, ὃς ἄρ' Αἰνόθεν εἰληλούθει

οὗτος δὲ τῶν Θρᾳκῶν ἡγεῖτο,

ὅσσους Ἑλλήσποντος ἀγάρροος ἐντὸς ἐέργει·

---

¹ ἥρως need not be emended to Πείρως, or Πείροος (cp. Kramer, Forbiger, Tardieu, and C. Müller); see the *Iliad*, 2. 845 and 4. 520.

definition of the term "Hellespont": in fact, there
are several opinions concerning it. For some writers
call "Hellespont" the whole of the Propontis;
others, that part of the Propontis which is this side
Perinthus; others go on to add that part of the
outer sea which faces the Melas Gulf and the open
waters of the Aegaean Sea, and these writers in turn
each comprise different sections in their definitions,
some the part from Sigeium to Lampsacus and
Cyzicus, or Parium, or Priapus, another going on to
add the part which extends from Sigrium in the
Lesbian Isle. And some do not shrink even from
applying the name Hellespont to the whole of the
high sea as far as the Myrtoan Sea, since, as Pindar [1]
says in his hymns, those who were sailing with
Heracles from Troy through Helle's maidenly strait,
on touching the Myrtoan Sea, ran back again to Cos,
because Zephyrus blew contrary to their course.
And in this way, also, they require that the whole
of the Aegaean Sea as far as the Thermaean Gulf and
the sea which is about Thessaly and Macedonia
should be called Hellespont, invoking Homer also
as witness; for Homer [2] says, "thou shalt see, if
thou dost wish and hast a care therefor, my ships
sailing o'er the fishy Hellespont at very early
morn"; but such an argument is refuted by those
other lines, "the hero,[3] son of Imbrasus, who, as we
know, had come from Aenus," [4] but he was the
leader of the Thracians,[5] "all who are shut in by
strong-flowing Hellespont"; [6] that is, Homer would

---

[1] *Frag.* 51 (Bergk).   [2] *Iliad* 9. 359.
[3] Peiroüs.   [4] *Iliad* 4. 520.
[5] *Iliad* 2. 844 and 4. 519.   [6] *Iliad* 2. 845.

τοὺς γὰρ ἐφεξῆς τούτων ἐκτὸς ἂν καὶ τοῦ Ἑλλησπόντου καθιδρυμένους ἀποφαίνοι. ἡ μὲν γὰρ Αἶνος κεῖται κατὰ τὴν πρότερον Ἀψυνθίδα, νῦν δὲ Κορπιλικὴν λεγομένην, ἡ δὲ τῶν Κικόνων ἐφεξῆς πρὸς δύσιν. (Epit. Vat.)

58. Κορπίλοι· Θρακῶν τινες. Στράβων ζ'. ἡ χώρα Κορπιλική. ἡ γὰρ Αἶνος κεῖται κατὰ τὴν πρότερον Ἀψινθίδα, νῦν δὲ Κορπιλικὴν λεγομένην. (Stephanus Byzantinus, s.v. Κορπίλοι.)

59 (58a). Τετραχωρῖται· οἱ Βεσσοί, ὡς Στράβων ἑβδόμῃ. οὗτοι λέγονται καὶ Τετράκωμοι. (Stephanus Byzantinus, s.v. Τετραχωρῖται.)

60 (58b). Λέγει γὰρ (scil. Στράβων) αὐτὸν [1] ἐν τῇ ἑβδόμῃ τῆς αὐτῆς πραγματείας [2] ἐγνωκέναι Ποσειδώνιον τὸν ἀπὸ τῆς στοᾶς φιλόσοφον. [3] (Athenaeus 14. 75.)

---

[1] αὐτόν (A), αὑτόν (PVL), αὐτός (Schweighäuser). Meineke reads αὑτόν ; and so does Kaibel, with the footnote "intellige Pompeium."

[2] τῆς αὐτῆς πραγματείας (i. e. τῶν Γεωγραφουμένων) is omitted by B ; Meineke following.

[3] The whole passage in Athenaeus is as follows : μνημονεύει δ' αὐτῶν (scil. τῶν Γαλλικῶν περνῶν) Στράβων ἐν τρίτῃ Γεωγραφουμένων, ἀνὴρ οὐ πάνυ νεώτερος· λέγει γὰρ αὐτὸν ἐν τῇ ἑβδόμῃ τῆς αὐτῆς πραγματείας ἐγνωκέναι Ποσειδώνιον τὸν ἀπὸ τῆς στοᾶς φιλόσοφον, οὗ πολλάκις μεμνήμεθα, συγγενομένου Σκιπίωνι τῷ τῆς Καρχηδόνα ἑλόντι· γράφει δ' οὖν ὁ Στράβων οὕτως· Ἐν Σπανίᾳ πρὸς τῇ Ἀκυτανίᾳ πόλις Πομπέλων, ὡς ἂν εἴποι τις Πομπηϊόπολις, ἐν ᾗ πέρναι διάφοροι συντίθενται ταῖς Κιβυρικαῖς (Κανταβρικαῖς, Strabo 3. 4. 11) ἐνάμιλλοι. Meineke strangely attributes the words συγγενομένου Σκιπίωνι τῷ Καρχηδόνα ἑλόντι to Strabo and retains them in the Fragment.

---

[1] The Cicones, themselves inhabitants of Thrace.

[2] The particular Thracians whose territory ended at Aenus, or the Hebrus River.

represent those [1] who are situated next after these [2] as situated outside the Hellespont; that is, Aenus lies in what was formerly called Apsinthis, though now called Corpilice, whereas the country of the Cicones lies next thereafter towards the west.[3]

58. Corpili: certain of the Thracians. Strabo, Seventh Book; their country is called Corpilice; for Aenus lies in what was formerly called Apsinthis, though now called Corpilice.

59 (58a). Tetrachoritae: the Bessi, according to Strabo in his Seventh Book. These are also called Tetracomi.

60 (58b). For he [4] says in the Seventh Book of the same work [5] that he knew Poseidonius, the Stoic philosoper.[6]

---

[3] The argument of this misunderstood passage is as follows: Certain writers (1) make the Homeric Thrace extend as far as Crannon and Gyrton in Thessaly (*Frags.* 14, 16); then (2) interpret Homer as meaning that Peiroüs was the leader of *all* Thracians; therefore (3) the Homeric Hellespont extends to the southern boundary of Thessaly. But their opponents regard the clause "all who are shut in by strong-flowing Hellespont" as restrictive, that is, as meaning only those Thracians who (as "Aenus" shows) were east of the Cicones, or of the Hebrus. Strabo himself seems to lean to the latter view.

[4] *sc.* Strabo.

[5] That is, his *Geography*, previously mentioned.

[6] This fragment and its context, as found in Athenaeus 14. 75, requires special investigation. If the text of Athenaeus is right, he misquotes Strabo at least once, for the latter " in his Third Book " (3. 4. 11) speaks of " Cantabrian," not " Cibyric," hams. Again, the readings of the Greek text for " he " (in " he knew ") present a grammatical problem; Kaibel makes " he " refer to Pompey, but it must, in the context, refer to Strabo. And did Strabo really say that he knew Poseidonius? Or could he have known him? (See 16. 2. 10, where Strabo speaks of Poseidonius as " most

STRABO

61. Ἔστι δὲ καὶ ποταμὸς ʿΆρισβος ἐν Θράκῃ, ὥσπερ εἴρηται, καὶ τούτου πλησίον οἱ Κεβρήνιοι Θρᾷκες. (Strabo 13. 1. 21.)

62. Τάχα δὲ (*sc.* ʿΡίπη) καὶ πληθυντικῶς λέγεται ʿΡίπαι, ἐὰν ὁ Στράβων περὶ ταύτης λέγῃ, ὅτι ʿΡίπαι οὐκ οἰκοῦνται. τὴν δὲ χώραν ʿΡιπίδα καλοῦσιν. [ἀλλαχοῦ δὲ σαφέστατά φησιν, ὅτι ʿΡίπην Στρατίην τε καὶ Ἐνίσπην εὑρεῖν τε χαλεπὸν καὶ εὑροῦσιν οὐδὲν ὄφελος διὰ τὴν ἐρημίαν (8. 8. 2).] (Eustathius on *Iliad* 2. 606.)

63. [Λέγει δ᾽ ὁ Γεωγράφος καὶ ὅτι τὸ τῶν Καυκώνων γένος ἐξέφθαρται τέλεον (12. 3. 9).] . . . ἔτι φησὶν ὁ Γεωγράφος καὶ ὅτι Καύκωνες οἱ ἐν Πελοποννήσῳ, Ἀρκαδικὴ μοῖρα, μὴ ἀνεχόμενοι τὸ Λεπρέου γένος κατάρχειν αὐτῶν—ἦν γὰρ πονηρὸς ὁ Λέπρεος—κατῆραν ἐκεῖθεν εἰς Λυκίαν. (Eustathius on *Iliad* 22. 328.)

64. [Πορφύριος δὲ Φθίου τοὺς ἐκ τῆς ὑπὸ τῷ Φιλοκτήτῃ Μεθώνης καλεῖσθαι ἱστορεῖ.] ὁ Γεωγράφος δὲ οὐ τοὺς περὶ Μεθώνην μόνους Φθίους φησὶ λέγεσθαι, ἀλλά, ὡς καὶ προείρηται, κοινῶς τοὺς ὑπὸ τῷ Ἀχιλλεῖ καὶ τῷ Πρωτεσιλάῳ καὶ τῷ Φιλοκτήτῃ. (Eustathius on *Iliad* 2. 716.)

65. Φησὶ δὲ ὁ αὐτὸς Γεωγράφος καὶ ὅτι ὁ Ἴστρος ποτὲ Ματόας ἐλέγετο, ὅ ἐστι κατὰ Ἕλληνας Ἄσιος· καὶ ὅτι πολλάκις μὲν οἱ Σκύθαι δι᾽ αὐτοῦ περαιούμενοι οὐδὲν ἔπασχον, συμφορᾶς

widely-learned of all philosophers of our times.") Moreover, how could Poseidonius have been an associate of that Scipio (Africanus Minor) who captured Carthage? Is not Athenaeus confusing Poseidonius with Polybius, who was with Scipio

61. There is also a river Arisbus in Thrace, as I have said before, and near this the Cebrenian Thracians.

62. Perhaps Rhipe is also called Rhipae, in the plural, if Strabo means Rhipe when he says that Rhipae is not inhabited. And they call the country Rhipis. [But elsewhere[1] Strabo says very clearly: "Rhipe and Stratie and Enispe not only are hard to find, but when found are of no use because of their desolation."]

63. [The Geographer says also that the tribe of the Cauconians has been completely destroyed.] And the Geographer further says that the Cauconians in the Peloponnesus, the Arcadian portion, could not endure to be ruled by the house of Lepreus—for Lepreus was a bad man—and so they sailed away from there to Lycia.

64. [Porphyrius records that the people from the Methone that was subject to Menelaus were called Phthians.] But the Geographer says that the people about Methone were not the only people who were called Phthians, but, as has been said before, the peoples subject to Achilles, Protesilaüs, and Philoctetes were so called in common with them.

65. The same Geographer says also that the Ister was once called the "Matoas"—that is, in Greek, "Asius";[2] and that, although the Scythians had often crossed over it without suffering any mishap,

---

[1] 8. 8. 2.   [2] "Muddy."

---

at the destruction of Carthage? Or is he not confusing Poseidonius with Panaetius (see Casaubon-Schweighaüser, *Animadv. in Athenaeum*, Vol. VII, p. 645)?

STRABO

δέ ποτε ἐπεισπεσούσης ἡρμηνεύθη Δάνουβις ἢ
Δάουσις, ὥσπερ τοῦ ἁμαρτεῖν ἐκείνους αἰτίαν
ἔχων. (Eustathius on *Dionysius Periegetes, l.* 298.)

66. Ὁ δὲ Γεωγράφος καὶ τὸν ῞Αδην ἱκανῶς
αὐτόθι ἐκτετιμῆσθαί φησιν. (Eustathius on
Dionysius Periegetes, l. 409.)

yet, when once a misfortune befell them, its name was changed to Danubis or Daüsis, as though it were to blame for their mistake.

66. The Geographer also says that Hades was much revered there.[1]

---

[1] In Triphylia, in the region of the Alpheius.

A PARTIAL DICTIONARY OF PROPER NAMES [1]

A

Abii, the, 179, 181, 189, 195, 205, 209
Abydon (Amydon), **341, 343, 345, 347**
Abydus, 373, 379
Acalandrus River, 117
Acanthus, 353, 357
Acheloüs River, 309
Acheron River, 17, 301
Achilles, Race Course of, 227
Acrothoï, 355, 357
Actian Apollo, temple of, 301
Actium, Battle of, 303
Adrias (*see* Adriatic), the, 151, 233, 249, 251, 267, 293, 329
Adriatic (Adrias), the, 109, 203, 257
Aegaean Sea, 295, 327, 353, 381
Aegestes the Trojan coloniser, 11, 81
Aelius Catus (*see* note 3, p. 209); transplanted 50,000 Getae to Thrace, 209
Aemilius Paulus Macedonicus, 293, 369
Aenus (Apsinthus), 279, 373, 375
Aeolus, Islands of (Liparaean Islands), 19, 63
Aeschylus (525–456 B.C.), the tragic poet, 191, 199
Aetna, 67, 69, 87
Aetna, Mt., 25, 63, 85, 91, 95
Aetolia, 289, 327
Agathocles (*see* note 5, p. 114), 19, 115
Agrianes, the, 271, 361, 363
Agrigentum (Acragas), 81, 91
Alaesa, 57, 81
Albian Mountain, 255, 259
Albis River, 155, 157, 159, 163, 171, 173
Alcmaeon, founder of Argos Amphilochicum, 305
Alcman (see *Dictionary* in vol. i.), 191

Alexander the Great (356–323 B.C.); his expedition against the Thracians, 201, 203
Alexander the Molossian, 17, 115
Alexarchus the son of Antipater, founder of Uranopolis, 357
Alorus, 339, 341, 345
Alps, the, 155, 165, 169, 251, 253, 255
Amadocus, the king, 371
Ambracia, royal residence of Pyrrhus, 303, 305
Ambracian Gulf, 295, 297, 299, 301, 327
Amphaxitis, 331, 345
Amphipolis, 359, 369
Anacharsis (*see* note 5, p. 201), 201, 207
Anaxilaüs (Anaxilas), tyrant of Rhegium, 494–476 B.C., 21, 23
Ancona, 133, 257
Antalcidas, the Peace of, 141
Antiochus (see *Dictionary* in vol. ii.), on the Phocaean colonists, 5; on Old Italy, 11, 13; on the founder of Zancle, 21; on the Siceli, 23; on the founders of Croton and Syracuse, 43; on the Achaean colonisers of Metapontium, 51, 53; on the founding of Tarentum, 107
Apennine Mountains, 27, 125, 127, 135
Apollocrates, son of Dionysius the Younger, 31
Apollodorus of Athens (see *Dictionary* in vol. i.), on Philoctetes as founder of cities, 11; on Homer's ignorance of geography, 187, 189, 193, 195, 209; on the origin of the name "Hellopia," 313
Apollonia, 265, 277, 279, 293, 307, 309, 355, 359, 379
Apollonides (*see* note 2, p. 234), 235
Appian Way, the, 125

---

[1] A complete index will appear in the last volume.

A PARTIAL DICTIONARY OF PROPER NAMES

Apsinthus (*see* Aenus)
Apuli, the, 127, 135
Apulia, 103, 127
Aquileia, 133, 165, 255
Aratthus (Arachthus) River, 303, 309
Archias, founder of Syracuse, 43, 71, 73
Archidamus (*see* note 3, p. 114), 115
Archytas (*see* note 1, p. 114), 115
Ardiaei (Vardiaei), the, 257, 261, 263, 271, 275, 325
Arethusa, fountain of, 75
Argeadae, the, 331, 341
Aristotle (384–322 B.C.), on the formation of river-stones, 193; his *Politics* cited, 289; native city of, 355, 359
Armenius, commander-in-chief of the Cheruscan army, 161
Artemidorus (*see* note 1, p. 130), on the distance around the Gulf of Tarentum, 39; on other distances, 61, 131, 133, 379
Asander (*see* note 1, p. 244), 245
Asius (fl. in seventh century B.C.), 53; epic and iambic poet, of whose works only fragments remain
Astae, the, 279, 285, 369
Ateas (Atheas), barbarian ruler, 227
Athamanes, the, 289, 307
Athos, 353, 355, 357
Augustus Caesar (63 B.C.–14 A.D.), colonised Rhegium, 27; his war with Pompey, 67; colonised Syracuse, 75; rebuilder of Ortygia, Catana, and Centoripa, 79; subdued all Celtica, 143; received Phraates' children as hostages, 147; friend to Marobodus, 157; permitted no generals to cross the Albis, 159; presented with kettle by the Cimbri, 165; sent expedition against the Getae, 213; utterly subdued the Iapodes, 259; burnt up certain Dalmatian cities, 261; founder of Nicopolis, 301
Autariatae, the, 251, 263, 271, 275, 325
Axius River, 311, 325, 331, 333, 341, 343, 345, 347, 361

B

Bargus (*see* Margus) River
Bastarnians, the, 151, 173, 215, 217, 221

Bato, leader of the Daesitiatae, 257
Beneventum, 123, 125
Berisades, the king, 371
Bermium, Mt., 349, 351
Bessi, the, 275, 369
Bisaltae, the, 331, 359, 361, 353
Bistonis, Lake, 365
Boerebistas (*see* Byrebistas), 211, 213
Boïhaemum, 155
Boii, the, 165, 169, 179, 211, 253, 263
Borysthenes River, 151, 153, 173, 221, 223, 225, 227, 233, 241
Bosporians, Cimmerian, 237, 241, 247
Bosporus, Cimmerian, 169, 227, 235, 237, 239, 241
Botteia, 331
Bottiaea, 121, 345
Bottiaeans, the, 111, 329, 341
Brentesium (*see* Brundisium)
Brettii (*see* Bruttii)
Bructeri, the, 155, 159, 163
Brundisium (Brentesium), 105, 117, 119, 121, 123, 125, 127, 133, 299
Bruttii (Brettii), the, 9, 11, 13, 15, 17, 35, 125
Bruttium (Brettium), 15, 17
Brutus (and Cassius), defeat of, 363
Brygi, the, 307, 311
Buthrotum, 299, 301
Byrebistas (*see* Boerebistas), king of the Getae in the time of Julius Caesar, 187
Byzantium, 275, 283, 285, 327, 379

C

Cabeiri, the, 371
Cadmus, 287, 307
Caenys, 21, 55
Calamis the sculptor (*see* note 5, p. 277), 277
Callatis, 273, 277
Callimachus (see *Dictionary* in vol. i.); calls Gaudos the " Isle of Calypso," 193
Callipolis, 361, 377
Camarina, 59, 81
Campani, the, 9, 27, 65
Campania, 11, 125
Campsiani, the, 159, 163
Canastraeum, Cape, 349, 353
Cannae, 135
Canusium, 123, 129
Capreae, 25
Caprus Harbour, 355, 359

A PARTIAL DICTIONARY OF PROPER NAMES

A PARTIAL DICTIONARY OF PROPER NAMES

Dodona, oracle of, 17, 313; anciently ruled by Thesprotians, 315; 323, 325

Draco, hero-temple of, 5

Dravus River, 255

Dromichaetes, king of the Getae and capturer of Lysimachus (*see* note 3, p. 203), 203

Drusus, son of Tiberius, 147, 155, 159

Dyrrhachium (*see* Epidamnus), 329

E

Edoni, the, 331, 359

Egnatia, 123, 127

Egnatian Road, 293, 309, 329, 333, 343

Eleus (Elaeus), 375

Empedocles of Agrigentum, the philosopher (fl. about 490 B.C.), 97

Emporium Segestanorum, 57, 81

Enna, 81, 85, 87

Ennius (b. 239 B.C.), the Roman poet; born at Rodiae, 119

Eordi, the, 295, 307

Epeirotes, the, 287, 293, 297, 333

Epeirus, 125, 299, 311, 329

Epeius, founder of Lagaria, 49

Ephorus (see *Dictionary* in vol. i.), on Locri Epizephyrii, 29; on Zaleucus, 33; on the Iapyges, 43; on Daulius, coloniser of Metapontium, 53; on the distance around Sicily, 59; on the earliest Greek cities in Sicily, 65; Iberians the first barbarian settlers of Sicily, 73; on the founding of Tarentum, 111; on the Cimbri, 167; on the Scythian modes of life, 205; on Anacharsis, 207; on the mouths of the Ister, 219; attributes founding of the oracle of Dodona to the Pelasgi, 313

Ephyra, 301, 339

Epidamnus (Dyrrhachium), 125, 265, 293, 307, 309

Eratosthenes (see *Dictionary* in vol. i., on Homer's lack of knowledge, 187, 193, 195, 197; false statements of, 269

Ericussa (Ericodes), Island of, 99

Erigon (Rheginia) River, 311, 331, 339, 345, 371

Eryx, 11, 83, 87

Eudoxus (see *Dictionary* in vol. i.), on the origin of the name of the Melas Gulf, 373

Euhemerus (see *Dictionary* in vol. i.), 193

Eumolpus, who once occupied Attica, 287

Eunomus, the cithara-bard, 35

Eunus (see note 3, p. 81), 81, 85

Euonymus, Island of, 97

Euthymus, the pugilist, 15

Euxine Sea (*see* Pontus); origin of the name, 189, 197, 327

Evanthes, founder of Locri Epizephyrii, 29

F

Fabius Maximus Cunctator (consul 233 and 228 B.C., and appointed dictator 217 B.C.), 107

Frentani, the, 127, 135

G

Galactophagi, the, 179, 181, 189, 195, 205, 209, 243

Galepsus, 355, 359, 363

Garganum, the promontory, 131, 133, 135

Gaudus, Island of, 103

Gela, 83

Georgi, the, 243, 245

Germanicus, son of Tiberius, 147

Germanicus Caesar, son of Nero Claudius Drusus and Antonia; his triumph over the Cherusci, 161

Germans, the, 153, 171, 173, 217, 221, 251

Germany, 159, 173, 223, 253

Getae, the, 157, 173, 175, 183, 185, 187, 201, 209, 211 (their history), 215, 251

Getae, Desert of the, 217, 221

Gorgus, founder of Ambracia, 303

Greece, in early times a settlement of various barbarians, 285, 287

Gyrton, 335, 337, 339

H

Haemus Mountain, 201, 251, 275, 279, 329, 361

Haliacmon River, 325, 331, 339, 343

Hannibal, 15, 17, 135, 141

Harpagus, general of Cyrus, 5

Hebrus River, 293, 329, 369, 373, 375, 379

A PARTIAL DICTIONARY OF PROPER NAMES

Hecataeus (see *Dictionary* in vol. i.), on the Inachus River, 79; his mythical " City of Cimmeris," 191; calls the Aoüs River the " Aeas," 265; the Peloponnesus inhabited by barbarians before the time of the Greeks, 285

Hellespont, the, 177, 249, 295, 373, 375, 377; definition of, 381

Helots, the, 107, 113

Helvetii, the, 165, 169

Heneti, the, 129, 131

Heracleia, 49, 51, 115, 117

Heracleia Lyncestis, 295

Heracleia Sintica, 361

Heracleium, Cape, 27, 29

Hercynian Forest, the, 155, 163, 165, 169, 173

Herodotus (about 484–425 B.C.), the " Father of History "; concerning Hyria, 121; on Idanthyrsus, king of the Scythians, 199; on the name of the Melas Gulf, 373

Hesiod (see *Dictionary* in vol. i.), his inventions, 191; mentions the Hippemolgi, 197; Galactophagi, 205; on the Leleges, 291; on the Pelasgi, 313

Hiero (tyrant of Syracuse 478–467 B.C.), 67, 69

Himera, 83, 91

Hippemolgi, the, 179, 181, 187, 189, 195, 209

Hipponiate Gulf, 13, 15, 37

Homer, 1, 17, 19, 97, 99, 177, 181, 187, 189, 195, 197, 199, 205, 207, 209, 243, 313, 317, 381

Horn of the Byzantines (Golden Horn), 281, 283

Hypsicrates (*see* note 2, p. 245), on the walling off of the Chersonesus by Asander, 245

I

Iapodes, the, 253, 255, 259

Iapyges, the, 13, 109, 111, 117

Iapygia (Messapia), 53, 55, 103, 121

Iapygia, Cape, 29, 39, 105, 117

Iapyx, leader of a colony to Italy, 121

Ibycus of Rhegium, the lyric poet (fl. about 550 B.C.), says the Asopus in Sicyon rises in Phrygia, 79

Idaean Dactyli, the, 371

Illyrians, the, 125, 143, 211, 215, 273, 285

Inachus River, 305, 309

Ionian Gulf, 29, 117, 267, 293, 307, 309, 327, 379

Ionians, the, 289

Ismarus, 365, 367

Issa, island of, 259, 267

Ister River, 143, 151, 153, 163, 165, 169, 173, 175, 201, 209, 211, 213, 215, 217, 221, 223, 249, 251, 253, 271, 285; name changed to Danubis or Datisis, 387

J

Juba (contemporary of Caesar and Pompey), ruler of Maurusia, 143

Julius Caesar (see *Dictionary* in vol. ii.), conqueror of all Celtica, 143; prepared expedition against the Getae, 187

L

Lacinium, Cape, 41, 117

Latini, the, 139, 141

Laüs, river and city, 5, 13

Leleges, the, 287, 289

Lemnos, 365, 367

Leontines, the, 85, 87

Leucani, the, 5, 9, 11, 13, 15, 37, 47, 125

Leucania, 3, 5, 13

Leuco (*see* note 3, p. 200), 201, 237, 243

Leucosia, 3, 25

Liburnians, the, 73, 259, 269

Liburnides Islands, 259, 269

Libyan Sea, the, 63, 297

Lilybaeum, Cape, 57, 59, 61, 63, 81, 103

Lipara (Liparae), Island of, 25, 93, 95, 97, 99, 101, 103

Liparaean Islands (Islands of Aeolus), 19, 91, 93, 95

Locrians, the Epizephyrian, 15, 29, 31, 35, 37

Ludias River, 339, 341, 345

Lyncestae, the, 295, 307, 309

Lysimacheia, 373, 375

Lysimachus (*see* note 3, p. 203), 203, 217, 279

Lysippus of Sicyon, the sculptor, 107

A PARTIAL DICTIONARY OF PROPER NAMES

M

Macedonia, 295, 327, 329, 333, 369
Macedonia, Lower, 331, 341
Macedonia, Upper (Free), 309, 331
Madytus, 377, 379
Maedi (*see* Medi)
Maeotis, Lake, 151, 153, 169, 223, 225, 229, 237, 239, 241, 245, 249, 281
Magna Graecia, 7
Mamertini, the, tribe of the Campani, 65, 67
Marcus Lucullus (consul 73 B.C.), carried off statue of Apollo from Apollonia, 277
Marobodus of Boïhaemum, 157
Maroneia, 365, 367
Marsi, the, 155
Medi (Maedi), the, 265, 275, 361
Medma, 19, 21
Melas, Gulf of, 295, 373, 375, 381
Melo, leader of the Sugambri, 161
Messapia (*see* Iapygia), 121
Messene, formerly called Zancle, 59, 63, 65
Metapontium, 13, 51, 53, 103, 105
Methone, 339, 345
Micythus, ruler of Messene, 5
Milo, greatest of athletes, 45
Minos, king of Crete, murdered at residence of Cocalus, 85, 109, 121
Mithridates Eupator (see *Dictionary* in vol. i.), 145, 223, 233, 239, 243, 247
Moesi (*see* Mysi), 181, 209
Molossi, the, 289, 293, 297, 307, 309
Mygdonians, the, 177, 361
Myscellus, founder of Croton, 43, 71
Mysi, the, 175, 177, 181, 187, 195, 197, 209, 215, 273

N

Naro River, 261, 269
Nasica, Cornelius Scipio, 261
Nauportus, 255
Neaethus River, 41, 43
Neapolis (Naples), 7, 353, 359
Neoptolemus, Tower of, 219; general of Mithridates, 227
Nestus River, 297, 355, 357, 363, 365, 367
Nicopolis, founded by Augustus, 301, 303
Nymphaeum, Cape, 353

O

Odessus, 279, 369
Odomantes, the, 359, 363
Odrysae, the, 369, 371
Oenotri, the, 7, 13, 23, 53
Oenotria, 11, 55
Oenotrides Islands, 5, 25
Olophyxis, 355, 357
Olympus, Mt., 335, 337, 339
Olynthus, 331, 351
Orestae, the, 327, 341
Orpheus the wizard, 339, 357
Ortygia, Island of, 75, 79
Ossa, Mt., 335, 337

P

Pachynus, Cape, 55, 59, 61, 81, 103
Pactye, 373, 375, 377
Paeonia, 251, 275, 325, 333, 361, 363
Paeonians, the, 295, 333, 341, 345, 363
Palacus (*see* note 3, p. 223), son of Sciluris, 223, 235
Pangaeum, Mt., 355, 363
Pannonia, 257
Pannonii, the, 165, 253, 257, 259, 271
Panormus, 57, 81, 267, 299
Panticapaeum, 225, 237, 239, 241
Parisades (Paerisades), lord of the Bosporus, 235, 237, 239
Parmenides (see *Dictionary* in vol.i.), 3
Parnassus, Mount, 327
Parthenium, the, 233, 241
Paulus (*see* Aemilius Paulus)
Pelagonians, the, 311, 369
Pelasgi, 287, 289, 313, 357
Pella, 295, 341, 345, 369
Peloponnesus, formerly inhabited by barbarians, 285
Pelops, 287
Pelorias, Cape, 21, 55, 57, 59, 61, 63, 65
Peneius River, 311, 325, 331, 333, 335, 337, 359
Perinthus, 363, 377, 379
Perrhaebians, the, 333, 335, 337
Perseus, defeated by Romans near Pydna, 345, 369
Peuce, Island of, 201, 217, 219, 223
Peucetii (Poedicli), the, 103, 123, 127, 135
Peucini (Bastarnae), the, 217, 223
Phalanthus, champion of the Helots, 107, 109, 121
Phanagoria, 225, 239

A PARTIAL DICTIONARY OF PROPER NAMES

Pharos (Paros), Island of, 261

Philip, son of Amyntas, father of Alexander the Great, 227, 285, 297, 341, 345

Philippi, 355, 363, 365

Philippopolis, 361

Philochorus (put to death by Antigonus Gonatas shortly after 261 B.C.), author of *Atthis*, a history of Attica from earliest times to 261 B.C.; says the region of Dodona was called Hellopia, 313

Philoctetes, founder of Petelia, 9; founder of Crimissa, 11, 81

Phoenicussa (Phoenicodes), Island of, 99

Phraates IV (contemporary of Augustus), king of Parthia, 147

Phrygians (Brigians), the, 177

Pieria, 331, 335, 345, 363

Pindar, the lyric poet (b. about 522 B.C.), calls Hiero founder of Aetna, 67; connects Arethusa with the Alpheius, 75; says the Boeotians were once called "Syes" ("swine"), 287; on the inhabitants of Dodona, 313; his conception of term "Hellespont," 381

Pindus Mountain, 311, 327, 335

Pithecussae Islands, 25

Plato, on a well-governed city, 205

Poedicli (Peucetii), 105

Polites, hero-temple of, 15

Polybius (see *Dictionary* in vol. i.), 39, 97, 133, 141; says that both seas are visible from the Haemus Mountain, 251; discredits Eratosthenes, 269; on the conquests of Paulus, 293; reckons 8½ stadia to Roman mile, 293, 295, 379

Pompey, Sextus (see *Dictionary* in vol. ii.), 23, 27, 67, 75, 79

Pontic Sea (*see* Pontus)

Pontus, the, 151, 153, 173, 189, 197, 213, 217, 219, 235, 249, 251, 275, 277, 281, 285

Poseidium, Cape, 299, 353

Poseidonian Gulf, 3

Poseidonius (see *Dictionary* in vol. i., 57, 59, 69, 87, 101; on the Cimbri and the Cimmerian Bosporus, 169; on the Mysi, 177, 179, 181, 185; on the sons of Scilurus, 235; on the mine of asphalt near Apollonia, 267; the Stoic, 383

Potidaea (Cassandreia), 349, 351

Propontis, the, 151, 249, 279, 295, 327, 373, 375, 377, 381

Ptolemaeus Soter (*see* note 1, p. 202), 203

Pydna, 339, 341, 345, 359

Pylon, marks boundary between Macedonia and Illyria, 293, 295

Pyrrhus (king of Epeirus from 295 B.C. till his death in 272 B.C.), 27, 115; defeated by the Romans, 141; his royal residence at Ambracia, 303; his lineage, 309

Pythagoras, the philosopher, of Samos (fl. about 540–510 B.C.); founder of a sect in Croton, 45; Zamolxis his slave, 185

Pytheas the Massalian (see *Dictionary* in vol. i.), false statements of, 175

Pyxus, cape, harbour, and river, 5

R

Rhaeti, the, 165, 253, 255

Rhegium, 7, 21, 23, 25, 27, 29, 65, 125

Rhemis River, 151, 153, 155, 157, 159, 161, 163, 171, 249

Rhesus, the king, 361

Rhipaean Mountains, the, 191

Rhizonic Gulf, 257, 263

Rhodope Mountain, 251, 275, 329, 361, 363

Road to Candavia, 293, 309

Rodiae, 119, 121

Rome, a sketch of its political history, 139–147

Roxolani, the, 173; "most northerly of them all," 223

S

Sacred Mouth, the, of the Ister, 217, 219, 249, 275, 277

Sagra River, 35, 37, 45

Salapia, 127, 129

Salas River, 159

Salentini, the, 103, 117

Samnitae, the, 7, 9, 13, 27, 51, 123, 125, 141

Samothrace, 369, 371

Sapaei, the, 367, 369

Sason, Island of, 119

Satyrus, dynasty of, 237

Sauromatae, the, 173, 205, 215

395

A PARTIAL DICTIONARY OF PROPER NAMES

Scilurus, lord of the Bosporus, 223, 233, 247

Scordisci, the, 179, 253, 255, 271, 273

Scotussa, 321, 361

Scylletic Gulf, 13, 37

Scylletium, 15, 37, 39

Scythia, Little, 241, 273

Scythians, the, 179, 189, 195, 197; most straightforward of men, 199; their modes of life, 205, 215, 247

Segestica, 253, 255, 273

Segimundus, chieftain of the Cherusci, 161

Selurus, the " son of Aetna," killed by wild beasts at Rome, 85

Selybria, 279, 377

Sertorius (see *Dictionary* in vol.ii.), 143

Sestus, 373, 377, 379

Seuthes, the king, 371

Siceli, the, 73

Sicilian Sea, the, 13, 21, 55, 61, 297

Sicily, 7, 25, 31, 55, 65, 73, 77, 81, 85, 95, 97, 121, 137, 141, 193

Sicily, Strait of, 7, 11, 13, 19, 21, 25, 63, 91, 95

Silaris River, 3, 13

Sinti, the, 361, 367

Siris (Seiris), 13, 49, 51, 53

Socrates the philosopher, 175

Sophocles the tragic poet (495–406 B.C.), on the Inachus River, 79; on Oreithyia, 175

Stageira (Stageirus), native city of Aristotle, 355, 359

Strongyle, Island of, 99, 103

Strymon River, 295, 297, 325, 331, 355, 359, 369

Strymonic Gulf, 353, 357, 363

Stymphalus, Lake, 93

Suevi, the, 155, 157, 165, 173

Sugambri, the, 155, 159, 161, 171

Suidas (*see* note 6, p. 317), on the temple of Dodona, 317

Sunium, 297, 333

Sybaris, 45, 51

Sybota Islands, 299

Symaethus River, 63, 81

Symbolōn Limen, 233, 235

Syracuse, 29, 59, 61, 63, 71, 73, 75, 87

Syrmus, king of the Triballi, 201, 203

T

Tamyraces (*see* Carcinites), Gulf of, 225

Tanaïs River, 151, 153, 223, 239, 241, 249

Tarantine Gulf (*see* Tarentum, Gulf of)

Taras (*see* Tarentum)

Tarentum (Taras), 7, 53, 55, 105, 107, 109, 111, 113, 117, 119, 121, 123, 125, 127, 299

Tarentum, Gulf of (Tarantine Gulf) 7, 9, 11, 105, 117

Tarquinius Superbus, 139

Tasius, Leader of the Roxolani, 223

Tauri, the, 233, 237, 241

Taurisci, the, 167, 179, 253, 255

Tauromenium, 59, 63, 67, 83

Temesa (Tempsa), 15, 17

Tempe, 333, 335, 337, 339

Tereus, who once occupied Phocis, 287

Thamyris, the wizard, 357

Thasos, 365, 369

Theocles the Athenian coloniser, 65

Theodosia, 235, 237, 241, 243

Theopompus (see *Dictionary* in vol.i.), 191; on the origin of the names of the Ionian and Adrias Gulfs, 267; his incredible statements, 269; on the Epeirotes, 297

Therma (*see* Thessaloniceia)

Thermaean Gulf, 297, 325, 333, 341, 343, 345, 349, 353, 381

Thermessa, Island of, 95

Theseus, legendary hero of Attica; coloniser of Brundisium, 121

Thesproti, the, 289, 297

Thessalonice, daughter of Philip, 343

Thessaloniceia (Therma), 295, 297, 329, 333, 341, 343, 347, 349, 369

Thrace, cleft almost in the centre by the Haemus Mountain, 251; consists of 22 tribes, 367, 371

Thracians, the, 175, 177, 179, 181, 195, 201, 209, 211, 243, 273, 287, 295, 329

Thucydides, the historian, on Amphilochus, 305

Thurii, 11, 13, 47, 49

Thusnelda, sister of Segimundus and wife of Armenius, 161

Thyssus, 355, 357

Tiberius Caesar, successor of Augustus, 147, 163, 165

Timaeus (see *Dictionary* in vol. ii.), connects Arethusa with the Alpheius, 75

Titus Flaminius (*see* note 2, p. 101), 101

A PARTIAL DICTIONARY OF PROPER NAMES

Tomarus Mountain, 311, 315
Tomis, 273, 277
Toronaean Gulf, 351, 353
Triballi, the, 201, 215, 263, 271, 273
Tricca, 311, 337
Tripolitis, the Pelagonian, 307, 311
Tymphaei, the, 311, 327
Tyndaris, 57, 81
Tyras River, 151, 217, 219, 231
Tyregetans, the, 153, 175, 221
Tyrrheni, the, 21, 141
Tyrrhenian Sea, 9, 11, 63, 91
Tyrtaeus, the elegiac poet, on the
    capture of Messene, 113

U

Uranopolis, founded by Alexarchus,
    357
Urgi, the, 221

Valerian Way, the, 59
Vardiaei (see Ardiaei), 263
Varus, P. Quintilius (consul 13 B.C.),
    161
Venusia, 11, 125

Veretum (Baris), 119, 121
Vibo Valentia (see Hipponium).
Vindelici, the, 163, 165, 253
Viriathus (fl. about 150 B.C.), a cele-
    brated Lusitanian brigand, 143

X

Xerxes, canal of, 355, 357; enumera-
    tion of army of, 369; Melas River
    insufficient for army of, 373;
    pontoon bridge of, 377

Z

Zaleucus, the law-giver (according to
    Eusebius, *Chron.*, fl. 660 B.C.), 33
Zamolxis (*see* note 3, p. 184), 185, 211
Zancle (*see* Messene), 65
Zeno (see *Dictionary* in vol. i.), a
    native of Elea, 3
Zeno of Citium in Cyprus (about
    345–265 B.C.); his emendation of
    the Homeric text, 191
Zephyrium, Cape, 29, 73
Zoilus the rhetorician (*see* note 2,
    p. 79); says the Alpheius rises in
    Tenedos, 79

ITALIA

0   25   50   75   100   125 Milis
100   500   1000 Stadia

GALLIA CISPADANA

Luna

Caesena

Ariminum

Luca

Pisa

Arnus F.

Sarsina

Volaterra

Arretium

Iguvium

Perusia

Clusium

Populonium

ÆTHALIA
Iª

Volsinii

Statonia
Volaterrae

Ameria

Spoletium

Interamnia

Carsulae

Narnia

Ocriculum

Trebula

Herculis Portis

Frentinum

Sutrium

Blera

Tarquinii

Graviscae

Pyrgi
Alsium

Sabata

Veii

Tarentum

Fretum

Fregenae

Roma

Ostia

Laurentum

Lavinium

Ardea

Lanuvium

Antium

MARE

CORSICA

SARDOUM MARE

Cercei Pr.

PONTIA Iº

PIT.

AGONITA

GOLGIA

SARDINIA

CARALIS

Sulchi

SICILIA

Diagebe

PARALII

TATIII III BALARI

Per.

Mylae

Solunto F.

Erycis

Papormus

Eryx

Cephaloedium

Alaesa

Agathyrnus

Himera

Egesta

M.

Mazara

Catina

Selinus F.

Enna

Longanus

Selinunto

Heracleia

Pelice

Catana

Thermae
Selinus

Agrigentum

Leontini

Emporium

Gela

Camarina

Pac.

SICILIA

Lilybaeum Pr.

Lilybaeum

Map V.

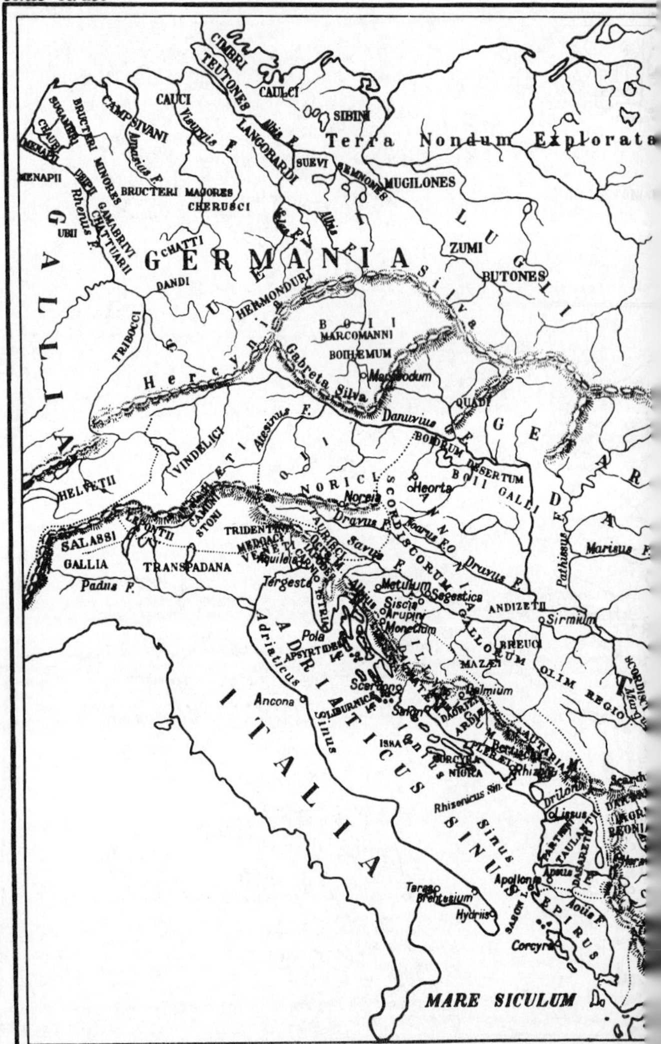
CIMBRI
TEUTONES
CAULCI
SIBINI
Terra Nondum Explorata
CAUCI
Visurgis F.
LANGOBARDI
Albis F.
SUEVI
SEMNONES
MUGILONES
CAMPSIVANI
Amasius F.
SUGAMBRI
CHAUCI
MENAPII
BRUCTERI MINORES
BRUCTERI MAIORES
CHERUSCI
Rhenus F.
GAMABRIVI
CHATTUARII
UBII
CHATTI
GERMANIA
GALLIA
LUGII
ZUMI
BUTONES
DANDI
HERMONDURI
BOII
MARCOMANNI
BOIHAEMUM
Marobodum
TRIBOCCI
Hercynia Silva
Gabreta Silva
QUADI
Danuvius F.
GETAE
VINDELICI
Atesinus F.
BOIORUM DESERTUM
BOII GALLI
HELVETII
NORICI
Noreia
Heorta
PANNONIA
Dravus F.
Savus F.
Noarus F.
Pathissus F.
Marisus F.
SALASSI
LEPONTII
CAMUNI
STONI
TRIDENTINI
MEDOACI
VENETI
Aquileia
CARNI
GALLIA TRANSPADANA
Padus F.
Tergeste
Metulum
Segestica
Siscia
Arupini
Monetium
ANDIZETII
Sirmium
Pola
APSYRTIDES
Adriaticus Sinus
ADRIATICUS SINUS
ITALIA
Ancona
Scardona
LIBURNICAE
Salon
ISSA
DAORIZI
ARDIAEI
Delmium
BREUCI
MAZAEI
GALLORUM OLIM REGIO
SCORDISCI
AUTARIATAE
PLERAEI
Rhizon
Rhizonicus Sin.
Ionius Sinus
Lissus
PARTHINI
TAULANTII
DASSARETII
Apsus F.
Apollonia
Aous F.
EPIRUS
Brentesium
Hydrus
Corcyra
MARE SICULUM

Map VI.

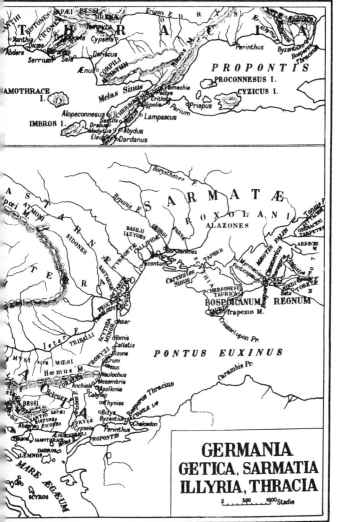

GERMANIA
GETICA, SARMATIA
ILLYRIA, THRACIA

0 ... 500 ... 1000 Stadia

Edward Stanford Ltd., London